# ONE FAMILY'S WAR

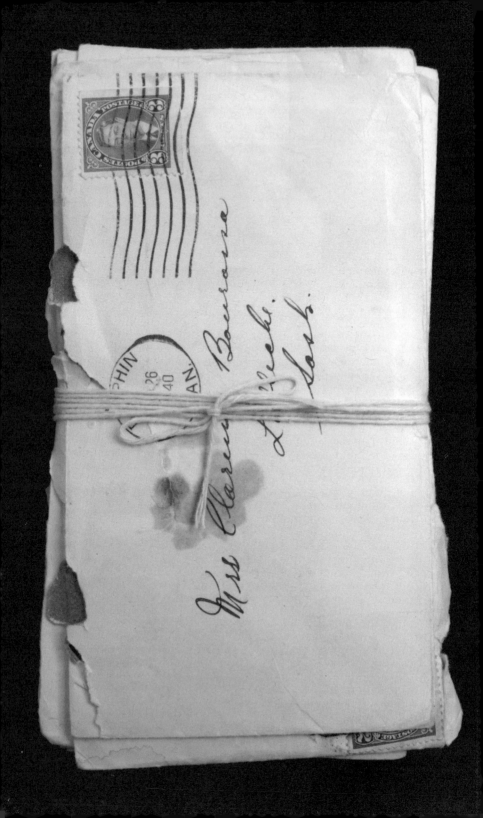

# ONE FAMILY'S WAR
## THE WARTIME LETTERS *of* CLARENCE BOURASSA

### 1940-1944

*edited by*
ROLLIE BOURASSA

*with an introduction by*
WILL CHABUN

University
of Regina

CPRC
PRESS

Printed and bound in Canada at Friesens.
The text of this book is printed on 100% post-consumer recycled paper.

Edited by: Rollie Bourassa.
Cover and text design by Duncan Campbell, CPRC.
Editor for the Press: David McLennan, CPRC.
Cover and section photos by Carolyn Pihach Photography.
Additional images courtesy Rollie Bourassa.

**Library and Archives Canada Cataloguing in Publication**

Bourassa, Clarence
One family's war : the wartime letters of Clarence Bourassa, 1940-1944 /
edited by Rollie Bourassa ; with an introduction by Will Chabun.

ISBN 978-0-88977-221-2

1. Bourassa, Clarence—Correspondence. 2. Bourassa, Hazel—Correspondence.
3. World War, 1939–1945—Personal narratives, Canadian.
4. Canada. CanadianArmy. South Saskatchewan Regiment—Biography.
5. Soldiers—Canada—Correspondence. I. Bourassa, Rollie II. Title.

D811.B675 2010    940.54'8171    C2010-902124-X

Canadian Plains Research Center
University of Regina
Regina, Saskatchewan
Canada, S4S 0A2
tel: (306) 585-4758   fax: (306) 585-4699
e-mail: canadian.plains@uregina.ca
web: www.cprcpress.ca

We acknowledge the financial support of the Government of Canada through the Book Publishing Industry Development Program (BPIDP) for our publishing activities. We also acknowledge the support of the Canada Council for the Arts for our publishing program.

Canadian Patrimoine
Heritage canadien

Canada Council    Conseil des Arts
for the Arts       du Canada

Mixed Sources
Cert no. SW-COC-001271
© 1996 FSC
FSC

# CONTENTS

*Dedicated to my mother,*
*Hazel,*
*Who Counted the Pennies*

# PUBLISHER'S PREFACE

On behalf of the CPRC Press it is my pleasure to bring to you the wartime letters of Clarence Bourassa. Replicating these handwritten letters on a typewritten page has proven to be no easy task, as it is somewhat difficult to capture all the nuances and sentiments that were originally conveyed by handwriting. But we have endeavoured to bring to you as true a replication of Clarence's writings as is possible.

Clarence often wrote in a sort of 'stream-of-thought' manner, and, at times, the letters are somewhat disjointed, but this reflects the kinds of less-than-ideal conditions in which Clarence would have written— in crowded quarters amid boisterous company, in a tent, upon his knee or leaning up against a wall. Often he would only be able to write a few sentences at a time between duties, and many letters were composed in starts and stops over many hours, sometimes over a few days.

The original letters lack punctuation, sentence fragments lack conjunctions, words which Clarence obviously heard in his head and intended to write are missing—grammar and sentence structure were clearly the least of Clarence's concerns. Sentences run into one another and Clarence often made spelling mistakes while writing on the fly— mistakes, you gather, he likely would not have made had he been able to write in normal circumstances. We have added punctuation for the sake of clarity, careful to respect Clarence's intentions, and we have also corrected some spelling mistakes. When we have been unsure as to where one sentence or thought ended, and where another began, we have simply left the structure as per the original.

There were times when we were unable to make out a word or two, and if this has been the case we have either indicated this by placing an ellipsis in the text or have placed a question mark in square brackets. Similarly, anything in the text that appears in square brackets should be considered an editorial insertion. Ellipses have also been used to indicate a larger block of text has been omitted, and this material, although it is not a lot, has been cut for two main reasons. The first reason is out of respect for Clarence and his wife Hazel and their privacy; Rollie Bourassa simply felt some matters were too personal. Secondly, Clarence and Hazel had some discussions of some people that would only confuse the reader, and it was felt cutting these references would not detract from the text and would be less awkward than numerous editorial asides. Additionally, pseudonyms have been used in some instances, but in most cases not.

Something must also be said about some of the language that Clarence used. Some of the expressions or words might today be seen as being "politically incorrect." But we humbly suggest these words or expressions cannot be judged from a 21st century perspective; Clarence's was the language of the day.

*David McLennan*
*Editor for the Press*

# ACKNOWLEDGEMENTS

There are a number of people whom I must thank for helping to bring this project to completion. First, I must thank Leanne Bonish for her work early on in the project; Leanne typed out some of very first excerpts I culled from my father's letters. I also need to acknowledge the work of Lisa Drinkwater and Amber Fletcher at the University of Regina; especially Amber, who organized and transcribed most of the letters and who sifted through and sorted the many photographs and artifacts. Will Chabun, of Regina's *Leader-Post,* must also be thanked for his belief in this project and for agreeing to pen the introduction. I am indebted to him for his contribution. And at the Canadian Plains Research Center at the University of Regina, David McLennan must be thanked for his knowledge, expertise, and, especially, for his dedication toward making this book a reality. I'd also like to express my gratitude to my wife Bea, my brother Murray and everyone else in my family who encouraged me and supported me over past few years. And finally, I'd like to thank my father, Clarence, for his caring, his thoughtfulness, and for leaving us this legacy.

*Rollie Bourassa*
*Regina, Saskatchewan*
*February 2010*

# INTRODUCTION

When I was a young reporter in Regina in the late 1970s, I learned quickly that the name of Rollie Bourassa was pretty well synonymous with fun-loving volunteerism. Everywhere I went, I would run into the ebullient Rollie: marshalling parades and acting as a volunteer at Buffalo Days, the annual summer fair in the Queen City.

This big-hearted gentleman has many special talents, notably the ability to talk easily and with others. But one day in the summer of 2006 Rollie seemed even more excited than usual. He knew of my interest in Saskatchewan history and military history—and was able to bring me some important news that combined both: he had prepared a book from the letters that his father (who'd served in the Canadian Army during the Second World War) had sent home to Rollie's mother—and it was to be published.

Some historical context is in order: no province was hit and battered as cruelly by the Great Depression of the 1930s—and by the accompanying drought and despair—as Saskatchewan and, in particular, its southwest. This farming area included the town of Lafleche, where Clarence Bourassa, his wife Hazel, and their two young sons, Rollie and Murray, were living as the 1930s drew to a close and brought a new challenge: a European war.

The Canadian economic boom that coincided with the arrival of the Second World War, with its demand for manpower and manufacturing output, did not necessarily filter down quickly—or, in some cases, at all—to small towns that had neither manufacturing plants nor military bases. Life remained hard in many parts of Canada. Thus it came to pass that young Rollie's father, Clarence Bourassa, born in 1913 and worn down by the Depression, enlisted in the Canadian Army during the first months of the Second World War.

Clarence was a member of the South Saskatchewan Regiment, a militia or army reserve unit that had its peacetime headquarters in Weyburn, southeast of Regina. Clarence and his comrades stayed there for several months—training, marching, being assigned to specific jobs or trades within the army, and reflecting on their lot. Loneliness clearly ate at Clarence. At one point that summer, he wrote to Hazel, "You and the kiddies are all I have and frankly this is the only reason I joined the army . . . so I would get away from Lafleche, where I was going to hell, and to give you and the boys a decent living."

The regiment—civilians could think of it as sort of a large extended family with its share of dynamos, eccentrics, malcontents and ordinary soldiers—moved for further training to Camp Shilo, near Brandon, Manitoba, then Toronto and Halifax, from which it departed for embattled Britain during December 1940.

At that point, our side was losing the war, to be blunt. In the previous 15 months, German troops had overrun Poland, Norway, Denmark, the Netherlands, Belgium, and most of France. Britain had been saved from invasion only because its Royal Air Force Fighter Command had fought the Luftwaffe to a draw; the German High command was nervous about trying to mount a winter cross-channel invasion with the RAF and Royal Navy still intact.

Important events, of course—but the endearing thing about this book is that it does not cover "the big picture" of the Second World War. Heaven knows there are enough books extant on the war's grand strategies and fateful decisions. Instead, this book derives its historical and social value from giving us an intimate, sometimes painful, look into war as seen through the eyes of a typical Canadian soldier. Much of what Clarence wrote in his letters revolved around his painful loneliness and the boredom that comes from being inside an army that trained and trained and then trained some more for combat. "What's the difference? I wished this onto myself and I've got to like it,"

Clarence wrote of his decision to volunteer for the army mere months after the war's outbreak.

The folklore of the Canadian armed services during the Second World War held that their officers and men were forbidden from keeping personal diaries lest they somehow fall into the hands of the enemy and divulge valuable military information. Letters were permitted, though. Like many other soldiers, Clarence became a dedicated letter-writer who would write frequently, sometimes daily, to his wife Hazel (who he often addressed as "Mommy").

Letters were not only permitted, but encouraged, as a morale-raising tool, though they were censored by officers to prevent sensitive military information from leaking out. Clarence was aware of this and likely "self-edited" his letters before mailing them home. Nonetheless, the accounts one reads in this book are often powerfully personal and sometimes vivid. They amount to the equivalent of a diary, one recording a strange and tumultuous time.

This collection of letters thus gives some fascinating insights into the daily life of a Canadian soldier during the long wait for the Allied invasion of France on June 6, 1944.

To be sure, there were some conscripts in Canadian Army uniforms during the Second World War. But the federal government, mindful of the tremendous strains on national unity unleashed by the conscription of soldiers in 1917, kept them at home until unexpectedly heavy casualties absorbed by the army in Italy and northwest Europe in the summer and autumn of 1944 forced the government to relent and send a small number of conscripts overseas. Thus the Canadian Army whose members were steadily sent to Britain between 1939 and mid-1944 was an all-volunteer force. But old soldiers and military historians know that by no means all Canadian volunteers had enlisted out of a sense of patriotism or a desire to stop ambitious, expansionist Nazi Germany. And over and over, Clarence tries to reassure his wife, and perhaps himself, that he made the right decision in enlisting. "I have a chance to make something for you and the kiddies in the future and God help me do this," he wrote to Hazel at one point.

Some of the things Clarence mentions in his letters definitely will not be found in proud regimental histories. At one point in 1940, he admits he "squandered" his meagre pay on "liquor and poker." There were more than a few thefts from Canadian servicemen, and Clarence tells his wife how a fellow soldier, who had been put in detention for bad behaviour, somehow got a rifle away from a guard and deliberately shot himself in the foot. He talks about how other soldiers (some of them married ones) were "fooling around over here," adding tartly that "the only thing ever discussed (plenty of literature) is how to protect yourself from VD."

The spring of 1942 brings the sad story of how a private in the SSR, returning from leave, not only ignored the challenge of a sentry, but covered his face, refused to reply—and was shot to death. Clarence makes plenty of references to "big shots," Canadian and British, who he seems to hold in considerable contempt. He begs for cigarettes, the currency of any army in those days, and for more mail, though he is always conscious that merchant ships crossing the Atlantic to and from Britain were being sunk at an alarming rate; the simple arrival of a convoy from Canada was deemed newsworthy in his letters.

As a lowly private assigned to duty as a stretcher-bearer or medical orderly, he seems barely cognizant of the world-shaking events taking place around him. Rather matter-of-factly, he notes in early 1941 that his regiment, part of the Canadian Army's 2nd Division, was being moved around southeast Britain in order to repel the much-feared German invasion (which, of course, never came). What was arguably the most important event of war, Germany's invasion of the Soviet Union in June 1941, is mentioned in passing in one sentence—and then about two or three weeks after the fact. The entry of the United States into the war in December 1941 is briefly mentioned several days after it took place. On a more poignant theme, Clarence—no word-smith, but an earnest, energetic writer—wrote touchingly of a six-year-old boy—an evacuee from the bomb-battered British city of Coventry, who befriended the Canadian soldiers, including Clarence. A few months later, he wrote: "Things are awfully quiet. You wouldn't think there was a war on only for what we read or hear."

Things were about to change.

The name of the South Saskatchewan Regiment is familiar to Canadian military history buffs for its participation in the bloody Dieppe landing on August 19, 1942. This was planned as a one-day amphibious raid—Clarence predicted it would be a "little mix-up with the Huns"—into the French port of Dieppe by a 6,000-man force that included some

British, American and Free French troops, though the majority (5,000) were Canadians from the 2nd Division. The intent of the raid was to test landing tactics and equipment, test German reactions and gather intelligence from German prisoners and radar sites and, according to many accounts, signal the Russians that their Western allies were "still in the game."

Due to a lack of surprise and poor planning assumptions, Allied losses were ghastly: the Canadian Army's official history of the Second World War says 907 Canadians were killed; more than twice that were captured. Clarence's account of how he escaped, while wounded, by swimming from a wrecked landing craft to an Allied warship is so anguished and painful that it is difficult to read. "It was terrible, Hazel," he wrote later. "I've always had a craving for excitement. I got enough in the few hours over there to do me four lifetimes."

In the aftermath of Dieppe, he was assigned to a job in the regimental paymaster's office. The workload and the unit's increased tempo of training for the inevitable invasion of France seemed to drain his energy and time for letter-writing. A lifeline for Clarence was the regiment's band and orchestra, of which he was a member. They played not only for official military ceremonies, but for dances and receptions. If it wasn't for music, Clarence confided to Hazel at one point, "I would go nuts."

The last letter in this collection was written on July 16, 1944, from the soil of Normandy, where Allied and German forces were engaged in a fearsome three-month summer confrontation that was, at times, reminiscent of the stalemate of the First World War. Clarence told Hazel he was "right in the thick of things and I'm fine, getting plenty to eat and plenty of sleep—if the guns don't get too noisy."

This story is not to have a happy ending. But we profit from reading Clarence's letters because of the insights they offer us, two generations removed, into the lot of a good man who was often tired, hungry, bored, frightened and, especially, lonely—but, nevertheless, did his duty.

And this, we realize with the passage of time, is what makes him and his comrades all the more impressive.

I thank Clarence for his sacrifices and his son, Rollie, for bringing to our attention his father's story.

*Will Chabun*

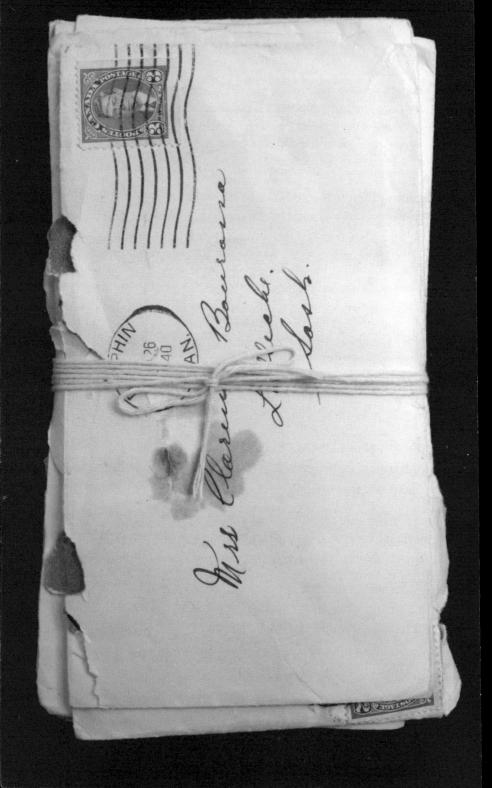

# LETTERS 1940

Pte. Bourassa, C.O.
L12541
S.S.R.
Weyburn, Saskatchewan
March 31, 1940


Dear Hazel,

Well, here I am. I get terribly lonesome at nights, but I sure am
kept busy all through the day . . . drill, march, P.T. [physical
training], drill, etc., etc.

How is Murray and Rollie? Is Rollie a good boy? I hope so. You're
well, are you Mummy? I really haven't much to say, only that I am
well and awfully tired—right now every muscle in my body aches.

I passed all exams and I applied for enlistment leave, but I don't think
I will get it because they said I had had plenty of time to do up my
business before I left Lafleche. But I applied for leave on the 15th of April
and I think that I might get that, but I won't know for a week or so.

Well, be good darling, and pray for me. In parting, you will get
a cheque for $79 May 1st, and see that our babies are well-fed
and well-clothed. So long my darling, I really love you and feel
pretty blue.

Your loving hubby,
Clarence

[P.S.] When you answer use same address as I wrote on top.
Love & kisses.

☙

Pte. Bourassa, C.O.
L12541
S.S.R.
Weyburn, Saskatchewan
April 7, 1940

Dear Hazel,

I'm sorry I didn't write any sooner, but I've been so darned tired at nights that I just simply go to bed. I came uptown once this week and took in a picture show.

I've read and reread your letters and sure enjoy them . . . I get pretty lonesome at times, and I go to sleep every night thinking of you and the kiddies.

Well, I'll tell you about myself. I like the army quite well and there are about sixty that have joined up lately that I know—some from Assiniboia and every town west to Meyronne. . . . [O]ur Sergeant Major told me that I was getting along fine and to keep it up because industriousness means promotion in the Army. And he told me that the conduct in or out of the Barracks is what the officers judged the men for [for] promotions. So you can really see that if I work at all seriously (which I will) there is a chance of earning some stripes.

I hope you didn't pay attention to what Steve was saying about stepping out, because I'm not going to, and I have no intentions to, because I've had a couple of long talks with Regimental Sergeant Major Strum and he says that it is more or less a curse of the Army that men step out and roust about, but if I would just take notice to the ones who have earned their stripes, that they were good steady men, and he said that that was the kind of men that he was looking for. So, please don't worry sweetheart, I will not step out now or later, even if this war lasts ten years. I've a chance to make something for you and the kiddies in the future, and God help me do this.

I hope to get leave in the near future—just when I know, and when I do get it, it will be on short notice so I may not be able to let you know before I get home. Sometime in the first part of May.

Lots of love to you and the kiddies. I hope Rollie gets over his cold soon. . . . I enjoyed Rollie's letter. Boy, I'm really getting lonesome right now. I will write Tuesday again. And tell the folks I will be writing again soon.

And please don't worry about me Mummy or about what Steve said, because what he does and is going to do doesn't mean to say that I will, because I'm not.

No, they do not read our mail here, so say what you want in your letters.

Goodnight Darling, I love you and I'm lonesome.
Your hubby,
Clarence

౬౨

Pte. Bourassa, C.O.
L12541
S.S.R.
Weyburn, Saskatchewan
April 10, 1940

Dear Hazel,

Young Turner and I are going to a show tonight, and while waiting
I thought I'd drop you a word or two to tell you I still am a little
lonesome, and that I miss you and the kiddies a lot.

How is Rollie? Is he good? Tell him Daddy is going to send him
something for his birthday, and tell him Daddy loves him all
"owser" ['owser' was Rollie's baby talk pronunciation of 'over'].

How is Murray getting along? Fine, I hope. Gee, I miss the dear
little fellow . . . his "gooing" and smiles. Does he still "goo" a lot?
I'll bet he is cute. I can't wait to see him. I will be home in about
three weeks—I expect leave in the first week of May.

Write often Darling. I cherish your letters, and I really do love you
more and more everyday. . . .

Well, here I am in the Army. I like it real well, and am doing fine,
only that I am quite muscle sore all of the time, but I will soon get
used to it. I've only been to town five times since I have been here;
we have all the entertainment we could possibly care for at the
barracks, so I just as soon stay here.

Write soon darling. Love and kisses for the kiddies. And for you . . .
love, kisses, and big hug . . . and more love and kisses.

Your loving husband,
Clarence

꿍

Weyburn, Saskatchewan
April 15, 1940


Dear Hazel,

Well I'm good and tired tonight, and we still have to study again.
I suppose that I will get to bed about one, last night it was two.
This school business is plenty tough, thank God it finishes next
Thursday. And, apparently, I'm going to last out, and so is Steve.
They have the school cut down to about 27, and it started with 63.
And they want 27 more NCOs [non-commissioned officers], so if
that is the case I'll stay in and I hope I pass the final exam.

Well, how are the kiddies? How is Murray? Is his cold getting any
better? Is Rollie good? And how are you? I've been waiting for a
letter from you and none yet; I suppose your [*sic*] waiting on me.
Gee, I'm lonesome and blue.

. . .

Can you possibly get down here next Saturday? Please do, because
we will be leaving here inside of ten days for Camp Shilo. Now that
I realize I'm gradually getting out of reach of home and you, I must
see you again. . . . It may mean a little expense; although, fifteen
dollars should be plenty: ticket, two nights in town, and five or
six meals. I want you to come sweetheart. I'm going to apply for a
weekend leave so that I can be with you all the time you are here.

Well, goodnight, I've got to get to work. And hoping to see you
Saturday on the train.

I love you,
Clarence

[P.S.] Kiss the kiddies for me.

℘

Pte. Bourassa, C.O.
L12541
S.S.R.
Weyburn, Saskatchewan
April 18th, 1940

Dear Hazel,

Well, here I am as I promised. I'm on the fire crew today so I
can't leave the barracks, so I'm writing in the recreation room.
You should hear the noise: a couple of radios trying to make themselves heard, and a piano and a bunch singing Roll out [the Barrel].
Excuse the omition [*sic*] of not explaining what the fire crew is. It is
a certain number of men that must stay in the barracks and watch
for fire, and, in case of fire, to man the fire hoses and to see that
everyone gets out. That sounds sort of absurd, this being a fire-
proof building, but it is being done all the same.

My trip was very uneventful, and all alone. Dolores [Clarence's
sister] was at the train in Assiniboia to meet me. Outside of that,
there was nothing doing.

I'm pretty tired tonight. We marched six hours with rifles at our
shoulders, and included in the six hours we had an hour of field
drilling . . . that is, advancing on the enemy, retreating and hiding.
Can you imagine looking for cover on an open plain? But, with our
uniforms, and making use of every little knoll, weed, etc., we did it
so well that our captain standing at two hundred yards couldn't see
a single one of my section. By my section I mean that I had 8 men
under me and they were to do what I told them about hiding. . . .
and when the order was given to "seek cover, aircraft in sight," . . .
[our] section was out in some sort of a slough and some of them
flopped right into the mud. What a sight when we all got together
. . . everybody got a big laugh out of it. One fellow especially was
plastered with mud clear back of his ears. . . .

How are you Mummy? Feel blue at times? So do I. How are the kiddies? Feeling better I hope. I was really proud of my Mummy at the station, she even stood it better than I did. I had a lump in my throat till I got past Melaval.

Well, I'll say goodbye darling for tonight. I will write again on Sunday. By the way, got your letter and the picture was swell.

Your loving Husband,
Clarence

P.S. I'm a little lonesome. And kiss for Rollie, Murray, and two for you Sweetheart.

જી

Pte. Bourassa, C.O.
L12541
S.S.R.
Weyburn, Saskatchewan
April 21, 1940


Dear Hazel,

Yes, I received your letter and I just don't know what to draw
from it. Yes, I'll admit I owe the money all right, but what I don't
like is your saying I bought something for some other woman with
the money. I most certainly did not. I just squandered what I did
get on liquor and poker, and as for the ten dollars goes, I intended
to send it back to pay up that account without causing any undue
worry to you. But, since they want there [sic] money practically in
one lump sum, you don't have to pay them a cent, because in the
Army Act, which I read yesterday, no one can garnishee a soldier's
salary or his dependents' portion on any accumulated debt before
his enlistment, and don't let anyone kid you otherwise.

Yes, I do want to see that paid, and for the present the best you can
possibly do is to pay them ten dollars a month, and I am going to
drop Dad a note to that effect. All I really can say is that I am pretty
mad about everything . . . you accusing me about cheating, gam-
bling, etc. Well, if you have no confidence in me I wish you would
say so right out plainly and what you are going to do about it, and
then I'll really know where I stand. After all, you and the kiddies are
all I have, and, frankly, that is the only reason I joined the army . . .
so that I would get away from Lafleche where I was going to hell,
and to give you and our boys a decent living. And if you think I'm
not lonesome and hurt your [sic] mistaken, because since I received
your last letter I've been feeling terribly bad, blue and lonesome.
Please Mummy, forget all this mess and tell me you love me.

I've two sore arms—inoculated in one for typhoid and diphtheria,
and vaccinated on the other for small pox. [And] was awfully sick
yesterday with it, but I feel much better today.

I'm going to drop Dad a note right now, and whatever you do enjoy yourself with the money and don't pay . . . any more than ten dollars a month. . . .

I love you,
Clarence

എ

Pte. Bourassa, C.O.
L12541
S.S.R.
Weyburn, Saskatchewan
April 25, 1940


Dear Hazel,

How are you now? I've been waiting feverishly for news. My last letter hasn't been answered yet, but I guess no news is good news.

. . .

How are the kiddies? Fine, I hope. Is Rollie a good boy? I miss him terribly . . . and does Murray still smile for you. . . .

Well, I've been feeling awfully punk lately. I've had a terrible cold and now my mouth has broken all out into cold sores. It hurt so much last night I could hardly get to sleep. My lower lip is swollen about an inch thick, but feels much better since the cold sores are drying up. The doctor here say it's from going out in the sun and in the cold while I was running a fever. He asked me if I had been feeling punk. I said yes, and he raised hell for me not reporting sick. Well, I didn't want to miss any more drill because they're going to choose some soldiers for stripes and I wanted a chance. Well, I was rewarded. Steve, Percy, and I were chosen from our platoon to go to the Non-Commissioned Officers School as the best prospects to make good NCOs. Of course, we haven't earned our stripes yet and we will have to do an awful lot of studying and drilling to pass the exams, which will be in about six weeks.

We were X-rayed yesterday, but haven't heard any results yet. So, I don't want to be too enthused about my luck, because I may still get a discharge for being physically unfit. At times I wish I was physically unfit and get sent home; because, after all, what I love the most in the world are you and the kiddies, and sometimes I get awfully lonesome.

Last night the ladies of Weyburn put on a play, tea and dance for the soldiers. I went to the play and had lunch after, and I watched them dance for about fifteen minutes, but didn't indulge. It made me so lonesome for you and home that I came back to the barracks and went to bed about 11:30.

We drilled around outside all day today and, boy, was it ever chilly. I was half frozen most of the time even with all the army woollens on.

Dad wrote me a letter saying that you had offered to pay him thirty dollars a month on that account, and said that whatever I thought you could spare . . . as I mentioned, $10.00 in the letter I wrote was quite all right . . . so whatever you do don't make yourself short of money. Your [*sic*] entitled to a lot more than you have had in the past. And now that you have the opportunity to have more clothes and money for yourself and the kiddies, don't pinch any more than necessary. And as far as putting money aside for when I come back home, that is entirely up to you.

. . .

Well, I will be getting leave around the tenth of May, because I believe, in fact, we will be leaving Weyburn for our summer camp, and no one knows where that is going to be just yet.

. . .

Your loving husband,
Clarence

☙

Weyburn, Saskatchewan
May 13, 1940

Dear Hazel,

Well, here I am, and I am awfully blue. I don't know why I feel
so darned lonesome—I guess it is because I love you.

. . .

Well, by all appearances we will be moving to Camp Shilo about
the 20th. And if you can possibly come down this weekend, please
do, because Lord knows it will be a long time before we can see
one another again. . . .

By the way, Percy was stricken from the school today. I don't
know what for . . . something must be wrong. I'm beginning to
have doubts if I will stay on through because it seems to be all the
recruits that have [been] stricken. I don't know what to think of it;
nevertheless, if they strike me from the school it sure won't be
because I didn't try my best.

. . .

It has been snowing and raining all day long here, and I was
marching around in slush all afternoon.

Well, I've got a terrible lot of notes to write and a lot of studying
to do tonite [sic], so I'll kiss you goodnight, and I will write again
tomorrow.

Your loving hubby,
Clarence

ᘒ

ROLLIE'S NOTE: *Dad had leave and made it home to Lafleche . . .*

Pte. Bourassa, C.O.

L12541

S.S.R.

Weyburn, Saskatchewan

May 23, 1940

Dear Mummy,

. . .

. . . Yes, I had a big lump in my throat when you left me, and I will never forget you disappearing around the corner when you turned back and waved . . . then you were gone. The bottom dropped out of everything. I felt awfully bad all day.

Well, I'm sure glad you are not pregnant. It will make things very much easier for you till I come back. And as what is going to happen to me in regards to where I'm going, I can't say a thing. The best thing we can possibly do is hope and pray that I don't leave Canada.

Steve Johnston and Vaughn Edmonds are leaving for Shilo tomorrow and apparently we follow them on Monday. Gee, I'm lonesome . . . I want my Mummy and my kiddies.

. . . Send me a picture of Murray as soon as you can, will you Mummy? Send me pictures of everybody as often as you get one. I miss Lafleche and home.

I've got to do some studying so I'll have to go—so, goodnight sweetheart. Love and kisses to you and the kiddies.

Write soon or right away. I'm so lonesome.

Your loving husband,
Clarence

P.S. Thank Adrien or the Legion for the pen set . . . I'm using them now. Tell him I'll write as soon as I get time. School keeps me too busy.

∾

1940.

1940.

CLARENCE IN UNIFORM, IN FRONT OF THE FAMILY HOME
IN LAFLECHE WHILE ON LEAVE.

Pte. Bourassa, C.O.
L12541
s.s.r.
Weyburn, Saskatchewan
May 27, 1940


Dear Hazel,

Well, school is all over and I passed. I don't know what marks
I made . . . fairly well, I believe. How soon I will get my stripes, I
don't know.

We are leaving for Shilo Monday morning at nine o'clock (this
morning to you sweetheart)—when you will be reading this we
will be well on our way. We've got to get up at 4 a.m., post time,
3 o'clock your time . . . kind of early, isn't it? Gee, I'm getting scared.
Compared to Shilo, this is close to home, and that is plenty far
enough to be from someone you love and your babies. I love you
Mummy and I am awfully lonesome and dead broke. I've had to
bum everything I needed, and by the time my next pay comes I'll
have a couple of dollars left again to do me another two weeks. Oh
well, what's the difference. I've wished this onto myself and I've got
to like it. The other night we had a banquet . . . all the boys of the
school put in $2.00 apiece and invited all the officers to it . . . I
didn't have the money and I didn't go, and I felt awfully cheap for
some reason or other. I guess all the big shots will be wondering
what was the matter with me. I was the only one missing. Gee, I
feel blue and so alone. I want my wife and my kiddies awfully bad.

. . .

As to staying in Canada darling, I don't know. I was speaking to
Colonel Wright, and he says my application was sent in, but
whether it would be accepted he didn't know.

How is Murray and Rollie? The whooping cough still bad? I hope not.
How is your little garden? Growing, I suppose. And weeds, too, I'll bet.

Say hello to [the] folks, Hazel. Tell them I will write as soon as
we get settled down again. Today, the barracks are in a turmoil . . .
and school all the last two weeks . . . I hardly had time to write
to anyone.

. . .

Yes, write soon darling. Address my mail to Weyburn until further
notice. It will get to me.

Thanks for the pictures. They are swell of Rollie . . . now, all I
want is a good one of you and Murray.

Love, sweetheart,
Clarence

P.S. I hope to be able to have you come and see me at Camp Shilo
soon. I'll write again as soon as I get there. Love and kisses to you
and the kiddies.

෬

CLARENCE'S CERTIFICATE OF MILITARY QUALIFICATION DATED MAY 24,
1940, STATING HE WAS PROMOTED FROM A PRIVATE TO A CORPORAL.

Camp Shilo, Manitoba
June 3, 1940

Dear Mummy,

I suppose you are wondering what happened to me not writing all
week. I feel foolish about it, but the truth is I couldn't do anything
about it. Being my duty week, that is to say, acting as Corporal, I
had to take roll call every night and I couldn't possibly find time to
write. But this week my evenings will be mine and I sure will write.
Oh, Mummy, but I'm lonesome. I want you and the kiddies terribly
bad. There are some women here visiting their husbands, and I feel
so damn bad that I'm all alone in my tent with a great big lump in
my throat, and I sure feel like crying. . . .

You will come up on Saturday won't you darling? You will have to
stay in Brandon, and I will be able to see you Saturday from 2 p.m.

to eleven at night, and the same on Sunday. I can't stay with you overnight, that is army regulations now. No one stays out over night.
. . .

Now for the bad news. I am slated to go overseas in about two weeks and I can't do a thing about it. I'm a section leader and I will get my stripes in the next few days. After payday, I had a $1.80 left, and tried to make money playing poker, and all I got out of it was to owe $7.00 and I'm dead broke. . . .

. . .

Camp Shilo is a big sandy plain with clumps of trees spread around, and the ground is practically all covered with creeping cedar, which gives the atmosphere a pleasant odour, especially in the mornings. There are about 5,000 men here, all under canvass. It is really something to see—about 1,500 tents.

. . .

How are the kiddies and how are the folks? Do you know I haven't written them a word? Say, by the way, drop word around the folks and tell them that cigarettes are certainly always welcome . . . just a hint sorta, eh! And tell them all that as soon as I get stamps I will write every one of them.

. . .

It's suppertime now,
. . . love and kisses to you and the kiddies.
Clarence

Camp Shilo, Manitoba
Tuesday Noon
[June 4, 1940]


Dear Hazel,

I got both of your letters today . . . I was awfully glad to hear from you and the kiddies . . .

As you read in my last letter I don't believe there is a very big chance of my staying in Canada, and further proof is that I am taking an anti-gas course, and when I get through with that I will be an anti-gas instructor. There are eighteen of us . . . so this means more study and no drill for the next couple of weeks, and then we will be in charge and responsible for 40 men apiece. That is to say we will have to train them in the use of the respirator (gas mask), and instil in them a natural instinct against war gasses. It's going to be quite a job, but the busier I am the less time I have to be so miserably lonesome. I have no stripes as yet, but I expect so in the near future.

Yes, I still want you to come down on to Brandon and be here Saturday and Sunday. And, listen, to make it easier for us to get leave from camp, you and Sarah pool in and send us a telegram that you are coming, and we will be able to get out and spend a few hours with you, which I want to do more than anything else in the world—and we are expecting you. . . .

. . .

You sure must be kept busy with the kiddies sickness and all. Well, I hope they get well soon.

As to guys trying to date you up, you will have to expect that because the average male thinks that a grass widow is an easy mark, and you will continually be pestered because they expect that some time or other that you will weaken, go out once, and then after the first time out, a drink or two, and from there you know what would happen. [Publisher's note: a grass widow was an expression used to refer to a person whose spouse was away for a prolonged period of time.] Men as a rule think that women can't resist sex after they have tasted of it, but thank the Lord you are above all such rot. Just simply tell them to go to hell and they sure won't be back. And don't trust a damn one of them as far as you can throw them. And, above all, beware of the ones that you might think never think of such things—they are the most dangerous. Well, it all boils down to this: avoid all temptations. After all, everyone is human, and temptations are always handy, and the opposite sex is always finding excuses for you, such as, "what's the difference," "he's doing" or "she is doing," and "do you expect her or him to be true to you for a year or more," "don't be silly, you only live once and why not live." You wonder why I say this, because I know that is exactly what you will hear and I've heard it myself, but I know that with you or me it is different. I love you, Hazel, and my only desires are for you, and will always be only for you.

Well, Hazel, please come to Brandon and see me. Find out the cheapest way, by car or something, even by Gravelbourg if necessary.

Well, so long, I will write again soon, and I want to say so much. So, you will have to come and we'll talk things over.

Your lonesome, loving husband,
Clarence

P.S. Beware of all male favours. There is always an object to any attraction offered any woman at any time by the average male. During the last war many families were wrecked by such things, and, please, let's not wreck ours. . . . So, Hazel, I pray and pray. I've never prayed . . . so fervently to God in my life to keep us straight and true to one another, and to see that we are together for ever and ever soon. I love you, please write.

Love Daddy,
to kiddies and the only woman in the world.

☙

TRAINING TO BE AN ANTI-GAS INSTRUCTOR
AT CAMP SHILO IN JUNE 1940.

Camp Shilo, [Manitoba]
Wednesday
[June 12, 1940]


Dear Mummy,

Just received your letter and am answering right away because
I believe we are moving out Monday. Where to, I don't know.
Anyway, that's the orders. We get paid tomorrow and then we
get 24 hours leave, and then we are to be confined to barracks
until we leave.

. . .

According to your letter you say mother is coming this weekend . . . why don't you come to [*sic*]? And if you do come you want to be leaving by the time you get this letter, because if you get here when we're confined to barracks I can't get out. You will only see me in camp—that would be a lot better than not at all. We get all day Friday off, free to go as far as time allows, and that isn't enough time for me to get home.

We went on a two day scheme to Souris, sixty miles from camp. I walked ten miles out and rode the rest of the way. On the way back I rode all the way (that's because I'm in the band) and the other men marched twenty five miles. They just got in . . . and talk about guys limping and groaning.

I'm sure glad I'm in the band. I didn't even have to march the ten miles. But it was so cold in the morning that I had to keep warm, and last night we slept under the stars. When I woke up this morning and peeked out from under the covers everything was covered with white frost, even my hair that was sticking out from under the covers. The water in the pails froze solid and I wasn't cold in the least. We had plenty of covers, but eating breakfast before sunrise was sure cold . . . my fingers were stinging. In fact, I've really just warmed up.

Well, we are to move from camp. Where to I don't know, but I sort of expect the worst—"overseas." So, I'm glad I'm in the band . . . we will see very little action. We are formed purposely to entertain the troupes [*sic*] returning from action. We are considered an important cog in the Battalion to keep up the moral [*sic*] of the troupes [*sic*], so I'm sure going to stick to the band in case we are going overseas. I hate the word "overseas." It means we will be much longer apart, and I'm too damn far from you now, leave alone England. Oh, what a rotten deal we've got . . . I can assure that whenever I make a move in my life again I will certainly think of what I am doing. If I had only listened to you when you asked me not to join up we would still be together, because they couldn't force me to join. I feel like a trapped animal. Worse than that, I can't get out of it. So the only thing I can do is make the best of it and try to look at it as an adventure with a happy ending.

If in all event I do go overseas you will be good and true to me, will you sweetheart? Lord knows how long I will be gone. And when I come back you will be just as I left you, will you sweetheart? I'll be true to you because I love you so much and you mean so much to me.

. . .

By the way, if I go overseas, make arrangements for me to get a thousand cigarettes a month . . . Winchesters . . . I believe it's $2.50 for a 1000. . . .

. . .

I will write again before you leave and give you my address. By the way, address my mail as "Private," because in the band I can't hold any other rank.

. . .

How are the kiddies? Fine, I hope. Gee, I'm lonesome tonight, and I want to see you all again before I leave. Oh, if only I could see you before we move from Shilo. I'm hoping against hope it's only to winter quarters in Canada, but I'm afraid it's England because our advance party is there—they landed last week.

Goodnight sweetheart. I'm going to crawl under my covers and I believe I'll cry myself to sleep. I feel so full inside that I believe I won't be able to keep a straight face much longer. I'm so lonesome and so much in love, and I've got two of the swellest kiddies in the world that I cannot enjoy. Isn't life mean.

Goodnight sweetheart. I'll write again before we leave and give you all the details about addresses, etc.

Your loving and lonesome Daddy,
Clarence

P.S. Rollie, be good to Mummy, and help Mummy. Kiss Mummy for Daddy. You're the only man left with her . . . and see that she is a good Mummy to you, Murray, and Daddy. . . .

"God, please keep them all good, healthy, and true till I get back to them." Please!

૮ა

Camp Shilo, Manitoba
[June 14?, 1940]

Dear Mummy,

Received your card, or Rollie's rather—the dear little tyke. It was really cute and there was a lump in my throat while I was reading it.

. . .

You asked if I wanted to go overseas—emphatically, no! I don't want to leave you and my family at all, and I'm sort of afraid I'll not have any choice.

I'm giving lectures on respirators today and am awfully busy. So, as long as I'm busy I don't get too lonesome, but at nights, I sure do, and I want you Mummy.

I've got to go and fit respirators on men now, so I'll be going. Write soon.

. . .

Your loving, lonesome Daddy,
Clarence

[P.S.] Write soon and often, I enjoy your letters so. I love you Mummy.

૮ა

Cpl. C.O. Bourassa
L12541
S.S.R.
Shilo Camp, Manitoba
[June 19?, 1940]


Dear Mummy,

Well Hazel, here I am at last. I suppose you are wondering what has happened to me. Well, first of all, Sunday, I couldn't write to catch the mail as [it was] after mass. Mickey, George Klein and I went fishing on the river and we didn't get back till 10 p.m., and to top it off we didn't catch a fish. Monday, it was 8:30 p.m. when we got off parade; in fact, this is my first opportunity since. I'm corporal of the guard and I have a little time to myself.

. . .

. . . I am writing a letter to Captain Hite [?] also asking about a transfer to home defence. I don't know how I will make out, but I am sure going to work on it and work hard. I'm going to write Dad also and see if he can't possibly do something to help. As to what is going to happen in the near future about moving, I don't know a thing. Please pray for me Sweetheart. I do want you to be with me always and sure will take you places, and we will do things just like sweethearts from now on—that is, when we are together again. . . .

. . .

Write soon darling. And, again, be careful.

Your loving husband,
Clarence

൦ഌ

Camp Shilo, Manitoba
[June 26, 1940]


Dear Hazel,

Well here I am and thanks for everything, I'm so excited we are
going to have a long weekend this week and I'm getting a pass to
Moose Jaw. It will take most of my money to get there, and I want
you there, so you will have to borrow a little and meet me there
Saturday night. And if you want to you can come in a car, say Dad's,
and we could go back to Lafleche for Sunday as long as I am back
in Moose Jaw Monday sometime in the afternoon. Everything will
be fine. Can you make it? I would like to see Lafleche once more.
Whatever you do I expect you in Moose Jaw Saturday night to
meet the bus which will arrive around eight. . . .

Gee, I'm excited, and if anything happens that I can't go I
will phone or wire. . . . See you this weekend.

Your loving husband,
Clarence

[P.S.] Be there, and I want to see Lafleche.

ROLLIE'S NOTE: *I have little information, but Mom got to Moose Jaw,
and she and Dad visited Lafleche and made it back to Moose Jaw in time.*

ℰↃ

Camp Shilo, Manitoba
[July 10, 1940]


Dear Hazel,


Well, at last here I am. I suppose you are waiting for me to write
before you do. I was terribly disappointed not getting a letter
any sooner. In fact, I haven't received one yet. That is, since last
Wednesday. What is the matter Mummy? As for myself, I can
explain. We were terribly busy. That is to say, I have been ever since
I came back. I could have written Wednesday night but there was
a movie on in camp, so I thought I would put it off until the next
night, and as it happened they put me on fire picket and I didn't
have time to write since. Sunday, one of the s.s.r. boys by the
name of Norm Kettol was drowned in the river, and a bunch of
us searched the river bed nearly all night last night. The body was
found this noon. Luckily, it wasn't me because I was swimming also.
There were about 200 of us and he wasn't missed 'til we got back
to camp about three in the afternoon. A few of us went back and
dragged the river for seven hours straight so I couldn't write yesterday. So, I'm taking advantage of the dark hours and a lantern to
write this. I really have been terribly busy. I had to wash some
socks tonight also.

I went to Brandon Saturday afternoon for a couple of hours and
inquired about apartments. I really didn't get much satisfaction
because time was short. The best we can do is $20 a month for a
suite. But I understand that at that price, you would get a very
clean and up [to] date apartment. How big I don't know, but I'll
get more details soon.


. . .


By all appearances we will be in Shilo for quite a spell, and I've
come to the conclusion that you must come to Brandon and stay
as soon as possible. I'll get something definite about apartments
in the next few days.

. . .

So the folks are put out because I didn't go over and say goodbye.
Well, I didn't really have time, and I told Francois [Clarence's
brother] to make my excuses.

Well, I have to sleep a little tonight so I'll say goodnight, and I hope
I dream of you in my arms, and I hope to have you there in person
soon if we can make any arrangements at all for you to move into
Brandon for the duration of my stay in Shilo.

. . .

Your loving and lonesome husband,
Clarence

❧

Camp Shilo
July 12, 1940

Dear Mummy,

At last, here I am. . . . and I feel like a heel because I didn't write oftener [*sic*] myself. But it seems that time is wanting as far as I'm concerned—I can't get about all these duties. But, today, I'm simply writing and will write whenever I have even a minute as I'm doing now, just after dinner, so it is.

We marched eight miles this morning and had a sham battle to boot. And we had the same thing again this afternoon. So, you can see that time is not wasted. And often at night we go out on some fool march, and when I'm not on these I'm on some camp duty that lasts a day or two.

I was going to go into Brandon tomorrow and inquire about apartments, but I don't think I'll be able to. First of all, I'm broke, and payday is Monday, and if I spend any more money than I have I'll be terribly short till next payday. So I think I'll wait till next Saturday unless I can bum a ride in. I'm so anxious to have you come down for a stay . . . I want you here awful soon. Don't you want to come as soon as you can? On second thought, I think I will go into Brandon and see about apartments right away. And as soon as you can get here you will be able to have me practically every weekend. And, of course, you can come to camp any night you feel like it—that is, till 9:30—then all women must be out of camp, much to my sorrow as far as you're concerned. . . .

. . .

Gee, I'm lonesome and blue. I miss you terribly, especially at night. Sometimes I could just jump up and hitchhike home I get so lonesome.

I received a parcel from Dodo, and a parcel from Mother same as yours (overnight cookies); from Dodo, cigarettes ["Dodo," pronounced 'Doodoo,' was a nickname for Clarence's sister Dolores].

How are the kiddies? Especially Murray? Gee, he sure [is] cute. I hated to leave the little fellow. How is Rollie acting? All right, I hope, because now is the time he can get out of hand. Raising kids is pretty tough isn't it sweetheart? I should be there to help you do it. We're all going to a show at the Salvation Army tonight ("Two in a Crowd"—sounds good.) There is something like that on every night now. That will help to break the monotony.

Gee, I'm anxious to have you near me soon. I need you so much, and expect you soon.

It's time to mail this, so I'll kiss you bye-bye. Be good darling, because I love you so much and if anything ever happened now— Oh, Lord, I don't dare think of it. . . .

Love and kisses, come soon,
Clarence

Camp Shilo
July 14, 1940


Dear Mummy,


Just read your last letter. And I've received all of your letters. I guess the postal service here is pretty rotten at times—they are always changing postmen. And, as it happened, my mail was sent to the wrong company and it didn't get back to me for four days. . . .

I went to Brandon yesterday and saw a few apartments, but I haven't seen anything I'm interested in yet. Rentals run around $25.00, some furnished and some not. . . . These apartments are all in private homes. The blocks are much higher. . . . There are some swell apartments in private homes. There is one fellow in the army who got an apartment with four rooms and a bath on the second floor for $25.00, and he says it is swell. Whatever you do keep packing and I will get an apartment somewhere. What we want and reasonably priced. The Knights of Columbus are looking around for me, I hope they find something suitable. The different clubs here put themselves out considerably to help out the soldiers. . . .

. . .

I met a lady here today, about 50, I'd guess. She told me that anytime I was in Brandon to go up to her place for our meals. She said her home was always open to the soldiers. Her husband is a railroad man and they have no children, and she says that if she had any boys she would be proud to have them be soldiers. She was rather nice. I thanked her for the invitation and so did the other boys. They said they would gladly accept the invitation. Personally, that was very nice of her, but I don't like this eating in homes—but an awful lot of Brandon Lady Societies are doing the same.

. . .

When you get here sweetheart, I promise I won't drink. And I promise to take you places. The district is sure nice: parks, lakes, picnics galore —we would simply have a grand time together. Oh, I'll be so darn happy when you get here. I simply can't wait. I see all the other fellows with their wives having such a good time that it hurts way down deep, because if you were here with the kiddies we could have a swell time. I believe I'd walk around holding your hand, I love you so much.

Yes, we may get a harvest leave, but that is just a rumour now. Nothing authentic yet. And you asked about winter clothing, etc. To tell you the truth, I would pack it up ready for shipment and have it come up later on if you decide to stay in Brandon—I mean, if we are billeted here for the winter. I don't think we will be, so it is best to wait and see. And as for the furniture, we'll have to get a furnished apartment, naturally. Because moving furniture around like we did before is too expensive and foolish, because as far as the rentals on furnished apartments there is very little difference.

An instructor and a student were killed here yesterday. Their plane crashed just north of the camp. It was a new plane. The authorities can't seem to explain it, because the instructor was an old pilot and the plane was just tested and found perfect. Probably, the student went haywire. Thank the Lord I'm not in the Air Force.

Well, I say goodbye sweetheart. Write soon, I simply live on your letters. Your loving daddy sends you all his love, kisses and hugs. And what is left over, split it up between our boys. Bye Mummy. I'm so lonesome, but the thought of you coming soon helps considerably.

Love and kisses,
Daddy

P.S. Hello Rollie. Are you good to Mummy? Do you play with Murray? You lucky little punk, you are with the nicest mummy in the world. And with the nicest baby. Daddy 'oves you all 'owser.'

꿍

Camp Shilo, Manitoba
July 18, 1940

Dear Hazel,

Received your letters and sure was tickled pink. I love you so much
and I am so lonesome, especially tonight because I have reason to be
blue and I know you are going to be terribly disappointed. But after
all, when I signed the oath, I pledged myself to do all possible for my
country. But it's not going to be as gruesome as it sounds. Here is
what I'm driving at: I can't get my transfer now. It was turned down
cold by the brigadier. . . . The reason for not considering my transfer
was that we will be moving out of Camp Shilo in the very near future,
and I was made to understand that it is to be next Wednesday, and no
one knows where to. Major White thinks we're going to Valcartier
near Quebec, because we are not ready for overseas. So, I still have a
chance to get on home defence. But Lord all Harry it sure seems to
be [a] hard thing to have done. And they make it as hard as they can
by insinuations, or guarded questions, such as, "are you afraid of lead
poisoning," etc. After all, I said to them I have a home and family,
and to my estimation they came first, and I figured my duty was to
serve God and my country, and I would do all I could possibly [do]
in Canada, and possibly much more to further our cause than by
going overseas and doing nothing as the rest of the infantry has been
doing—that is, over there where they have more soldiers than they
know what to do with. And the answer I got was, "you plead a good
case," and I had, "no immediate worry," and I was dismissed.

So, Hazel, I'm afraid that all our plans for the future—that is, about
Brandon—are all blown to hell for the time being. And I hope that
this last news is just another rumour and that we will be here for
a time yet. So please, Darling, don't take it to [*sic*] hard, because
when I got the news it hurt me terribly, and we will have to face the
fact I'm in the Army and the Army is cruel. It spares no feelings or
individuals. I got myself into this, and I don't seem to be able to do
anything about it. . . . So please Hazel, [don't] hold this against me,

although I am to blame. And if in the event we do move from here, don't leave distance draw us apart, because you are all I have in the world. And under the circumstances, don't leave this get your spirit and make you say, "oh, what's the use, I'll never see him again." Because I know the Lord will not take us away from one another and keep us apart much longer, because he is all just and I am putting all my faith in him. And I know that later on in life we will look back on this as a bad dream. And, oh, darling, won't we be happy with our little family growing up around us and looking up to us as good examples, which I am certainly going to strive hard to give them. And no doubt you will, poor Sweetheart. Oh, Mummy, I love you. I've got awful big tears in my eyes, and there are other boys writing here so I have to keep my head well down over the paper. . . . it's the Army sweetheart, and whatever happens from now on don't be surprised. I'm beginning to realize that, and that we will have to take it on the chin with a smile regardless to what happens. And the best we can do is live in the hope and love for one another. I hope this letter doesn't hurt too much Mummy. Lord knows it took all of my courage to write to you and tell you we would have to cancel our plans for the time being. But I still have a strong hope of staying in Canada. Let's pray and hope for the best. That is, that we are together soon and forever. . . .

. . .

Don't cry, Mummy. Please kiss the kiddies for me. A big hug for all you. The biggest for you Mummy. The picture is swell. Please don't go all to pieces darling, I know this letter is going to hurt, but we must face some things. Oh, the world is cruel. Why must there be wars???

I love you,
Daddy

P.S. Write a letter Mummy telling me you can be brave. And pray for Daddy. I wish I was [there] with you to tell you these things. Love, love, please be brave. I'm crying now myself.

I'm going to a show now, "The General Died at Dawn." They say it is very good. It's free in the YMCA building. You should see the camp now. You wouldn't recognize it. Again, it is all new buildings, simply hundreds of them. We will soon be in them as sleeping quarters. No more tents, thank God. There are about two thousand carpenters here hammering away all day—it makes a terrible noise. Hoping you see it Sunday. I'll pray for a miracle, and that is that you get here, that is, Brandon. And I'm sure I can be with you two or three days. . . . Bye-bye, till tomorrow.

Your loving Daddy

☙

Camp Shilo, Manitoba
August [4?], 1940


Dear Mummy,

I just read your letter bawling me out about not writing, but I
simply have been terribly busy. I am orderly corporal, and that
means work.

Practically all of the s.s.r. are on weekend passes and I stayed
here and took over the orderly job so some other fellow could go
to Weyburn on his leave. And I didn't care to go anyplace since you
aren't there. Gosh, I'm lonesome and blue. I want you near me and
I'm afraid! Afraid that if you don't get up here we won't see each
other for a while, because I'm sure we're moving in the near future,
and all the harvest leaves for the s.s.r. have been cancelled for the
present. . . .

Yes, I joined the Army and the Lord only knows what I've gotten us
into. At times I think it's not true—that it's only for a day or two,
and then I'll be back with you. As I notice it is quite true—I'm here,
you're there, and God only knows when we will be together again.
The big trouble is I don't know a thing—where we are going if we
go, if it's overseas, if it's east coast or west coast—this uncertainty is
driving me nuts. I want you so darned bad. I want to kiss you, hold
you in my arms. But no matter how hard I wish or want, I can't do
a thing about it. As I said in my last letter if you were to move to
Brandon, it would just be our luck that the s.s.r. moves away. Oh,
darling, I need you, and the only satisfaction I have is knowing that
you love me and that I have two nice kiddies to come back to—
soon, I hope. And I have faith that you will be true. And pray for
me so that we can be together soon . . . if I were to go home now
I'd be with you so darned much you'd be sick of me hanging around
and I'd smile to myself thinking of how you would get loved, etc.,
etc. Gee, I love you sweetheart, and for some reason I'm terribly
proud to have you as my wife. By the way, I've received several

compliments as to the girlfriend I had here two weeks ago today. Do you remember who the girlfriend was? I do, and wish you were here now.

By the way, excuse the paper, but it serves the purpose. And I'm supposed to be on duty, so I'm sneaking this time as there is no one around.

. . .

Say hello to the folks and tell them to write once in a while, even if I don't always find time to write myself.

. . .

Love,
Daddy

☙

Camp Shilo, Manitoba
August 6, 1940

Dear Mummy,

Received parcel and letter today. . . .

. . .

I still notice in your letter that you are expecting me on harvest
leave. Oh, damn, darling, it is cancelled and I'm awfully afraid we
are moving awfully soon. Advance parties are under three hour
notice, all stores are packed, and everyone is in camp. No leaves
are given whatsoever, and anyone that was on leave was called in.
Everything looks awfully suspicious. Where our destination is,
Lord only knows.

Don't worry darling, something in me says I will see you soon
and under much better circumstances. I just feel that way. . . .

. . .

. . . please darling, remember when I joined the army we were
down and out. You and the children going short on everything,
bad company, no future, and no living. Now, I've given you security
. . . what a terrible cost to both of us. . . .

Hug the babies for Daddy and write him a nice loving letter. He
is awfully lonesome tonite [sic]. In fact, he is nearly crying. Oh,
darling, I love you and I need you.

Bye-bye,
Clarence

Saturday
August 16th, 1940

Dear Mummy,

Gosh, I feel terribly blue. Mickey and George are home and I'm
still in Shilo. Neither one of them are married and they got the
pass which I didn't get. They are about the only two who did in the
whole s.s.r. They were awfully lucky, they beat the weekend cancel-
lations by the matter of minutes. I was about fifteen minutes too
late when I went to get my pass from Major White. He showed
me the brigade order stating that all weekend passes were to be cancelled. The major said he couldn't possibly let me have mine. I told
him I knew of some passes that were issued and he said the only
way they could have been issued is that they were signed and delivered before the order was given out. I chewed the rag with him for
almost an hour and he said he couldn't possibly do a thing about it,
but seeing how badly I wanted to get home he would try to get me
away on Monday on a four-day leave. Gosh, but the Army regulations are cruel. I told him so, and I asked him if my conduct was
bad, and, if not, why can't I get a leave like the rest of them. He
agreed that I haven't had a fair deal and will try to let me get
away Monday. . . .

. . .

I went to Communion Tuesday morning and I prayed for the
safekeeping of our love and that I see you again soon. Do you go
to church Hazel? Or are you letting it slip with the excuse you have
no one to keep the kiddies? If you do, please go to church often and
pray for us. Will you Sweetheart? It certainly helps. I've got big tears
in my eyes now.

. . .

How are the kiddies? Swell, I hope. I'm just dying to see them again.
Do you remember when I left last time Rollie wouldn't kiss me

goodbye. That hurt way down and has been bothering me ever since. Of course, he is only a kid, but I do love those little tykes and I'm afraid they will forget all about their daddy. That hurts too. . . .

Your loving husband,
Clarence

P.S. Pray that I get home Monday . . . no matter what the circumstances are I'm coming home, even if it's to see you for just a minute. . . .

෩

ROLLIE'S NOTE: *Dad did make it home on leave.*

Camp Shilo, Manitoba
August 27, 1940

Dear Mummy,

I suppose you are wondering why I didn't write sooner. In fact, I have, but tore it up, because I got into a rumpus with the R.S.M. Strum—you remember the guy that wouldn't give me an extension? It was all over returning to camp Saturday morning. When I came in I didn't hand in my pass. And even when I was on parade they put me up as AWOL and charged me a day's pay. And then Sunday they had me on as orderly corporal and Strum took after me and gave me a hell of a bawling out for not advising the next sergeant for guard duty. I got mad and thought out loud. Apparently, I said too much, because they put me on orders again and I lost my stripe for a few days as a lesson they say. They called it insubordination and contempt of a superior officer. And the colonel said he'd make an example of me to other NCOs who sometimes think they are running this Army. I'm still plenty mad about this, but all the other NCOs stick back of me, and so does Major White. He told me to watch my step and I would have my stripe back soon, and that he was surprised that I lost my temper. He says that he thought I was quite level-headed, but that at times Strum got pretty overbearing. Another sergeant threw his stripes in Strum's face. I don't know what the argument was. I haven't heard yet. Probably some fool thing, and the sergeant wouldn't take Strum's dirt and decided a private's life was easier. It is much easier, but a guy likes to advance. I'm rather disappointed in myself, but still I had the satisfaction in blowing up.

The trip back was very uneventful. . . .

Gosh, I was lonesome Sunday, knowing I was up for orders for the second time in two days. And I was afraid I would lose my stripe, and it rained all day. I wrote a letter and decided to wait and see what was going to happen to me, so you see the reason I didn't write.

Please, don't worry about the stripes. I'll get them back if I stay here. . . .

Gee, I'm lonesome and blue. I watched Lafleche till it was out of sight. I dreamed of being with Rollie and Murray last night— when I woke up the world seemed so empty. I looked around [at] all the severe cold walls and cots—I could have screamed. I felt so terribly alone. No real friends. And the wind was blowing; in fact, howling. The more I see you on these leaves, the harder it makes Army life. . . .

Now that I have no duties for a while I can write often. I'll write again tomorrow. You may get two letters together because I might be too late to catch the mail.

Do you love your Daddy all over? I love you so darned much and feel so miserable without having you around.

Write soon, I need your love so much.

Your loving Daddy,
Clarence

P.S. Love and kisses.

෴

Camp Shilo, Manitoba
August [29?], 1940


Dear Mummy,

Gee, your letter hurt. I'm sorry if I seemed not to care, but the truth is
I do. Oh, so much. And the reason I didn't write sooner was that I
didn't know what was going to happen about me losing my temper. So I
waited to find out if they were going to take my stripe before I did write.

Yes, I'm a private again, and let me tell you it's a hell of a lot less
responsibility and I don't have to take any dirt from everyone and
do all the dirty work. Just the same, I am sorry I blew up, because
I wanted to advance instead of just always being at the bottom of
the ladder. I suppose you are ashamed of me. Are you darling?
Please don't be, because it's no disgrace. The only thing that
really bothers me is that I lose the extra pay. . . .

. . .

By the way, one fellow asked me if I went AWOL to Lafleche and I lost
my stripe. That's what is going around camp. But I told him, no, that's
not why, and to look at part 2 orders and he would see it in black and
white. This is how it reads darling, "L/Cpl. Bourassa reverted to ranks
charged with insubordination and insolence under Article 11–5-7."

Strum made it a strong charge. I guess I must have made him mad.
And I just had to take it or make it worse. I feel like a sap about it
all the same.

. . .

It's raining buckets, has been all week. And I feel awfully lonesome
and hurt and disgusted with myself.

. . .

Love,
Your Daddy

August 31, 1940

Dear Mummy,

Received your letter and feel very much better.

. . .

I've got to go soon because we have a route march tonight—11:00 o'clock, what an hour—but it is to be done all the same. I've got to polish my brass and clean up for the inspection.

. . .

Excuse the shortness Sweetheart. Write soon and write often. I get awfully lonesome, especially at night.

. . .

Love and kisses,
Your lonesome Daddy

[P.S.] Spent my last 20 cents for stamps, need tobacco— ain't I a bum? . . .

೭ා

[

[September 3, 1940]

Dear Mummy,

You asked me about putting up fruit, etc. Well, put some up if
you want to. It may be, would be, cheaper than buying it canned.

I'm in the Army band now. . . .

Excuse the writing, I'm sitting in bed with a box for a table and
writing is quite sloppy.

Yes, the house should be quite warm with a few layers of paper and the
siding put on tighter than it is. All I can say is, I hope you don't have
to live in it this winter [and could] be with me instead. Don't you?

. . .

We have band practice tonight, so I haven't much time left just now.
I'll write again tomorrow.

How are the kiddies? Gee, I get lonesome for them. I want them
so bad. I sure do, and I need my Mummy awful bad too.

. . .

Write again soon, Sweetheart. I reread and reread your letters, it
makes life more bearable. When you get those pictures developed,
don't forget I want to see them, and then I'll send them back.

Bye Sweetheart, words of love and kisses—not much to offer when
it's on paper—but oh how I mean it, I simply ache for you.

Love and kisses to you and kiddies,
Love,
Daddy

p.s. Write often.

☙

Camp Shilo, Manitoba
Thursday
[September 5th, 1940]


Dear Mummy,

I said I was going to write yesterday, but due to a concert given in
the Y[MCA] I didn't get around to it.

. . .

Since I've joined the band I haven't done a thing but play music.
I'm playing the baritone and I am getting along as well as any of
them, and that's not too bad. So, you can see I'm having a soft time
now—no dirty work, no parades, no drill, and a swell bandmaster.
Even with all the soft times I still am very lonesome and I want my
Mummy Sweetheart and kiddies.

By the way, you will have to send me some stamps because this is
my last one and I want to write you some more. I'll have to borrow
one to write you on Sunday.

Received two packages of cigarettes from Mother and a little note
saying simply, "Love, Mother." I'm going to enclose a note for the
folks—you give it to them, will you?

. . .

We expect to be moving someplace soon, everything is in readiness.
But according to the news last night, I doubt if we [will] move
anyplace but in Canada. The move I would like to make would
be to the Air Force, then to the coast with you and the kiddies.
Wouldn't that be swell? But after all, I don't expect anything so
nice. Everything else has gone wrong, but I'm going to try anyway.

. . .

Bye-bye Sweetheart,
Daddy

P.S. I'm awfully lonesome tonight. I wish I could crawl into bed and reach over and find you there—isn't life mean? Pray for me and that I may get the transfer. Love.

ℰ℘

Camp Shilo, Manitoba
Sunday
[September 8, 1940]

Dear Mummy,

. . .

Well, you insist I answer your questions. Well, here goes. Yes,
my lady friend is fine, I hope, but I don't get to see her very often.
I was in to Lafleche to see her three weeks ago and she was fine then.
And I think she loves me very much, but she thinks that I am quite
reserved and didn't act as she expected a lover should. She says I
seemed so quiet. But I wrote her and told her if I was reserved and
not so ardent, there was a reason. And to tell you the truth, I love
her an awful lot. A lot more than she realizes. And I want her to
come and live with me soon and bring the kiddies too. I get so
darned lonesome here, especially today—it's raining and cold,
and to top it off I've got the blues.

. . .

As for a furlough, I'm applying for it on Wednesday. There are quite
a few who have furloughs coming now, and a move being imminent
I doubt if they will grant them. I'm going to ask for mine anyway,
and if there is any hope of getting it I'll bet you know the best I can
say now is let's hope.

About the transfer, we won't know a thing till it's put through,
if ever. We've the wheel a rolling, but if anything happens, I have
my doubts. I'm really not counting on it too much because I've
learned that the Army is the most disappointing thing in the world.
All I'm looking forward to is that we can stay in Canada. We will
know soon and then I'm going to have you move to where I am. In
fact, if we are still here the first of the month I want you to come to
Brandon and stay. We should be able to get board and room for you

and the kiddies for about $10.00 a week, and there are apparently quite a few places. I'm so sick of this being apart that I may go nuts, I want you so bad.

Well, I am going to bed now and be lonesome lonesome. The rain is drumming on the roof and everybody seems to feel blue. Yes, I wish that the dream you had was true. Let's hope it materializes and we get together forever awfully soon.

I'm sending the snaps back . . . I wish to God I was with my wife and kiddies who need me, and where I belong.

Write soon darling,
Daddy

℘

Camp Shilo, Manitoba
[September ?, 1940]


Dear Mummy,

. . .

Well Hazel, when I received your bawling out I was really mad.
I couldn't just seem to figure it out for a while, and then I started
to realize what it was like not hearing from me. Because, I certainly
look forward to your letters and parcels, and when I don't receive
a thing I'm disappointed myself. But, please believe me it was
through no fault of my own that I didn't write.

. . .

Well, for the next week I will be, or am, battalion orderly corporal,
and that is going to keep me terribly busy. But I'll find time to write
if I'm not too flat broke to buy stamps. By the way, I received your
cigarettes. They sure come in handy because I'm broke flat between
now and payday. So, I guess I'll have to bum smokes for the next
few days.

Steve and George Turner went to Brandon today. That is, they have
a weekend pass and wanted me to go too. I didn't. I hate Brandon
without you, and there is only one reason I can see for anyone
going to Brandon and that is women. And not being interested
in any way, I stayed in camp.

Mummy, I am awfully blue and lonesome all alone in my tent.
And I see men (soldiers) and their wives and sweethearts wandering
all over the place—it makes me feel worse. And if it wasn't for being
kept pretty busy I could never stand being away from you and
the kiddies.

I'm sending you a locket, not so hot, but the best I could afford.
And I saw some that were swell and I did the best I could, but I'm
sending all my love with it. Please keep it nice. And I've kissed it for
you sweetheart.

As for leaving camp within 72 hours, that is all baloney, just a
rumour started in camp. No one knows a thing. We are simply
under 72 hours orders; that is to say, when the order to move is
received we have to be out of camp within that time. And according
to the last we received, in all probability we will be stationed somewhere in Canada. I read the wire myself.

How is Rollie now? Is he feeling better or is he just spoiled?
Now whatever you do, don't spoil him or let him get away with
anything—be firm.

. . .

Write soon and a kiss for you Sweetheart, right here—x

Your lonesome Daddy,
Clarence

☙

Saturday
[September 14, 1940]

Dear Mummy,

I just read your long letter and I feel terrible about it all. You seem hopeful that we might stay in Canada, but I really think we are going overseas because they are discharging anyone and everyone who is the least bit physically unfit, and they are checking our equipment over and making sure everything is in perfect order. And made us all sign our wills—what little we have. I naturally signed you as beneficiary, rather gruesome you can see, but I've got myself into this and only the Lord will see me through to my wife and kiddies.

When you phoned last night I couldn't possibly imagine what it was—either somebody sick or you were coming to Brandon. But I sure was tickled to hear your voice. I was prickles all over. Oh, I love you so much, and you sounded so disappointed in me, as if I didn't care to come home. Yes, Hazel, I feel like a heel because I didn't go. I know you wanted me to, and I wanted to terribly, but I just couldn't get the money from anyone. I tried all over, but since there is a possibility of moving everyone is hanging onto their money. So, I just had to stay in camp. Steve made money playing poker, so he paid for his and Tom's way.

. . . What a hell of a life, and I don't know how to make the best of it. The only consolation is that I'm in the band and the risks are much smaller.

. . .

The Cameron Highlanders are all lined up outside with full equipment and they are going away—where, they don't know. They are in the same brigade as we are so that means we are moving for sure.

. . .

Monday

. . .

How are the kiddies? I suppose Murray is getting nicer and cuter everyday, and Rollie is getting longer legged and all neck and full of the devil. Thank God they have a good mother, so my worries about a bringing up for them are few, and I love them so.

Write soon Mummy, and don't stop because you think I might be gone. Because as far as this damned army goes, they say we're leaving, and I don't believe a thing anymore. The only thing that makes me mad is that we can't find out anything definite.

Well bye Mummy, I'll write again tomorrow. I expect a letter from you.

Love,
Daddy

☙

Camp Shilo, Manitoba
[September 19], 1940


Dear Mummy,

My not writing I suppose makes you think I left Canada. Well,
we are still here. And if I'm judge of anything, we will be in
Canada all winter. Where, I don't know. . . .

. . .

Tonight, we are giving a Band Concert for the Officers. We have
been quite busy with the music, but it's quite interesting and not
hard work. I wish I knew what was going to happen in the future;
and, as you suggested, if I could get into a band that would stay in
Canada we could be together. Wouldn't that be swell. I want to
stay in Canada so bad that I'd grab at any chance.

I've got to go now, it's about time to go and play. I'm getting
along famous. The Band Master says that I've developed a very
good tone on the baritone and to keep it up. And that I possibly
could develop into a very good player. Excuse [the] writing, I'm
standing up and writing against the wall. Will write again
tomorrow. I love you all over.

Write often. I enjoy your letters, and the last one was swell.

Clarence

ⅽↄ

Dauphin, Manitoba
[September 26, 1940]

Dear Mummy,

You probably are worried sick about what happened to me. Well, to tell you the truth we've been on a war scheme all over the province of Manitoba. We've been down to Killarney, Boissevain, Portage, Minnedosa, Neepawa, Clear Lake [and] Riding Mountain National Park. The scenery is really swell, but we were always out in the open, freezing at night, and we couldn't get a chance to write at all.

The Band Master let me have a few minutes to write you a note a nd let you know why I couldn't write. In fact, on this scheme we're not supposed to communicate with anyone. We are supposed to pretend we are in actual warfare, and we are not even allowed out of the bivouac grounds. I'm writing in a drugstore in the auto camp here, and I'm afraid to get caught because I'm out of bounds. I supposed it's like this overseas—if a person wishes to write to anyone they would have to hide or have special permission.

I suppose you were getting pretty sore and imagined all kinds of things. The fact is I haven't heard a word from you since we left camp, eight days today. But I know there will be a letter or two bawling me out and accusing me of something or another, because I haven't written for over a week. Last week I said I was going to write tomorrow, and that tomorrow found me about 300 miles from camp, and I didn't have a possible chance to write till now.

Well Mummy, I still love you terribly much. And I get lonesome, especially at night looking up through the tall pine trees at the sky and feeling so all alone, thinking of you and the kiddies and worrying about not writing and wondering if you are terribly disappointed in not hearing. Anyway, I love you darling, and no one else will ever interfere with my love for you, come what may.

Clear Lake is just grand sweetheart. I made a vow that someday you, the kiddies and I would go to a place like that for a few weeks some summer. It's simply swell. There's such marvellous trees and scenery, a grand lake and beaches, swell fishing, etc. Some day we will enjoy those things together.

Well, I'll have to close now and will write as soon as we get back to Shilo; and again, I feel quite sure we'll be in Canada for the winter.

By the way, someone stole a pair of my shoes, a sweater and hold-all, and in kit inspection I was shorted those, and I suppose they will take it off my pay check [*sic*], so that won't leave me much.

Bye, and oodles of love to you and the kiddies,
Your loving hubby,
Clarence

❧

[Camp Shilo, Manitoba
October 10th, 1940]


Dear Mummy,

I'm awfully lonesome and blue today. I don't know why, because I expect to see you soon. That should make me feel better, but I don't know when that will be. Apparently, we are going to Toronto for the winter, so as you see the rumours change every day. All I can say is prepare yourself to move someplace soon. I've got to have you near me soon or I will go nuts, I love you so much.

. . .

We might get furloughs after we move, and I hear that you can travel for half-fare being a soldier's wife—find out! If so, you will be able to come soon when we get settled.

Love,
Daddy

[P.S.] Hello Rollie. Are you a good boy? Kiss Murray for Daddy.

જી

*Postcard*

October 16th, 1940

Hazel,

On our way to Toronto. Received your letters and will answer as soon as I get settled down in our new barracks. How are the kiddies? Better, I hope.

Love,
Clarence

☙

*Postcard*

October 18, 1940

Hazel,

Well, we are in Toronto—a little busy for a day or two! Will write tomorrow and it won't be a card. Our address is s.s.r., Exhibition Grounds, Toronto. How are the kiddies? And yourself? Write soon.

Love,
Clarence

☙

Toronto, Ontario
[October ?, 1940]

Dear Mummy,

Received your two letters today—one was forwarded from Shilo. Yes, I'll admit you must be wondering what was the matter I didn't write sooner. Well, your suspicions are all wrong, because I do love you and it wasn't because of anyone else. The reason I didn't write before we left Shilo was, or were, Friday, the band played for a funeral. A young fellow (soldier s.s.r.) by the name of Carlson died of a carbuncle. . . . Saturday, I went to Brandon to see what I could do about the Air Force, got back Saturday night 11 o'clock. Sunday, had dinner with Bob and Kaye [Clarence's brother Robert and his wife] so Sunday was gone, and Monday, we were terribly busy getting ready. And Tuesday, away. So as soon as we were settled down in the train I mailed a card, and another as soon as we got here, and a letter on Sunday.

Maybe the officers did choose Toronto for its night life. Well, to tell you the truth there certainly is a lot of entertainment for the troupes [*sic*]: circuses, vaudeville, boxing, wrestling, shows, boating, cruising, etc., etc. All innocent as you see. Of course there is the social side also, if a person wants to look for such things, but I haven't come in contact with any of it and I don't intend to. Maybe you believed what Robert said or told you regarding some address in Brandon. Yes, he did ask me if I knew where he could pick up a girl or "woman" for the night, as he put it, and I answered him very plainly that I knew of no one personally, but that I had heard of two sisters living in Brandon, and I told him the address. The reason I knew of the name and address was that it was common knowledge among the troupes about these two sisters on 312 Princess. I believe that is what I told him. You know how it is among men—if there is such a place in the city it gets known, so I sent him there. And that's not excusing myself, because I don't know these women, and if he tried to make you believe that I said I knew them he is a damned liar . . .

Anyway, you're coming here right away so keep about fifty bucks—beg, borrow or steal—there is a cheaper rate of transportation if I get it for you from this end. Just a minute, I'll go and see if I can't find out anything definite right now. Can't find out anything for sure just now, but this is what I have decided. Just as soon as I get the necessary papers from you re: Air Force, I'm going to apply for acceptance into the Air Force and I should know for sure by the 5th of November if I am to be accepted. In the mean time busy yourself with the idea you are going to be with me for the winter, because you are. That is why you will need about fifty. If you can get more, the better. Rentals here are very cheap compared to the western cities. Also, cots are much cheaper. What we considered luxuries there are staples here. So hang on to our shirts for a few more days and I'll know for sure what to do. At any rate I must have you with me sweetheart. The only thing is when you do come you will have to furnish the money to buy the ticket. I don't know what takes so much money at this end. As far as I'm concerned the little I get just sees me by. It is enough though, so you needn't worry about me asking for any to spend on myself.

. . .

Bye Sweetheart, write a nice letter, and assure yourself you will be with me for the winter. Where there is a will there is a way.

I love you,
Daddy

[P.S.] Hello, Rollie. Give Murray a big [hug] for Daddy and be a good boy for your Mummy.

Love and kisses. Bye, write often.

ભ

S.S.R.
Exhibition Grounds
Toronto, Ontario
[October 23, 1940]


Dear Mummy,

Well, here I am, as lonesome and blue as I can possibly be, and so far away from you sweetheart. Miles and miles and I haven't heard a word from you. Maybe it is because I didn't write. I hope so. I suppose you feel lost too with me so far away.

Well, it was a long tiresome trip up here. Rained all the way and is still raining. . . . Mickey and I went to the zoo yesterday and did it ever remind me of our honeymoon. You remember the big lion there, well, they have it here, the same one. Don't I wish we could start our married life all over. I'd love you and kiss you so much you'd beg for mercy. . . .

. . .

We are quartered in the Horse Palace at the Canadian National Exhibition Grounds. It's terribly large. There are about 8,000 men in this one building, and what style they had for these horses. Silver, nickel, chromium, and oak, and so clean. But its quite a joke around being quartered in a barn, and is it ever an expensive place. $2,000,000—can you imagine? And ultramodern.

. . . . We are right on the shore of Lake Ontario, is it ever a lake! The most water I've ever seen.

. . .

Love,
Daddy

Exhibition Grounds
Toronto, Ontario
October 25, 1940


Dear Hazel,

Well, here I am again. I'm Infirmary Orderly tonight, and I'm
taking time out to drop you a line . . .

This evening I was standing on the shore of the lake watching the
steamers going back and forth (by the way our barracks are on the
shore of Lake Ontario) and I was thinking wouldn't it be swell if
you and I could go to Niagara Falls on one of them and have a
second honeymoon, and it only costs $1.50 return. And let me tell
you sweetheart it would certainly be a honeymoon all over again.
Tonight I'm so lonesome and blue and I feel as if I were at the end
of the world; although, when I think of you coming to me soon it
makes life much easier. I still haven't found anything about railway
fares yet, but as I said in my last letter to be prepared to be with
me for the winter.

Yes, this is really pretty country. The trees are still green and it's
quite "summery" . . . and the lake is only about two hundred yds
from here. It is more water than I have ever seen. The Air Force
training field is only half a mile from here, so we hear a continual
drone of planes overhead and I sort of enjoy watching them. While
watching a 'sham' battle between two planes the other day, one of
the young pilots lost control of his ship and crashed into the trees
about two miles south and was killed. I read it in the papers the
same night. Let me tell you it was an awful thing to watch.


. . .

Well, I guess I'll close, wishing I could crawl into bed with you and cuddle up and keep warm. Sometimes I lie awake and miss miss you, and I get so lonesome and blue, but let's hope it won't be for long. Do you love your daddy? He loves you.

Hug kiddies for me and tell them I think of them a lot and hope to be with them soon.

Love,
Daddy

∽

c.n. Exh. Grds
[Canadian National
Exhibition Grounds]
Toronto, Ont.
[October 28, 1940]


Dear Mummy,

. . .

You ask me again if I love you. Please, darling, I do. Oh, so much.
I'm going crazy here and I want you with me right away, so please
come. I need you and you need me, and why live apart when we
don't have to. And as you say I may go overseas anytime, and if
that's so, why waste more time about this foolishness. Why not
take advantage of it while we can be together. Even if it's for just a
month. Am I not worth it? So come. I'll help financially at this end
as much as I can, and that will be something. What I spend eating
downtown, shows, etc., we could use to help get squared up, and,
furthermore, you will be out of Lafleche.

I suppose Murray is getting real cute. I can't wait to see the little
darling. And Rollie I suppose is getting to be quite the man. Please
come Mummy. Hurry and answer back so that I can let you
know what to bring. . . .

I love you and want you here.

Love and kisses to all,
Daddy

☙

S.S.R.
C.N.E. Gr[ounds]
Toronto, Ont.
Sunday
[November 3, 1940]


Dear Mummy,

You are probably wondering what's the matter this time—well,
first of all I'll answer your letters.

Yes, of course, there are burlesque shows in town, and I saw
one and it's all show and talk. There is nothing to them; in fact,
I consider them disgusting, especially these 'stripteases' as they are
called. So, you can ease your worries about them, because I am
quite sure that I wouldn't waste a nickel on one again.

And as for the women['s] beer parlours—yes, there are quite a number
of them. But I haven't seen the inside of one, because the only way you
can get in is with a lady escort. So, if Steve and Tom have been to
them—you can judge for yourself—they must have women friends.
So, don't worry about that because the parlours I've seen are for men,
and what I know about the women's is just what I wrote above.

. . . you must make up your mind to come to me at once, because
I'll go nuts if I'm disappointed . . . I'll be with you all of the time
you are here, every evening, and two nights a week, and every
other weekend. Gee, I'm lonesome and blue. I see a lot of our boys
strolling around with their wives from Saskatchewan, and some of
them have kiddies. So, if they can come, some even with babies two
and three months old, you can come with ours too. And if they
have apartments, we can get them too.

I went to the hockey game last night between [the] New York Rangers
and the Toronto Maple Leafs. And do you know what? It cost me $3.00,
but it was a great game and at that price I don't think I'll go again now
that I've satisfied my curiosity and I can say I've seen big league hockey.

...

Are you being a real good girl? Yes, I'm good—too good. To please some of the guys around here, my worst doings are the odd glass of beer and the odd picture show, and I haven't been to anything like a dance or social, which the people put on for the "Westerners" as they call us. I just don't feel like going anyplace until you get here, and then I'll only want to be with you.

Yes, my birthday will be on Tuesday and it's going to be awful quiet. I'm not even going out of barracks. Wouldn't it be swell if you were here and we could go to some nice dine and dance place for the evening on my birthday, where we know no one but us and have us to ourselves for a whole evening. I believe I could be quite the lover.

...

Bye,
Daddy

P.S. Enclosed pictures of our band and I suppose you can pick me out easy enough.

*Toronto 1940.*

CLARENCE, THE TALL FIGURE JUST TO THE RIGHT OF CENTRE,
IN FORMATION WITH THE SOUTH SASKATCHEWAN REGIMENT BAND.
ACCORDING TO CLARENCE'S NEXT LETTER, THE PHOTOGRAPH
APPEARED IN TORONTO'S NEWSPAPERS.

Canadian National Exhibition Grounds
Toronto, Ontario
[November 5, 1940]


Dear Mummy,

Well, here I am. Not much more. . . .

Received a card from Mother today and received your letter
Monday, and it was a swell letter darling. I have reread it about
ten times. Yes, I want you here . . . I get so lonesome without you.

Yesterday we played for a colonel's funeral, some guy of the
Toronto Queen's Rangers, and we were complimented on our
playing and today we have our pictures—that is, the band—in all
the Toronto papers. Next Saturday we play for a football game,
and next Sunday for a Armistice Parade in downtown Toronto.

. . .

Well, I'll close now darling and I will keep you informed about
transfer. The band is going to a fight tonight in the Coliseum—
Air Force vs. Army—should be good.

Write often.

Love,
Daddy

P.S. Hug Rollie and Murray for me. I'm lonesome and will be
with you soon. Love.

ॐ

[November 8, 1940]

Dear Mummy,

Come now! I've got a room and kitchenette in a home with a couple our own age. That will do for as soon as you get here. About 15 minutes walk from here, and if that isn't just what you would like, we could look around when you get here. $5.00 a week and bathroom is next door to ours and there are no other boarders.

If I get into the Air Force, it is going to be a long while I'm afraid. I've made my applications all over again and they were very frank with me and told me that they were not taking on soldiers unless an expert in some line. But, they would put my application through just as soon as I had birth certificates of my two children. So you will have to get those from the priest too. I could have got in as a gunner or observer, but that is worse than what I'm in. So come, and get all the money you can because we will need it. I can pay one week's rent on the 15th.

When you come wire me from someplace on the way down so that I can meet you and arrange to get you to our rooms. Bring blankets—that is, all you can—and linen, towels, clothing, and kitchenware, dishes, no furniture, bring baby carriage.

Gee, I can hardly wait. Come as quick as you can, I'm terribly lonesome today.

Your loving Daddy

P.S. Hurry.

⁓

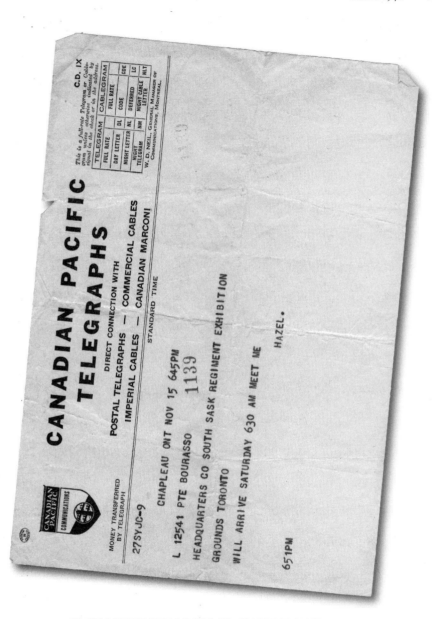

CANADIAN PACIFIC TELEGRAPHS

DIRECT CONNECTION WITH
POSTAL TELEGRAPHS — COMMERCIAL CABLES
IMPERIAL CABLES — CANADIAN MARCONI

STANDARD TIME

MONEY TRANSFERRED
BY TELEGRAPH

27SYJC-9

L 12541 PTE BOURASSO

CHAPLEAU ONT NOV 15 645PM  1139

HEADQUARTERS CO SOUTH SASK REGIMENT EXHIBITION

GROUNDS TORONTO

WILL ARRIVE SATURDAY 630 AM MEET ME

HAZEL.

651PM

CP TELEGRAPH FROM HAZEL TO CLARENCE SENT WHEN
SHE WAS EN ROUTE TO TORONTO. THE TELEGRAPH WAS DATED
NOVEMBER 15 AND WAS SENT FROM CHAPLEAU, ONTARIO.

ROLLIE'S NOTE: *I remember we were going to Toronto—a young mother with a five-year-old and a baby. It was 48 hours on a crowded train, my mother making lunches, changing diapers and trying to keep me occupied. Even after all these years I have vivid memories of our trip. Our "apartment" was the second floor of a two-story house; the "kitchenette," a wooden table with chairs; and there was a bedroom separated by a curtain. It was Christmas in the big city and I remember sitting in the upstairs window watching streetcars, and milkmen and paper boys making their deliveries. And watching squirrels running along power lines and through trees kept me entertained for ages. I also remember going with Mom and Dad to the Armouries for Christmas parties and shows, and a movie, and being terrified and refusing to go up to Santa at Eaton's department store. And then a week before Christmas, my Dad's orders came to embark for England. We watched from the house as Dad walked down the street to the barracks, turning back to wave. The war was now very real.*

❧

*Postcard*

[December ?, 1940]

Mrs. C.O. Bourassa
10 Sorauren Ave.
Toronto, Ont.


Dear Hazel,

Well, by the time you get this we will probably be in Halifax. The scenery has been very nice. I'll write the first opportunity I get!

Love,
Clarence

P.S. A hug for each of the kiddies. All feeling well, I hope.

❧

C.O. Bourassa
L12541
South Saskatchewan Regiment
C.A.S.F.
[Canadian Active Service Force]
December 27, [1940]


Dear Mummy,

Here I am in England and you in Canada. I can't realize we are
so far apart in such a short time. Well, I'll tell you about our trip.
The train ride was alright. We saw a lot of country. The only thing
that spoiled it is that we were getting further apart. And no sooner
landed from the train, then we were herded (if I can use the word)
aboard ship and actually packed like sardines. There was three times
more men aboard than the ship could accommodate. And so the
meals were terrible, but being in the band and playing for the officers' mess we got—that is the band—one good meal a day. Thank
God for that or I would have starved. Our passage over was very
rough and most of the boys were sea sick—and were they sick. To
tell you the truth it was simply awful, crammed in the boat as we
were, and only a few of us well enough to get the cots and to keep
the place clean enough so not to choke, or rather smother, with the
foul smell, or simply the stench of the sections. Frankly, when I
set foot on land here, I could've rolled in the dirt with pleasure.

While I'm thinking of it, the mail service is terrible, so we will
have to write often. And I suppose a lot does not reach its destination due to sinkings, so the oftener we write we will be sure to get
letters often. And please send all kinds of cigarettes and razor
blades. The cigs are terrible here and awful expensive.

Just heard our first air raid warning—the "Fritzies" must be flying
towards London, not so far away from here. They claim we can
see the anti-aircraft from here.

Just came in from outside. Heard planes flying overhead and heavy explosions in the distance. There never has been a raid here as yet, and no one seems to worry.

How did you make out after I left? It must have been terrible for you. How are the kiddies? I'm worried because I seem so cut off from the rest of the world here. And news of home are certainly scarce. I'm already looking forward to letters which I suppose will get here about the 15th of January. I don't know how I'm going to wait for news of you and the kiddies. Dear little tots, I'll sure miss them, especially Murray. Send me pictures of them and yourself and the folks and all the news you can think of about everyone I know. And as I've already mentioned, as I told you before I left, and if anyone sends me anything, tell them cigarettes.

I'm going to write to the folks Sunday, and to you again, and I'll give you all my impressions of England. I've seen nothing yet, so expect a composition. I'll write twice a week so you will get letters regularly. After they start coming, or rather whenever ships go over to Canada, you should get four or five at a time because there is a convoy every four or five weeks I suppose, and it must be the same coming here. So if you send cigarettes send plenty of them and often so as to catch all convoys coming over.

Well, I guess I close and sit me down to write a nice, decent letter Sunday.

A kiss and a hug for the kiddies, and love for Mummy,
Daddy

p.s. Hello, Rollie. Be a good boy for Mummy and say a little for prayer for Daddy before going to bed for Daddy and give Mummy a goodnight kiss every night for Daddy too. Bye-bye, and be a good boy.

Love and kisses,
Clarence

My address is:

Bourassa, C.O.
L12541
South Saskatchewan Regiment (note: in full)
Canadian A.S.F.
c/o Base Post Office
Canada
(and mark the envelope across the right side below the stamp
with England)

&

England
December 29, [1940]


My Dear Hazel,

I said I'd write often—well, I am. I don't know whether you
have received my first letter or if you ever will, so to make sure
you know, I'm fine, and we have good quarters and substantial
meals. And England is nice, the climate mild. And I'm safe and
secure. In fact, where we are at you would never know there was
a war on—it is so quiet and peaceful.

I feel quite lonely, the holiday seasons away from my loved ones,
and especially you darling. So let's pray and hope for a quick
ending to this, so that we can be together again soon for keeps.

How are you darling? Fine, I hope. And the kiddies? I suppose
Murray is getting cuter every day. Do I ever miss the little tyke
and that grin of his. Does he walk yet? If I could only be there for
his first step. How is Rollie behaving? Is he still as naughty as ever?
I suppose he keeps asking for me. Yes, I feel quite lonely without
the kiddies around. In Toronto I was really happy and contented
with you.

Well, I suppose you are in Lafleche, and the trip back must have
been terrible for you with two kiddies. And I suppose the house
was cold, and is cold. Are you staying alone? Or have you Kaye
or someone with you? Or are you out on the farm with your Dad?
I've a thousand questions to ask, but I'll wait for a letter which
I suppose or hope will tell me all I want to know.

Did you get he card I mailed on the train? I suppose you were
awfully worried about me not writing—no news, and your
imagination didn't help either I don't suppose.

Well, it's getting quite late . . . so bye-bye for now, I'll write twice a week. How many you'll receive I don't know. Don't forget cigarettes, lots of them.

Your lonesome Daddy

P.S. Rollie, give Mummy a hug and a kiss for Daddy, and Murray too. Be a good boy. Love.

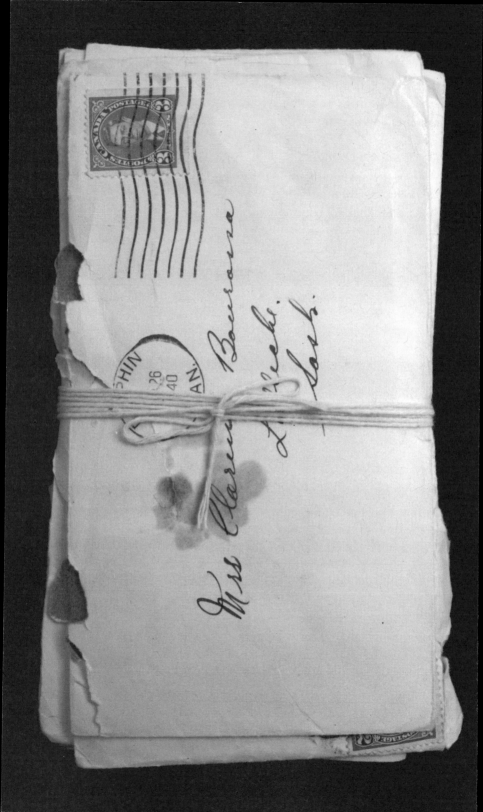

# LETTERS 1941

England
January 5, 1941

Dear Mummy,

I hope you have received my last letter, as the mail service is a little
unsteady you may have got the other one first. . . .

Well, I get pretty lonesome for you and the kiddies—more so
today—some of the boys got mail from Canada today. I really don't
expect any before the first of February, because you didn't know if
we were going over or not, and I wasn't sure either till we got out
from port. I felt I was stepping off the end of the world as I
watched Canada disappear on the horizon.

I've seen nothing of England yet, just what is around our camp, and,
frankly speaking, give me Canada any day. It is damp, chilly, and an
awful lot of fog, and these confounded blackouts, you can't see a
speck of light. And if a person gets away from camp I'd imagine he
would have an awful time of it finding his way back.

Well darling, I suppose you feel terribly lonesome yourself, alone in
this terrible mess with a couple of kiddies. Well, I don't know just who
is the worse off of the two; you have the kiddies to fill part of the ache
in your heart, while I only have their pictures and sweet memories. Yes,
I think of you and the kiddies constantly, and am already looking forward to my return to you. When that will be I haven't the slightest idea.

Did I tell you that all the boys in this hut pooled their resources
and bought a radio. We listened to "Major Bowes Amateur Hour"
here the other night. It was a rebroadcast of course, but awful nice
to hear. Another piece we hear a lot is, "I'll Never Smile Again."
When I hear it over the radio it makes me awfully lonesome. The
author of the piece was a girl from Toronto who lost her husband
after 6 weeks of married life. So I suppose his dying was the reason
she wrote such a sad tune. Now, I understand she is to marry Bert
Pearl of the "Happy Gang." Maybe you knew all of this.

Well, here our training is certainly much heavier than in Canada. All of the NCOs and Officers are taking special courses, and the men are drilled and lectured etc., from day in to day out.

The war news was just on—and they sound very encouraging. The Wops are sure catching hell in Africa—just a few more days and they should be out of it.

Well, Sweetheart, how are the kiddies anyway? Fine, I hope. I look at their pictures daily and I've got yours with me all the time, and it isn't one of your latest so please send me pictures regularly of yourself and the kiddies. I'm going to have some taken of me and send them to you.

Well, darling, I went to communion this morning and prayed for the safekeeping of you and the kiddies and that we will soon be together again.

I'll close now and write again in about three days, and what I really want to stress is I love you terribly and pray constantly for a happy return to you and ours.

Love,
Daddy

P.S. Go to church regularly sweetheart—for me, will you? Rollie, are you a good boy for Mummy and do you play nice with Murray? Say your prayers tonight, and don't forget to mention Daddy to Jesus and give Mummy a big kiss for Daddy.

Bye-bye

ᏋᏏ

January 8, [1941]


Dear Hazel,

Well, here I am again. This is a break in band practice and I'm
in the Salvation Army hut, so I'm going to start this letter.

We have been here two weeks now and I haven't received a word
from Canada, and probably you haven't heard from me yet. But I
suppose I will hear soon. In fact, I don't know what I'll do if I don't
hear awful sudden, because I'm terribly lonesome and aching for
news of you and the kiddies.

We got news from Canada Monday night. I understand that south
Saskatchewan has had a two-day blizzard and that the roads are all
blocked and that it is terribly cold. Gosh, Darling, if you're staying
in our house you must be nearly froze solid. Can't you arrange for
someplace warmer? Because it must be terribly cold for the kiddies.
And if anything should happen to the kiddies, I'd go wild. And I
would like to be able to say, well, at least if not happy, my sweetheart and boys were warm and comfortable. Are you being good?

The weather here is snowing, cloudy and damp. In fact, it's miserable out of doors. I haven't been any place at all. But, I expect to
see quite a little of England soon, because I'm getting a six day
leave starting the twenty-first of January, and free transportation.
I'm going to Glasgow for a couple of days, then Edinburgh for
another couple of days, and on my way back I'll stop and see a
little of London, although they say London gets an air raid
practically every night. I'm going to look it over in the daytime
and then come to camp where everything is nice and peaceful.
Really and honestly, I would just as soon stay in camp, but apparently everyone must go on this "Landing Leave." So, I'm going to
make it a sightseeing tour. So I can at least talk about, or rather
say, or tell the people, I have seen England and Scotland when
I get back to you and good old Canada.

Nets Brailsford just received a telegram from his girlfriend in Toronto wishing him a happy new year, and did that ever make me feel blue. But one consolation I have, is that I know you are mentally sending me all your love and best wishes everyday that we are apart. Len Myland is sitting behind me playing "I'll Never Smile Again" on the violin, and it is sure a swell piece. It always seems to fit in with my mood, and frankly I don't think I'll ever forget the tune.

By the way, I started writing this letter this morning and since I've had my first taste of basketball. I played a game of it this afternoon and really enjoyed myself for the first time since leaving Toronto. And yes, what I wouldn't give to be with you tonight. Nothing else matters, just you and the kiddies and I can't do a thing about it.

All the boys are gathering around the radio waiting for news from Canada—funny how practically everyone of us were impatient to get over here and now they are all lonely for good old Canada. By the way, how are your financial difficulties? Getting them ironed out?. . .

How is Rollie behaving? Having any trouble with him? I suppose he should be in school soon. He is just about the age where he will be hard to keep track of, and if he is anything like I was you will need a special detective. He sure is a swell kid all the same. And Murray, the sweet little tyke, does still clamp his teeth and grin? I don't suppose I'll recognize him when I will see him again.

Are you saying a prayer for me every night before going to sleep? And is Rollie giving you that goodnight kiss for me?

. . .

Your loving and lonesome,
Daddy

P.S. Hey Rollie, what did you do all day today? Were you over to Nino's or playing in the snow? And are you a good boy? Do you miss your Daddy? And I forgot to ask you before, did Santa Claus bring some nice things for you? What did Murray get? When Mummy writes Daddy write a little note for Daddy— that's a good boy! Bye-bye, Daddy.

Writing again soon. Oh, yes, I would like a scarf and a sweater, size 38. I would buy one here, but wool is at a premium and easier procured in Canada. Remember the list I left with you before I left? . . . English smokes are terrible. Could you arrange it so as I could get a thousand a month? And if that is too many, I'll let you know and you could hold back one order. Order them through a store at $2.50 per thousand, and ask for a receipt and let me know when you order them (Sweet Caps or Exports).

Love,
Clarence

❧

January 10, 1941

Dear Hazel,

I'm writing with [a] gas respirator on; we have just had a gas
alarm. Drill, I suppose, but never-the-less we must wear them
till the all-clear signal is given.

How are the kiddies? Fine, I hope. Or have they got colds? I've got
a real one just starting—it hurts terribly when I cough. If it gets any
worse I'm going to report sick, because I understand that colds are
hard to get rid of here.

"Fritzy" was over again last night and we were out of doors watching
the searchlights and anti-aircraft fire in the distance, and we could
hear the dull booming of the coastal guns in the distance. According to the news this morning, and considering all the noise, the
Germans did no damage.

Last night I did all my laundry and mended socks. It took about
two hours. I'll be quite the handy man when I get home. Frankly,
I sure will be glad to get back and even mend and wash my own
duds just to be with you and the kiddies.

By the way, I haven't tasted onions or coffee since I left Canada.
And I understand onions are a luxury here and expensive (about
6 pence a pound—12 cents in Canada). And we never hear of
hamburgers and hot dogs—beg your pardon, they have hamburgers.
Four pence for one as large as Murray's hand. What I wouldn't
give for a feed of hamburger and onions and good coffee.

Sweetheart, you worry about me, don't you? Well, listen, we are as
snug as "bugs in a rug": roomy quarters, single spring beds, no one
over top anymore, steam heat, swell showers and baths, and plenty
of air raid shelters if we ever need them.

Yes, and another thing. Yesterday, someone stole my respirator and steel helmet, which [we] are supposed to have with us all the time, and, therefore, I had to get another one, and I had to buy it. Sixteen dollars for the respirator, three dollars for the helmet, and one dollar for eye shields. Twenty dollars, all told, to come out of my pay within two months. That means I get one pound a payday, about $4.50 till it's paid for. Worst of luck. That will not happen again. I carry both with me all the time: to cot, to the showers. There have been quite a few disappearing so I'm not taking any chance at all. I'd sure like to catch one of these sticky-fingered guys. Well, just what I'd do to him, I don't know, but it certainly won't be pleasant.

Band practice now, so bye-bye, and write every other day. I am, and if I can't see the kiddies I would like to hear of them from day to day.

Love,
Daddy

೭౩

January 12, 1941

My own sweetheart,

Six p.m. here, which means 10:00 a.m. there—you are probably just up trying to get the house warm. . . . Boy, oh boy, that house must be cold. It wouldn't be so bad if I was there to cuddle up to and keep warm, would it? And get up and get the house toasting warm. Oh, how I would like to be there and do just those things.

Have I ever got a cold. I don't ever remember having one so bad. I stayed in bed all day yesterday, and today I got rid of the fever, but it still is awful painful to cough. Practically, all of the boys have colds. I guess it is the change in climate. It is terribly damp here and rain, much more so than Toronto.

Well, I'm still in the band and we practice plenty now. Although, the band is no larger than it was in Canada.

. . .

Well, I still haven't been any place to see anything yet. So, I can't write very much as to the country and landmarks. But, I'm going to Scotland on my leave on the 21st, and I'll write a long letter telling you all about it.

So bye-bye, and be good and pray for daddy.

Love,
Clarence

లు

January 14, 1941

Dear Mummy,

Well, here I am again and I haven't a word from you yet, and am
I ever anxious . . . this being cut off completely from my loved
ones is getting me down, so please write very, very, very often.

. . .

We go out on a brigade scheme tomorrow. Where to, I don't know.
But if we see any new country or sights, [I'll] write all about it.
On a route march the other day I saw for the first time an old
English castle. I don't know the name of it or who it belongs to.
It was an immense building, and so old, all covered with moss
and old, old creepers. Yes, no doubt England is very interesting,
as to history and old legends we have read about. And, as I believe I
wrote before, everything practically is still green. So, I'm wondering
what it would be like in summertime. It certainly must be beautiful.
The flowers and trees will be blooming in another two or three
weeks. Yes, if you were only with me and this war a thing of the
past it would simply be wonderful, and as it is it could practically
be called drab.

Well, I guess I'm just about out of inspirations, so I guess I'll
close with all my love,

Clarence

[p.s.] Rollie are you always good? Do you always say your prayers
and go to church Sundays with Mummy? Well, say a prayer for
daddy and kiss mummy and Murray for daddy every night before
going to bed. Bye-bye, write daddy, love.

☙

January 20, 1941


Dear Hazel,

Received two letters from you today and I'm hurrying to answer.
Boy, oh boy, it was a long wait. When the corporal was handing
out the mail, I think I was holding my breath 'till [he] hollered
my name.

You say you didn't receive my cards that I mailed on the train.
Well, I sent one from Rivière-du-Loup and one from Halifax.
I can't understand why you didn't get them. Of course I didn't mail
them myself. I handed them to men on the station platforms.
I can't figure it out; you really must have been disappointed,
and still you are so nice about it. Gosh, I love you darling.

. . .

So, Daniel Lamonte has been around, has he? To tell you the truth,
I expected it because he seemed concerned about when I was going
to leave. But, these things do not worry me, because I know you
and your love for me, so I have no worries.

And the kiddies? Yes, they will have to go to school, and that will
be a problem we will have to cope with when they get older. And
of course we will have [to] start making provisions for that now.

. . .

Received mother's letter enclosed also. I will write her again, I have
twice. I received an Xmas card from Yvonne [Clarence's sister] and
I have written her too.

Yes, I made a promise I would write faithfully, and I have I hope.
And as far as the cards go, I can't explain it.

So, Tom did take you to a show, but as I said you know my opinion about those things, and you know how to take care of yourself and what I expect, so I'm really not worried, but a little jealous because it wasn't me.

Yes, I can see the kiddies didn't have the Xmas I would've liked them to have, but there are other Christmases.

Re: that watch, I don't want one of those—I would like a nice watch though. About $25 would get a shockproof and waterproof watch: a Westfield or Bulova. The one I have I took to the jeweler, and he said it wasn't worth fixing, so I'm without one. But what I really am wanting is good Canadian cigarettes. And of course a watch is very handy in the army.

. . .

Yes, darling, save all the little nickels you can because I will be back and we will need something to start us up in business of some sort. As you say, Toronto certainly has its possibilities.

So you didn't get to midnight mass; well, neither did I. We were anchored off the British Coast Xmas eve, and landed Xmas day and arrived at our destination, or camp, Boxing Day, so I certainly didn't enjoy Xmas either. In fact, I was terribly lonely both Xmas and New Years Day. In fact, I have a lump in my throat all the time. I long for you and kiddies continuously.

. . .

Well, I went to a show last night for the first time since landing. It was Spencer Tracy in "Edison, the Man," and it was a very good picture, but it made me very lonesome. When we started for the show it was snowing and cold, and when we came out it was pelting rain and warm. That sure is just like England. Snow, rain, fog, sun, clouds, etc.—generally, miserable weather.

A bunch of the boys went to see Windsor Castle today, but I stayed in and had a good nap. I simply don't care to go anyplace. I'd sooner lay around barracks and daydream when I get the chance—in fact, as I have mentioned in previous letters, I haven't been out of the camp area.

Wednesday, Kohaley and I are going to Glasgow for a couple of days. A sightseeing tour, and I'll write and tell you all about it. Anyway, I guess I'd better move around a little if I want to see England [and] Scotland before going back to Canada.

. . .

How did you make out financially till you got your cheque? And how did you make out on the way to Lafleche? And I suppose everything was cold. And did anyone help you get settled down again? I can just visualize the mess you had to come to. Life is a mess, isn't it? But, as you say it will be until Hitler gets his ears pinned down, which is being done slow but sure.

Well Mummy, I guess I'll close now with all of my love. Don't worry about me as I'm snug as a bug in a rug. Am looking forward to coming home sooner than most people expect.

All of my love,
Daddy

P.S. Rollie, did you say your prayers for Daddy and did you give her a kiss for me? Well, bye-bye, and be a good boy, send me a picture of Mummy and Murray and you too. Love.

～

January 29, 1941

My own sweetheart,

Well, I just got back from leave and there was a letter from you waiting for me. It was the first one you wrote after I left and it was a swell one.

Yes, Darling, I do some funny things. When I look back at the day we left Toronto, I left you early in the morning, I tried to smile as I stepped out of the room. In fact, I don't remember. I couldn't think as I walked out of the house. All I can say is I cried like a kid. A good thing it was dark out. It was terrible leaving you. And when I got back to the barracks I was going to phone back and have you come to the barracks and see me off, but didn't. I simply couldn't have stood it, because I didn't want to go and I was afraid that I would do something at the least temptation.

Several times before leaving I started for the phone, but hesitated. And finally I didn't phone. I wished I had of now. But then I don't think I could have spoken a word to you once you were on the phone because the lump in my throat would have choked me. Yes, darling, I do love you, and if, as you say, when I was with you in Toronto I was swell, what will I be like when we are together, because I'm going to be sweller. You say you have a few nice memories of my leave in Toronto. Well, I say I have a lot of swell memories of my leave in Toronto. And I dwell among those memories.

Yes, darling, you promised me something when I left—I, visa-versa. And for my part it will be kept to the letter. And I have no doubts about you, I know you won't let me down.

Well, I've had my landing leave. I enjoyed my trip and I did an awful lot of traveling. In fact, I slept on the train every night between stopping points. We traveled the first night to Newcastle Upon Tyne and spent the day touring all its historical spots and

waterfront that night. We went to Nottingham and looked that
city over (Private Kohaley and I); the next night we went to Glasgow and looked that over in daytime. The next day we went to see
the famous Loch Lomond, and that is really something to see: the
swellest scenery, just like a dream, mirror-like lakes and mountains,
castles in the distance, and white thatched-roof bungalows here and
there through the trees. It is swell even at this time of year. I wonder
what it could possibly be like in summer when everything is in full
bloom. The next day we looked Edinburgh over, which was real interesting to see. The city is built on mountains I guess, because you
are either climbing or going down steep hills. On the whole, Scotland is prettier than England as to scenery, and now I am back in
camp and haven't seen London yet because I haven't had time.
And all the way through our trip I saw one bomb scar, and that
was on a residential street.

Well, I haven't seen a bit of sunshine in eight days now, and it is
forever raining. I'm getting sick of it and hoping for summer and
the sun and heat. It's terribly damp all the time. I'm lonesome
terribly. I'm going to a free picture show tonight in the Salvation
Army hut, and I hope it doesn't make me lonesomer than I am,
because life, as you say, is long enough without to much of that
before we are together again.

I must be pregnant, I've had heartburn for over a month—a little
every day, and some days it's terrible, especially tonight. It's that bad
that at times it brings tears to my eyes. One of these days I'm going
to see the M.O. [Medical Officer] and have something done if I don't
feel any better. Oh, before I forget, I have had a photo taken while
in Glasgow. When I get them, I'll send them on to you. I do hope
they are good, and if not I'll have more taken.

How are the kiddies? Fine, I hope. I suppose Murray is walking
now and into everything—I'd sure would like to see him. Do you
know I haven't heard from anyone but you since I've been here.
I'm beginning to wonder if they know I'm still alive, or if they
give a darn. I got a card from Yvonne and not another word from

anyone. So I am not going to write any of them until they do. You can tell them for me. I was especially disappointed not hearing, or not even an Xmas card, from any of them.

And please, darling, look over the list I sent in a previous letter— especially cigarettes. The ones here are terrible, also chocolate bars. The grub is there as to quantity, but I still get hungry for something nice, homemade anything. And if you do send anything, wrap it solid, sew it in cloth if you can.

Well, I'll say bye-bye for now, and hope to hear from you awful soon. Pray for Daddy.

All my love,
Clarence

P.S. Hello Rollie. Write Daddy and give Mummy a kiss for me. Bye.

ℰ↷

January 30, 1941

Dearest Hazel,

Just twenty four hours ago I was writing you and here I am again.
I could write much oftener as far as I'm concerned if it wasn't that
I would just be repeating myself. But one thing I will always be
glad to repeat, and will repeat, is that I love you and miss you,
home, and the kiddies.

Well it's still cloudy out and right now it's pitch dark out, and what
I mean is that it's [so] dark you can't see your hand in front of your
face and everything is just slush. If you happen to step off the road-
way [you] squish mud over your boots, so you should see mine now.
I just went to get this paper to write, and being a soldier and always
supposed to be neat we are forever polishing and cleaning boots.
Boy, oh boy, wouldn't I just like to see a dust storm for a change.

. . .

Well darling, I understand we will be broadcasting a piece or two
over the radio some time in the near future. Just what date it will
be I do not know, so keep your keep your eye on the [Regina]
Leader Post for a date if you get this letter before we broadcast—
anyway, I suppose you listen to all the overseas programs.

Yes, I'm still in the band and getting along fine. We don't have to
play for route marches anymore because we have no more route
marches—concentration of troupes [sic] in England is not allowed
because of possible air raids. So they don't allow us to bunch up.
We play for church parades and the different messes.

Here I am again, broke, but don't need money. I can get by because
now that leave is over I have no place to go and don't care to go
anyplace. I'll get along all except for these blasted English cigarettes,
which I will have to buy, so I'll have to borrow a little. . . . I have

two pounds, 10 shillings coming, which I suppose is probably all
Dutch to you. But I've got this English money business down
now, at first I had the very devil of a time to figure it out.

. . .

I'm still waiting for those photos from Glasgow, will send them
on as soon as I get them. Going to bed now and lie and think of
you and the kiddies. Bye. Love.

xoxxo
All my love,
Clarence

February 2, 1941

Dearest,

. . .

Well, believe it or not the sun is shining, or rather, it was shining all day, the first time since I've been in England. And was it great to be able to sun ourselves on the south side of the buildings after 13 days of rain, fog and snow. I'm terribly lonesome today for you and the kiddies, the days seemed so terribly long. We played for two church parades this morning and I slept a couple of hours this afternoon, but even at that the hours seemed to drag.

I understand we are to broadcast over the radio sometime in the next ten days. I do hope you get to hear it. Now that I think of it, you haven't a radio, and that is one of the first things you want to buy. Get that instead of a watch for me. It will help fill in the time and [you'll] get the news of everything going on over here.

Well, how are you keeping anyway darling? Having any colds? And how is that house of ours? I suppose you are half froze most of the time. Gosh, I do worry about you, I'm always afraid everything isn't quite all right. Oh, do I wish I were there to take care of you and the kiddies. This war I believe, or I know, is much harder on those left behind. All the anxieties and cares, children growing up, money matters, all for a woman to look after over and above keeping house. It doesn't seem fair to me. I really shouldn't worry, because I know you can do it, probably much better than I could. But I do wish I were there to help sweetheart.

I got those photos and they certainly aren't flattering. In fact, if they picture me, I'm decidedly a homely guy. I'm really disappointed so I'm going to have more taken by someone who knows his business. The guy that took these was just after the soldiers' money. I've seen several different photos and they are all rotten. So I guess maybe I really don't look as bad as this enclosed photo shows. I will send them all over to you one at a time in case one or more of my letters get lost.

Well, I've another army qualification now. I'm a qualified stretcher-bearer. That's three—corporal, musician, and stretcher-bearer—if they mean anything. Yes, I know how to apply splints, patch up broken ribs, stop hemorrhages and bandage wounds. But I do hope to never have to use the knowledge.

How are the kiddies? I suppose Murray is getting cuter and cuter. Are they both well? I certainly hope so.

Well, I'll close now with all of my love. I understand there is more Canadian mail over here now, so I expect an armful, and mostly from you darling.

Bye, write often.

Hugs, love and kisses,
Clarence

P.S. Hello Rollie, are you a good boy for mummy? Do you help her a lot? Does mummy send you downtown to get things for her? You lucky little fellow. You can be with her everyday and do things for her. You better be real good to your mummy, because you always want [to] have a mummy. Someday, you may be far, far away like daddy is, and then you will miss your mummy. So you better be real good to your mummy, because she is a real nice mummy. Give mummy a big hug and kiss for daddy, and always remind Jesus of daddy in your prayers. Bye, love, daddy.

By the way, anytime that you want to get in touch with [me] urgently, you can wire me direct darling. This is what you do: just send it cablegram through Spence [Herb Spence, the CPR telegraph agent at Lafleche] to me at—that is, to Pte. Bourassa, C.O. L12541, South Sask. Reg., C.A.S.F., at Morval Barracks, Cove, Hampshire. I believe that is quite clear. The name of the town I will repeat is *Cove, Hampshire,* County.

Bye, with love. Are you lonely? I feel terrible tonight. Bye, and write often, often. Love.

ROLLIE'S NOTE: *We finally got a radio, and I remember we couldn't receive anything but static at first. Mr. O'Neill (my third Grandpa) came over and ran a wire up the wall and across the ceiling to the chimney on the kitchen stove—and voila, the miracle of the airwaves was now a part of our lives.*

ↄ

February 7, 1941

Dear Mummy,

Here I am as tired as I can remember being. I'm writing this being in bed. We just got in from an all-day scheme. We wallowed around in slush and mud all day, and my feet were soaking wet and my clothes all mud, and we have just got back now. It is now 9:00 p.m., about 3:00 p.m. at home.

Yes, most of the boys got mail from Canada today, but I didn't. But I shouldn't feel too bad, because there is tons of it to be sorted yet—so there must be several letters for me, no doubt. And cigarettes too, I hope. Because I'm broke and nothing to smoke, only what I can bum. When I am tired like this I'm just so terrible lonesome. Oh, what I wouldn't give to be with my darling sweet and loving mummy, even for just an hour. Oh, for the day when we will be together again. What say mummy, are you lonesome for me?

Well, yesterday I spoke to you over the radio. That is, my voice was recorded with a lot of others to be rebroadcasted in Canada sometime in March. So write to the CBC in Winnipeg and get the exact dates, because there will be two different broadcasts. In the first program, I didn't get the opportunity to say a word because the band played; but I had a chance to speak in the second and I hope you hear it, because I was so excited when I spoke that I really don't remember what I said, and I could just picture you sitting in front of a radio and hearing my voice. I wish I could hear yours the same way sometime.

You'll have to excuse my writing, because in this position I find writing clumsy. And my eyes simply won't stay open. But still I couldn't possibly go to sleep without writing a word or two sweetheart.

I sure hope there is a letter from you tomorrow because I'll go nuts if there isn't. I'll say bye for tonight and write again tomorrow. I'll probably have plenty to write about after your letters, and I'll probably be more awake, and I hope you don't write me too many letters after coming home from dances. Frankly, I don't mean not to write whenever you feel like it, but what I mean is I love you so much that I can't help being jealous. I haven't been to a thing social here and I don't intend to—simply not interested. I'd sooner sit, write, and think of you and the kiddies.

Bye darling, I'm just about asleep. I wish I could go to sleep and dream of you and only wake up when I'm back in Canada.

Your loving Daddy,
Clarence

&

February 10, 1941

Dear Mummy,

. . .

Well, I start by answering your first letter, one you wrote on Jan.
5th and which I received on February the 7th. You probably
wonder why I didn't answer as soon as I got it. I really wanted
to but was sent out as medical attendant on a scheme and we didn't
get back until last night, and I have a terrible cold and can hardly
talk right now—I don't feel too bad though. Tomorrow, I'm going
on dental parade—a few fillings, I want to keep my teeth for a
while yet, because I can't play a horn if I get them pulled, and I
think that there is a possible chance of the band being withdrawn
from active service and used for ceremonial parades, church parades,
and entertainment of the troops. That will be nice if it goes through,
won't it darling? It's in the fire now, and will soon be official, I hope.
I will let you know naturally, the bandmaster is really working on
it and seems to think that he will win out.

. . .

So Jackie beat it, did he, couldn't stand the pressure. Did you get
any details as to cause or would it be that his wife was starting to try
and run him. Well, thank God our troubles are over—and that first
five years was a tough session for you darling. Thank God it's over
and those kiddish stunts of mine will never happen again. I love
you too much, and I'm real glad to hear that you say nix to liquor
and dances, and I have been doing the same and intend to 'til we
are together again. And you mentioned Wilfred losing his girl, she
found another guy, and that things like that do happen. Yes, they
do, but not to everyone. At least it isn't going to happen to us. And
now Wilfred will be seeking consolation and sympathy, so beware
of the guy because he doesn't dislike you, and at times kind of queer.
Well, I have no worries there. I know what you think of him and

how much you love me. And as far as Lucien Boudreau goes, yes, I'm glad he is gone, because he could certainly be a pest to you and he is not what I would call above doing anything to gain his own ends. And as I always have said, a married woman or, that is, a soldier's wife, they consider very vulnerable. Why repeat all this? You know what I expect as you said in one of your letters. You expect me back as I left you in Toronto, and darling, I expect to find you as I left you.

So, Lafleche is the bunk you say. Yes, I'll admit it is, but the summer will soon be here, and you will be on your feet this summer. So go someplace, visit your relatives, and see something, because no doubt Lafleche will get terrible to live in all alone if a person don't get out and around.

. . .

I guess I'll close now, sending you and the kiddies all my love.

Your hubby,
Clarence

❧

February 13, 1941

My own Mummy,

Received a letter from you and Mother yesterday, and that swell
Valentine tonight, and did it ever hit the spot. It left a terribly big
lump in my throat, and I suppose darling Rollie signed it, didn't
he? And that was a swell poem too, and the song, "When London
Lights Shine Again." Oh darling, I love you for those nice little
things you do, which shows that you love and miss me a lot. And
please don't ever think I get tired of hearing from you. I could read
and read your letters day in and day out and enjoy every moment.

Yes, Hazel, send plenty of razor blades, these English blades are poor.
And, of course, candy, smokes, shaving material, anything that a
man might use will certainly be appreciated—and don't forget eats.

Well, darling, I feel bad about not sending you a Valentine when
I thought of it. It was too late for you to get it on time, but to me
you are my Valentine, and will always be my own only Valentine.

. . .

We are leaving for a scheme sometime darling. The night, where to,
I don't know. How long, I don't know. We are standing to all night,
so I am going to get some sleep right away and will write as soon as
we get back—to Mother too.

. . .

. . . Wishing you a happy birthday Mummy, and sending you my
undying love.

You loving husband,
Clarence

P.S. Hello Rollie . . . I liked the Valentine. Write often, Rollie.

Love,
Daddy

February 18, 1941

Dear Hazel,

Gosh, it seems a long time since [I've] written. A whole five days and I've been just aching to write you. Writing you seems to help considerably, because I know you look forward to my letters as I look forward to yours.

Well, we went on a three day scheme through the country. Just travelled around, not much of importance or even interest to write about. And then Monday we went on a route march to Maiden-head (quite a name) and back 40 miles, and I walked every inch of the way. Got back last night, should have written then, but was terribly tired, aching bones, and blistered feet; in fact, I went to bed without supper and slept the whole night.

We left here Monday morning with full equipment and marched on paved roads for 20 miles, and then to bed on a wood floor with one blanket between me and it and one over. So, between cold and aches I didn't sleep much. Tuesday morning back pounding pavement all day. In fact, I still ache in every muscle, but I guess I'll have to take it because we expect these route marches to increase weekly until we can march seven days in a row at about twenty five miles per day.

. . . Gosh, I'm terribly blue tonight. I want you darling, and the kiddies. At times I could simply cry with all this mess, which at times seems so hopeless—you away over there—and I love you so much and I know you feel the same too. But the way things are shaping up, I wouldn't be surprised to see this over soon and we will be together soon—awful soon wouldn't be too soon for me. Well darling, I've got all my equipment to clean up and polish for some big inspection tomorrow. I believe it is the King and Queen, so I'll have to cut this short and get to work and will write again tomorrow.

. . .

Bye Mummy, I love you,
Clarence

P.S. Hello Rollie, tell mummy to send a lot of cigs. Daddy is always
bumming and borrowing Canadian cigs. . . . Well darling, I may
seem selfish about this, but all of the boys . . . have been receiving
cigs regularly by the 1000s, and to date I haven't had some yet.
Oodles of love. xxx Write every day if you can find time.

Bye,
Daddy

ఌ

February 20, 1941

My own Mummy,

. . .

Well darling, there is an awful squabble on in the orderly rooms: whether they keep the band, send us to "holding," or break it up completely. Strum is the big agitator, but so far we are still a band. And according to the Colonel, as long as he can "within army regulations," he will keep the band as auxiliary first-aiders. He is also trying to get us through as a band of the Canadian Forces attached to the s.s.r. with no other duties than to play. That would certainly be swell, wouldn't it—but sounds too good to be true. I sure pray and hope to gosh it does go through, so I am just simply waiting and afraid to say a word.

Last night I stood out back of our quarters while the Heinies were making an air raid somewhere to the east of us, and watched them dropping flares to find their targets. I could hear a few bombs exploding but the anti-aircraft fire soon chased them away. In fact, the Germans seem to be catching it from the English; our planes even go up after them in the dark and shoot them down. Germany is losing an awful lot of her planes, and it gets me how they ever get nerve enough to come over here because there is always a few planes that never get back. Yes, there is no argument about it at all now: who is going to win this war. Germany just hasn't a chance. Everything is going against her and the British are getting stronger everyday in every way. So I sort of expect that '41 is the year when this will be all over and me back home where I belong.

Well, how are the kiddies today? Fine, I hope. And I suppose you are in the pink of conditioning. Take care of yourself, the very best care of yourself, because I am doing so just for you.

. . .

Say, I am already making plans for our future . . . the only thing
that we must have to start is a few dollars and then we will go out
on our own. To hell with all this "pull" stuff and depending on
someone else to get me a job. So, I am occupying my spare time
in figuring out all kinds of angles to make a dollar or two. Just what
it will be I don't know for sure, but one thing certain is that I am
going to make money for you and the kiddies. You just wait and see.
And I'll be my own boss, or rather, we'll be our own bosses dealing
with the public and we'll make money. I'm just beginning to realize
how gullible the public really is: give them service and a smile and
they will pay for it. So darling, if you can possibly save a few dollars
after you get squared away—do for our future. And think up something and let me know: snack counters, cigs and tobaccos and con-
fections, groceries, insurance, etc. With my own sign writing to
boot, I think we should make a respectable living and put some
away, don't you? Of course, it will take a lot of thinking out and
work from both of us, but we will do it. So whatever you can think
up write me about it, and that way we can start discussions in writing, which will give us time to think them out and when we decide
just what it will be we will really get our plans straight and stick to
them. Do you get the drift of this long breath?

Well, I'll say bye for now. And think everything over darling,
and write often.

Bye, and love to you all,
Love and kisses mummy,
Daddy

౨

February 23, 1941

My dearest Mummy,

Received your most welcome parcel and letters. Yes, everything is coming through fine, and I sure am waiting for those Canadian cigarettes. . . .

. . .

Well, all this blarney about Hitler doing this and that is just wind. Hitler has his hands full the way things are.

Received two razor blades and bars all safe and sound, and did I ever enjoy a good Oh Henry! and a chew of Canadian gum. And now for a decent shave. Pulling the whiskers out by the roots isn't very pleasant and my whiskers are getting much more plentiful and tough, so I'll always appreciate good Canadian blades.

. . .

Listen darling, I haven't been anyplace with Steve or [any] of that crowd. I go to the odd show when I can afford it with some of the band boys—the closest theatre is about 3 miles and costs a shilling return and a shilling, two pence to get in, so I don't go very often. That is the extent of my amusement. Just last night Steve went to a dance and got into a scrap and got hit over the head with a bottle for his troubles, and he sure is all cut up and quite proud of himself. He says, "you should see the other guy"; of course, we've got to take his word for that. Well darling, don't worry about dances, and remember your advice, "they are bad medicine."

Don't worry about London and its clubs, I value my neck a little. The Heinies have a nasty habit of bombing the place, and it's much healthier here and much quieter, and what I have seen of London doesn't interest me at all.

So bye-bye for now, and oodles of hugs and kisses for you and the kiddies, and I miss you a lot.

Your loving husband,
Clarence

☙

February 28, 1941

My own sweetheart,

How is my little darling this morning (the middle of the night
in Lafleche)?. . .

We started out Tuesday night—a bright starry, chilly night—in
trucks. We travelled till about midnight and then unloaded, and
[were] taken to a haystack and told to make ourselves comfortable.
Well, I couldn't see how I could make myself comfortable, so four
of us started to snoop around an adjacent farmyard for a decent
place to crawl into, and the farmer came out and we started to
hightail it the hell out of there, because the farmers have had poul-
try disappearing and soldiers were to blame. So we expected a load
of buckshot but the farmer called out to us, "are you with the soldiers out in the field? If you are looking for someplace to sleep I
might be able to accommodate a few." So, we turned around and he
took us to the hayloft and we made the best of that. At least [it] was
warm and dry, because about three in the morning it started to rain,
and all the [other] boys were in it. And did it rain! I now know
where the saying comes from: "sheets of rain." And it rained like
that for two solid days and nights. In fact, it's still drizzling. Well, it
was rainy and we were on a scheme. The first night I kept dry, but
no sooner outside to get something to eat and I was wet to the hide.
And then we marched for two miles in the rain and mud and our
trucks kept getting stuck. And between pushing them and falling
flat on my face in the mud every now and then—I even had an ear
plugged with mud and we ate standing in the rain. And the funny
thing about eating was that when I got tea I couldn't seem to drink
it all. I'd get a cupful and take a big drink and set it down and then
take another drink and set it down—it kept getting weaker and
colder but the cup was always just about full. So, the second night
I didn't try to sleep. So when we got back last night, after carrying
my equipment and rain-soaked great coat—which weighed about
forty pounds—and wet blankets, and I didn't sit down for fourteen

hours in one stretch—I was a tired soldier and my shoulders
were aching just like a toothache practically all of the time, carrying
about fifty pounds of equipment and pounds of water. My conclusion is soldiering is certainly no picnic, but I am back safe and
sound. There were two motorcycle riders killed due to rain, mud,
and darkness, and a truck upset, and most of the men are in the
hospital with broken bones, but no one seriously hurt. I [was]
surprised there weren't more hurt, because there was about a million
troops on the move on this scheme. And with all the mud, rain,
and travelling in the dark, so many trucks, and travelling without
lights because Fritzie was overhead practically all night and we
didn't care to have him drop a few among the trucks—so, no
lights—no wonder a few got hurt.

Well, I feel alright today, dry and clean, and I had a good night's
sleep and no bad after-effects outside of a few stiff muscles.

. . .

Love to you all—the kiddies are fine, are they?

Your Hubby,
Clarence

March 5, 1941


Hello Darling,

. . .


Well darling, this is going to be a short letter. I've just got back
from a scheme and I can hardly keep awake and I will write again
tomorrow. Received your parcel and we are making coffee now,
and will have onion sandwiches too—the bandmaster and I.
And when I get that eaten up, to bed and dream of you darling.

Gee, I'm lonesome tonight for you. At times, I wished I was a
kid again and have a good cry, seems that might help. Oh, for you
and the kiddies. What I wouldn't do outside of murder to get back.
I love you, I love you so much it hurts.

. . .


Well, I'll write again tomorrow; I have a lot to write about.

Bye darling, all of my love, and don't worry about dances or me
stepping out, my love for you wouldn't allow me to even take
time to even think of it.

All of my love,
Daddy

ை

March 9, 1941

My Dearest Darling Mummy,

Here I am again, terribly lonesome and blue tonight. The sun
shone all day and another fellow and I went for a long stroll
over the countryside.

Whoops, there goes the air raid alarms. Boy, oh boy, what a
weird sound. They give me the creeps. [They] are rightly named,
"Moaning Mona[s]." The whole countryside is moaning. There is
a siren about every mile all over the country, so when they all start
wailing together it sure is a terrible blood-chilling sound. But this is
all we ever get here, is just the warnings. They fly right on over
about four or five miles up.

. . .

. . . Got a letter from the Banks with a bunch of addresses of their
folks in Scotland. I may go up and visit them. They told me to be
sure I did. . . . Got a letter from Dodo too. And received a letter
from some guy in England that worked for Fogals in '27-'28-'29,
and said Mrs. Fogal mentioned me in her letter to him. So he
wrote me to get my address so that he could come down and see
me. Says he knows Dad and Granddad. So I answered him and
got an answer back the next day. He lives in London and will be
here next weekend and says he will take me out motoring and show
me the country. His name is Percy Starbuck and [he] works for the
Department of Food Supplies, is married and has three children. So,
I'll write all about it after I meet the 'so-called' Mr. Percy Starbuck.
And, yes, darling, those snaps, I didn't eat them but I sure devoured
them with my eyes. I have them in front of me now. And that one
with you and the kiddies—oh, so natural—and the one of you
alone. Darling, it just makes my arms ache to hug and kiss you.
The picture gets the kisses, but it's only a picture. If it could only be
you, you darling, my all. And you look so natural, maybe a little sad.

It makes my heart swell up great big. I was so tickled getting
them and so proud that I showed them to everybody present when
I opened the letter. . . . Received the bars and cheese—that sure was
swell too darling. You seem to be able to feel just what I want most;
and may I add, send writing paper. I don't like writing you with this
stationery at all, and what we buy downtown is so cheap looking,
sort of a dirty grey colour, and that is all they have. The other
paper is all commandeered by the War Department they say.

Well, this afternoon I went for a four-hour stroll over the countryside. The day was swell, sunny, no wind or rain for a change, and,
darling, is the scenery ever beautiful. If you could only be here with
me to see it. I enjoyed the walk, only for a little lump in my throat
that seemed to say, "Hazel would enjoy this immensely," and I
would have more if you were with me. Yes, a fellow by the name
of Dick Nunn, also in the band, and I went for this stroll. The trees
are just breaking into leaf, and the flowers, Hazel, especially, the
crocuses—millions of them. And, to my surprise, different colours.
They grow all over: along the footpaths, roads, lawns—all over!
About the same size of a blossom as the Canadian crocus, but what
colours! Deep purple and varying shades, to mauve, even white, and
some yellow. I picked a few of every colour (and they are all crocuses all right), and flowers by the name of snowdrops: the blossom
is shaped like a lily, only in miniature. These snowdrops grow in
patches as thick as snow too, and have a very delicate perfume.
They remind me of Ben Hur perfume. I once had a bottle of it—
college days, you know. And the daffodils are all in bloom. And
the rhododendrons—more of a tree—something like the willows
we see along the rivers in Saskatchewan, but with leaves about the
size of an oleander leaf. And their blossoms are shaped like great big
bleeding hearts—red, white, and pink—and you can smell the perfume of them all over the place. We walked about four miles down
a country lane and I found it very beautiful. Such marvelous trees
and lawns, rock gardens, ivy covered cottages, and lawns just like
thick carpets. Yes, it sure is beautiful, but it needs to be to make
up for all this dampness, and the people claim that it will be much
prettier as the season advances.

Well, now for the sordid side of it all. Tuesday morning at about 1:30 a.m., I was rudely awakened from my sleep and told to get into battled dress and full equipment plus stretcher and medical kit. We were going out on a scheme, so nothing else to do but get ready—about seventy pounds of equipment and stretcher to boot. I was loaded down proper and at two o'clock loaded into a bus and away. We got to our destination about eight and marched back four miles toward camp before we had breakfast, which was at 10—long time between meals (five o'clock, night before). So you can imagine I was hungry. After breakfast it started to rain, and rain it did. In ten minutes I was soaked to the hide, but the scheme must be carried out. We were the attacking party, so we hit off across country through bush, swamp, swollen creeks. We didn't look for any place to go around, we were so wet we just waded right through them and when we came close to our objective we had to crawl and drag that stretcher, all our equipment, rifle, and about fifty pounds of water that our clothes and equipment soaked up, and this went on till seven at night. I was so tired, water-logged and wet, that I could see spots in front of my eyes. I was too tired to eat and we had to march back to camp 18 miles. It took us till 1 a.m. to make it, and Hazel, to tell you the truth, I don't know how I made it nor does half of the others. The other half fell out and had to be picked up by the escorting trucks. A year ago it would have killed me to go through that, and they claim that we will be getting more of the same things and worse to toughen us up. In fact, I'm still muscle sore from that scheme yet a week ago, but outside of that I'm fine. I wore the bottom right out of the pair of socks I had on and my feet were one complete blister. By the way, I need socks badly.

Enough for that. We had all the next day off to recuperate and I needed it. So Wednesday afternoon I was having a nap and was awakened by a terrible racket of planes and machine gun fire, so out I goes to look on [and] had a ringside seat watching an air battle between four spitfires and two German bombers. I never dreamt that planes could swirl around so much and stay in one piece—up, down, around, upside down, standing on end, looping over—how they did it without crashing one another, I don't know.

But they were up a couple of miles and a mile or so over to the
east, so, naturally, they would look awful close together. Continuing
with my story, the spitfires looked like sparrows after a hawk. Then
suddenly, one of the German bombers fell out with a long trail of
black smoke behind it. Down, down, down it came at full speed,
both motors wide open. It seemed to be heading towards us and it
split up or burst into a million pieces, and a minute or so after a
shattering blast was felt more than heard. The windows rattled and
the buildings shook—the bombs exploded that it was carrying. The
other bomber, in the meantime, tried to run for it, but soon [was]
overtaken by the spitfires and it surrendered and landed in a nearby
airfield. So, I heard that night the crew of five were taken to a concentration camp and the members of the other plane were all killed.
None of them were seen to bail out. That's as close as we have ever
come to the war. If it wasn't for the odd plane flying over, I would
never know there was a war on. Everything seems so quiet and
peaceful here.

. . .

Well, how are my smiling kiddies? Fine, I suppose. And Murray
no doubt gets into everything including the coal pail. Oh, the dear
little tyke, what I wouldn't give for one of his wet kisses or nose rub.
Is Rollie behaving alright? He doesn't try to perform surgical opera-
tions on the cat does he? Yes, I noticed the cat even posed on the
snaps, and I would have never noticed it in Rollie's arms if you
hadn't mentioned him being there. I take it he's a him.

Well, I'd better close because I'm really outdoing myself, and
better save up a little energy to write about Wednesday again.

So bye-bye Darling. Love, hugs and kisses.
All my love,
Clarence

☙

March 19, 1941

My dearest Mummy,

Gosh, I feel ashamed I haven't written for a week. I didn't through
my fault though, we had that sixty-mile route march. It took 3 days
to make it, and then we rested one day, that made it Friday. We got
back and then Saturday I got a long weekend. Went into London
to meet this Percy Starbuck and he took me around the city all
day Sunday and Monday, and got back Tuesday morning, and I
am writing today so I do hope you aren't sore darling. So, I will
start answering your letters now. . . .

Oh, by the way, I had a tattoo while in London. In fact, Percy
and I each had a tattoo. I'll enclose a picture of mine, or rather,
a drawing. It is a red heart with your name over it and mine below,
and the whole garnished with green laurels. I think it is quite nice.
And at the time I felt so blue that when Percy suggested a tattoo
I decided to have something put on my arm with your name.
So, now I've got your brand Mummy. . . .

. . .

. . . By the way, a few ships have been sunk going to Canada lately
and there probably might have been a letter or two of mine on
them . . .

Haven't you heard my voice on the radio yet? I spoke to you and
Lafleche when the recording was made here. And last Saturday,
while in London, I went to the Maple Leaf Club to see if I couldn't
say hello over the radio, but they had been bombed out the night
before, and that it would be a few days before they would be in
operation again. . . .

Yes, I went to Scotland. Of course there are women there, but
I wasn't interested. I was out looking the country over, not the
inhabitants, least of all the women. What I saw of them, they look

like any other to me. And again, I repeat, I'm interested in only getting back to you. . . . Please don't worry darling, my thoughts are all for you, morning, noon and night.

So, Murray is a lot of fun? I guess I am missing the best part of his life. Gosh, I get lonely when I think of all I'm missing—you and the kiddies—if this would only end. No doubt at times Rollie is hard to handle. I know I should be there, but what can we do? It's up to you darling, and do your best, and let me tell you when I get back will I ever make up for the misery you are in now.

. . .

Last Monday, or rather a week ago Monday, we started out on the 60-mile march, went 18 first day. Felt alright that night, washed my feet, changed socks, and to bed about 8:30 out under the trees, and thank God it didn't rain . . . The next day, we climbed over a mountain ridge and down to the sea shore where we could see France across the channel. Stayed there for two nights and rode back to camp Friday . . . the next morning the bandmaster said it was my turn to go on weekend pass . . . I went into London and met Percy Starbuck—what a name, but a nice fellow. Quiet, teetotaller, to my surprise . . . Saturday afternoon we went to a show. "Waterloo Bridge" was the title. Made me feel terribly lonesome it was so sad. After the show we went for lunch, and that took about an hour and a half. First, Percy ordered a sweet cider cocktail, then fish and chips. About 15 minutes between courses, and then ices or frozen milk with a lemon flavour, and was the place ever swanky, real high class. Unless in uniform, you must be dressed in evening clothes, and they had a floor show as well—step dancing and singing. It cost Percy about 17 shillings for the two of us and then I went to the Union Jack Club where I got a room. The Union Jack is a swell hotel for soldiers or men in uniform only. Marble floors, tiled walls from end to end, and the rooms were fifty cents a night—small, but neat and clean, single bed, linen sheets, hot and cold water, and a dresser, and quiet, no drunks allowed . . . Sunday, I went to cross the River Thames to mass in the chapel of St. Thomas Hospital, a beautiful but small chapel, and Hazel

I couldn't believe it, the next wing to the chapel had been blown
flat by a German bomb two days before and what a mess. A wing
of that hospital is twice as big as the Gravelbourg hospital . . . well,
after mass I walked around the wreckage and asked questions from
the men working, building it up again, and they seemed quite used
to these bombings. And they asked me if I would consider a hospital as a military objective for bombing. Of course I wouldn't. I was,
in fact, shocked at the sight of such wreckage and the thought of
so many helpless victims being caught in the hospital that I can
hardly believe my eyes. In fact, it will always be in my thoughts.
No one can realize what this country is putting up with till they
see it. From there, I went and saw St. Andrews and then the
Parliament Buildings and Big Ben—all still unscathed. . . .

. . .

Yes, I saw London. Had quite a weekend there. Saw a lot of
bomb wreckage in some places. Terrible, mostly homes again.
I went to Madame Tussaud's waxworks with Percy Monday—
zquite interesting. Effigies of every notable person in the world,
and to perfection, even Mackenzie King. General McNaughton
reproduced in wax to perfection. From there we went to the zoo,
an immense thing, from elephants to the smallest insect. It took
us eight hours to rush through it. Every kind of an animal, reptile,
or fish can be seen in their natural surroundings, and all alive. Oh
darling, I wish you could see some of these things, and, oh yes,
it was at the zoo that I got tattooed.

. . .

Well, bye darling, I'll seal this up and get it away tonight. Bye,
take care of yourself and go to communion often. I do, it seems
to help, doesn't it?

Bye, your loving, lonesome hubby,
Clarence

The tattoo I got on my arm

HAZEL Blue

Red

Green

CLARENCE

Rather rough but will give you the General Idea

CLARENCE'S DRAWING OF HIS TATTOO THAT HE SENT TO HAZEL
WITH HIS MARCH 19 LETTER.

Pte. C.O. Bourassa
L12541
Bn. H.Q. South Sask Reg. C.A.(O)
March 21, 1941


Dear Mummy,

Darling, excuse paper, but it was all I could get for nothing.
The S.A. [Salvation Army] is out, and the stuff we buy is terrible.

I'm wandering around today with my heart all swollen—it hurts.
I'm so darned lonesome, I look around see this and see that, try to
read, play games, but that don't help. I'm simply so lonesome for
you and the kiddies that I'm nearly sick. Oh darling, if this would
only end. Frankly, I want to go home now. Sweetheart, I can just
see you in the doorway, waving out the window, etc., etc. Today,
is the worst I've had. I haven't received any mail from you for two
weeks. Should be some soon, tomorrow or the day after—it won't
be too soon. I have reread every one of your letters today and
gazed at the pictures of you. It's terrible isn't it, darling? Loving
and being separated so, so far apart and not knowing when we
will be together. I hope that this general feeling around in England
that the war will end this year is true. I suppose you feel awful
blue most of the time too. . . .


. . .


We are having a big general inspection on Monday the 24th, and
of course the band will play. And a general inspection takes about
three hours and they are swell to watch, and of course with our
band it will be much nicer. But I'm not looking forward to it
because three hours of continual playing is awful hard work.
We had a rehearsal yesterday and my lips are still swollen and sore.


. . .

Well, I guess I'll close and write again Sunday—to the dearest little mummy in all the world.

. . .

Bye darling,
Clarence

March 22, [1941]


Dear Mummy,

This card [a birthday card for Hazel] has every ounce of me in it—
I love and love and love you—darling, I am so blue.

. . .

Oh, I wish I could take you in my arms and hug and hug you till
you screamed for breath—rather caveman-ish, but that is where
you belong, safely cuddled in my arms. Oh, darling, I simply
ache with longing for you.

To be continued in a letter.

Love,
Daddy

ROLLIE'S NOTE: *The following is a birthday letter that accompanied a card that my father sent to me and that was included with the note above. My mother's birthday is at the end of March; mine is April 11th.*

March 22, [1941]

Hello Rollie,

So you're five now, getting to be quite a little man. Daddy is sending you a card, and he wants you to be the best little boy in the world for your mummy.

Daddy thinks of you every, every day and he wishes he was with you everyday to play with you, and hopes to be home soon, too. Daddy sees a lot of little boys here but they just make me lonesome for you and Murray. And be good to Murray too, he is smaller than you are so look after him, and look after Mummy too.

Bye, and be a good boy, and say a prayer to little Jesus for me so I can come home soon.

Daddy

❧

March 24, 1941

Dear Mummy,

Received your letter with all the sad news about Mush [Clarence's
cousin, whose plane went down]. I went to communion this morning and offered it up for him. I also sent a cablegram to Aunt Olive
from the boys of Lafleche and I—I worded it, "We have heard your
bereavement and are sending our deepest sympathies. He shall not
be forgotten by the boys from Lafleche overseas."

Darling, I don't suppose all of that helped you any did it, me being
over here and your imagination? I can just see you worrying, but
listen kid, don't worry about me. I am not in the air. My feet are on
solid ground and in the safest part of the Army, the infantry, and a
stretcher-bearer, and if this band goes through as Brigade Band . . .
well, I'll be set. So, don't worry, I'll be back, and more of a man
than when I left.

. . . I'm just continually putting in time for the day we will be
together again. I put in an awful lot of my time reading and writing.
I went uptown yesterday for the first time in months it seems. . . .

. . .

Gee darling, you seem to be having an awful hard time financially,
but winter being over your expenses will be much lighter so you
should soon be caught up. Yes, Hazel, I received the socks, gloves,
and sweater. Thanks, they were swell, but whatever you do don't
forget the smokes. I'm just about out and will be before long. I
don't want to sound like a chiseller, so make sure I get cigarettes—
these English ones are terrible.

. . .

I hope you have received my birthday cards, one for you and
one for Rollie.

. . .

Well, tomorrow is the big inspection and I still have my horn to clean before bedtime. I should have done that this p.m., but slept all afternoon instead. . . .

. . .

Gee, I'll bet Murray is cute, walking from chair to chair. I can just see him looking up and laughing, and so excited, I'll bet. At times I get practically desperate to see you and the kiddies.

Well, bye for now. I'll write again Tuesday so that I'll be sure you get plenty of letters from me.

Your lonely and loving hubby,
Clarence

သ

March 24, 1941

Darling Mummy,

. . .

Yes, darling, I am lonely tonight. I heard Bing Crosby sing
"Only Forever" and did it ever get to me, especially the words to it.

Well, darling, on top of feeling awfully lonely I have a plenty sore
jaw. During the night one of the latest fillings started to ache and
did it ever ache. I didn't get any more sleep after it started and I
stood out on the parade square for hours and played my horn for
the General's inspection, which went off very well. Only I didn't
enjoy it in the least, standing there with my tooth beating a tattoo
on my brain. So, this p.m. I got it pulled and feel pretty punk now,
but no toothache, and as you have been having a lot of fun with
yours you certainly have my sympathy. It is certainly no joke.

. . .

Have you been juggling your brain for any ideas of what we will
do after the war? I keep continually thinking of it and I always
dwell on the thought of a store, something like that, and be our
own bosses. Whatever happens we will get by, and swell too.

. . .

Your lonesome Hubby,
Clarence

℘

March 25, 1941

Darling,

Here I am again, not much to write about, but it's the nearest
I can be to you, so I'm writing.

Today's orders came out that our passes were due, and that one
and one-half per cent of the Battalion personnel could go each day
starting on Thursday the 27th of March. I see my name on the list
for the 25th of April, a month from today, and I think I will go up
to visit the Banks' relatives in Thurso, Scotland. I looked it up on
the map of England and it's on the extreme north tip of Scotland.
Quite a ways, but my transportation is free, so why not see some
country. And it will put in time and may be interesting, although
I'm not looking forward to it at all.

I have no enthusiasm for anything over here. I'm lonely most of
the time, and when I go anyplace I wish I was back in camp with
the boys. Why, I don't know. I guess it's because they are from
Canada and feel like I do; that is, some of them. I often sit and
chat about home, the kiddies and you. I've never really realized
what you mean to me till now. Every bit of me aches for you
and . . . the day when I set foot on Canadian soil.

I went to a variety show tonight in the camp theatre. It was put
on by the Canadian Legion and it was very good. Really high-class
entertainment: everyone is an artist, a swell orchestra, swell dancing
and singing, a magician, a ventriloquist who puts Bergen and
McCarthy in the shadows. The Legion are going to put on these
shows for us every Monday and Tuesday. These shows would cost
about $5.00 in any of the cities in this country (a lot of them were
American). Judy Garland was the star tonight, so you can judge
by that what kind of shows they are putting on for us. Good
shows and all, [but] give me a chair in the corner beside the stove
in a little brown house in Lafleche with you in my lap and the
two kiddies at my feet.

. . .

Bye-bye, your loving Daddy,
Clarence

P.S. Smokes, bars, gum, etc., etc., sure would be appreciated. Does
that sound too selfish darling? Love and kisses, your lonely big baby.

℘

Canadian Army Overseas
s. Sask. R.
March 25, 1941


Hello Darling,

. . .

You mention two parcels of shirts. I've just received the one,
mermaids will be wearing them [the others] by now.

Well, don't worry about me going on a spree of Canadian liquor.
I believe I'm cured from drinks. I've tasted all they have here and it
frankly is terrible; and, [in] fact, that I mentioned I'd like to go on
a spree on good Canadian liquor was just something to write about,
and when or if I ever decide or take a drink you will be along and
certainly not trailing. You mention that I may hear some silly thing
and try to drown my sorrows. No darling, that just aggravates
things. I believe in you, and as far as talk goes there will always
be that, and I've learned plenty since I've been away. So you
needn't worry on that score. I'll believe you and not what I hear.

I'll admit darling I didn't know what a wife was until I left you,
and am I ever sorry.

. . .

I'll bet Murray is real cute now. I got a big kick out of the
maple syrup.

Well darling, I guess I'll call this a note. And I love you. Hugs
and kisses for the kiddies. I should be home to look after Rollie.

All my love,
Clarence

P.S. Thanks for the promise of plenty of smokes. xxx

March 29, 1941

Dear Mummy,

I'm late in writing darling. I said I would write on Wednesday and today is Saturday. But I couldn't help it because last Wednesday we had to clean our equipment for an inspection, so that didn't leave time. And on Thursday we were inspected by Their Majesties. There was no formality to it at all. We just lined up any old way and they strolled among us, talking to one and then another. The King stood about four feet from me for about five minutes talking to a major, so I sure had a very good look at him. The Queen just passed by, I just got a glimpse. Oh, yes, of course we were playing, but after the inspection I had an accident: I can hardly talk, leave alone smile. We were tussling around and I ran into a fellow and the edge of his tin helmet hit me on the mouth and smashed my lips to a pulp. I bled like a butchered pig, blood all over me. The doctor didn't stitch my mouth, but I have one bad cut on my upper lip about one and one-half inches long just below my moustache. I am afraid that it will leave a scar. And of course I can't play my horn with my mouth like this so I've been working in the hospital, but expect to be playing in a few days.

This afternoon as I was washing clothes in the hospital they brought a fellow in who had shot himself in the leg with an army rifle. The bullet entered just over his shoe top and emerged through the sole of his shoe . . . I thought he was going to bleed to death. I had to take, or rather cut, his shoe off and sock too. The mess his foot was in nearly turned my stomach, and blood flowing all over 'til we applied a tourniquet. Then the doctor washed the foot, or what was left of it, and sent him to a hospital in Reading. The Doc says he will be crippled for life, maybe lose the foot. And as it happens the fellow was in detention and was due for a court martial, so apparently took one of the guard's rifles and deliberately shot himself so he could get a discharge. Well, no matter how badly crippled he is now, [it] will not get him a discharge. In the Army, a self-inflicted

wound with a bullet is five years penal servitude minimum, unless
he can claim an accident, which I don't think he can. Nevertheless,
the guy must be nuts to try such a thing. And, as I understand, he
was in and out of detention regularly. Well, enough for all these
gruesome details, but still my mouth is plenty sore.

. . . I'm forever hoping this ends quick and apparently it isn't going
to be so long now. The Balkans are against the Axis, and Italy is taking a licking, so no doubt it will be soon, I mean within 12 months.
But, gosh, that's a long time to be without my mummy and kiddies.
Gee, I love you darling. That's all I can think of. Oh boy, oh boy—
when I get back, just look out.

Well, I'm going to try a picture show tonight. The boys say it's
good: "Let George Do It," is the title of it. Like any others I've
been to, I'll come out feeling bluer than ever. It's terrible isn't it
mummy? The only consolation is knowing that you love me too,
and you are true to me. I have no doubts about that, thank God.

. . .

Write oftener than often, I haven't had any mail now for
fifteen days.

Love to mummy and the kiddies,
Daddy

&

Sunday,
March 30, 1941


Darling Mummy,

Just a line darling, to tell you I'm lonely for you and that the day
was awful long. I went to church at eight this morning and read
and slept the rest of the time. Say, we had our Christmas dinner
tonight. The dinner that the Canadian papers said we had on
Boxing Day. Yes, we had that tonight. Chicken, as much as there
was, spuds, gravy, dressing, and diced pineapple for dessert.
The best meal we've had since we landed here.

Well darling, I expect about a half a dozen letters from you
tomorrow or the day after—cigs too—because a Canadian
convoy came in last Thursday, and being as I haven't received
a letter for over fifteen days now, I'm sure anxious.

. . .

Well, it's bedtime darling, so I close. Wrote to mother tonight.

All my love,
Clarence

☙

April 1, 1941

Dear Mummy,

Well, some mail came in, but Pte. Bourassa, C.O., went without.
But, I hope I have some tonight. I was awfully disappointed
because I have written an awful lot of letters to different people
and haven't heard a word. But I suppose they are just as busy or
lazy as I was in civilian life and just can't settle down to write,
but will eventually. Well, I guess I'm just in the dumps.

Well, we are waiting for orders to move someplace on some other
fool scheme. We were supposed to leave an hour ago, but it's snowing out and wet. Mud, mud, mud—we were all issued with gum-
boots to keep our feet dry, they do, but are awful hot. Well, regards
to the scheme, I suppose they will wait till the middle of the night
and then decide to move. All the same, we've got to be ready to
load and move out in fifteen minutes.

Darling, I think the band is going to break up thanks to Strum. Our
four best players enlisted as bandsmen, and he decided to have them
take a test as musicians. They did, and passed, but were grabbed up
by the Netherhall Band and aren't with us anymore. So, I have my
doubts if the band will stay in the s.s.r. Strum tried to break us up
before but the bandmaster jumped him and Strum said, "all right
for now, but there will come the day." Well, I guess that day is here.

I've had some snaps taken, and as soon as they are developed I will
send them to you two or three at a time, just in case the mermaids
take a liking to them.

Well, my mouth is healing up swell, but will have a little scar on
my upper lip. I don't think it will be very noticeable though. I tried
blowing my horn this a.m.; I can, but it hurts like the devil yet. Gee,
I hope the band don't break up, it was the only thing of interest in
this darned Army.

Well, have you been using your pretty little head as to what I will do when this is over? It will be someday, and we have to think of the future. My mind always seems to dwell on retail business. I sure would like a store of my own, but that would take at least $1500, and that we would have to save, beg, borrow or steal. What do you think darling?

. . .

Your lonesome Hubby,
Clarence

೧൦

[April 5], 1941


Dear Mummy,

Just a few lines to tell you I'm lonesome for my darling and kiddies, mostly my darling. The weather here is getting awfully nice, and as we played through town today I noticed that the fruit trees are all in bloom and the parks are marvellous. It reminded me of the Wascana Park when we were in Regina, and do I ever wish I could live that through again. Oh, how different I would be. Yes, sweetheart, all the scenery is so nice and I'm here and you're there. It would be so nice if we could enjoy this together. As it is, I'm alone, so alone, and funny thing or maybe it's only natural, all the beauty spots and nice scenery I see always reminds me of you and makes me awful lonesome. Do you remember the park in Minot? How swell that was? Well, the scenery here is much nicer, more natural, more luxuriant: lily ponds, rock gardens, flowers, lagoons, brooks, swans, beautiful driveways and promenades. Oh, if you were only here, how we would enjoy all of it as it is. Repeating myself, it just makes a lump rise in my throat—an ache, darling, a way down deep that keeps me calling for you—yes, you, my little darling Hazel.

Well, I'm lying on my tummy writing this so naturally the writing won't be any too neat.

. . .

Well darling, I'll say nighty-night, sending all of my love and kisses.

Your loving hubby,
Clarence

P.S. Rollie, write to Daddy again. You have only written once so far and Daddy loves his little man. And don't forget that goodnight kiss to Mummy every night for Daddy either. Love, Daddy.

April 6, 1941

Darling Mummy,

Writing again, it seems to relieve my loneliness. I slept all afternoon.
Do you know that Sunday is my busiest day. I go to mass at 8:30
and then I play for the s.s.r. church parade from 9:30 to 10:30, and
then the Cameron's Church parade form 10:30 to 11:30. Quite a
bunch of church business if you ask me, and it is becoming quite
monotonous—just sitting and listening to some guy in a falsetto
voice monotonously praying away, and then a dry sermon, that is.
The Anglican church parade—it's so darned empty, a few hymns,
a public confession, and a very uninteresting sermon. I'm going to
ask the bandmaster to excuse me from going with the band on these
church parades. I don't believe they can force me to go, but I don't
want to antagonize the bandmaster either, so I'll have to use tact.

. . .

I got a letter from D.S. Dallas today inviting me to stay with them
during my leave. He is the Scotchman we met at Banks' the day
we were there for supper. . . .

. . .

Gosh, I'm just starved right now. The meals today were the bunk,
and the canteen is closed so I'll have to wait for breakfast, really the
only meal I enjoy. It is usually mush and bacon and jam, and cocoa
without sugar. To sweeten the mush, I eat my jam with it.

. . .

. . . I like strolling around with some other chaps, talking of home
and lying on the lawns. I am indeed getting quite settled. I don't
care to go anyplace, I just like to take it easy and loll around when
off parade. . . . How about you? Are you being good? Real good?

At times I'm afraid you will get too lonely and something might happen. Life like this is quite lonesome, especially when one loves the other and [is] separated as we are, and imagination and suggestions may prove disastrous. So, the only thing to do is hope, pray, and place full trust in one another. I trust you darling and I know I will never let you down. And I avoid all temptation and invitations here and there, and feel pretty good about it all. . . . I cherish our love and when I come back to you—soon I hope—it will be with a clear conscience, the same as when I left you in Toronto. . . .

. . .

Nighty-night darling,
your loving hubby,
Clarence

☙

April 8, 1941

Darling Mummy,

. . .

Last night, I went to another of those Legion variety shows and was it ever swell. A grand orchestra and swell singers and comedians— no striptease! Now this isn't Toronto, but some of their jokes were definitely two-sided. . . .

But that orchestra, one of the best in England. They played all the pieces I liked: "Stardust," "In the Mood," "Careless," "When London Lights Shine Again," "I'll Never Smile Again," etc. And it sure hit a tender spot way down inside—I'm afraid I'm hopelessly in love darling.

Well, today we have our Army tests to see if we are completely trained. All those who do not pass will be sent to a training unit for six months, which I understand is certainly no fun. Well, I'm not worried because I'll pass without any trouble, although I'm not in- terested at all. My mind is definitely not in England or the Army, it's in a little brown house with the nicest mummy in the world.

. . .

Boy, oh boy, you should hear the noise. The boys have cornered a mouse. They've their bayonets out, brooms, etc. There they go, over the beds— the mouse got away. You would have thought they had cornered Hitler.

Well, I'll say bye for now darling, I understand there's more Canadian mail in. I can hardly wait for it.

Love to the kiddies. They are fine, I hope.

Your loving hubby,
Clarence

P.S. Did you receive those birthday cards? Love.

☙

April 8, 1941

Darling Hazel,

. . .

You mention about us going to Greece. Well, we are still here, and
being in the Army we don't know a thing or where we are going.
In fact, we are quite ignorant of what is going on and we can't do a
thing but do what we are told to, with a smile if possible, and hope
for the best. But, I feel quite safe and content in the fact it could be
a devil of a lot worse.

I went to a show in the Salvation Army hut tonight, "Doctor Takes
a Wife." Loretta Young and Ray Milland—a real good picture I
thought. It sure hit the spot with me. Quite comical with a touch of
sadness. Isn't it funny how a show makes one feel so blue and lonely
when they are away from their loved ones? Yes, I go to them to kill
time, and afterwards I'm sort of sorry I went.

. . .

So, Bob is quarantined is he? Don't I wish I was quarantined. In fact,
if I was to come home, or even if I was home, I wouldn't mind being
quarantined with you. And when I do get home they might as well
stick up a quarantine placard on the door, because I'll just stay right
with you until you kick me out. Now, how would you like that?

So, you have seen the newsreels of London burning and air raids.
I've seen it being done, and not on a film either. It is terrible and
I don't care to dwell on the subject at all.

. . .

Well, I close for tonight and I hope for more letters tomorrow and
I will write again.

Your loving hubby,
oodles of love,
Clarence

☙

April 13, 1941

Sweetheart,

I certainly hope you get this letter. We were made to understand
that all of the mail going to Canada during the month of March
was sunk, and I wrote you ten letters in that time so you probably
will go quite awhile without hearing from me. It sure disappoints
me because I know what it is like. I'm short seven of yours and all
those parcels and cigarettes which probably went down too. Well,
we are lucky it was only mail, and that hurts plenty too, because I
simply live for your letters and when they don't get here, well, it's
awful disappointing, and I'm right out of smokes. Don't give up
sending them, and plenty of them too, because the majority will
get through and maybe I can get ahead enough to make up for
what might go down.

I'm going out on the range tomorrow as first aid for any possible
casualties. Quite a soft job: just lay out in the rain and mud, unless
maybe the sun will shine. It did today, but two days running would
be too much to expect. . . .

Well darling, I went to mass this morning and we had quite a nice
sermon on what our wives and families are doing back home. It
was real touching, gave me the blues, which I drowned by washing
clothes for two hours this afternoon. And then a couple of hours of
sleep and a picture show tonight, "My Girl Friday," a light comedy
with plenty of laughs.

So, it is getting late and the lights will soon go. I'll write real often,
every day or so, so that some of my letters will be getting to you
regularly.

Gosh, I do love you darling, and quite blue most of the time, but
I expect to be home a lot sooner than one dares to hope.

Your lonesome hubby,
Clarence

[P.S.] Rollie—Are you real good to mummy for daddy and do you still give her those good night kisses for me? Well, be good, and hug Murray for me.

∾

April 14, 1941

Darling Mummy,

Is everything alright with you darling? Are you really sure everything is as it should be? Something seems or feels wrong to me.
It came on me last night—this feeling, is it what they call
premonition or is it just my imagination?

Well, I said I would write again last night so here am. I was out
on the range all day. It didn't exactly rain, but it was cloudy all
of the time and the odd drop of rain. Nobody scratched a finger,
so I had nothing to do but keep myself comfortable.

Oh yes, I forgot to mention we had a chicken dinner on Easter
Sunday and was it ever good. But they have nothing on you as
for dressing. I'm afraid that when I get home I'll just simply eat
myself sick.

. . .

Well, I just got myself in wrong with our Corporal and he claims
he is going to make me step around here. He came in here slinging
his lip and I just couldn't stand it and I spoke my mind. So now
I'm going to have to step around carefully. Well, I don't give a rip.
I can see to it that he won't find any reason to stick me up on orders.

Well, we have lost our Bandmaster and one of the boys—fellow
by the name of Munday has taken over and he is all right. . . .

. . . we are going on a five-day scheme in the morning so I won't
write for that time, but I have your pictures with me and that helps
a lot. Gosh, this is terrible writing—I'm writing with the paper on
my knees!

Well darling, I haven't really much more to say, only that I miss you and love you more and more as time goes on. How are the kiddies keeping? I suppose they are outside most of the time now. The weather has improved considerably here, and the fruit trees are all in blossom and more flowers than ever. I understand we are going out on coastal tactics, which will be quite interesting, so I will write all about that in my next letter.

. . .

I do hope you get this letter darling—if any more of my mail goes down I'll go nuts. You probably are wondering what is the matter now not hearing. I understand more mail has been sunk again going to Canada, but that may be just talk I hope.

Well darling, I'll close sending all my love to you and the kiddies. And do be good.

Hugs and kisses,
Daddy

☙

Sunday,
April 20, 1941


Dear Mummy,

Well I'm back off of that scheme, and what a grand and glorious
miserable time I had. I'm still shivering with the cold and wet—
I'll tell you all about it later. I must answer your letters . . . which
I was afraid had went down. And your parcel, it was grand and just
on the spot too. I came in from the scheme half starved and was
handed the parcel, and I sure wasn't long in eating most of it.

. . .

. . . So, I'll tell you all about the scheme.

We left here Wednesday noon, the sun was out in all its glory. We
were transported by lorry all afternoon. That night were unloaded
in the swellest district: trees and lawns, meadows, beautiful estates
and flowers. The primroses are all out now and the countryside is
just simply loaded with them. The sky was clear when we rolled in
under the stars, but as England would have it, it started to rain
about 2:30 a.m. Thursday. Well, I got soaked and cold—my blankets were all wet—so I didn't get anymore sleep then till about 8:00
in the morning. The sun came out hot all through the day, and at
10:00 p.m. we were again loaded into the trucks and away till about
2:00 a.m., and then we marched the rest of the way. And of course
it had to [be] cold and foggy. And to top it off, loaded down . . .
with all that equipment. We had to climb to the top of a ridge
(about a two-mile climb), and when we got there, no blankets, and
it was a lumbering camp. We had to sleep under the stars again (no
stars, clouds, and cold). I tramped around through trees all night
till daylight, then we made fires and lay down around them. Could-
n't make fires during the night because that would be inviting a
Fritzie bomb. So thanks to Hitler we froze all night. But no sooner
did daylight come so did the rain, and it's still raining this morning.

So we stood around all day Friday soaked to the hide and cold. I'm lucky I didn't get pneumonia, but I have a swell cold all the same. And Friday night we started a retreat, marched six miles, downhill this time slipping and sliding in the mud and water. And, oh yes, all we had to eat Friday was two sandwiches and two chocolate bars and tea. After the six-mile march we were again loaded into trucks packed like sardines and moved back a few miles and then stopped, and we couldn't get out of the trucks awaiting further orders, which came the next morning about 5:30. The order was at 8:41 proceed back to camp and then we had a hot meal for breakfast. So I didn't sleep all of Wednesday night, none of Thursday and none of Friday. So you can see I had a wonderful time: cold, wet and hungry (I had some beer that I bought off of the lumberjacks on Friday that helped a little). So when I got back to camp, dry clothes, bed, and your parcel and letters, it was like heaven.

I'm enclosing the yellow primrose and the purple primrose and the daisy—I hope they keep some semblance of their colours and shapes.

So Blackie is going to have kittens. I'll bet Rollie is excited. I suppose he will want you to keep them all.

I'll close soon darling because I understand there is more mail to come today, so I don't want to run out of ideas and items of interest.

So, love to you and the kiddies, and hope for plenty more mail tonight including Mother's parcel which I haven't received yet, and more cigarettes—I've been smoking English ones for two weeks.

Bye Mummy. Hugs and kisses,
Daddy

April 22, 1941

Dear Mummy,

You ask me if you are writing too much and ask if I am getting tired
of receiving so many of your letters. Darling, you can't write too
often. I enjoy every word of them and the more I get, the better I'll
like it, so keep on writing as often as you have, oftener if possible.

. . .

Listen darling, don't let this get you down. Do something to occupy
your mind. I think that doing a little work for Dad through the
summer months will help you kill time and take your mind off of
this mess a little. It is much different here. We are kept busy with
schemes and the band. It helps keep my mind off of our worries
and troubles. It is awful hard darling, I know, but what can we
do but make the best of it and pray for an early reunion.

Did you receive the birthday cards and Easter cards? I understand
some of our mail didn't reach its destination and I'm afraid they
were among it.

. . .

And yes darling, I did receive the sweater, gloves, and socks.
They were all swell. I've the sweater on now and it fits like a glove.
Couldn't be better for style, colour, or fit. Thanks a million.

So, Aunt Olive received the telegram. That's swell, I was afraid she
wouldn't. How is she feeling now? Getting over Mush's death I hope.
How does she look? As tired as ever and getting older I suppose.

So your financial troubles are gradually dwindling. Don't leave
them worry you darling, they will all straighten out and everything
will be rosy.

Yes, you tell Rollie that the King's house is bigger'n all the houses
in Lafleche put together, but that I wouldn't change houses for
anything. That little brown house of ours holds all sorts of
cherished memories for us, good and bad.

. . .

So the folks have moved? What does Mother think of it? I suppose
Rollie will be tickled. He can go and see Grandma every day on his
new bicycle, and I suppose Murray will be wanting to ride it too
pretty soon. Does he show any temper yet when he wants anything?
I can just see the cute little fellow fighting with Rollie over something. I'll bet he is sweet.

. . .

So Murray is having his baby sickness now is he? I'll bet it keeps
you busy on top of all your housework. Dad says Murray is an
awful big fellow and heavy set. He looked as if he would be at
Toronto. Oh, if I could only be home to see his babyhood and
the different stages of boyhood. Hazel, I do get terribly lonesome
and blue, at times I can hardly stand it. . . .

. . .

. . . I've been looking at my hair and it is quite grey. I'll be white-
headed pretty young I suppose. Do you think you will still love
me with white hair when I'm about 35?

. . . I'm trying to borrow a camera for when I'm on leave to take
pictures or have a bunch taken of myself. I suppose you are anxious
for snaps from me of me, and I feel like hell for not sending you
any . . . I would like photos of you and the family—snaps will
have to do—and I could stand plenty of them.

Well darling, I will close now sending you all of my love, and
I will write again tomorrow before going on leave and as soon
as I get back to tell you all about it. . . .

So bye and love,
Daddy

P.S. Rollie, that was a swell letter you wrote daddy. Do it again, eh!
Daddy likes to hear from his little man, and be good for Mummy.
Bye-bye.

❧

ROLLIE AND MURRAY IN FRONT OF THE
"LITTLE BROWN HOUSE" IN LAFLECHE.

*Picture Letter Card*

May 2, 1941

Hello Darling,

I'm away up on the northern tip of Scotland and just had tea with Jack Banks' brother in this hotel. I've enjoyed this tour immensely. The scenery is grand. Took a few snaps, which I will send right away. But I'm awfully lonely just now—I want home and the kiddies, mostly you.

Writing on Sunday, all of my love,
Clarence

❧

May 4, 1941

Sweetheart Mummy,

Gosh, I feel awful blue and guilty for not writing more than just that folder I sent you while I was on leave [Clarence is referring to the picture letter card above]. . . .

Well darling, I'll tell you all about the trip. When I landed at Thurso it was snowing and colder than blazes, while when I left here it was warm and hot and sunny. But, I must admit Thurso is a long way north of here. When I arrived Mr. Dallas met me and we went out to his place away up on a hill, a white bungalow with a red roof, very modern to my surprise, but with the inevitable fireplace in every room. I had a very nice room, cozy and warm. I'd sit at the fireplace every night and read and look into the flames and think of home, and many a time with tears in my eyes . . . I just don't seem to grow up. I get so blue at times I'm nearly desperate, and sweetheart your last letter upset me pretty bad—you seem to have given up hope to ever see me again—I don't know what to make of it. Please darling, don't feel like that. I'll be home again, and don't forget my arms will be there for you where you belong and no one else will be in them but you. Yes, liquor, I naturally had a drink or two, to be exact nine drinks over six days with Mr. Dallas. I didn't even feel it. And then when I did drink them it was because someone I was introduced to insisted we must have drink[s]. Hazel, sweetheart, I do wish you could learn to trust and believe me. Of course there are women in England, but I'm not interested in any of them, not in the least. Listen, Sweetheart, I love [you], and only you. You always ask about women and liquor around the camp. I never touch liquor. First of all, I don't want it, and, furthermore, I haven't the money. Please believe me. I love you, and I will be back to you as I left in Toronto.

Well, I'm roaming all over I'm so lonesome, but I want to tell you about my leave and what I saw.

Caithness County looks like Saskatchewan, flat and all farms, scarcely populated. I met thousands of Scotch people who have relatives in Canada, so it was a continual round of visiting, dinner one place, tea another, and supper another (I can't remember hardly any of their names), and back to Dallas's at night. In the mornings I'd help him with his chores, and about noon into his car and we'd have dinner someplace else. I've never witnessed such hospitality and friendliness in my life, and I was forever answering questions. Some people would say, have you met my brother in Hamilton; another would have a sister in Saskatoon, etc., etc. They think Canada is something like England, I guess. The longest time I spent with anyone outside of Dallas's was with James Banks. He was in Lafleche for several years after the last war and knows Dad well. I spent the afternoon and Wednesday night with him. He is a widower and an invalid from the last war (gassed and wounds). He has two grown-up daughters, 19 and 22. The youngest one is working on some farm. I didn't meet her. The oldest one, a delicate, awfully thin girl, stays with him, but James and I talked away about Lafleche for hours that night. In fact, after he took me touring throughout the scenic spots we sat and talked Lafleche and its people and my family till 3:30 in the morning and then I went to bed. And Mr. Dallas called for me early next morning to take me visiting his son a few miles away. We had dinner there, and then back to Dallas's for my last night there. Yes, I enjoyed myself while I was on leave: good eats, nice people, and, above all, a rest and a change. But I was awful anxious to get back to camp for your mail and parcels and a chance to write a decent letter. I think this covers pretty well my trip—the train ride was awful monotonous and tiresome, it takes 48 hours either way.

So, now I'm back in camp and to the same old routine and dying to get home, and a lot of time to write you darling.

Well, sweetheart, your last letter had an awful disappointing undercurrent. You seemed to be impatient and despondent as if you were in jail or something. Please be careful darling, don't do anything you will be sorry for. Above all keep yourself busy with tennis as you say you are going to take up, play golf, etc.—all of those things. It would help a lot to take up your spare time and surplus energy, and you would feel an awful lot better. It is different with me—the band, schemes, drill and route marches—I'm kept plenty busy and my bed always looks good at nights. And I love you.

Your parcel was just swell and on the spot; especially, the peanut butter—absolutely none in England for sale. Well, all in the parcel was swell.

. . .

Well, I'll close for now darling, sending you and the kiddies all my love and thoughts, and you especially—oodles of hugs and kisses.

Bye Mummy, be good and write often, I will,
Love, Daddy.

*ᘓᕠ*

CLARENCE WITH JAMES (JIM) BANKS IN NORTHERN SCOTLAND IN EARLY MAY 1941. JAMES HAD SPENT TIME IN THE LAFLECHE AREA FOLLOWING WORLD WAR ONE; HIS BROTHER, JACK BANKS, HAD TAKEN UP A HOME-STEAD SOUTH OF LAFLECHE IN 1908.

May 6, 1941

Darling Mummy,

I was just looking through the snaps I have of you and the kiddies and I'm awfully lonesome. Do you know sweetheart you are actually good looking and those snaps show it up plain. At any rate, you are swell and I love you. And thanks for the gum, bars, sugar, coffee, etc., etc. I'm making coffee now. I'm [an] orderly in the hospital tonight so I've got the alcohol stove going. If I get caught I'll catch hell, but there is no one around, no danger.

. . .

So, you have had your summer coat fitted. I'll bet you look swell in it, and I'd bet you could get the coat all mussed up in my arms. I sure wish you could too—my arms just ache to hug you darling. I'd like to muss your hair too. I'm afraid that when I do get back to you, I'll want to eat you right up. I'm sure looking forward to that day. Excuse me, I've got to dress a fellow's boils—I'll only be minute.

That's done. Tomorrow, I'm going to ask to be allowed to try that musicians' test and also ask our major if he will let me transfer to the holding band if I pass. . . .

. . .

How is Rollie doing? Getting bigger and heavier every day I suppose, and now that he has his bike I suppose you have quite a time keeping track of him. If he is anything like I was, you will have a lot of fun keeping your eye on him. But Rollie is a good boy outside of a little temper. The guy that's going to be naughty is Murray I'll bet. He sure had little devils in his eyes at Toronto. I'll bet he is getting big too. Oh darling, you don't know how I miss those little tykes, the feel of their small soft hands and hugs. I'll be such a stranger to them when I get back that I'm afraid they will never really know me

as a daddy. They learn to love a daddy when they are babies
and I'm missing their babyhood.

. . .

So bye, be good, I love you,
Clarence

కు

May 11, 1941

My Darling Sweetheart,

Mother's Day! Greetings to the swellest little mother in the
world. And I've had some swell compliments about your looks and
actions from the family darling. Mmmm, I love you sweetheart.

. . .

So the Pope spoke over the radio and says the war will be long
and drawn out. Oh, I do hope he's wrong—I've been away from
you a darn sight longer than I care to.

. . .

. . . And when am I coming [home]? That is hard to answer darling.
I'm physically sound and in good health, worst of luck, so it seems.
By the way, I've [an] infection in my left hand now. The doctor
drains the matter out every day. I cut the palm of my hand the
other day and infection set in overnight. It doesn't hurt much and
they are keeping an eye on it.

. . .

So, you didn't buy yourself a new hat for Easter—why? Darling,
I'm afraid you are so anxious to pay up your bills and save that you
are making too many, too many, unnecessary sacrifices. I want my
darling to look just as well-dressed as the next, and I understand
that you look swell in your coat since you have made it over. Oh
darling, I do so want to be with you and see all these things myself,
be able to tell you how much I love you instead of writing about it.

. . .

Well, yes, we were on a scheme for three days . . . freezing nights, there isn't much good to say about it. These fool schemes of crawling around through bush, etc., etc. are getting my nanny, and I sure hope this fool war calls a halt. And, personally, I don't see how it can last two years more at the longest. They can't keep it up and [I] still can't set a date at all as to when I will be back as much as I would like to.

. . .

So, Rollie is dressed up as a soldier man, is he? I'll bet he is doing his strutting. And so darling, Murray sends me a kick in the tummy and a nose rub. Tell him they were swell.

. . .

Your loving hubby,
Clarence

ROLLIE, AGE FIVE, IN HIS SOLDIER'S UNIFORM,
AND HAZEL, MURRAY AND ROLLIE, LAFLECHE, 1941.

May 13, 1941

Darling,

. . .

I've just come back from the show, "The House Across the Bay," the one you were telling me about in your last letter. A very good and touching picture. When I came from it I felt terribly low and still do. Why it should get me as it did, I don't know. All the way through the performance I could practically feel you sitting beside me. Oh darling, I miss you so. Isn't it terrible darling, this continual longing. Is it ever going to end? Soon, I hope. I'm down in the dumps tonight, am I not darling? But when I stop to think of who loves and is faithfully waiting for me in a little brown house away across the sea in a little country town by the name of Lafleche, Sask., Can., I take up new courage and try to make the best of things as they are, and look forward to the day when we will be back in each other's arms again with our kiddies at our feet. Won't that be swell mummy?

. . .

By gosh, I've got a pair of sore feet tonight. I tried a ten-mile route march with new boots on. I made it, but towards the last I was sweating blood. But the shoes are broke in, in case we have a four or five day march. Yes, when this war is over and I'm back with you, it's going to be a wheelchair for me in the house and a bicycle or something for out-of-doors, and if anyone ever mentions going for a stroll I believe I'll get mad.

Taking good care of yourself are you mummy? Do. And how are the kiddies? Fine, I hope.

. . .

Love,
Clarence

☙

Wednesday,
May 14, 1941

My Own Sweetheart,

Here I am again. I wrote a letter last night, but I'm writing again
because we are going on a scheme. That is four. First-aid men
are going out with part of the battalion on a four-day scheme,
so I won't be able to write till Saturday or Sunday.

Yes, I had a bad cold last night, but this morning it was practically
cleared up. It is now 2 p.m., but for a runny nose I feel fine and am
now going to bed because we will be travelling all night to the coast.
So tomorrow darling, I'll have the whole day on my hands to sit
and think of you while waiting for someone to get hurt. Funny, in
all these schemes I've done nothing more than maybe put Aspirins
in water for some fellow or iodine on a scratch. But this scheme, as
far as first aid is considered, [is] to be a picnic and the weather is
fine. So, I may enjoy myself as much as can be expected without
the only girl in the world.

I had my left hand cut open by the M.O. (Medical Officer) today—
there seemed to be infection there from a scratch. He took out a
big piece of flesh and skin so that it would rebuild and heal up, and
then he poured iodine into the open wound—my, my, my, oh my,
did it make me sweat.

One fellow in the S.S.R. from Swift Current just got a divorce from
his wife, or rather divorced her, on the grounds that she wasn't true
to him. He had mentioned it to me about two months ago, saying
that he wired to some Army organization in Canada to look into
these reports he had received re his wife, and they apparently did
and verified the rumours about his wife being unfaithful. He was
pretty upset and filed [a] divorce suit, which only took three weeks
to go through—cutting his wife off the Army pay and separation
allowances at no cost to him. The Army officials claim that it is only

fair to the soldier away from home to have some protection against such happenings. Very drastic, but effective, and it will no doubt go hard on a lot of these old and young chippies who married young, foolish soldiers for the security there was in it, hoping that the soldier gets killed and then they will have the widow's allowance and still step around, which an awful lot of them do anyway. Thank heavens I don't have to worry about you stepping out darling. I have all the faith in the world that you never will and I love you all the more every time I think of you sitting in Canada, lonely and blue waiting for me to come back, which I will without a doubt.

Take care of yourself for me mummy and write often. Often, even if at times letters don't come, it will be because they were sunk.

Bye, bye Sweetheart, oceans of love,
Daddy

❧

May 16, 1941

Hello Sweetheart,

Well here I am back from the scheme earlier than expected, and there was a letter of yours waiting for me, a letter you wrote on the 5th of April . . . which I had given up as lost. I guess that with all this trouble of convoying across the Atlantic we must expect the mail is to be very irregular.

It's now 15 to 10 p.m. and the sun is still shining (will be for a half hour yet), and it was real nice and warm today. But yesterday was chilly and windy, so out on the scheme wasn't pleasant at all. Yesterday, I nearly froze, and last night I did. We travelled from midnight till four in the back of trucks and there was an exceptionally heavy frost for this country. So I froze with the blossoms on the fruit trees. Yes, I understand that last night's frost has practically ruined all the fruit crop for this year—everything except the apples—so we will have to go short on fresh fruit on top of the rest.

. . . While I was on the scheme, and yesterday strolling around the countryside, I came across a group of children playing under the trees, chaperoned by a nun. The children were all about 3 or 4 and they came running up to me and asked all kinds of questions. Then the nun or Sister came over and started asking me questions of Canada. If I was married, etc., etc. She was real nice, and those kiddies, Hazel, reminded me so much of ours that I could hardly speak to the Sister without a catch in my voice. The children these Sisters were taking care of were children whose parents had been killed in the blitzed cities. It was terrible pitiful to listen to their chatter about going home, their daddies and their mommies. One little fellow about Rollie's size named Ronnie told me his daddy was coming tomorrow on the bus to take him back home. Yes, England has many and many a sad story to tell. I thank my lucky stars my young ones and you darling are safe and sound away from this mess.

. . .

You say nobody knows how lonesome you are. I know sweetheart.
I care too, because I'm awful lonesome myself and it's terrible.

. . .

So bye-bye darling, take care of yourself religiously and physically.
I love you.

Your hubby,
Clarence

P.S. Tell Rollie to write again and that the little boys and girls at
the orphanage promised Daddy that they would pray for him to
get back to his little boys soon and safe and sound. Oh Hazel,
I'm lonesome and I'm going to bed with a great big hurt way
down deep. Bye-bye sweetheart, I love you.

෴

May 19, 1941

Dearest Mummy,

Just a note before we go out on parade. I was going to write yesterday, but understood there was more mail in so I waited and received
the cigarettes and a parcel from Dodo of peanuts, candy, bars, and
fruitcake. And you know, I actually like fruitcake now, or maybe it
is the hunger I have for sweets. And the smokes sure were a godsend.
I was broke and would have to bum or borrow smokes. In the Army,
the fellows are nice enough, but they can't stand a bum and make
no bones about it either. . . .

. . .

Oh yes darling, do send some decent stationery once in a while.
I'm tired of asking for this stuff and it isn't just what I'd like to
write to you on.

. . .

Saturday afternoon the troops were called out to fight a bush fire
a few miles from here. When we got there it was pretty much under
control, and when a few hundred soldiers armed with shovels got at
it the fire was soon put out. So, we have done something of value at
last instead of sitting around.

. . .

Your loving hubby,
Clarence

May 23, 1941


Dear Mummy,

. . .

Well, here I am, 5 p.m.—we packed all our equipment in blankets
for nothing I believe, because I had to unpack all mine tonight. This
afternoon we were out on the ranges having target practice. Do you
know what I did this p.m. at practice? I wasn't doing so good and I
said to myself on one shot, "if Hazel loves me, I'll hit the bull's eye."
And I did, smack in the middle, so I guess you love me.

. . .

Re: money when I get back. The government pays all return soldiers
about $75.00 a month for three months—anyway, this I am sure of.
And the longer one is overseas, the more you get when you get back.
That is, the government pays you for more months after. Just what
the details are, I'm going to find out and let you know. So you
needn't worry about the immediate [future], and surely within six
months I should be able to get something furthermore. I'm taking
the free commercial arts course, started last Wednesday. Don't know
much about it yet but I think it is what I want, lettering and poster
writing. Anyway darling, save some if you can, it will all help.

Haven't you heard my message yet? I understand the s.s.r. program
was broadcast and I had a special message for you. I wish you had
heard it. . . .

. . .

Received a long letter from Aunt Olive today so I'll answer it right
away. She seems to feel pretty bad about Mush and wants me to
write her often, which I will, that is to say about every fifteen days.

I wish you were or had been here to kiss my mouth better. It was pretty sore for a while and it did leave a small scar on the red part of the upper lip; not noticeable unless I laugh, then it shows up white.

. . .

Well, I guess I'll close for now and write again Sunday. . . .

Your loving husband,
Clarence

∽

May 26, 1941


Dearest Mummy,

. . .

So you have received the birthday cards. I was afraid that they were having a salty bath. So Rollie was pretty tickled with his. Good boy, he likes his Daddy, doesn't he?

Yes, I wrote about Mush's death. Did one or more of my letters not get to you?

Yes Hazel, there are a lot of things I could write about etc., but can't because if ever they intercept a letter going out with military information the party responsible will have some tough explaining to do, and all further mail would be opened and censored.

Do you ever stop to think that every morning when you open your eyes it is one day closer to the day when we are together again? I do, but the thought always mars the pleasure of it, that there will be how many days, weeks, months, etc. Sometimes I really get disgusted with it all, but I'm not letting it get me down or make me do anything I'll be sorry for, because I want to come back to you better if possible than when I left you.

You say in your letter that if you ever get a hold of me again you will never let me go. And you won't have a very hard time to hold me because I'll be quite willing and content.

I've lost three hundred of your cigs darling.

Yes, I sent my love to you over the radio and if you don't happen to hear it my intentions were good and I sure meant what I said.

. . .

So you wish you had me with you to feed. Well, don't I wish I was there. I'd probably get something to eat. At times here the meals are quite uninviting, and we don't eat what we like, we eat what we can darn well get.

Yes, I can remember the day when you walked in on me in the café in Brandon. Don't I ever wish that that was today.

So Murray is quite the guy, eh! I can just see the expressions on his face as he gets mixed up with the stuff in the cupboard.

Yes sweetheart, I got the Aspirin box. I'll admit I couldn't figure out what was in it till I opened it. I got quite a kick out of it and I'm keeping it.

Hazel, please, I am not sold on England. I'll admit that the scenery is grand to anyone from the prairies, but the climate and the average Englishman—nix for me. . . .

. . .

Well darling, I'll say bye for now, and I am hurrying home as fast as I can.

Your own daddy,
Clarence

P.S. Hugs and oodles of love and kisses. Get some little knick-knack for Rollie on the quiet and say it was me who sent it. Love.

❧

England
May 31, 1941


Dear Mummy,

Received your swell parcel and three letters today, and that typed
one was sure swell and is going to take a lot of answering. And
thanks for the writing paper. It's a treat to write on something
else besides Sally Ann paper.

. . .

Yes, the parcel was swell and everything in it was swell. And I don't
think you're cheap about the smokes, because if I would receive all
the smokes people say they are sending me I would have plenty. . . .

So, you are still doing a little typing. Are you getting anything
for your trouble, and, furthermore, are you playing tennis yet?
It would do you a world of good.

. . .

Of course I don't mind your typing a letter to me. When I first
saw you it was over a typewriter. . . .

So you are having thunderstorms over there and a lot of rain. It
must be good for the crops. They must be all in long ago, so the
farmers should be rather glad. I'll bet you wished you could have
cuddled up to me darling the night of the storm. Well, I'd like to
be there every night, storms or no storms.

Gosh, by the trend of your letters the kiddies are quite interesting.
It makes me awful blue and as if I'm missing something which I no
doubt am. I'm missing the kiddies at their nicest age and when they
are really cute. And Rollie and his bike, I'm glad he thinks I sent it
to him for his birthday. And send a lot of snaps of the kiddies. I'm
depending on them to give me an idea of what they look like.

So the yard looks nice and you apparently have a lot of garden if half of the yard is garden. The fence is fixed and that mess at the back is straightened out and the screens painted etc., etc. So you are going to make the place look respectable. And do shingle it this fall if it's the last thing you do. And get the foundation fixed, it would make the house much warmer.

. . .

So, Ridgways are having an addition to the family, and you say they have a system for a girl. I hope they won't be disappointed. Darling, I hope to be [the] father of your daughter someday myself; in fact, when I do get back I'm going to try—what do you think of it?

. . .

So, things are going up in price in Canada too. It's unbelievable here. Two-thirds of the price of anything is tax. I don't know what this is coming to. I'm afraid it's going to be tough a long time after this war is over, and I hope to gosh it don't last as long as they expect it to.

. . .

Well bye-bye sweetheart, I love you, and I'm lonesome.

Your loving husband,
Clarence

&

England
June 5, 1941


Dear Mummy,

It's another dreary, rainy day here. We had a thunderstorm last night which made me feel awfully blue. I reread all of your last letters, and the one about the storm you had there made me feel all the worse, and later I went to the show, "Bachelor Mother." I had not seen it before and did it ever make me think of home and the baby. Yes, as you say, we go to shows to kill time, and after it's over we feel worse.

Do you know that on Wednesday, June 3rd, we could see our breath, it was that cold. I put my winter undies on and wore a scarf all day. And yesterday afternoon was so warm and sultry we could hardly move around. England is like that, being so far north.

. . .

I suppose you are figuring out what you will do when I get back. One thing I know we are going to do is another and better honeymoon before I even think of doing any work. I ache for you so much at times that when I do get you in my arms I'll probably hold you so tight you won't be able to breathe.

. . .

I haven't received the smokes yet you sent 1st of May and I'm getting low. There is more mail in so I'll probably get them today or tomorrow. In your next parcel send peanut butter again. Send some often. I like it with bread before going to bed. And darling, I'd like some summer underwear. I'd like a couple of pair of broadcloth shorts, size 32, and buttonless cotton shirts, short sleeves with a crew neck. We can't buy them here because they are rationed and we can't get ration cards for clothing in the Army. . . .

Well, I've got band practice so I'll close, and I hope to have letters to answer of yours tonight.

Your loving hubby,
Clarence

P.S. Hugs and kisses, sweetheart.

൫

June 11, 1941

My own Mummy,

Hello sweetheart, do you know the sun is actually shining today in all its glory. The weather is grand and we are having organized sports this afternoon—more interesting than drill. I'm playing baseball.

. . .

Enclosing two more of those snaps which Mr. Banks sent me from Scotland. Give them to Jack Banks if you have received the other two. I think the pictures were quite natural, so you have an idea what Mr. and Miss Banks look like (both invalids too). And as for the girl, I hope you don't misconstrue the fact that I had a picture taken with her. And what do you think of the pictures of me? Rather a nice looking snap at a quick glance. He was in Scotland, but his heart was in Lafleche. Quite conceited, eh!

Enclosing a rhododendron blossom and a leaf. I put a whole bunch of kisses in it before I pressed it. Did you get the other pressed flowers I sent—primroses and daisies? Yvonne wants to have a pressed primrose; I can't send her one because there are no more, so if you still have them show them to her.

It's nearly time to go now, so I'll close this with all my love darling. Keep your chin up sweetheart and please take care of yourself. And I do hope your trouble clears up quick, I'm worried.

Love,
Clarence

P.S. I promise to draw some pictures for Rollie—I will next letter. Hugs and kisses for my little boys and mummy.

～

England
June 13, '41

Darling,

I've just come back from a swell show, "The Amazing Mr. Williams."
It was full of laughs and a few sad parts. Joan Blondell was the
actress. Hazel, of one actress she certainly reminds me of you in
a lot of her actions, and am I ever blue and lonesome now.
I simply could bawl. Oh, I love you, I do, I do, I ache.

Boy, oh boy, is there ever an electrical storm. It's simply terrible.
It would drive you wild—just crash, flash, crash. It has been doing
that for an hour, no rain. They say that England has a lot of electrical storms in summer, practically every day. I frankly don't like
them and it makes me feel all the lonelier. Do you remember when
I was with you at home nights when storms would come up how
we would cuddle together close, close like a couple of frightened
kids. Don't I wish that was now. Say, it started raining and is it
ever. Just looked out my window and the square is a lake. Just
over a minute. I didn't know what it meant "to rain" till I got here.

How is your garden? Eating any of it yet? Boy, would I go for a
few green onions and radishes. Haven't had any here yet—they call
green onions 'scallions' in England. They should have a fancy name,
they are scarce enough.

How are the kiddies? Darling, but I'm lonesome. I've tears in my
eyes and I'm not ashamed of it. I'm downright lonesome for you.
Today, on the way to band practice, I could just see Murray tod-
dling around the yard after Rollie. Oh Mummy, I want to come
home to you and the kiddies.

Bye sweetheart, write often, often, I need your letters.

Love, hugs and kisses,
Daddy

P.S. Rollie, give Mummy a big hug and kiss for Daddy, and a nose rub to Murray for me too. Be a good boy, Daddy.

త

England
June 14, 1941


My own Mummy,

Received your air mail letter last night telling me about the
broadcast. Darling, I don't remember what I said, so if you
have memorized it, write me whatever I said.

So Rollie wants me to come, the little darling. You tell him that
Daddy wants to come home in the worse way, but that a bad man
won't let him. You have heard my voice, and don't I wish I could
hear yours.

We are going out on a three-day scheme sometime today, so that
will be a weekend that I can't write. So, I'm writing this morning,
and I will write again as soon as I get back.

So you have been quite a while without hearing from me. On
the first of May some English mail was sunk, so maybe some of my
mail went that way. Some did, no doubt, because I do try to write
real often. So, if you don't get all of my mail, it's another score you
will have to settle with Hitler.

Don't forget to send more writing paper, these pads don't seem to
last very long. Onion skin is what I would prefer—am I too big a
bum darling?

. . .

Well darling, I'll close now, time I started to get ready. Bye-bye.

Love,
Clarence

England
June 22, 1941

My own Mummy,

Gosh, it has been a long time since I have written—eight days—but I couldn't help it. We went on a scheme last Saturday and didn't get back till Friday, and was the weather ever hot, heavy and sultry. And we were marching through forests, up and down hills—the scenery was grand. In fact, a picture. And I'm sending you some pressed buttercups and a four-leaf clover that I picked on the southern shores of England.

Gosh, it is warm today. I haven't a stitch on and [I'm] sweating like a horse. How would you like to have me roaming around the house this way? I know I sure wouldn't mind. Yes, the days here are very warm and sultry, but the nights soon cool off and we can sleep.

I'm all alone in the hut. Everybody is away to swimming pools, ballgames, etc., but I'd sooner stay in and be cool. I tried the air raid shelter but it is too cold down there, so I stripped and am sitting between a window and an open door and the breeze keeps me half alive. I suppose it is terribly hot in Lafleche and I'll bet the boys are tanned nut brown by now. I'm as dark as an Indian myself. A whole week under the sun and stars, I should be.

Gosh, it has been quiet in England lately. No air raids, not a thing. I hope it's not the lull before the storm. Anyway, I'm not worried, being in the medical department and band.

Boy, it's warm, just absolutely suffocating. My hands are wringing wet. I'm afraid to make a mess of this letter.

How are the kiddies darling? Full of pep, I suppose, and keeping you plenty busy I'll bet, especially Murray. I'll bet his face at times must be comical to see—all dirty, and that mischievous glitter in his eyes. Gee, I wish I was home. I envy those two little fellows because they are with the nicest mummy in the world. . . .

Gosh, it's twelve whole days since I've heard from you. I hear there is mail in, but it is quarantined due to some illness on the boat. So, it will be a few days yet. And looking at my smokes—I have three packages yet—enough to do till Thursday. I hope I receive more soon.

. . .

Well darling, I really haven't much news. Nothing ever happens. And I can always write about my love for you, but that is not news anymore, it's a fact.

Bye Sweetheart, write often. I need your letters and you.

Your loving husband,
Clarence

☙

June 24, 1941

Sweetheart,

. . .

How is everything there, darling? Is the garden swell? How are the trees coming? No doubt, plenty of weeds. (Excuse paper, we are at band practice with our respirators on. Can't play, so I am writing on the only paper available.)

We played for an inspection of the s.s.r. by the Duke of Gloucester, the King's brother. There is quite a resemblance between the King and the Duke. The latter is heavier and wears a moustache. The inspection was very informal and short, he didn't speak to anyone.

. . .

Next week we are going on coastal patrol; that is, the whole battalion for about 10 weeks in the nicest part of England, where we had our last scheme. So, I'll be able to keep cool swimming in the ocean. The boys are pretty tickled about the change. Life was becoming quite monotonous here.

. . .

I was just thinking the sports and picnics must be in full swing around there. Have you taken in very many of them? Boy, wouldn't it be swell if we could take them in, dances and all. We sure could have a grand time. And, as it is, life is just misery. I don't go any place but to shows and swimming.

. . .

Gotta go now, so bye sweetheart. Love to the kiddies, and all of me for Mummy.

Love,
Daddy

❧

England
June 25, 1941


My own Mummy,

At last darling, I received four of your letters today. It should make
me feel just tops, but as it happens I'm so darned lonesome for you
sweetheart. I think of the funniest things I'd like to do if I were
with you, such as run my fingers through your hair, smooth the hair
back on your temples, kiss you on the ear. I'm madly in love with
you darling. Oh, for the nearness of you, feel you cozy and loving
in my arms. Does it all sound foolish darling? I'm just aching to do
those things, and the way things are going here now, I don't think it
is going to be very long. Hitler will soon be on his knees. Oh, for
that day.


. . .


So Rollie gets pretty naughty, eh? I should be there I'll admit, but
kids will be kids. And Murray, you say I should see him. The folks
say he is grand. The lucky little punks are with you—I'm not—
I envy them and miss them.

I guess I'll close and write again tomorrow. In the meantime, be a
good sweetheart, and when you feel exceptionally blue remember
I love you.

Your hubby,
Clarence

∽

England
June 26, 1941


Dear Mummy,

. . . Received a registered letter from the R.C.A. Force with all my papers today, and a letter stating that they couldn't consider my application anymore, being on active service in England. So you needn't ask them for the papers as I asked you to.

Well, next Wednesday we will leave for our new quarters in southern England on the coast. I understand some summer resort in peacetime. We will be on coastal guard in case of an invasion. I'm anxious to get out of here to this new place for a change. The entertainment here is nil; while there, there is fishing, swimming, a swell scenery, and we will be busy doing something worthwhile and not this monotonous training day in and day out.

It is 10:15 p.m. and the sun is still shining. In fact, it doesn't get dark until 1 a.m. Seems funny, going to bed in daylight.

I was speaking to Hammond today and I really feel bad for the chap. He is a nice chap. He received some cake, eats, and tobacco from his wife and felt pretty good about that. He talked about his kiddies and wife, how lonely he got, etc. If he realized how his wife was carrying on, he'd go nuts. He showed me a picture of his wife taken in Lafleche—she does look hard doesn't she? And as you say, she is.

How are the kiddies doing? Send some snaps of them and yourself again soon, I'm sending more as soon as I get mine.

. . .

Take care of yourself and be good. Hugs and kisses to my kiddies, and all my love.

Your hubby,
Clarence

July 1, 1941


Dear Hazel,

I've wanted to write the last three days but we can't mail anything
till we will be down in our new quarters. But, I couldn't wait any
longer. Today is Dominion Day, the 1st of July, a great day in
Canada and a holiday for the Canadian troops overseas—and I've
reread and reread your last two letters. They were swell, and I'm
sorry if you haven't received any mail for such a long time in June
and the later part of May. I didn't write while I was on leave, I'll
admit, but I did as soon as I got back and I've written regularly ever
since. I'm enclosing another picture of the band boys . . . and I'm
also enclosing a rose I picked the other day. It is rose time here now
and there are millions of them. I hope it retains some of its original
shape and scent. Anyway darling, there is a kiss under each petal.

. . .

Gee, it is warm here. All I have on now is those fancy shorts we
bought, "you and I," in Brandon. Do you remember them? It is the
only way I can keep cool outside of the showers. Yes, if I was home
on these warm days I'd probably be sprawled out on the bed with
no more on than now. I wouldn't mind, would you? And I don't
think I'd be sprawled out alone very long if I were there now.

Excuse paper, I borrowed this because I've all my stuff packed
waiting to move, which will be anytime tonight or morning. And
I understand our new billets will or are swell. Two men to the room,
hot and cold running water—schools that have been evacuated
someplace near Brighton on the south coast. I'm sorry but that
is all I know about them so far.

Yesterday evening I tried to get a photo taken. I went to three different studios and they were closed, "no film." The film shortage here is
terrible . . . most of the boys get theirs from Canada, so you can send
me a film now and then, size 120. I can borrow a camera. . . .

The other night [it was] too warm to sleep. We were talking away and eventually started thinking up something to do. So, noticing one fellow was asleep, we picked his bed up to give him a scare. He didn't awaken so we decided to change its position. We did that and he just grunted, so we decided let's take him outside. That we did and he still was snoring away peacefully. So we took his bed out in the middle of the parade square, which is about 600 feet square, and set his bed down gently. And in the morning we got up early to see if he was still in his bed. He was, and we watched him till he woke up, and what a laugh we got out of that. There was no movement in the bed for quite a while, and then, wham! He jumped straight up in the air and came running full tilt for the hut as the Lord clothed him and scared blue. He admitted that when he opened his eyes, looking into the sky and the square, he didn't know what was happening. The first thing he thought was an air raid and he hit for the shelters. And he said when he saw us all standing around the hut, what happened dawned on him and he wanted to kill someone, and he finally had to laugh too. It really was funny darling.

I'm going to have another shower now darling and then try to get a little sleep. We'll have plenty to do in the next twenty four hours.

Haven't received your parcel or cigarettes, and I'm in need— send often.

Your loving husband,
Clarence

[p.s.] Bushels of hugs and kisses to the kiddies too. Write often darling, your letters are swell. Love and more love. Well, in comes the rose and it's smothered with kisses.

౨

England
July 4th, 1941

My own Sweetheart,

Just got up from the dentist's chair. Had all the old fillings
removed on the upper teeth and new ones put in. My gums
were froze and still are.

Well, we are in our new quarters and are they ever swell. It's a
white building, a hotel in fact, in the nicest part of England. I can
see the ocean from where I am sitting. There is only 30 of us in the
building. Of course, it is used as a hospital as well, that's why we
have a dentist, and he is a good one, from Calgary. . . .

The country here is really beautiful. The grounds around the hospital are simply grand: millions of flowers, mostly roses just now,
beautiful hedges and lawns, big oak trees, cedars, birch, and a rock
garden, lily pond with gold fish in it—pretty swell, eh! And separated from the rest of the battalion by two miles in fact. The set-up
is practically too good to be true. Now for the building: L-shaped,
3 stories, white, red tile roof, a terrace in the inner side facing the
ocean, and a swell beach there too. Haven't been in yet, but expect
to tonight. My room—that is three of us, Dick Nunn (sax player),
Kayo Symons (bass player), and myself—is a large room overlooking the grounds with a bay window to the south and another window looking over the town about a half-mile away. Adjacent: tiled
bathroom with built in tub, hot and cold water taps. And modern
washbowl in the room, a swell fireplace (the room is about 14 × 20),
quite large clothes closet, but no curtains on the windows—so this
afternoon we are going shopping for some. We have several vases of
flowers through the room, two swell bouquets of poppies, roses (all
shades), Canterbury bells, foxgloves, larkspur, cornflower, iris, and
marigolds—the room is a riot of colour. Someday I hope to show
you this country, it can't really be described. I'm going to take pictures of the hospital and grounds and send them on, and of course
I'll include myself in some of the pictures.

CLARENCE, IN FRONT OF THE NEW QUARTERS NEAR BRIGHTON.

By the way, I have a film being developed back in Aldershot. I hope they send them on down here and I hope they are good—I've had two films go haywire on me. The first, a soldier tried to develop it and of course spoiled it, but gave me another, [but] when I sent it in to [be] developed it was all blank.

Oh, yes, we have a big garden too, and a gardener, so we don't have to weed that. So, we are getting green peas, lettuce, radishes, onions for a change, which makes the meals more inviting. And with two cooks for thirty men the meals are much better. And a swell kitchen, all tile, modern stoves, Frigidaire. This is a great building. Our quarters are on the top floor; administration and doctors, second floor; hospital, or sick bay as called here, on the first floor.

The weather has been grand. At night we open all the windows and the sea breeze blows through the room so I sleep comfortably. Oh yes, we have fruit trees too: apples, pears, crabapples, plums and cherries, and blackberry bushes, gooseberries, etc., etc. So, we should get a feed or two of fresh fruit later on.

Yes, sweetheart, it is beautiful here and comfortable, but not cozy with it at all. I'm still lonesome for you and the kiddies. All these beauty spots make me more lonesome because I know you would enjoy it and the kiddies would go wild on the velvety lawns and sandy beach.

Hazel, I miss you terribly. I love you, I do, and all this means nothing without you.

. . .

Well, bye for now sweetheart. I'm closing with all my love and a couple of blossoms off of a bleeding heart bush, and a kiss with all of my love is on each one.

Bye, your loving husband,
Clarence

❧

July 6, 1941

Dear Mummy,

Just got back from playing a band concert down on the beach.
The weather was grand and we had a swell audience—that is, an
appreciative crowd. And we are to play at some cove next Sunday
afternoon on the invitation of Lord somebody. I forget his name—
a tall, lanky Englishman with "rawthas" and a monocle.

Well darling, we do nothing here but wait for something to
happen, such as an invasion. So we do a lot of band practicing
and laying around in the sun, and watch the R.A.F. flying over by
the hundreds to return Hitler some of his bombs, the same way
he dropped them on some of the cities here. Today, a squadron of
bombers flew over. There was 23 of them flying to Germany. When
they came back later there was two missing. But most of the time
they all come back.

So, the R.A.F. is doing alright and the way things are Hitler is having
an awful hard time. And it's going to much worse for him soon.
Wait till the Russians start moving back after they are mobilized.
The next few days will tell. I really don't think that this is going to
last another year. I'm honesty looking forward to being back with
you and the kiddies in 1942, maybe sooner. I do hope not to be
disappointed.

Well, I've finally had a few good fills of green onions, lettuce,
and radishes, and out of our own garden back of our billets. I hope
you get the letter I wrote day before yesterday, because I told you
all about the layout. Frankly, it's swell compared to barrack life.
The unit is spread over an eleven-mile area, so we are on our own
and we don't have to contend with Strum and that's something.
Our regulations are much tougher though. If I want to go to a show
I've got to have a pass that states I'm going to be at the show, and if
anyone is found anyplace else he is AWOL and that means detention.

We can't go strolling any further than a quarter of a mile from our quarters and we can't be out any later than 10 o'clock and only 15 per cent of us can be out of the grounds at once. I don't mind at all. I'm comfortable here and I never go anyplace, and the beach is only a hundred yards away. But with it all I get awful lonesome, terribly lonesome. At the band concert a little fellow about four came over and stood at my elbow while we were playing. I picked him up, he was fair with deep blue eyes, real cute and chubby. I asked him his name and he said, "Dievie," for "Davy" of course. Well it sure made me lonesome, and on the other hand I'm sure glad that my sweetheart and kiddies aren't over here and I wished I wasn't here.

Well darling, I haven't received your cigarettes or parcels of May and June yet and I'm out, but I suppose they will catch up to me with all this moving. Send more writing paper, toothpaste, shaving cream, blades, etc.

How are the kiddies darling? I sure stare at those last snaps you sent and it makes a great big lump in my throat. Gee, I'm lonesome sweetheart. I ache all over for my mummy especially. And how are you feeling? Better, I hope. And stay that way darling.

I love you,
Clarence

೧

England
July 7, 1941

Dear Mummy,

Since we have been down here we are kept fairly busy. That is to say being just the medical staff in the hospital. We, the stretcher-bearers, have to do all the fatigues and night guards. Today, I was in the kitchen and I had plenty to do. I was real, or am real, tired and I have to go and guard from 10:30 to 1:00, but tonight I don't mind. I received three of your letters tonight, which I can read and reread and dream of home while standing guard. And I received your swell parcel darling. It just shows me how much you love me. . . .

It's six o'clock here and I'm sitting looking out over the trees and grounds. I can see several large boats out on the ocean, the sea is calm, and smoke from the ships is streaming out back of them to disappear over the horizon. A nightingale is singing to beat the ears someplace close, the boys are rolling around in shorts out on the lawn, some are playing golf—that is, there is a practicing green out in front—and the flowers and the scent of lavender is heavy in the air. I'm going down and get a few blossoms of lavender to enclose in the letter, and I hope the scent is still with them when you get this letter. Darling, it's so peaceful, beautiful and quiet, a person just can't realize there is a war on. Oh, oh, here is a reminder coming over a way, way up. Yes, I can see them, just silvery specks a way up and that dreadful drone of a bunch of bombers going over to hand Hitler some of his own. I said a dreadful drone; in a way, for the people here it is a pleasant sound to hear their own planes returning some of the past favours to Fritzie. Outside of the continual drone of planes going back and forth everything is very peaceful. As I sit here looking at all the beauties of nature, I realize how much I miss you. Wouldn't it be swell if you were sitting with me at this same window shoulder to shoulder? Oh, I miss you darling, and if it was the kiddies out on the lawn, those two little bundles of fun and love—if, if, if—when is this going to stop?

I'd better get that lavender before I forget. How did the rose keep? And the scent was swell, wasn't it? Got the lavender. They aren't in full bloom yet, but I've actually kissed every one of them and you will notice that the scent is nice, but not as nice in comparison as my love is true for you.

. . .

You said you heard me cough on the broadcast. The fact is Hazel I did, although I tried hard not to. So you can even recognize me by my cough. You know me in all ways, don't you darling? And I love you all the more for it.

Well darling, I guess I'd better get my equipment ready to go and guard. It's got to be all spic and span.

Oh yes, I had to drop that art course since we are on coastal patrol. It wasn't much of a course anyway, and so slow it would take two years to complete. . . .

. . .

Love and kisses to the kiddies, hugs, two great big ones. . . .

All of me,
Daddy

∽

England
July 8, 1941


Darling Mummy,

It is another grand day, and another day of loneliness. . . .

The other night we stood to, a practice in case of invasion, and
I and three other stretcher-bearers were sent out as first-aiders to
'B' Company. Their headquarters is in a tower on the shore. In fact,
the sea laps at its base. We were sent there, I went out on top of the
tower and looked at the sea in the moonlight. It was real calm and
silvery. The night was real clear. As I stood there all alone I could
imagine or feel you beside me, your warm little shoulders against
my side. I looked west over the ocean and a great big lump formed
in my throat. I actually had tears in my eyes. To my left was France,
trouble and sorrow, and to my right, Canada away way over the
Atlantic, a country of peace and plenty where I could be so happy
with my wife and family. Yes darling, I do love you.

The s.s.r. are forming an orchestra and have bought me a saxophone. The bandmaster picked seven out of the band and said, "you
are the orchestra." I wasn't very enthused, but when he said the only
duties you will have will be orchestra, band, and stretcher work, I
didn't mind that, because here we were doing fatigues every day and
this being a hospital we were kept quite busy. And hard enough
work at that—being nursemaid to a bunch of men, carting water
bottles, bed pans, etc., and rubbing their backs, bathing them, etc.
I didn't like it so the orchestra is a welcomed change. . . .


. . .


How are the kiddies? As mischievous as ever? I'll bet you get plenty
cranky with them at times: when Rollie refuses to come in and
Murray [is] mauling the cats, upsetting the coal pail, and pulling
stuff off things—at that, I'll bet he is awful cute. Give him a big
hug and kiss for me, and tell Rollie to write his daddy.

Well I'll say bye-bye for now sweetheart, I'm lonesome.

Your loving husband,
Clarence

૯૭

July 12, 1941

Dear Mummy,

. . .

So Murray is getting independent enough to walk downtown without holding his mummy's hand. I'll be he is cute, but if I was home I think I'd rather hold my mummy's hand.

Good, you are playing tennis at last. It will do you a world of good and never mind what the public think[s]. Go ahead, to hell with that Lafleche crowd, and if I was home I'd sure play with you myself. And when I do get back we will be together and do things together a lot more than we ever have. Will you like that? I'm look-ing forward to that now. "That will be the days," won't it darling.

You say you expect me home in '42. I feel quite sure I will, Hitler is up against a wall.

. . .

You mentioned the art course. I'm sorry, I had to drop it because we were moved into active service and have no time for anything, or rather given no time for anything, outside of the barrack area.

. . .

Well darling, I'll close now, and don't work too hard and take care of yourself.

Hugs and kisses to my mummy and kiddies.

Love,
Clarence

England
July 17, 1941


Dear Mummy,

. . .

Now, I've done quite a few things since last Saturday. Sunday afternoon we gave a band concert in the town park and we had quite a
crowd. The park is grand. We had a picture taken of the band just
before the concert. I will get a couple of them to send home. I've
also had another film taken of me and some of the boys and I've
another film to take yet, so I will have a bunch of pictures to send
home. Monday, I went to Brighton with [the] bandmaster and
bought a saxophone. I've had some pictures taken with it, it is a
gold finish. Brighton is a very nice city, reminded me of Regina.
Swell stores and streets, and the Brighton beaches are famous the
world over. They call Brighton the "California of England."

And Tuesday night we played for a dance and did remarkably well,
but we're not going to play for any more for a few weeks till we learn
a bunch of orchestrations. I picked out a bunch of pieces myself: "I'll
Never Smile Again" and "London Lights Shine Again," were the first
two I picked, because you like them and when I play them I do it for
you darling, and I play them with my heart in every note.

There is some talk of getting dress uniforms for the band, but we
will have to pay for them ourselves—and ten shillings a pay day,
roughly $2.25—and we can keep them after the war is over. I
agreed to buy one that way. They cost about $30.00 and would be
a swell souvenir when this is over, which no doubt will be soon the
way things are going now.

I'm supposed to be on kitchen fatigue today. I was and have
sneaked a few minutes to write. I picked and shelled a bushel
of green peas, great big juicy fellows, I believe I ate as many as I
brought in to the cook. And we are having new spuds for supper
too, out of the garden. Radishes and onions too, so our meals are
much better since we are away from the rest of the battalion.

Gee, I hope I get some mail soon darling, I get so darned lonesome and our anniversary less than a month away. Oh, if I could only go home to you and the kiddies. This is getting me down.

Say, we put up curtains in here, that is, our room, this morning. Bright cretonne, makes it look more like home and cozier.

We have to play for another concert on Sunday, so between band practice and orchestra and hospital duties I'm kept pretty busy and I prefer it that way. Time passes much faster, the faster the better till I get back with you.

I was just looking through my snap album and it makes me ache all over, especially that picture of you taken with your winter coat on and the badge on your hat, the badge I gave you before I left. You look so swell and loveable and neat, I sure would like to mess you all up with hugs and kisses every time I look at the picture.

ROLLIE, MURRAY AND HAZEL IN FRONT OF THE BOURASSA HOME IN LAFLECHE. HAZEL IS WEARING THE WINTER COAT AND THE HAT WITH THE BADGE THAT CLARENCE DESCRIBED IN THE LETTER ABOVE.

How are my little men? In the best of health I hope. Give them each a big hug and a kiss for me. Well, bye-bye darling, write often and long.

Your loving daddy,
Clarence

એ

July 22nd, [1941]

Dear Mummy,

. . .

. . . I haven't received even a letter but I suppose that now that we are on coastal duties the mail service will really be rotten.

We had our band concert last Sunday and we nearly made a flop of it. We were all out on an overnight scheme with the Home Guards and therefore no sleep, so we weren't in the best of shape. Last night I went to bed at 5:30 p.m. and never woke up till 6:00 this morning, so I must have been tired.

I've just borrowed a camera to take another film of pictures. The weather is grand, so today is the day for picture taking. I have some being developed now, I hope they turn out. The developers here won't develop a negative unless it is perfectly clear and [of] no military value. So we have to be careful when we take a picture that it is perfectly innocent of landmarks or military objects that may be of value to the enemy.

Say darling, could you get me some E♭ alto saxophone reeds (mediums)? Sax reeds here are very hard to get and of poor quality. Send me a dozen if you can get them from some music firm; you know of some we dealt with through the store.

How are the kiddies? Say Rollie, are you a good boy for mummy? Daddy might be coming home awful soon because that bad man Hitler is getting a licking. So, I may be home to see you pretty soon now, so be a good boy, because daddy don't like bad boys.

Well darling, I'll close now because I haven't any news of interest. Haven't seen any of the boys for a long while now we are so far apart, and I'm being good. Oh yes, I had two glasses of beer Sunday night with the Mayor of Seaford, where we gave the band concert Sunday. Are you being that good?

Bye darling, all my love and kisses,
Daddy

જી

July 29th, 1941


My own Mummy,

I'm having rather a hard time writing, I'm all cramped up. I broke
a rib yesterday, a rib up under my right arm and I'm all stuck up
with adhesive tape so tight that I can hardly breathe, and is it ever
itchy. Outside of that it doesn't hurt much unless I move around
too quick. Yes, and I broke it fooling around in the room. Kayo, my
roommate and I, got wrestling around and I rammed up against the
door and that is what happened. But I didn't know it until I went
to bed. Every time I'd move it was if someone stuck a knife in my
side, so I didn't get much sleep till the doc fixed me up this morning. I find it hard blowing either sax or euphonium and I have to
play for a dance at 'A' Company gym tomorrow, and the band has
to pay at the divisional meet (athletic meet) next day. I'm excused
all other duties but they do expect me to play. I got through band
practice today without dying, but at times when I blew fairly hard
my ribs gave me hell, and being the only eupho player and leading
sax, I'm going to have to go through with it. The outlook isn't
pleasant, just two days and it will be all over.


. . .


As for you, the things I write that you like, I mean them, and have
ample time to think things over, so, again, I mean them—every last
word. So expect the lover of your dreams when I get home.

Dick Nunn, my other room mate, is going to pick my pictures up
in Brighton tonight, so I hope to have some snaps to send home in
my next few letters.

So Murray is sprouting more teeth. I'll bet he is getting to be quite
the man. Oh boy, for those Toronto days again. That would be swell,
and, as you say, it would be nice to be away from Lafleche, which
we will because I can't see any possible future there. Suit yourself

about moving darling, but don't forget I haven't that job yet and where it will be I don't know.

. . .

So, our trees and shrubs are coming nice. Do you know that some day those lots may be pretty nice?

And Rollie is starting to notice things is he, the little beggar? Tell him daddy misses him a lot and wants him to be a good boy till daddy comes home and then he can be as bad as he wants to. . . .

Love and kisses,
Clarence

eɔ

England
August 5th, 1941

Dear Mummy,

A few pictures of the town we are billeted in and surrounding
scenery. I'll have a whole raft of snap shots to send home about
Thursday—three films, I hope they all turn out.

We are moving away from here next week. We are going under
canvas for few weeks in the midlands. It is going to be a drastic
change from the comfortable billets we have here and the swell
surroundings, but I understand we will be back here for the winter.
I hope that is true, because the band was sure well received here.
We played a band concert every Sunday night and after each
concert the Counsel put [on] a supper for us. Swell eats, so we
will miss that part of it for sure.

Well, I've had a real busy week of it. That is, music since last
Monday night. We played, that is the band played, for the changing
of the guard and then at the officers' mess for two hours, so that
took till 9:30. And on Tuesday we played a band concert two hours
from 7 to 9 p.m. on the beach. And Wednesday, we played for a
garden party at the officers' mess. We were stuck in a corner of the
lawn and played all evening while the officers entertained some of
England's nobility and big shots. Thursday, we went to the divisional athletic meet and played all afternoon and it rained cats and
dogs for awhile, so we got good and wet. And, by the way, our
brigade won the meet and the S.S.R.'s won most of the meets or
contests. After the meet we came home and played for the dance
in the 'A' Company's gym. Friday night, we played retreat and for
a dance at 'B' Company; Saturday night, we played for an officers'
dance in some Mrs. Singe's home, an old house with about sixty
rooms in it. The house was called, "The Keltons." Mrs. Singe's husband was a general in the last war and his forefathers were soldiers,
generals, marshals, etc. The house was just simply littered with old

weapons, medals, and trophies. Well, the party was quite the affair. All the elite were there with their "rawthas" and "I declares," etc.— just as we have seen them in picture shows in Canada.

Yesterday, Sunday, we played . . . at Div. headquarters, and last night we played our last band concert here and they had a banquet for the band afterwards. So, you can see that with our ordinary duties and band practices we have been plenty busy. And I enjoyed it, it sure was a change to the monotony of the army, which we are going back to on Sunday.

I'm on kitchen fatigue today, so I'll have to close till later on in the evening. Supper is about due.

I'm lonesome darling, I do love you. Do you love your Daddy? Did you get my telegram? I'll write a letter tonight.

Love,
Daddy

August 5, 1941

Dear Mummy,

Did you get those pictures I sent of Seaford? And did you get my cablegram? I hope it didn't scare you too much before you got it open. I sure was aware that the seventh of August was coming up, and I couldn't really figure out what to send, so I decided on a cablegram. [Clarence was speaking of their wedding anniversary. He and Hazel were married August 7, 1935.] Yes, Thursday is our anniversary and look where we are—you in Canada and I'm in England. Oh darling, if I were only home with you (what I wouldn't give to be back with you). The scenery here is wonderful I must admit, but it is empty. I don't enjoy it as I would like to. I see so many nice things that I know you would enjoy, and if we were here together we could both enjoy it and have a swell time. As it is we are both eating our hearts out for one another and the day I get you back in my arms "will be the day." Are you looking forward to it as much as I am? I love you, and I'm lonesome.

Steve was up for a medical yesterday. He is going to school again and he is a sergeant now, and boy is he ever struttin'.' Give me what I am doing now and they can use their stripes for enemies. Although I believe Steve has earned the stripes. He has, and is well-liked by the men. But the responsibility gets heavier with every additional stripe and the risks are that much greater. He was telling me that if I had stayed in 'B' Company I would have three stripes myself, and I told him, no Steve, I'm glad I'm in B.H.Q. and the band. The work is nicer, cleaner, and the band work is a pleasure. No, no rifle company for me. He agreed . . . and sort of wished he could have played an instrument when they started up the band and he could be in it too. But as it was he did the best he could and got more stripes. One thing I might add, he sure has been celebrating them lately. He said that it cost him twelve pounds to "wet" them as they call it here. He can have his parties and liquor. I'd sooner play for a dance any day. We have a good orchestra, swell music, and the boys like our music and I get a big kick out of playing. Steve suggested we get together some night and go out on a tear. When I said I'd rather not, he asked me if I was getting old, or was it through faithfulness to you. If so, not to be a sap, she isn't going to sit and wait for you till this is over. All I said was that I chose to believe and think differently and that when I get back to Canada that I would be able to look at my wife and children and frankly say I'm back the same as when I left you. He didn't seem to like that a bit, but said nothing more than "well, I've got to be going, see you around."

Now, don't you ever say anything to Sarah because it comes right back. Yes darling, when I get back to you I will be able to say, "here I am sweetheart, just as I left you," and honestly say it. Darling, I love you and nothing in the world would ever make me do any-thing you wouldn't like, even if you would never find out. I don't do things because I'm afraid you might find out, I don't do them because I love you and my boys. I feel terribly blue today, I guess it's because I miss you terribly.

I'm sending Rollie some transfers [stickers, temporary tattoos]. Directions are on the back, and I tried one on this letter, a spit-fire—we sure see plenty of *them* here, by the hundreds in fact. And do they ever travel. Just a streak and a roar—one is going over now.

. . .

Well bye-bye darling and thanks again for the pipe. I'm smoking it now. I'm enclosing a couple of carnations, they are all over the place here. All colours, and what a scent.

Love,
Daddy

[P.S.] Expect a parcel soon, I'm gathering up little souvenirs, etc.

August 7, 1941

My own Mummy,

Hello darling, today is our wedding anniversary. The sixth year, so if the old saying is right we certainly should get along swell now, and we have had a year and more to think over our shortcomings, etc. So, when we are together again it is going to be ideal isn't it sweetheart? Oh, will that day every hurry around? Anyway darling, on the occasion, "Congratulations for having put up with me as long as you did, and all of my love."

Gee, the weather the last while has really been rotten. Today, it rained all day and still is. We have our fireplace going in the room, which makes it quite comfortable, but I wouldn't say cheery be-cause everything is damp. And anyway, today my thoughts are all in Lafleche and no doubt your thoughts are all over here, or are they, because I haven't heard a word in over three weeks. . . .

I have some pictures of myself here which I am enclosing—not all, I'll spread them over letters because we do lose some of our mail, and we have an awful time getting film. And when we have them developed they only make one of each, and when we try to get reprints we have to practically beg, so I'll be sending my negatives along later.

How are the kiddies anyway? And Rollie, I suppose, is getting all growed up. Is he starting to act like a little man yet or does he still kick and squeal when you want him to do something, the dear little tyke. Even at that I really don't believe he is half bad.

You should hear the noise right now. A bunch of bombers flew over with an escort of fighter planes, about sixty all told, heading for Germany I suppose.

Yes, on Thursday we move out of here for canvas for a couple of months. Boy, that is going to be a let down after what we have had the last six weeks.

I was just playing "Stardust" on the saxophone. I sure like that number and I make a good job of it I think. When I play it I play it for you. (There goes another flight of bombers, eighteen of them.) Oh darling, I don't know how I stand being away from you, I could go wild sometimes. I'm all alone in the room tonight and the weather miserable. The other boys are at the show, "Irene." That last time I saw it was in Brandon with Bob and Kay. That was the second time, so I didn't care to go again.

Well, I guess I'll close for now darling and write again on Sunday.

Bye-bye and all of my love,
Your Hubby,
Clarence

P.S. Write often, I need your letters.

❧

August 10, 1941

My own Darling,

Gee, I've just noticed I've written you nine letters without writing
to anyone else, so I'd better get down to business and quit lolling
around in the garden and on the grounds.

I was on guard last night and it just simply poured rain by the
buckets and I had to walk the beat once every ten minutes for two
hours. After the first two trips, rain cape and all, I was soaked to
the hide . . . I might just as well have stood out in it all night all the
time. When I came in I filled the tub with nice hot water and got
a real soaking, at two in the morning, a rather odd hour for a bath,
but I had slept all afternoon Saturday and I was wide awake after
standing out in the rain.

This morning I played in a quartet with the euphonium at Blatch-
ington Parish church, an old, old stone building completely covered
by vines. It looked quite large on the outside, but when we entered
it was small. The walls were six feet thick and all fixtures were . . .
hand-hewn oak hundreds [of] years old. After that, we went out to
'C' Company for an open air service, and if you look at the picture
I sent, you will find the "Seven Sisters" [Clarence is referring to
landmark series of chalk cliffs on the coast in the Seaford area].
Well, we had the service on the first one [of the Seven Sisters],
about a hundred yards from the edge. That is at quite a height too,
about six hundred feet above the water. The weather was swell.
After [the] church parade, I and [a] few others crawled over to the
edge on our tummies and looked over. The sea was calm, but a long
way down. I looked away over to the west and said to the others,
"can you see Canada?" We couldn't, but all agreed that when we do,
it won't be too soon.

I ate a few pears right off of the trees this afternoon. They will soon
be ripe but we will miss all that. Just three or four more days here

and back to the parade square and miserable schemes, on top of sleeping under canvas in this country with so darned much rain. Yes, when I get back to Canada they will have one hell of a job to ever root me out of it again for anything like this. But one must learn. Well, I don't want to learn anymore especially. Experiences like this may be nice to look back on sixty years from now, but it is hell to go through. Oh, some of the fellows are having the time of their lives, but they mustn't have anyone back home to love or who loves them. Sure the scenery is grand—they can have it all. . . .

I'm not enclosing any snaps in this letter, but the next, because I don't want the snaps to go over all on one convoy. I sent four or five in the last letter, did you get those?

Say, how about our little tyke Murray? Is he showing any of his daddy in his make? Mother told me I was quite the lad, and if Murray is like that maybe I'd better come home and look after him and take some of what I used to hand out. Wouldn't it be swell if I could just say, "I guess I'll go home, I'm needed there," and just go. Wishful thinking, but someday this will be over, and soon.

Well, so long darling, be good and take care of yourself. Are you feeling better now?

All of my love and a big kiss (see, I smeared the ink with my lips).

Love,
Daddy

ço

August 11th, 1941


Dear Mummy,

. . .


So the mosquitoes are bad are they? Here, we are bothered with
a sand flea, and do they bite! They leave a welt like a hive! They
get into your clothes and eat a guy right up. I'm just covered with
bites, and do they itch the privies, and all the boys are bothered
with them.

. . .


It rained all day today and we are going back to the midlands under
canvas. And then I suppose we will be wet and in muck all the time
we are there.

Well darling, I'll mail this letter and wait for the others and answer
them as they come. Is everything as it should be darling? Your last
letter sounded or read rather queerly. I'm so afraid something might
happen to mess things up for us—I'm sure making sure I don't.

All my love,
Clarence

. . .

ℰↃ

August 18, 1941


Dear Hazel,

Hello sweetheart, it is a whole week since I have written and a lot
has happened since. We have moved away from Seaford where we
have been for six weeks. We are now in tents, and to make things
really miserable it rains practically all the time. And I'm not enjoying the mud in the least. We wear gum boots, and slop, slide, and
slush around in the mud. This is the first decent evening we have
had. It isn't raining, so all the fellows aren't in the tent and there is
room to write and a little peace. I was going to write on Saturday;
it rained all day and Sunday too, every thing was just soaked and
even in the tents we had to cover everything over with ground
sheets on account of the leaks. I'm not going to go anyplace, not
even a show while I'm under canvas. It is only for two or three
weeks and I have leave coming up, and I'd like to get away for a
few days so I've got to save my money. Where I am going, I don't
know. I sort of counted on visiting Banks' again. . . .

Received the pound of tobacco darling, it is swell. I haven't smoked a
cigarette since, and this a swell pipe too. I think I'll light up and
smoke one on you sweetheart. Well, it's glowing. Now to answer
your mail . . . with all the clippings, they were all swell darling.
And the pictures are great. Boy, oh boy, but Murray is growing.
I can't believe that it is the little tyke that gave me the nose rub the
morning I said good-bye. Did you notice that in every picture he is
pointing? And the picture of Gary and our boys is grand, especially
Murray. What a grin! And he looks great, full of the devil I'll bet,
and Rollie sure is sprouting. And what in the dickens is Murray
doing with the kitten anyway, choking it? It seems to be fun
whatever he is doing. I take it they are our kittens, five of them,
and they look cute.


. . .

Did you get my cablegram? Gee darling, I wish I could have been
there. What did you do in way of a celebration? I stayed in all day
and played for a dance . . . and drank three bottles of beer, the most
since I've been over here. And with it all, I went to bed awful lonesome and blue at eleven. I love you all over.

So, you intend on going to Moose Jaw for the winter. By all means,
if it suits your dear little heart, go darling. I realize what it is like
for you to have to listen to all this foolishness in Lafleche. What
will you do with the house? Rent it? Are you going to have Piché
fix it up? His price sounded cheap enough, but if you don't intend
to stay there, don't you think it is kind of foolish to fix it up for
someone to rent it at five dollars a month?

. . .

Well, I'll say bye for now, and again thanks for everything. And
write often and don't forget a parcel or two. We are back on straight
army rations, and smokes are always welcomed. I haven't been out
now for over two months, but all I have left now is the pound of
tobacco and a few cigs which should do a month, and I hope to
receive more by then. . . . I haven't danced a dance in England and
I don't intend to darling. Just the thought of someone else in my
arms disgusts me. I want you and can't bear to think of anyone
else, so I don't dance.

Well bye darling, be good,
your lonesome husband,
Clarence

August 22, 1941

My own Mummy,

Received your letters . . . tonight so I am answering them now.
So you have sent me a parcel on the first, I'll no doubt get it tomorrow. I'm sure anxious for something good to eat and right now my
tummy is in need of filling. The meals today weren't so hot, they
haven't been ever since we have been under canvas.

I'm enclosing a picture taken at the door of our tent. Rather blurred,
but it is me nevertheless, and I'm wearing the sweater you sent me,
smoking your pipe and your tobacco, and smiling at the camera for
you. Do you notice the size of the tent? Same size as we had at Shilo,
and eight of us sleep in there like rats if you ask me. And the floor
boards are about two inches apart, and nothing but a few ply of
wool blankets between it and my thinly clad bones, so I don't sleep
any too well. But next Wednesday we are moving to better quarters,
billets I understand, so I guess I can stand it a few more days. The
doctor condemned our camp here as being unhealthy, so we are
moving out—thank heavens.

Gosh, you are having an awful time both financially and physically.
Yes, $79 a month doesn't go very far, does it darling? Doctor bills
and all sure eat it up. It must make things hard for you. And the
upkeep of the house, clothes for the kiddies, etc., etc.—it's surpris-
ing where it all goes. But don't leave it worry you darling. Just per-
sist and it will all clear up. I hope you went to the fair. You need a
holiday sweetheart, regardless to what people think or say—they
will always talk. Go ahead to do as you please, don't worry about
them. As long as it is innocent fun there is no harm in any of it.
As long as a person's conscience is clear, to hell with other people's
opinions.

. . .

Yes, I've received all the parcels from everybody, and I've written
and thanked the Banks for them. Didn't they or you get the folder
of pictures from John O'Groats that I sent when I was in Scotland?
I'm going back next week, September 4th, I suppose. So I will send
more pictures to them through the Army postal service. They will
no doubt get them this time. Yes, I'm going back to Scotland for
my leave. I haven't much money, and I can stay with them for
nothing, and they keep continually writing me to come up. So,
I'll go up and stay a night here and there. They seem to think we
Canadians are just the thing, and one feels so at home, and anything for a change is just the thing. . . .

So, Mrs. Hammond is doing some stepping is she? I feel sorry
for her husband. He is such a nice chap, quiet and even tempered.
Probably, that is what the trouble is.

Really darling, when I come to think of it I don't know what to
suggest for you this winter. You say that you hate the thought of
winter—coal bills, etc.—and you have a notion of going someplace
else. And your financial troubles—sit down and figure it out. Can
you stay in a city cheaper than in your own home? No rent for one
thing, and a few people you might call friendly, etc. And on the
other hand, in the city or wherever you are, there is rent, light, and
water in most places, and . . . complete stranger[s]. And the kiddies
to worry about and room enough for them to play. You say you are
having a hard time to get squared away. Don't you think you should
stay in Lafleche till all our bills are squared away and the house fixed
up. It may be worth something sometime, and it is the only thing
we own. True, if it wasn't for that house we wouldn't be in Lafleche,
and on the other hand we had sorrows aplenty in it and trouble too,
and also a lot of pleasure. And it's home, our first home, and I
frankly hate to think of the little place belonging to someone else
now. Maybe that is too sentimental, but every little bit of it is part
of you in my heart darling. You say you have no real friends in
Lafleche and that they insist on talking about you, etc. All small
towns are the same, they haven't enough to keep them occupied
outside of teas and bridge parties, which naturally includes a bout

of gossip. While in a larger place, people haven't the time to bother with that kind of foolishness—in that sense, city life is much pleasanter. But the kiddies—Rollie will soon be of school age and that is a problem in itself. And my opinion is you can't beat nuns for elementary education, and I want the boys to learn French properly while they are young, because it is much easier then. And if I were you darling (of course whatever you decide is fine with me), but if I were you, I wouldn't let Lafleche get me down. Get yourself squared away and whatever move you make do it with the kiddies in mind—a good school! Gee darling, this is a hard thing to write about. If I could only be with you these things wouldn't have to worry us near as much.

You ask about money. Well, that's easy. Pay all your bills, see to the kiddies and yourself, and put aside what you can. Just don't worry. When this is over we will get by. And the government has to help all return men according to their dependents. I understand it is seventy-five dollars a month for three months for the first year of service overseas, and an additional month for every other year, as well as a complete set of civil clothes: suit, shoes, socks, underwear, and coat, etc. On the other hand, one can stay in the Army back in Canada until he secures a position with the government's help. So, the set-up isn't as bleak as you make it. When I get back you can set your mind at rest about that, but whatever more we can have set aside will certainly help too.

. . .

I suppose you are back from the fair and weren't bothered too much by would-be boyfriends. I suppose there are still some hanging around.

Well darling, I'm going to call this a letter. It is getting too dark to see. Bye-bye. . . .

Take care of yourself. I love you,
Daddy

*top:* CLARENCE, THIRD FROM LEFT, BACK ROW, SMOKING HIS PIPE
AND STANDING IN FRONT OF THE TENT HE DESCRIBED ABOVE.

*bottom:* ANOTHER PHOTOGRAPH SENT TO HAZEL. IT SHOWS CLARENCE
SITTING IN THE DOOR OF HIS TENT, AGAIN SMOKING HIS PIPE, AND
WEARING THE SWEATER THAT HAZEL HAD SENT TO HIM.

August 24, 1941

Dear Mummy,

. . .

. . . I've got such a pile of letters that I'm going to have to dispose of them. I have half a kit bag of them and finding places to keep them and my equipment is getting to be quite a problem. I don't want to, especially yours, but I guess a lot will have to go to the incinerator.

So Rollie is starting kid tricks is he? I'll admit a person rather has a time of it to know just what to do. Rollie isn't quite old enough to understand about that jug and money. Whenever that happens again, or anything like it darling, don't let your temper get away with you. Reason with him, tell him in a nice way he shouldn't do those things. Whatever you do don't scare him about what you will do, because he will try to lie himself out of a lot of corners. So whatever you do, don't frighten him with threats. Gain his confidence, makes him feel cheap and ashamed. It may not work the first time or first few times, being so young, but it will work and spare us a lot of grief later on. Above all things, don't make a liar out of him. He no doubt at times is hard to handle. Just don't make any fuss when he starts his stubborn streaks when you ask him to do something. Be firm and make him do it even if you have to help him and make him think he did it himself. Don't ever bribe him into doing something. He is old enough now to realise he can get things by raising a fuss. He has started running away has he? I guess all kids do that—don't strap him. When he wants to go someplace let him go on his own with your permission for a while, not any place of course. Supposing he wants to go over to Grandma's or something like that. Let him go, and with the understanding he is to stay there and be back at such a time and see that he does it. I admit it will be nuisance for a while, but he will learn to always ask to go and you will know where he is. And whenever he doesn't do as he should, don't let him go again and tell him why. It is up

to you darling. I know I should be there when the kiddies are
beginning their pranks, but I'm not. I reread and reread your letter
and did a lot of thinking about Rollie and I know it must get on
your nerves at times, but always count ten before administering
any punishment. This advice may sound easy because I just have
to write about it; frankly, it worries me and it makes it hard for you
and you have to bring them up without letting them become little
brats. It's a job isn't it darling?

Yes, I understand mail posted here on the 10th, 11th, and 12th of
June was lost. In that time I sent you two letters. And the parcel
with the little pillow and hanky and seashells—you got that,
didn't you, I hope. . . .

. . .

You ask if the advice I gave you re loneliness, drink, etc., is from
experience. Oh no, darling, not that bad, but I see a lot of queer
things happening around me and I sure don't care for what I see.
And furthermore, some fellows here that I thought were tops do
things. That is, I've seen them out with women, and it always happens when they have been drinking. Speaking to some of them,
they admit they are ashamed and say it will never happen again—
"I love my wife, and I do those [things] only when I get tight." They
all have the same story. So judging from that it must be human nature and liquor which makes such a bad mixture. Don't worry darling, I've avoided women easily. The only lady I even stopped to
chat with for an hour or so was an old lady evacuated from Paris.
She couldn't speak a word of English, and one night at a band concert she was there and asked in French if any of us spoke French.
I was the only one, so she began speaking to me, asking all kinds
of questions about Canada, my family, and how she appreciated
us Canadians. And she went on to tell me all about France and her
troubles. Her name is Madame DeLeverge, about 70. She invited
me up for tea. She was staying at Seaford House, a hotel, so I went
down the street with her to the hotel and she ordered tea for two.
I was there about an hour. She was quite nice and asked me for my

address, and anytime I was in the vicinity to make sure I dropped
in to see her. When I got back to barracks the boys sure teased me
plenty—such as, where did I pick up the girlfriend, etc., etc. The
boys keep kidding me about her yet, asking me if I'm going [to]
spend my leave with the dream girl, etc., etc. But that is the extent
of my associating with women, and if that's the worse I do you
certainly shouldn't have any worries in that line. . . .

. . . I wrote a letter to mother last night. It rained all day yesterday,
but Mr. Sun came out today and we went out on a river fording
scheme—a long drawn out, damp affair. We crossed a river in
canvas boats large enough for nine men and equipment. The whole
battalion crossed. Only one boat upset, [and] it was really funny.
Nobody drowned—they were fished out right away—but there
sure was a lot of blubbering and splashing. You can imagine with
all that equipment on they thought they were going to drown.
All they got was a soaking and lost their rifles; of course, those
are down in the bottom.

. . .

You talk about it being hot, windy, and dusty. Well here, it's chilly,
windy, and raining most of the time. They say September is a nice
month here so I'm looking forward to it.

. . .

Well darling, it is getting quite dark . . . I have no light, so bye-bye
my darling. I was rereading some of your letters of June and noticed
one with a kiss on the corner to keep me warm on some cold route
march. I like rereading those letters. I took the kiss today for about
the fifth time I guess. I was so darned lonesome thinking of home,
your troubles, and me so far away. And you must be lonesome, because I miss you all the time, and if I ever get my arms around you
again they are going to need a derrick to spring you loose. Oh yes,
I opened up that Aspirin box and took a kiss from it . . . the one
you packed so many kisses in the last night we were in good old

Toronto. Oh, if we were there now on the same terms. Oh, why do I dwell on those things? It just hurts all the more a way down deep. I'll never forget the walk back to the barracks that morning, I knew I was going overseas and I actually cried most of the way back. I ached all day to have you come up to the barracks before we left, but I couldn't face it. I never want to go through that again, so I'll always be with you when I get back.

So, bye-bye sweetheart,
your loving hubby,
Clarence

[P.S.] A bunch of warm kisses and hugs darling. Be good, I love you.

⁃℥⁃

England
August 25, 1941


Darling,

Received your swell parcel darling, and will it ever fill my tummy,
everything is just grand. The parcel was badly damaged and the
cookies, some of them, were all squashed. And thanks for the writing material. And boy, are those snaps ever swell. Murray is getting
to be quite the man. And that is quite the wagon they have too,
I'll bet they have a swell time with that.

. . . you thinking of working. Well, that is up to you. In a way it
would help while away the time, but are you well enough darling?
And I suppose you would have a girl working for you. As I said, it
may take up your spare time and you wouldn't find time so long.

You mention sending more tobacco. I hope you didn't order fine
cut, because I want pipe tobacco, which is coarse cut. And you say
I should receive a thousand cigs a month. I've received the ones you
sent the 1st of June and the ones of the first of July, but none for
August yet. Yes, darling I have been doing fine as far as smokes go,
and if I get too many ahead I'll let you know and you can stop the
shipment for a month or as long as I say. Is that all right darling?
I'd like to have enough smokes ahead to do me a couple of months
in case some of them don't make the grade or we get off in the bush
someplace without mail service. So don't weaken on the smokes yet.

So Rollie is full of mischief? All kiddies go through those things and
the best a person can do is watch and shame him and make him try
to understand. No use trying to browbeat him, it just won't work if
he is anything like I was.

You mention our anniversary. Yes, that was three weeks ago.
Did you get my wire darling? The one I sent from Seaford?

Thanks for everything darling. I owe you a lot of hugs and kisses for all these nice little things you are doing for me, so lookout, I'll repay with interest when I get back. And I don't believe Adrien and his ten years, I'll be home a long time before that.

Love to the kiddies, and hugs and kisses for you darling,

Your Hubby,
Clarence

☙

England
September 1st, 1941


Dear Mummy,

Received two of your letters this morning and I'm going on leave
today too, so I'll sure have plenty of time to read and reread your
letters. I'll be on the train 24 hours, I'm going to Thurso again—
anything to get away from the Army for a few days.

I'm taking this pad with me on the train and I'm going to sort of
make a diary of my leave so that I don't forget anything of interest
to you sweetheart. I'll be going in a few minutes, so this letter won't
be very long.

How are the kiddies? Is Rollie still naughty, and did you get the
letter with all my fatherly advice? The advice I should be 'doing',
instead of someone else doing it for me. Gee, it sure must be hard
for you all alone, and two growing boys, and Rollie will be hard to
handle. Pray God this ends soon, so that I can get back to you and
the kiddies. I should be sort of tickled going on leave, but I'm
lonesome for you and home all the same.

We played for the officers' dance last night and didn't get to bed
till 3:30, and had to play on church parade this morning so I'm
plenty tired. I'll no doubt sleep most of the time on the train.

Well darling, I guess I'll call this a letter, I've got to shave yet.
Bye-bye sweetheart. And I'm waiting for more mail—for when
I get back, there should be quite a bunch of it.

All my love,
Daddy

☙

England
September 1st, 1941

Hello Darling,

Well, here I am waiting for the train to pull out. I'm sitting
looking out at the thousands of people along the platforms (in
Euston Station, 24 platforms). I'm in the train at platform 12.

I had three hours to wait in London—away we go, just pulling
out, on my way. I had three hours in London, I wandered around
and the city is real calm. A few bomb scars are still visible, but no
rubble laying around. Everything is all cleaned up and new buildings and repairing all around. There is a noisy smart guy in this
compartment who is getting on my nerves, I hope he doesn't ride
all the way. We're still in London. It's such a big place, we seem to
be traveling hours before we leave it behind. I guess I'll stop for a
while and get acquainted with the other three chaps with me (one
sailor and two soldiers). 'Till later—I feel like having a nap as well.

Hello darling, it's late now, about midnight. Had a sleep [and] a
few sandwiches I brought along. Can't sleep well—it's too stuffy in
here—and the rumbling, no place to stretch out, the blinds are all
drawn, can't open the windows (blackout). I've been traveling eight
hours steady now without a break. I'd like to get out for a walk. I'll
have to wait till we get to Edinburgh, about 6, I guess. I hope we
are on time so as to have a few minutes for a meal and wash. I feel
all sticky and dusty. Are you lonely darling? I am. If it was only you
sleeping beside me instead of the snoring sailor. Can you hear him?
At times he makes me jump. Oh darling, I'd have my arms around
you and your head on my shoulder. I guess I'll try and sleep. Love.

Good morning. Just leaving Edinburgh. Had a bath for 3 pence,
6 cents, feel much better and I can watch the countryside. We are
in the mountains now. We can see the lumbering camps. On both
sides of the way pine trees mostly and beautiful scenery, and the

heather is in bloom. I'll have to get a sprig or two to send home.
There must be some at Thurso too. Just went by a waterfall down
the mountainside. The scenery here is much like Banff only on a
smaller scale. I'll be in Inverness about ten. I'm going to look out
the window. The scenery is grand and the sun is out in all its glory.
Bye for a minute.

Hello, had dinner in Inverness at 11 o'clock. Will be in Thurso
about six. I guess I'll put this away till tonight darling.

Well, I'm at Dallas's. Same room and same fireplace, and I'm sitting
in front of the fire now and I'm awfully tired. They met me, that is,
Dallas met me, at the train. Had fried chicken for supper and quite
a chat about Canada, you, the kiddies, and Banks, MacKays, and
Sutherlands. How are the kiddies tonight darling? Rollie and Murray would get a big kick out of the fireplace here. And the night is
quite chilly too—Thurso is so far north. I'm on leave and sure feel
all alone too. I wish this was a leave home. As I watch the flames
licking up the chimney I get all the lonelier. I love you Mummy
and I need you awful bad Mummy. I could just about cry. I haven't
felt this bad for quite a while. Oh, if this would only end. Tomorrow, Mr. Dallas is going to take me around and I'm gong to visit
with James Banks Friday and Saturday. Have to leave Saturday
afternoon for camp. I'll say nightly-night now Mummy, my
eyes just won't stay open any longer, bye.

Wednesday night. Got here Tuesday, in case I didn't mention it
sooner. Sure met a lot of people. Had tea seven different times.
Wherever I went we had to have tea. The first place we went to
was to a blind chap's place (I met him the leave before) by the name
of MacKay. No relation to Tim, but he sure asked plenty about
Canada. Then we went to Heuston's [?], then to Duncan's, etc., etc.,
and tea every time. They all know Jack Banks and most of them
knew MacKay, and they all wanted me to stay the night with them.
Of course, I refused. I had so many invitations that I'd need six
weeks leave to keep them all. I ran out of ink and had to get some
from Mr. Dallas and had a cup of tea again. I'm beginning to like

tea—about time—I must have drank an ocean of it since I've been over here. And tomorrow for breakfast we are going to have some of the coffee you sent me in your last parcel. And do you know that I had breakfast in bed this morning? I was embarrassed at first, but they insisted that I have my breakfast before getting up, and I must let them know what time I want to be awakened. I said tomorrow at eight, but could manage to get to the table for breakfast. But no, they said they always give their visitors breakfast in bed. A queer custom—apparently everyone does it—so tomorrow morning: bacon, eggs, toast, and coffee in bed. Pretty nice! I think I'm going to enjoy my leave. Tomorrow we are going rabbit hunting with rifles. We saw a lot of them today. They are small like the Canadian bush rabbits and are supposed to be great eating.

Well, nighty-night sweetheart. A big hug and kisses, and give the kiddies a big hug and kiss for me too. Bye.

Hello darling, walked miles and miles over hills and creeks—as they say here, "o'er brae and burn"—and we shot one rabbit. I shot that, and I'm to have it for dinner tomorrow. And then I'm going to Castletown for the rest of my leave. It's twelve now, we played checkers all evening and I'm going to bed now. Bye, all of my love.

Here I am again, writing on my bed. It's 3 a.m., I'm at Banks's. Talked all evening, going fishing in morning for trout, and the girl whose picture I sent, Miss Helen Banks, is under doctor's observation. I believe she is a suspected TB case. In my opinion, she looks it. She just sits around unable to [do] a thing in the line of work. Mr. Banks and I cooked our own supper. James is always fussing around the girl seeing to her comfort, etc., etc.—drafts and so on. All he said to me about her is that she is a very sick girl, nothing like her sister Mary who I met this afternoon. I should say she isn't. Mary is about five-foot-ten and big. She works on some farm near here. I'll bet she does the plowing, etc. She is hefty enough. She was in a few minutes before supper to see her sister. By the way, I got some heather yesterday too. Some purple and white which I'll enclose in this letter when I get back to camp. I'm leaving tomorrow afternoon at 3:30, will be back in camp Sunday night. So, night-night for now darling, and till I get back to camp, love.

Well, here I am two days back in camp and the trip was tiresome on the way back. The train was awful crowded. No sleep at all and being Sunday I had hardly anything to eat. All the station restaurants were closed. Ate chocolate bars that I got from a canteen in Thurso, tasted like baking chocolate. Good thing I had them or I would have starved. Oh, yes, I got two trout Saturday morning, little fellows about a pound each and we had them for dinner before leaving Thurso, and I enjoyed my leave.

Next week the band is going to the Saskatoon Light Infantry—some place in England to play for the Presentation of their colours. We are going up three days before the Presentation to rehearse, probably the King and Queen are going to present them with their colours. We must be getting fairly good for them to pick us for the job. Well, I'm looking forward to it. All these affairs are interesting—never seen a "Presentation" of this sort before.

I suppose you are wondering if we are the Canadians that took Spitsbergen, the Norway Islands. No we aren't. We are going back on coastal defence in the next fifteen days for the winter, back to Seaford I hope—we had swell billets there.

Well, there is plenty in this, [so] I guess I'll quit for now and write again tomorrow.

I'm going to orchestra practice now, haven't blown the sax for about fifteen days.

Well, bye darling, I'm going to play "Stardust" first. I like that tune, it's a sax solo and I'm going to play it for you Mummy. By the way there was no mail waiting for me when I got back, I was really disappointed. Write soon and often, send parcels, I haven't enjoyed a meal since my leave. Always the same eats—stew, stew, and stew—quite a variety! Maybe beans once in a while.

Do you love me? Are you lonesome? I sure am.

All of my love,
Clarence

[P.S.] It took over seven days to write this Sweetheart, love.

∽

THE SOUTH SASKATCHEWAN REGIMENT BAND REHEARSING AT SEAFORD,
EAST SUSSEX, IN 1941. IT APPEARS CLARENCE IS SEATED FOURTH
FROM THE RIGHT, PLAYING THE EUPHONIUM.

England
September 14, 1941


Hello Mummy,

I promised to send you heather. In fact, I said I was going to enclose it in my last letter and forgot. I noticed it right after mailing the letter, it is going in this one.

Received your letters, and, darling, you mentioned parcels and smokes. I've received everything you have sent so far and I wish you had more on the way. I'm not out, but hate contemplating that I might run out. I've got enough till the first anyway, and I hope I get more by then. A thousand sounds big, but spread that out over a period of forty days or so. . . .

. . . And re my being home right after the war, don't worry. The married men are shipped right off, just the single men are kept here, at least that is what I understand. As soon as this is over they will have a hell of a time keeping me here. I've contemplated beating it already. I get so darned lonesome for you and the kids. . . .

. . . Yes darling, it will soon be a year since I said goodbye and I hope it isn't another year before I say hello.

Gosh darling, you are having a devil of a time financially and you say you wish I had never gone away. Don't worry, I wish the same, and it will sure have to be something desperate that will ever drag me away from you again.

. . .

How are the kiddies? I'll bet Murray is cute with his Buster Brown haircut.

All my love darling,
Daddy

England
September 15, 1941


Dear Mummy,

Just a note by air mail to see what the service is like and to tell you
I've received all smokes and more always appreciated. Sent heather
from Scotland in a letter yesterday, tell Mother I've received parcels
and smokes.

Say, didn't you get the telegram I sent on the 5th of August? You
didn't mention it in any of your letters, they said you would get
it on the 7 or 8th. I so wanted you to get it on our anniversary,
I hope you did.

Be good, I love you, hugs and kisses for the kiddies too.

I'll write again tomorrow. Tell me by same if you have received this
in short enough time now that the trans-Atlantic service is running.

I'm fine, had a nice quiet leave in Scotland which I wrote all about
last week. You will get the letter soon. A quiet time fishing, hunting,
and talking about Lafleche.

. . .

Bye-bye darling, all of my love, send something to eat, I'm hungry
as the devil right now for something good. More smokes always
welcome.

Be good,
love,
Clarence

ço

England
September 17, 1941


Dear Mummy,

Well, I've received two letters from you and one from mother
and one from Yvonne, but that's all and that was a week ago.

Did you get my telegram of August the 5th and the air mail letter
of September 15th? Rereading your last letters you didn't mention
the telegram so I naturally figured you haven't received it, and I
really wanted you to get that on our anniversary—I am disappointed.

I really haven't an awful lot to write about. Yesterday, we played
for the brigadier's inspection. That took all morning and it sure
was tiresome. We played and played, and to boot we practiced slow
marches all afternoon . . . and played for [an] inspection last night
and change of the guard and retreat, so we really had a day of it.
My mouth feels as if somebody had punched me one.

This is the third trip I've made around the stores and photo
shops to get films and have my photo taken. But they have no film,
haven't had any since August 1st, so pictures are scarce of me. No
matter how good my intentions are I simply can't get me taken in
any shape or form, but I have put my order in four different places
for films as soon as they get some, and I've paid in advance so I'll
probably get a film somewhere.

Well, Friday, we go to the Presentation of Colours for the Regina
Rifles. I understand at Pearly near London, and we sure are practicing band drill and slow marching, and all the officers keep remind-
ing us, "make a good job of it, be gentlemen," because we are
representing the s.s.r. I suppose.

I'm enclosing some of the negatives I have of myself so that you
can have more finished if you want them. I was just looking at my

collection of snaps and was wondering if Rollie would remember his daddy when he got back. And Murray doesn't even know I ever existed—he was so young when I last saw him. How are the kiddies? Rollie giving you much trouble? I hope he isn't too bad because things are certainly hard enough for you as it is.

Steve looked me up last night and borrowed some cigarettes. I suppose you know he is a sergeant now and apparently having a swell time. He mentioned something about a bang up of a party on Monday night and how he has met a swell girl, the best yet, and asked me to go with him last night. And I used the excuse I was dead tired, had a tough day, and anyway I haven't the money—"you must remember, I'm still a private." He said, "it won't cost you a thing," but I didn't go, told him I'd rather not and he said, "life is short, I'm going to have a time while I can." My answer was rather sarcastic. I said, "Steve, do you know I love my wife and I know she loves me? In fact, I'm just beginning to realize how my life is centred around Hazel and the kiddies, and as you say life is too short. It is too short to spoil my happy home for the future over some foolishness. This war isn't going to last forever and I intend on going home to my wife the same Clarence that left her, a little older no doubt, but much the wiser I hope." Well darling, he left after that saying thanks for the smokes, "I'll return them when I get some from Sarah." I'll get them all right, I've loaned him some before and I've borrowed some from him.

. . .

The weather lately has been grand, but the evenings and mornings are awfully chilly. It is dark here at 6 a.m. I can sure feel winter coming; I hope we will be in nice warm quarters, Seaford, I hope. Have you looked it up on the maps yet? A little to the east of Brighton, which is on the south coast. We expect to be there all winter, the billets are swell. I need gloves. Can you get me a decent pair of leather ones? I take size eights. And wool ones too? They are rationed here. Soldiers have to wear issue stuff and they are made with hemp. Course grey things, ten sizes too large. I'm ashamed to wear them if they are to be seen. And when you think you can, send me a couple of khaki dress shirts size 14 ½. I've worn out the ones I had bought here, I can't get any more. . . .

Well bye-bye darling, take care of yourself, don't work too hard and write often, often, I need your letters.

Love, kisses and hugs for the kiddies, and as for you I would like to find words to really put down how much I really miss you. Darling, at times it's terrible and the only ray of hope is someday I'll be back. . . .

I love you,
Clarence

ल

England
September 21st, 1941

Darling,

A bunch more mail came in again last night and I was left standing
after it was all distributed empty-handed. Gee, that's disappointing,
the third mail in a row. I hope the next mail will mean an armful
for me. I count on your letters so much.

Well, we were to go to the Presentation of Colours this weekend
but it has been postponed. So instead, today, Sunday, they are
sending us out on the firing ranges. A pleasant pastime for
Sunday. I'd sooner read or go for a long walk.

We are stationed near Reading now, we have fair quarters. Have
to walk about ¼ mile for our meals and the meals are more to my
liking just now. We get a lot of fresh tomatoes and cukes, lettuce,
etc., which sure helps at times. The meals are sure plain—stew
and potatoes and rice pudding day in and day out.

Yesterday afternoon I went to Reading. It is a large place and awful
busy. We went out along the Thames and hired a punt and went
rowing. So I'm all muscle sore this morning. I saw some grapes
in a store window and went in to buy some and they asked for 8
shillings, 6 pence a pound, which is $2.04 a pound, can you imag-
ine? So I didn't buy any. I tried to buy film but they wouldn't sell
me any and asked me to leave my name and they would save one
or two for me on their next allotment. As it was, all they had at
present was spoken for.

You should have seen the fog here day before yesterday. Our
quarters are under large oak trees, and standing fifty feet away from
them we couldn't see a thing. Just like a blanket, all traffic was at a
standstill. I started downtown to get a package of Oxydol (I still do
my own laundry); I got down there alright by following the curbs,

but got lost coming back. Couldn't see a thing, the houses were just dim shadows. It took me two hours to get back, which should have been five minutes. So the fogs are sure thick—the worst I'd ever seen. It is quite foggy out just now. My laundry is hanging on the line—it has for two days—and is still as wet as when I put it out. I'll have to bring it in and dry it by the stove I guess, if the sun don't show up.

How are you feeling now darling? Any better? Are you getting used to the fact that I am away? Are the kiddies being good? Not giving you too much trouble? Well, as for me I am fine but never happy. I won't be till I'm home with you and that will never be too soon. I'll never get used to the idea that I'm away from you. I continually think of you and the kiddies and I worry a lot lately about how you are making out. Your letters sound rather disappointing (your health, finances, and our family). I should be home, you need me, and I feel so useless here. Anyway, "I love you," and always will, come what may.

Write often darling.

Bye-bye,
Clarence

P.S. Love and kisses for the kiddies.

☙

England
September 23, 1941


Dear Mummy,

Received your letter. . . . Gee, that was a long wait between letters.
I've received one letter in seven weeks so I sure ate it up.

Thanks for the cigs and tobacco you've sent, I'll get it next mail
I suppose.

Well we are on the move again to our winter quarters. Where they
are going to be I don't know. They keep all these things quiet till
we get there. We're going to be out on manoeuvres for ten days
starting in the morning and from there we go to our new
quarters, so I won't be able to write over the scheme.

We played for a dance in Bramshill House, a castle near here, and
what a place. About the size of the G-bourg [Gravelbourg] convent,
with wonderful grounds surrounded by a high stone wall and a
moat. The castle was renovated in '35. It was built in 1365, all rock,
about five stories high. Inside is all hand-carved oak and stone,
hand-hewn solid marble stairways wide enough to drive a 4-horse
outfit up. Arched ceilings, huge marble pillars, and marble fireplaces,
there are as many windows in it as days of the year and as many
chimneys as weeks . . . the ballroom . . . was about 30 ft by fifty,
oak floor and the walls were completely covered with tapestry—
worth millions with all the history. And the highbrows that were at
the dance! It was a flop, even with all the highballs and punches,
liveried servants and officers—everything was done in style. The
dances were announced by an undertaker-looking butler who
would march into the middle of the room as stiff as a board and in
a funeral voice would say, "Next dawnce is a wolse," the melody is
to be "Love is All" by "the name of the composer, etc., etc." And for
a tag dance, they call it an "excuse me dawnce." Yes, it was a flop as
far as pep may be. The aristocrats, monocles, "beg pawdons" and

"I do declares" had a good time. If they did, I wonder how they would act at a funeral?

I've got to pack up yet tonight, but this letter won't be very long.

How are the kiddies? Was just looking a their pictures, and yours too darling. I love you all over. I'm enclosing a few pictures again. How is everything darling? Everything under control and you're all well I hope?

Dropped my pipe and busted it all to the devil, so I need another.

. . .

Well darling, I've got work to do. So bye-bye darling, I'll write as soon as I get the chance.

I love you,
Clarence

P.S. Say Rollie, are you a good boy for Mummy? She says you are pretty naughty at times and she has to spank you. Shame on you! And you have the nicest little mummy in the world. Be good to Mummy. Rollie boy, you're the only man she has with her just now.

∽

ROLLIE'S NOTE: *The next five letters were mailed in one envelope on October 7, 1941, and arrived in Lafleche on November 5th or 6th, 1941.*

[Saturday]
September 27, 1941

Dear Hazel,

Well, here I am sitting under an immense oak tree in a cow pasture. We have to be awful careful where we sit down. The weather is grand. It is 1 p.m. now, and warm. We have to stay here overnight and all day tomorrow, and then we start on some scheme through the night. I wrote a letter a few days ago, but all the postal services have been stopped till the scheme is over. . . .

Yes, we are sleeping under the stars tonight. Two blankets and great coat for covers and mattress—oh damn, but this gets me down. A swell bed at home and you, the kiddies, and I have to do this. Oh, it certainly won't be any too soon when this is over and I can [be] back to you and home life. This tromping around being hollered at all day and inspected like a herd of cattle every so often—if there was any novelty to Army life the newness has certainly worn off.

We started from camp or Hartley Row at 7:30 this morning with a slice of bread and a slice of bacon for breakfast and stew a few minutes ago and I sure was hungry. As bad as it was I enjoyed it. Everything during these schemes is cooked on the run practically, so by the time this is over next Sunday I'll be eating bark. They call it part of training because some day we may have to do it.

Hello darling, just had supper: corned beef, cheese and spuds, tea and molasses, cake for dessert—not too bad that—I've got a tummy full. This p.m. we strolled around through the trees and ran into a patch of blackberries and ate and ate. The berries were as big as my thumb and nice and sweet. I'm going to soak my feet in the brook at my feet, it's cold, but crystal clear. Another chap is sitting beside me beside this brook writing his wife too. L/Cpl [Lance Corporal] Miles of Moose Jaw. Just stopped daydreaming—watching the water bubble and gurgle over the stones, and thinking of home and you darling. I've got my bed made up like a cocoon on the thick grass; I hope it doesn't rain or fog up. I may be warm and cozy, but it would be much nicer if you were with me. Gee Hazel, but I do get awful lonesome for you, terribly so, especially when I'm out like this. The weather is grand, the scenery marvellous, all of which you would enjoy immensely. Every time I see something nice I always think of how Hazel would enjoy this, and you would darling. I'm sitting under the branches of an oak which spreads out about a hundred feet; we don't have these in Canada. They are very pretty, but fall is here, the leaves are starting to fall. The vines on the houses—and the same houses as a rule are buried in vines—which are fiery red just now, which is really something to see against the deep green background of the trees. Well darling, I'm going to soak my feet and then make hay; that is, sleep. I'll continue this tomorrow. Goodnight sweetheart, love and kisses. Are you lonesome? You're not leaving our being apart get you down, are you Hazel? I love you Mummy.

Sunday
September 28, 1941

Hello Sweetheart,

Here I am under the same oak, sitting on my pack and writing on my knees, so the writing isn't much. Had a good sleep last night from 8 to 7 this morning. No rain, plenty of fog, but between ground sheet and gas cape, which is a huge cape of oilskin that we are to wrap over ourselves in case of a gas attack from the air (if it's gas proof, it is water proof), so I kept dry. There was no Catholic church parade this morning so I didn't go to church, and as it was it started raining, rained till three this p.m., so I'm a bit damp just now. As soon as it quit raining I went picking berries for our cook (blackberries). There are millions of them just now and sure are good. I ate as many as I brought in and that was over a gallon. And I found a bunch of hazel trees, so I was sure reminded of you, and ate a bunch of those; that is, filberts. When I got back from berry picking after walking through the wet grass my feet were soaking, so I changed socks.

I don't suppose I will get much sleep tonight. The ground is all wet and I believe that we will be on the move some time during the night. So I think I'll roll up in my coat and ground sheet and try to get some sleep that way. And to boot the sky is cloudy and it will no doubt rain. This is quite a place. There is three cows about a hundred feet from me looking on very interestingly. They've been sort of staring at me for the last five minutes.

Saw Tom this morning and he was telling me about a girlfriend of his that he likes an awful lot, and that he is trying to get a divorce from Pearl and hasn't heard from her since, and is worried that Pearl won't give him his divorce. He said he would never go back to Pearl etc., etc. As far as Tom and Pearl go, I don't suppose she is doing the right thing by him. Anyway, nevertheless, they are married and have a child. What is going to happen to the kid? Tom don't seem to give a damn, he is so taken up with this dream of his, which I have never seen. Well, I've got to admit they are quite a crowd.

Well darling, you may have doubts and worries about me that I may be stepping around too, but you needn't worry or doubt Hazel, I don't and do not intend to. And I haven't since I'm in the Army. Regardless of what you hear from your so-called friends, who are just waiting for an opportunity to tell you they heard this or that, that someone wrote to someone etc., I love you, no one will ever change that. So, I'm still repeating, whatever some of the Lafleche boys over here do doesn't mean I'm doing it too. I'll be with you again tomorrow darling.

Bye-bye, love and kisses, xxxxx. I'll think of you while I'm on guard from 12 to 2 a.m. (just was notified).

Tuesday
September 30th, 1941

Hello Mummy,

I was going to write yesterday but didn't have the chance, we were on the move all day.

Sunday night I didn't get any sleep at all—rain, rain and rain. I was soaked to the hide even with all the protection of ground sheet and gas cape. It came in around my neck in rivers. I was on guard for a couple of hours, so I decided to stay up. All the other fellows got soaked trying to sleep so I had a wonderful time. We were better off standing in the rain, because under the trees the rain kept dripping off the leaves in pails full. I sure enjoyed breakfast at 5:30, hot cocoa especially, and then we built a fire of dry oak . . . which we couldn't do during the night, blackout you know. But as soon as daylight came we sure got a fire going, and the rain stopped so I stripped down to my trousers and dried off for an hour. And then into the buses. We travelled about a hundred miles and the irony of it was the sun was out all day and I slept most of time and we landed here about 6 last night and it was clouding up again . . . no trees, so I went to a house beside where we were bivouacked and asked if we could use their garage as a dry place to sleep. I strung quite a sad story and they let us use the garage. Nine of us slept in it. It was dry—even if the floor was cement and didn't give much—I had quite a good sleep I was tired enough, but at that the cement was darned hard! My hips are still sore. Just my coat and a blanket between me and the floor, but it was nice to look out and see water sitting all over [and] we were dry. Before going to bed last night Cpl. Miles and I went for a stroll along a river bank, sat there and talked about Canada, our wives and families. He has one child, which he hasn't seen, and gets awful lonely.

I spoke about you, and how I wished I was home, and about my two boys. The river (I don't know the name of it) was covered with water lilies and swans were paddling around in it. It was really nice to see. I sat there and dreamed about home. A couple paddled by in a canoe laughing and talking away as happy as you please. I watched them round a bend, thinking with a big lump in my throat if it were only Hazel and I, oh how happy I would be too.

Well the sun is out today and I'm leaning or sitting up against the house where we stayed last night and it's nice and warm. We just had tea and chocolate cake that the maid brought out for us five stretcher-bearers. A whole twelve-inch cake and was it ever good. The people of the house seem awful nice. They gave us five books and a Toronto Star, last month's of course, and said we could sit out on their lawn which we are doing. And are the grounds ever swell. The lawn is like a carpet. And flowers! Roses (frankly, I don't know the names of any of the others), great big blossoms, size of a softball, all colours, and rows and rows of lavender, the scent of it is all over.

The lady of the house just came out and told us to go and see our cook and tell him he could have what he wanted from their garden—green beans, beets, carrots, leek—so Cpl. Miles has gone over and we are offering to gather what ever he wants. We might have a good dinner yet.

I understand we will be near London tonight and no doubt in the open again, so I'll probably be the one to scrounge around again for a dry place to sleep. I don't fancy it, but it's better than sleeping outside.

Around here is plenty noisy. The air is full of planes. I can count eleven from where I'm sitting, all types. There is a four-motored bomber going over now. Between them and motorcycles, trucks, buses on the London road just in front of here, the racket is terrible.

Well, here they come with pans etc. to gather the vegetables, so I'll say bye for now.

Love. xxxx

Friday
[October 3, 1941]

Hello Sweetheart,

Well we are still on the scheme. It is over now, but we are waiting
for orders to return back to our billets. Thank heavens it hasn't
rained since Monday night, and I'm sure anxious to get back to
camp. There must be mail waiting for me. I've been two days without any smokes with me. I brought some but not enough and I'm
just about out. Anyway, I had to buy some English ones this morning if I wanted a smoke, and it was the first opportunity I had to
buy them at that. Everybody was out of smokes, and as far as these
smokes go, a person might just as well be without.

Well, on Tuesday we stayed at the same place and sat around and
slept on the same cement floor the next day. Wednesday, we travelled all day, slept out at night, had a good sleep at that. Fritzie was
over us—we could distinguish the markings in the moonlight. He
was that low and going to beat the devil. Just skimming the tree
tops. Probably running from our night fighters and crippled too.
The next day, yesterday, we moved up on the attack (scheme), captured an enemy patrol before sunset, but that was all till after dark.
Then we captured a whole column of artillery, and later a petrol
column and the companies of the medical corp. You probably don't
understand this, but part of the English Army were our enemy and
they wore steel hats or helmets, while we wore our wedge caps.
According to the judges we did fine, and that we were the only
regiment of the second div. left intact according to the scheme
rules. So, the s.s.r.s are doing all right.

The colonel just drove up. I wonder if he is going to say go home or
wait. Rumours are flowing around that we will be here for a couple
of days yet, and it's four days past payday now and everybody is
broke—no smokes, etc.

Gee, the sun is swell. I'm sitting on a bus and writing as you see.
The boys are all hollering, "let's go—what the hell is this, a Sunday
school picnic?" The Colonel is speaking to some of them now. I
hope it's "let's go." The kitchen is cooking dinner under the trees;
I don't believe I've told you about our field stoves. Well, they are
like a very large blow torch run with gas, and it blows a flame about
six feet long which they direct down a tunnel made by steel sections
about two foot square that fit into one another. Each section has an
oval opening at the top and the side. We cover with sod to keep the
heat in, as well as the end. They cook a dixie of spuds, one of meat,
and one of pudding—five dixies in all. A dixie is an oval pail that
holds about seven gallons. It takes about an hour to cook a meal for
150 men. No work, no fuss with wood, ashes, etc.—so they have a
good outfit for cooking. And when the stove is tore down it would
fit into a suitcase, only for the pressure tank, which is about as large
as a pail. Dinner, so bye-bye for a minute.

Hello, have had dinner. Roast beef, dry spuds, rice pudding
with currents (gravel), and tea, bread and margarine, not too
bad, got a fill anyway, and we were issued two cigarettes a piece
("Sweet Caps").

Dinner was early—eleven—so maybe we are going to move off.
Hope so, this sleeping on the ground under trees with all sorts of
bugs as companions I don't care for. I'm all covered with bites and
dirty. I've quite a high tide mark on my neck and arms [and] need
a bath something terrible—these schemes don't lend to cleanliness.

Well darling, I don't know where we are going to for the winter.
I've heard a hundred different rumours. One thing certain is that
we are going to the coast for six weeks, and then—Lord knows,
but it will be on the British Isle somewhere.

I've got my pocket full of beech nuts. They lay around under the
beech trees an inch deep and are very good. Rather hard to shell,
so they will keep me busy for the afternoon.

They are forming up the convoy now, so I'd better get packed up. Will finish and mail this tomorrow. Bye, love and kisses.


October [?], 1941


Sweetheart,

Well darling, we are back in camp, or our billets, and all the rumours about us going to the coast were baloney because we are to be here another month yet.

Well, I've had a swell bath and am going to do laundry tonight. Just lit my pipe and a bit of hot ashes dropped on the first page and burnt a hole in it. Anyway, I put a kiss right over the burn.

Thank heavens the scheme is over and we can stay dry for a few days—till they think up something else just as foolish.

Darling, I've received no mail [for] two months now and I'm out of cigs too. I've still got some pipe tobacco, so at least [I can] smoke, but I do want some of your letters terribly. I hope some come soon —tonight, I hope. I understand another convoy landed last week, so here is hoping.

Love and hugs for the kiddies. How are they anyway? Bye-bye, write often. I should get a dozen letters in the next mail.

Love,
Clarence, xxxx

℘

s. Sask. R. B.H.Q.
c.a.(o).
October 9th, 1941


Dear Mummy,

I'm really disappointed tonight, mail has been coming in quite regularly the last few days. I received yours and mother's parcel last night, but not a written word. Oh, I hope I get some mail, I mean letters, soon. I've been so darned blue and lonely of late. I've been going to write every day for the last week, but then mail started rolling in so I just waited so as to answer your letters, but couldn't wait any longer without writing so here I am and I'll no doubt get a dozen letters at once. I love you darling. The old saying: "if you love your wife, kiss her and tell her so"—I can't kiss you or tell you so, but the next best thing, I can write you so. I love you darling, and here is the kiss, x. See, I even smeared the mark.

Thanks for the eats in the parcel, they sure came in nice, especially the peanut butter. I don't know who sent me the tobacco, it was swell but awful expensive, when for the same money they can send me 300 cigarettes through the tobacco companies. If you ever want to send me any tobacco that way always remember you can buy tobaccos and cigarettes for half the price through the companies. At any rate darling, the parcel was swell.

How are the kiddies? I sure am reminded of them often here. At Hartley Row there are a lot of evacuated children here, all about Rollie's age. One little chap, 6 yrs old, follows me around a lot and is quite entertaining. His mommy and daddy are in Coventry and he speaks real old English—"rawthers," "blimeys," etc.—and he asks no end of questions about the Indians and my boys and if I'd like to be home. I gave him one of the bars yesterday and he has been around all day. I sent him home to supper just a few minutes ago. I suppose Murray is [a] real little man by now. Do they still ask about their daddy or have they forgotten all about him? I suppose they have. Murray must have, in fact he never knew me. I'll be quite a stranger to you all. I've changed an awful lot since I last saw you. I never go out any place except the shows in camp and to play for dances. And darling, everyone remarks as to how grey my hair is. Quite grey on the temples and over my ears, but my hair is still staying with me so I may come home the distinguished-looking gentleman if this lasts much longer.

Well darling, we are going to the same place we were this summer for the winter I understand. I'm glad because things were really handy and comfortable there, but, as usual, rather lonely. I hate it here without you darling and will never be satisfied till I'm back with you and the kiddies. So damned far away and worried more or less that things may not be all right. In your last letter you mentioned being fatter, but nothing about your troubles. Are you fine again darling? I do hope so. As for the kiddies, I suppose they are as healthy as you please.

Gee, the boys are noisy here right now: a couple of horns going full blast, a mouth organ, fiddle and accordion in one corner, and one chap singing for all he is worth—and they keep asking me if they are bothering me. Really, if there wasn't any noise around I'd be all alone. These guys here just simply root and toot all day.

Thanks for the film. I'll have some pictures taken as soon as we get to our old home on the coast and send them on.

Take care of yourself darling and all of my love.

Your loving hubby,
Clarence

P.S. Rollie are you being a good boy? You better be because if Mummy tells me you aren't I'll be mad. Give Murray a big hug and a kiss for me.

Bye-bye, write too.

☙

s. Sask. r. c.a.(o).
England
October 11th, 1941


Dear Mummy,

Received two of your letters last night and I was sure tickled. I got them just as we were leaving to play for a dance so didn't get a chance to read them till we were ready to play . . . I was simply starved for your letters.

Tomorrow, we leave for the coast and then I'll have pictures taken with that film you sent. By the way, if you send me more films make them 120. Dick Nunn, one of my pals, has a 120 Kodak and said I could have it any time I liked.

So you are still having financial troubles, are you darling? Yes, I suppose the little you get don't go any too far does it? But don't worry mummy, as long as your debts get a little smaller each month.

I understand that there is an awful lot of that sleeping sickness and infantile paralysis in Canada, worse than ever. If it isn't one thing, it is two. Do you know I woke up in a cold sweat the other night. I was dreaming Murray had infantile paralysis. I was sure glad it was [a] dream.

How are the kiddies anyway? Gee, I miss them mummy. Mother was telling me in one of her letters that Murray is talking a little now and growing like a weed, and that Rollie hasn't changed much. I sure won't know them when I get back I suppose.

. . .


I'm sitting by the stove writing. It is a real fall day. The leaves are laying around ankle deep, and cold, a little spitting rain, so the fire is swell. I'm having quite a time to concentrate on writing, the boys are pulling wrists on the floor and making a devil of a racket.

Bye-bye sweetheart, xx, I love you, take care of yourself, love for the kiddies too.

Love,
Clarence

ॐ

England
October 16th, 1941


Dear Mummy,

Well here we are in the same room, the same room mates and the
same fireplace, which sure is swell. The weather here has been nasty.
So far, we have been here three days and it has been chilly and windy.
Looking out of the window I see the channel and it sure is rough.

Well darling, we rented a Philco radio with push buttons, 5 shillings
a week, and [a] gate-leg table and two cushioned chairs for an
additional two shillings a week, which we pay every payday. . . .
I haven't taken the pictures with that film yet, the sun hasn't been
out yet but as soon as it shows I'll take them.

On guard last night I had a big lump in my throat; some chaps got
a little mail, I didn't get a thing—I was a little blue as it was. I was
on the 3 a.m. shift and I paced back and forth with my mind in
Lafleche. My arms simply ached to hold you close darling; and the
kiddies, I keep wondering just how much of their lives am I missing.
Sometimes darling, I get frantic. I do miss you and the kiddies so
much, and what can we do . . . Lord, is this ever going to stop.
I guess the best is to make the best of it.

Tomorrow night we will be playing for a dance, I really enjoy that.
It kills time and [is] fun to boot. If it wasn't for the band and orchestra I would go nuts. The band is getting larger. We have four
new players added, which makes it easier for us. As we were before,
no one to relieve, we had to play continually through a piece, while
now with more playing the same parts one can get a breather.


. . .


Well bye-bye darling, take care of yourself.

All my love,
Clarence

October 26, 1941
Sunday


Darling,

Received three of your letters and the parcel of eats. Also, a parcel
from Mother and the letter from Elnora [another of Clarence's sisters],
but what has happened to all the mail from Sept 2nd to Sept 22nd?

Well darling, I've been over ten days without writing but I have
been away on a band trip near London. We played for the Presentation of Colours by the Queen to the Saskatoon Light Infantry. I
enjoyed the trip; we were away for a week rehearsing a few days
with the S.L.I. The weather was swell till the actual Presentation and
then it was colder than the dickens. I shivered and shivered and my
fingers were stiff with cold. We all were cold, but no slip-ups were
made. Everything went over swell. I saw the Queen again. She spoke
to the band master. She looks as fresh as ever and moving pictures
were taken of the Presentation of Colours, which will be shown to
the world over. We were taken marching and playing for the "march
past" the Queen. So, you may still see me on some news reel. I hope
to see the picture here some time soon, I'm rather curious. Well,
after the whole thing was over and we were back home we were
congratulated by our officers for the grand display we put on. And
to show their appreciation we are to get three extra days leave on
our next privilege leaves. Mine is to be about the tenth of November, and this time I am broke. I believe I'll visit Percy Starbuck in
London. It is close to home and when I go broke I can get back
quick. I had to buy cigarettes since I haven't received any cigs for
two months. I bought six hundred from a fellow who didn't smoke
Sweet Caps sent him from Canada. I paid two pounds, all of my
next pay. I suppose I'll be half broke till Christmas now.

And darling, I've been casting around to get you something nice for
Christmas, and frankly it is awfully hard. I don't know what to get.
Everything I look at is a way beyond my finances; this war tax

business is making it hard to be able to get things like presents. I'm afraid darling it will have to be something like a photo of me— I hope you won't be too disappointed.

Gee, I've been awful lonely today. We played for [a] church parade this morning. It is a dull day, cold and miserable. We have the fireplace going full tilt so the room is bearable. I had a three hour nap this p.m., and I don't suppose I'll get to sleep before two or three. I'll sit up and read that magazine you sent me, "Your Life." I read a little of it before dinner and it was swell. Send them as often as you get a hold of them.

The boys and I—that is, Dick, Kayo, and I—are going to have toasted chicken sandwiches for supper, I mean midnight lunch. We swiped a pound of margarine, a fair substitute for butter, and with the coffee and sugar and a loaf of bread and a pint of milk I bought, and the chicken, thanks to you, we should have a decent feed for a change.

Do you remember the sweater you sent me? Well darling, someone was kind enough to swipe it when we moved down here, plus a pair of my army boots, which I will have to buy this time. (No one else around in our bunch with shoes or rather feet [the] same size as mine; the sweater was in need of a little mending at the elbows and it would have been as good as new, but it is gone.) I believe it was one of the English chaps whom we relieved here. I had sent it down with, or in, my kit bag. When I got here, someone had been through my stuff and took it and my extra shoes—"the fortunes of war." All I can say is "damn the luck" and take it—can't do anything about it.

So you may send Rollie to school? I hope he likes it to start, because if he don't, he will be a little nuisance. Whatever you do after he has started, don't leave him stay home. See that he goes every day and don't pamper him or bribe him to go, just make him go—it is the best. He is endowed with a certain amount of intelligence, and make him understand he has got to go and will. Under the circumstances it is the best thing for him. You may have a little trouble starting him off—kids will be kids—and, furthermore, if started young enough they soon take it for granted, while if they are left till they are too old they develop the habit of doing nothing such as playing and nothing else. I started when I was five and I am none the worse for it. Boiled down, it has to be done sometime. So why not at once and make a good job of it. I sure wish I was there to see him off for his first day at school.

So Murray can get into mischief too. I'll bet he is a little darling, even upsetting tubs of rinse water. I'm forever looking at his pictures, especially the one of him standing in the backyard dressed in bloomers only. He is quite cute and is forever pointing his finger. He is pointing at something in all of them.

Having financial troubles still, are you? Don't worry about them darling, but whatever you do don't skimp on yourself. The people you owe are no doubt in a better position than you are. Above all things, don't worry darling.

. . .

Yes Mummy, it is my birthday on the 5th and I certainly hope it is the last [in England]. I sure am sick of it all, trying to make the best of things, but at times I get terribly disgusted and lonely. I'm just beginning to realise how big a cold, cold world this is when you are away from your loved ones and home.

So Sarah is having her troubles with Steve. All I can say is he certainly isn't being fair to her in any shape or form. I never see him, only sometimes I'll see him going by.

Just turned the radio on and the music is swell. I'm going to sit back and listen. They are playing, "You and I." I wished you were beside me listening. I've actually tears in my eyes. I love you Mummy. Do you love me? A big kiss right here, x.

Well, here I am again as lonely as ever. Elnora, in her letter, said she hoped I was getting used to being away and that I liked England now. As far as England goes, the country is beautiful, but it's not home, never will be without you or the kiddies.

Thanks for the parcel darling and the swell letter, and thanks for your best wishes on my birthday. And I'll certainly not stay away any longer than I can help, every additional day I'm away is too long as far as I'm concerned.

So Rollie is going to send me a coloured picture. What does he say when someone asks him, "where is your daddy?" I'll bet he is quite the little man.

So the bazaar is over and it didn't go over so good. I understand things are pretty tough there again this fall. What is this world economy coming to?

That was swell of your dad to do the house for you and it will no doubt be much warmer, and when you paint it in the spring it should look swell.

Thanks for the reeds darling. We had, that is I had, an awful time playing with these old rags of reeds we had here. I played an hour or so after supper.

So, it took 18 days for an air mail letter to get to you, not a terrible lot of difference so I guess I won't use the air mail again. I didn't receive your air mail letter.

. . .

No, I didn't go to Spitsbergen, but I have met some of the chaps who were there. One was from Saskatoon. . . .

No doubt some of my letters are being censored so I must be careful that I don't write about something I shouldn't be—might get into some hot water.

Yes darling, I'll be careful—I don't know what you mean re: VDs, because I never intend to be anywhere near anything that may give it to me. One fellow came into the M.O. [Medical Officer], and when asked how did he get it, he said off a toilet seat. The M.O. said, "that's a queer place to take your girlfriend." So it can only be picked up by contact, so I have no worries and you needn't worry either, I won't.

I'll bet it is cute to see our kiddies saying their prayers, side by side.

Well darling, I'll say bye-bye for now. And send plenty of cigarettes [and] pipe tobacco every other month.

And thanks for everything, I love you more for all of it.

And darling, when you mention going to dances, oh, how I wished I was at them with you. Some other punks have the pleasure of dancing with you, while the one that should be, or rather have you in his arms, has to be miles and miles away. Have a good time darling, but do be careful. I love you and I trust you, I've opportunities to go to dances but never do. I play for them but never ever dream of taking any other women in my arms to dance. I don't know why I should be like that but I am.

Bye-bye Mummy. Be Good.

All my love,
Clarence

෴

Canadian Base Post Office
October 28, 1941

Dear Mummy,

Here I am all by myself. The boys are all away playing ball against
the Royal Canadian Engineers. So, I've been cleaning my equipment and doing laundry. I kept out of sight till they got away, it's
such a miserable day, cold and cloudy. So I'm in my room with the
fire roaring in the fireplace and all my stuff cleaned up and it's cozy
but plenty lonely.

At noon today I listened to a Canadian broadcast from Canada—
wives and sweethearts speaking to their hubbies and boyfriends
over here. It came from Winnipeg this time. I listen to these programs every Wednesday in hope that I may hear the voice that I'm
so lonely to hear—yours, Hazel. Have you ever had the opportunity
or the invitation? You couldn't have, or you would have. I keep listening as often as duty permits in case you do get the chance. If
ever I get the chance I'm going to. Sometime when I get into London I'm going to enquire how to be able to send a message over. So
someday you will hear me saying over the air, "I love you Mummy
and I miss you." And how I mean that, darling. But I'm lonesome,
especially on days like this—bleak, windy and cold. I need you
darling, nothing seems to matter anymore. I want you and home.
I'm just marking time and hoping for the day I get back. Gee, the
ocean sounds mournful coupled with the swish of the drying leaves
on the trees. It is really a depressing day. I'm looking out to the west
towards Canada over the sea, which really is in a turmoil, heaving
and churning, spray flying. It seems to be leering at me and saying,
"you want to go back don't you? But you can't, even if you deserted
you would have to swim me, and you can't." Oh, Lord, but I do
want to get back to you and the kiddies. Yes darling, to have you
beside me, someone to love and cherish and be loved by that same
person. As I said in a previous letter, "it is a big cold, cold world
when you are away from the ones you love."

A rather depressing letter isn't it Mummy? But I'm in the best of health and I feel like any loving husband should feel under these circumstances.

How are the kiddies? Is Rollie away to school yet? If you do send him are you going to see him to school on those blizzardy, cold days this winter? That isn't going to be so pleasant is it? I wish I was there to do it. It would be fun to take my own son to the door of the same school I went to, holding his little chunky hand and answering his never ending flow of questions. Hazel, when I get back to my kiddies I'm going to really be a daddy to those boys. I don't want them to be afraid of me as we were of T.H. [Clarence's father].

Yes, Dad was always so stern when we were young, to the extent that we never really got to know one another, and less, confide in one another.

Well darling, I believe I will close and call it a letter. Write often darling and don't forget smokes. I'll write you a letter on my lonely birthday.

All my love,
Clarence

P.S. Hugs and kisses for the kiddies.

☙

Canadian Base Post Office
November 1st, 1941


My own Mummy,

Hello darling. I love you—a big kiss (right there). It is the best I
can offer, but all of my love and heart are in it darling.

Wednesday, I will be 28; another two years, I'll be in the thirties.
Time doesn't wait does it mummy? Even my hair is greying quite
noticeably, but as plentiful as ever and I hope to be home to celebrate my 29th birthday. Yes, it will soon be a year since we parted
and what a long year it has been. And I certainly don't care for anymore like it either. Over three hundred days of continual longing
and loneliness, and if you miss me like I miss you, it was the cru-
ellest thing I've ever done when I enlisted. Little did I realise what I
was letting myself in for. And leaving you to all the family responsibilities, two kiddies to look after. Well, I guess there is no use crying
over spilt milk is there? Only thing, why must we learn through experience? If you ask me it is a plenty rough school. Dinner time, bye.

Had dinner and a two-hour nap. It is now 3:30. Just lit a fire in the
fireplace, the weather is miserable again, the sun was out all morning. I was thinking of going for a stroll along the shore—brrr, not
now, it is too comfortable in the room. How do you like the piece,
"I Don't Want to Set the World on Fire"? Quite nice isn't it, and we
hear it a lot over the radio.

We are going to have some big inspection next Friday the seventh
and we have started rehearsing for it. We were out yesterday afternoon and the band just stood in one place for three hours in the
cold wind playing for the regiment going through its paces, and it
sure was no fun. . . .

Is the house any warmer since you have it all fixed up? I certainly
hope so. Wouldn't it be swell if we could sit side by side on these

long winter nights toasting our toes in the oven. Do you remember us doing just that? And we did very little of that, but when I'm home again you can rest assured that there will be a lot of evenings of just you and I. I love you Mummy, and when I get a hold of you again you will realize I do.

Well bye-bye darling,
your hubby,
Clarence

∽

Canadian Base Post Office
November 10, 1941

Dear Mummy,

Received three of your letters tonight, rather another long wait.
I'd been feeling terribly rotten that last three or four days. I haven't
the least idea what is wrong. No fever, no cold. Probably, I need a
good physic[al]. And I'm losing weight, maybe I should [go] out
more. I stay in days at a time without a glimpse out of a door.

I really feel punk tonight, so this letter will not be overly long.
I'll answer your letters though; thank Rollie for the paint job,
it is really good.

Two of your letters are missing . . . I hope they show up.

I wish you hadn't shown Adrien that letter I wrote about the
Legion. At that, I hope it wakes them up.

Re my Christmas present darling. I really don't expect one for
the simple reason I'm not sending a thing myself more than a few
Christmas cards. Presents are so darned hard to find and money
always seems to be a question too. I had my photo taken this week
and received a proof today. I'm enclosing the proof, not so good I
don't think. But I'm having a few more printed and getting mounts
as well. It will be a couple of days yet, so you will probably get them
all at once; I mean, with this letter. You asked about a photo in your
letter . . . but I beat you to it because I had the proof before the letter.

I'm sure glad to read that you are feeling better darling. You can't
be feeling too bad at that. I notice you take in the odd dance so you
can't be feeling too bad. And that news is good news. Do you have
fun at the dances darling? I hope so. A person can't go into her-
mitage because wife or husband is away. I've a lot to keep me occupied and I have fun playing for dances. We have a grand trumpet

player and can he swing it. And I don't mind doing a bit of swing myself, so we have fun tearing all these hot numbers to pieces such as "Bugle Call Rag," "Loch Lomond," and "Hut-Sut." We play for two dances a week and practice new numbers every other night. I went to Brighton on Saturday and bought some new ones, "Down Forget-Me-Not Lane," "I Don't Want to Set the World on Fire," "My Sister and I," and we make a swell job of playing these new ones and they are all nice. I prefer playing these sentimental numbers. Do you know I can actually close my eyes and play for you at dances. I've done it, and I've often wished I would open my eyes and see you smiling, enjoying the music while you dance. I always dedicate the nice pieces to you mummy. I love you darling.

Well darling, I'm going to have a bath and then to bed. Hope I feel better in the morning.

Looking forward to smokes and the Christmas parcels darling. I'm hungry right now and breakfast is in the morning.

. . .

Well, bye-bye sweetheart, love and kisses.
Truly in love with you,
Clarence

P.S. Hugs and Kisses for the kiddies. Be good!

Canadian Army [Overseas]
November 24, 1941


Dear Mummy,

Hello darling, I've been away on leave. I spent it at Gravesend with
Percy Starbuck and had a real good and quiet time. He is a stay-at-
home. Doesn't drink or smoke, so I did have a quiet time. Saw a few
shows and went to a dance and danced two dances with his girlfriend. She is about 39, real nice. She is a private secretary to some
big shot in London and very much in love with Percy, so I suppose
she will be marrying him soon and be a different kind of secretary.

I had a swell room and grand eats for a change. Percy stays with his
mother (an invalid), and his sister [Dorothy], an old maid about 45,
but very pleasant. Percy is 6 ft. 4" tall and his sister is 6 ft. 2" tall
and big to boot. No wonder she is still single. But they were very
nice and want me back for Christmas. It is real close to here so I
will probably go there.

I'm afraid this won't be awfully long darling, we have orchestra
practice in a few minutes and four dances to play for this week, and
five next week. So, we will be awful busy. Anyway, I'll write oftener.

Received your letter . . . and tobacco. Thanks darling, I was in
need of smokes.

I'm sending pictures of all the places I visited on leave: Canterbury
Cathedral, Rochester and different places. I enjoyed it all, but the fact
still remains regardless to where I go or what I do there is a little someone who always creeps into my thoughts, and how I miss that little
someone. Yes darling, I love you. Did you get my Christmas card?

The radio is playing "A Small World"—if you ask me it is an
awful big one or I would get to see you once in awhile. Gee
darling, I could scream I get so darned lonely.

. . .

How is the house for warmth since you fixed it up, any better?

I'll close for now, I'll write again tomorrow, the boys are waiting.

Love and kisses to the kiddies,

Bye-bye,
love,
Clarence

ॐ

Canadian Army Overseas
November 25th, 1941


Dear Mummy,

. . .

Thanks for the parcel mummy, it was swell. The cake was grand; that is, it looks grand, I'm putting it away for Xmas unless we move again. . . . Oh mummy, mummy, I love you and I'm terribly lonesome. Oh kid, I don't know how I stand it. I'm just a sappy kid yet, I suppose I could have a good cry. Darling, I feel so lonely at times that I am simply miserable. Damn, I guess there is no use feeling that way, I can't do anything about it, just pray and hope for a speedy reunion. And to make me feel worse, just 30 more days before Christmas, and I owe you a Christmas. Darling, I've made your last two Xmases hell, and when we have a Christmas together I'll sure make it all up to you to darling.

We played for a dance tonight and I made a poor job of it. I just didn't feel up to it, and we have to play for a Red Cross dance tomorrow, a big affair, so I hope I'm in the mood.

The weather here is miserable. The trees are all bare, the lawns stay green the year around, but it is awful chilly just the same. So, I don't think I'll be going any place much other than band and orchestra work, our room here is so cozy.

I'm enclosing another picture of myself. Did you get the others? Not much as a Christmas present, but it is all with my love darling, and I'm not forgetting your birthday either Mummy. Expect a nice present, I've got something in mind.

How is Murray? I was just gazing at his pictures; I can't believe I'm the daddy of two boys. Rollie looks like quite the man now. Mother sent me a snap of him working in O'Neill's garden, real good too. I'll have that film you sent me taken, and I'll send them to you.

Bye-bye darling. It is quite late, I'll write again tomorrow.
Do you love me?

Hugs and kisses [for the] boys, and love, Mummy,
Daddy

ॐ

Canadian Army Overseas
December 1st, 1941

Dear Mummy,

I'm on guard today, and between shifts I hope to catch up on my correspondence. Between band, orchestra, practices, and dances, I have very little time to myself. I'm glad of it, it makes time pass much quicker.

I'll go through your last six letters and answer them line by line.

So, the Legion went in the hole with their dance for us chaps over here, and Adrien figures we have more loose cash than they have. He should try it under these circumstances. Yes, we draw four pounds a month, approximately $19.00. I spend most of it in the canteen having lunches—I've got to fill up somehow. And when a person has to buy cigarettes, as I am doing now (about 40 cents a day), $19.00 soon disappears. Yes, re smokes, I haven't received a cigarette from Canada for over two months. You say different people are sending me some; well, those different people are the same, they just talk. I'm smoking the pipe a lot, but when I'm out any place the pipe is so unhandy and smelly that I leave it home.

You are mistaken about the five pounds limit on parcels to the Canadian troops; that is just to the civilians. Nevertheless, five pound parcels are welcome at all times. I'm getting terrible, am I not darling? But we certainly look forward to them. Received a swell parcel from mother. . . . Mother sent gloves, towels, hankies, socks, bars, chicken, cheese, gum, and writing paper, quite nice, eh!. . . .

. . .

You mention photos in your letter. I've sent you a couple and will enclose another, and will have others taken when I get to a photographer again. There are none here.

Yes, I would give plenty for last year. At this time we were happy and I was on furlough too. Little did we know at this time last year that I would be here now. Yes, it was December, Friday the 13th, the day or morning I walked away from [you]. I stopped at the corner and looked back up at our window, all I could see was a crack of light. I knew then that I was slated for overseas. I knew I loved you, I had tears in my eyes and a big, big lump where my heart should have been. I never want to go through anything like that again—I love you darling.

Received your telegram the eve of my birthday. It was swell, still is—I have it at my elbow.

Yes, Hazel, I received the butter Bankses sent me months ago. Thank them again, it was swell.

Dear little Rollie, I'm glad to hear that he doesn't forget his Daddy. The only thing is, I wish I had been a better dad [to] him.

. . .

So, Mrs. Hammond is put out about her husband finding out about her stepping out. Serves her right. And if things are as you say, I'd sure let her know I knew and tell her what she could do about it.

Cecil Johnson, Officer of the Peace, in the Village of Lafleche. Does he wear the star? Boy, oh boy, I'll bet he is struttin'.

You mention Murray in his sleepers walking into the kitchen about 10 p.m. pretty proud of himself. I'll bet he is cute. All these little things you write about the kiddies I sure enjoy, and they make me awful lonesome. Nevertheless, I like it. I enjoy every word you write about them.

You say you are going to have chicken for Xmas. You probably have ate it by the time you get this. I wish I could be with you and eat some of your dressing, not mentioning the chicken, which is something you would call just a memory.

You mention Dec. 13 in your letter of the 30th Oct., and you are wishing me a nice one. I do hope it will be better than the last. One thing I'll be spared, the agony of parting. Now it is just an ache, a steady lonely feeling, and a prayer that I get back to you awful soon. . . .

. . .

Well, bye-bye Mummy, I'll close now, sending all of my love. And we are changing billets. I'll write you from there, a few miles inland; we are being relieved by another regiment of this brigade.

We played for a dance last night (Red Cross dance). It was a good dance and the people seemed to really enjoy our music. Now that we are getting on as a dance band and in demand, we are being moved to some strange place, and we were certainly comfortable here.

Bye sweetheart, I love you, and tell Murray I'd sure enjoy one of his damp kisses.

Well, love and kisses and hugs for the kiddies, and for you darling, a long, long, close, close kiss.

Bye,
Daddy

☙

England
December 10, 1941

Dear Mummy,

Well, we have moved and are we ever busy now. I'm . . . on the go
night and day, doing guard work, stretcher work, piquets, band and
orchestra; the latter two, of course now, is done on our own time.
Our new colonel is sure stepping on us, everything is changed. I
don't think I'm very fussy about the s.s.r.s under the present set up.
It has got to the point that writing letters is getting hard to do unless we write after meals or after lights out—it is eleven now. I was
on kitchen fatigue today; yesterday, on guard; the day before, fire
piquet; tomorrow, I've got to go out with 'C' Company for two
days on some scheme.

Darling, there has been mail for the last six days and so far I haven't
received a card in this bunch. I was beginning to wonder, but I always console myself with the thought tomorrow I'll get a bunch.
I no doubt will, but I hope that that tomorrow *is* tomorrow.

We are still near Brighton, a few miles from the coast this time, and
I understand we are to move again soon. And, furthermore, we are
to keep on the move.

Things are sure happening now with Japan in the mix up and the
Russians putting on a push. I don't know what to make of things;
I hope it doesn't tend to make the war longer.

How is everything with you darling? And the kiddies? I suppose
everything is on the rush, Xmas being so close. I'm sure not looking
forward to it, it will be just another day to me, I'll probably be
lonely and blue.

. . .

Well darling, I do love you and only you, but as it is I probably could write much oftener. But I really can't find an awful lot to write about; that is to say, that I can write about due to censors, and I just keep repeating myself. Do you know that we were even asked not to mention weather conditions. Why, I don't know. I guess as far as that goes we needn't, because it is always rain.

Well darling, I'm just about out of smokes and certainly could do with a bunch anytime now.

Well, bye darling, I suppose I'll get a bunch of letters to answer of yours tomorrow.

Love and kisses to the kiddies, and a long, long kiss for you darling.

Love,
Daddy

&

Canadian Army Overseas
December 16, 1941


Dear Mummy,

Received 300 Wings cigs from you darling and are they ever swell.
I haven't received any others though. Thanks darling, I have some
for Christmas now.

We had some excitement here yesterday. Dick, my roommate,
took the wrong medicine by mistake. He took tincture of camphor
instead of camphorated cough syrup, and did he ever go into fits.
Foamed at the mouth, just simply went wild—it took three of us to
hold him down and [we] stuffed warm water and mustard into him
until he began to throw up, and he has been plenty sick since. In
the ruckus yesterday, Dick punched me on the nose and split my lip.
He didn't realise what he was doing, so I don't feel so good myself.
I've a slight head cold and my nose insists on running and I can't
blow it or wipe it so I'm feeling more or less miserable.

Received a letter from James Banks yesterday telling me his
daughter Helen is in a sanatorium some place in Scotland. He
didn't mention the name of the place, so if you see [the] Banks
you can tell them.

Gee, the weather here is swell today. The sun is shining, the lawns
are vivid green, and you should see the holly trees. They are simply
grand and loaded with those red berries. Such shiny green—there is
a holly tree just outside my window. Roses are still blooming here,
Hazel. There has been no frost to kill them yet; can you imagine
roses in December?

Ten days to Christmas darling and I'm afraid I'm going to be awfully lonely. We are going to make up a meal of our own; that is,
Dick, Kayo and I. Canned chicken, canned tomatoes, sausages
(canned also), canned fruit, your fruit cake, etc., etc.—all saved up

from parcels we have received, so at least we will have a good meal.
But the thought of turkey dressing, cranberries, swell dressing,
makes my mouth water. I still believe I will be home in 1942 darling.

How are the kiddies darling? Are you skating? And I suppose
the weather there is terrible. How are the curlers doing? Are
you curling?

I'm going to write to the Red Cross now and thank them for
the parcel.

Bye-bye Darling,
love and kisses, x
Clarence

Canadian Army Overseas
England
December 19, 1941

My own Mummy,

Received your airgraph of the 10th today—nine days, pretty good time.

Gosh, that is sad news about Uncle Henry. Gee, Aunt Olive must
feel terrible. Two deaths within a year and her two remaining boys
in the services. It must be driving her wild. I can't imagine Uncle
Henry passing away so easily so your letter says, he seemed so
strong. The town of Lafleche must have taken it hard. He was so
well-known and well-liked. Do you know it is the third relative of
mine that has died in the past nine months. I hope it stops now. . . .

Wired you a Merry Xmas and a Happy New Year this morning, and
I'm going to wire again for the New Year. In case you don't get one,
two will be better than none, won't it Mummy?

Sergeant Ring is writing his wife wondering how come she has received only two letters in three months. He is a chap about 40 and
say he writes at the very least once a week. And I'm sure I write that
often, so I don't understand why you don't hear from me oftener either.
I hope they aren't lost. And since I've lost my little note book where
I've kept track of my letters I haven't been numbering them so we have
no way of checking, so I'm numbering from now on, this is one.

Lord, it's hard to settle down and write. The fellows keep coming
in and out, the radio is blaring away, but I'm still trying.

We are going to play a band concert in Seaford tomorrow night, the
first one in quite awhile. In Lewes here they have no halls available
for us, so we don't play band concerts or for dances. All halls large
enough are all booked till after the first of the year, so I've been
staying [at] home. But we are kept plenty busy. One day I'm on
guard at B.H.Q. [Battalion Headquarters], and then on kitchen fatigue here at the hospital. And next day guard here, and then sick
bay orderly, and then fireman, and so it starts all over again. When

night time comes around I'm glad to see my bed.

So Murray has a new coat. Does he say daddy yet? And I suppose when he gets it on, he struts and pats his chest and says "ni-ni" as Rollie did. So Rollie is sending me one of his teeth; so that is the beginning of him growing out of childhood. I hope I get home before he is big enough to beat up on me for joining the Army, which I justly deserve.

The news is on now and sound[s] very good—I hope the Ally successes continue, it means a quicker return home. And apparently we do not leave this island for the duration, so we may see very little action, if any.

We are moving to other quarters out in the country someplace near. Some of the boys don't seem to think much of it; as far as I'm concerned it is all the same to me. And I hope our duties will be lighter; if so, I'd prefer the move. Maybe I'm getting lazy; I believe it is mostly that I'm sick of it all, and how.

Well, bye-bye darling—I feel pretty blue as we are drawing near Christmas. Oh, by the way, I went to Brighton to a show night before last, and as I was trying to buy matches, going from one shop and no luck (matches are terribly scarce), in a drug store after the clerk said I'm sorry but we are out as usual (I asked him for a light), an elderly lady offered me a small box of matches and we began chatting about Canada, and she finished up by inviting us to her home for Christmas dinner—that is, Dick, Kayo and I. We accepted. It seemed good to us. She was well-dressed and appearance was good, and after she went out we asked the clerk about her, and [apparently] they are well-to-do, have a nice home, and that it should be a very nice dinner. She told us she had two boys in the Navy and hoped that they could have a nice Christmas dinner somewhere, and she felt sure our mothers felt the same. A Mrs. Hewett was the name, so I'm to have a Christmas dinner anyway.

Well bye-bye darling, got to tend fires now.

Hugs and kisses,
Daddy

CANADIAN PACIFIC
TELEGRAPHS
*World Wide Communications*

CANADIAN PACIFIC COMMUNICATIONS

STANDARD TIME INDICATED

W.D.NEIL, GENERAL MANAGER OF COMMUNICATIONS, MONTREAL.

CD 1X

CK EFM Via Comml

Great B ritain

S WU Dec 23rd 925

Mrs. Clarence Bourassa

Lafleche, Sask.

Love an d best wishes for Christmas and the N ew XXX
Year to all at home all well.

Clarence Bourassa

Canadian Army Overseas
December 27, 1941


Dear Mummy,

Well, Christmas is gone by and I didn't leave camp Christmas Day.
We are out in the sticks and no bus service or train service. We have
to walk a mile and a half to the station so I don't bother going any
place at all. We are busy playing for plenty of dances. On Boxing
Day we played the British Legion dance in Lewes, and for the first
time since I've been over here I got a real glow on. While we were
playing, the Legion members kept feeding us Scotch. I was more or
less down in the mouth over the rotten Xmas I had, so didn't refuse
any drinks, and the outcome was I got plastered practically and I
was having a whale of a time playing. It was soon over and back out
in the country we did plenty of singing. Then Kayo started a crying
jag about how he was lonesome and hated this. He got me going
too. It must been funny to see a couple of soldiers in one another's
arms trying to console one another. The next morning I sure felt
plenty tough and did we ever get kidded about the sob business
of the night before. That was yesterday and they are still at it, and
"how I have the nicest little wife in the world" and "how I loved her,"
etc. According to the boys I must have really put on a show.

In one of your letters you said, or rather asked, "Do you really love
me or are you just building me up in your imagination?" I don't like
that and I can't figure out why you wrote it. What I remember of
Toronto is certainly not imagination.

Xmas Day we had a swell turkey dinner in camp and plenty of it:
turkey, gravy, mashed potatoes, cranberry sauce, and mince pie, and
did I ever enjoy the meal. Outside of the meal, Christmas was awful
lonely. I had a good sleep in the afternoon; at night, I went to a
show for the troops and it was terrible, I didn't wait for the finish.
I came back here and played the sax for an hour and then to bed
because we had to play for a dance Boxing Day. So, I had a terrible

Xmas darling, and was, or am, I ever lonely. We are out in the
country and it rains every other day, freezes every night, and thaws
out in day time. So, we are really in the mud! Slip, slide, slush, in
gum boots and denim overalls. We have been digging trenches, so
you should see the shape we are in most of the time. I'm forever
scrubbing up and washing clothes, I've socks soaking now.

Received a cablegram from Aunt Olive last night wishing me a
Merry Christmas. It took only two days to get to me. It sure raised
a lump in my throat when I thought of the sorrows she has to bear.
I'm dropping her a line tonight.

Did you enjoy your Christmas mummy? Did you get tight too? Did
the kiddies enjoy themselves? Oh damn, but I do miss them. I can
just see them playing hide and seek and playing with their toys—
isn't life hell darling? I sure put my foot into it the day I signed that
dotted line.

I suppose there is a lot of excitement across the pond over Churchill,
the papers here are just full of it. I believe he is to speak to the
Canadians tonight about their boys over here, and according to the
news over the radio he is to bring back some special pleasant news
for us over here. There are rumours going that we may be recalled
for coastal duties (if that could only be true!) and I'm afraid it is just
a rumour.

Gee, but I'm behind with my correspondence. I've received no end
of letters from Canada, even a card from Bessie Galbraith with a
hanky in it. Between dances and duty nights I get very few to myself. I could have written last night I suppose, but felt too punk between hangover and loneliness.

We are playing for an s.s.r. dance tomorrow night, and [a]
New Year's Eve dance in Salmestone, and one on Saturday for the
Foresters Club in Lewes. And I'm going on leave on the 5th, so I'd
better settle down and write. For my leave I'm going to visit Percy
Starbuck again. It is close and I haven't a devil of a lot of money.

And these leaves sure burn up the little we do get and I'm forever borrowing a pound or two to go on these leaves. At the price we pay for railway and bus fares, a few meals, and smokes—everything is confounded high-taxed here, taxed there—I get by at that.

Well, I'll say bye for now darling. Take care of yourself Mummy— love you all over. Love and kisses. Couldn't you cuddle up on a cold night like this darling? There will come the day, and soon, I hope.

Night-night sweetheart,
Love and Kisses,
Daddy

[p.s.] xxx—I love you and am lonesome.

# LETTERS 1942

Canadian Army Overseas
January 2nd, 1942


Hello Mummy,

. . . Happy New Year darling.

Well, I'm sick and tired of dances and rehearsals. Thank heavens
that is all over with. A dance to me now is getting to [be] something I dread, although I do like playing. And now for a decent
leave. I'm not terribly rich but my keep is all taken care of. All I
have [to] look forward to is bus fares, shows, and a photo, which
I had promised a long time ago.

So, I should have quite a long letter when I get back off leave. I'm
going to Motherwell, which I think I mentioned in a previous letter.
I'm not using those airmail forms anymore as they take just as long as
any other letter. Some of yours have taken as long as eight weeks too.

Excuse me for a minute, there is one hell of a rumpus in here—
wrestling, singing—I'll wait till this New Year spirit wears off the
guys (more to follow).

Well the boys are all settling down—writing, sleeping, and reading.

The Brighton dance went over with a bang. There were three bands:
the Regent's own band, a sixteen-piece band, and a small six-piece
band. We held our own and were complimented on all sides. Of
course, the bands all didn't play at once—an hour at a time. We
played from 8 to 9 and 10 to 11. And what a dance hall. The floor
was like a mirror, about 60' long by 100', completely surrounded by
alcoves and tables and palms—the nicest hall I've ever seen. And the
boys were all real tickled to be able to say we have played in the Regent Palais. The charge to get in to dance was 10 shillings per head
($2.50)—five bucks a couple—so, that might give you an idea what
the dance was like. And 1200 dancers were there! You should have

heard the noise as the new year came in. The dance broke up at 12:30—war restrictions. The next day, New Year's Day, we stayed in Brighton and went to a show and a vaudeville. Got back at 10:00 p.m. no richer. Got paid a pound, six shilling, and spent a pound, ten—[on] rooms, shows, and eats—but we had fun.

We were supposed to play for a dance tonight in Kirdford—thank heavens not, I'd like a rest. Tomorrow, the brass band plays for Church Parade—I see music in my sleep as it is. Thank heavens I'm going to leave for a few days, I won't look at a note or instrument for a week.

Tomorrow, I'm going to spend the day ironing shirts and uniform and great coat for my leave.

Well, it is a New Year mummy—'42—is it going to see us together again? I do hope so.

I get a big kick out Rollie's crayon work, how is he doing at school? I see my name on the list of parcels lost in the fire, I wonder what it was. I haven't received December smokes, nor the civvies, but I have received everything else you have sent (I'm still borrowing a pen), but no Xmas telegrams so far, just the one from Wilfrid.

Did you get a raise in your check at all lately? There is to be a 20 cent a day raise in a private's pay and I get half, so you should be getting a $3.00 raise. Not an awful lot but will help.

Gosh, I'm behind with my mail. I owe everybody a letter. As soon as my leave is over I'll have to settle down for about 10 nights writing and nothing else. The orchestra and all is very amusing but takes up a little too much time.

Well Hazel, I'm fine, and as for the Army it is just everyday ordinary training, same routines, no news or rumours.

The news are good. I hope they keep up. Everything seems in our favour at present; I hope we are not due for disappointment. The Allied successes in the past didn't amount to much, but I do believe that we are on our way now and the end is clearly in sight. So, I hope it all ends soon.

Well Mummy, I'm getting sleepy. I'll be closing now with all my love, and to bed with me to lie and think of home, Mummy and the kiddies. By the way, Miss Starbuck received your parcel and wrote me about it. She was really tickled—stockings just aren't procurable here.

Bye-bye Mummy, I'm away on leave and will tell you all about it when I get back.

What kind of a New Year did you have? Any of the old gang around, or are they all away? Where did you go for your New Year's dinner?

Well, I've started to end this a couple of times now. It's late, the fire is out and my bed is handy.

Nighty-night darling, my bed is handy, but I'll be alone. Do you still keep my half of the bed warm and cozy for when I get back? Gee, I'm lonely. I am most of the time. They say a person can get used to anything after a time; one thing [for] sure, I'll never be used to being away from you. Someday soon, I hope so. Keep my place warm and cozy. Mmmmmmmmm.

All of me,
Clarence

ᜅ

Canadian Army Overseas
January 4, 1942


My own Mummy,

Received two shirts and a swell sweater from Dad last night, and
300 cigs from Mrs. Brunelle, and a nice letter from you. . . .

I've received everything you say you have sent to date and I get
your letters in bunches too. Hazel, I go six and seven weeks
without a letter and then they come in bunches for a few days.

. . .

Didn't you get my photo yet? Maybe it was too soon. Since you
wrote this letter I sent you a couple of them, and you no doubt
have received the cablegram I sent for Christmas.

Yes Hazel, I meant, "yes it is my birthday on the 5th, and I do
hope it is the last," [but] over here I meant, not my last birthday
[Clarence was evidently referring to a comment he had made in an
earlier letter, one which had upset Hazel.] Well, I haven't given up
hope yet. Things are still very much in favour of the Allies, more so
of late. So, I still expect to be home sooner than you say—Lord
knows I've been away plenty long enough.

. . .

I'm glad the house is warmer and more comfortable, and it helps to
hear that you are saving on some ends; such as, you say your meat
bill for December will be practically nil.

What kind of a time did you have [at] Xmas and New Year's? I
suppose there were some plenty wild parties. Be careful of Brett
Matlock. I know him like a book and I know his parties and his
ambitions, and I also know what extent he will go to to obtain his

ends. Ask Janet about Brett. That is the main reason I don't like
her as a companion of yours. I believe I mentioned it before—oh,
what's the difference anyway, I'm probably just down in the dumps.
I know you darling, and I believe in you, so I don't see why I should
worry. What got me into the blues was your letter and another
chap's, who was reading his while I was reading yours, and he
jumped up and started to curse—one of the chaps of the band: serious, good-looking, nice personality, and true to his wife. He never
went out and was continually writing to her. Well, he went wild
and is away someplace tonight. He has been burning wires with cablegrams, seeing the colonel, etc., etc. This noon I asked up, "what
is the matter old kid?" And he showed me a paragraph from a letter
he received from the chap he used to work for. This is what it said,
"Sorry Dick, but I feel it is my duty to tell you this, 'your wife is
about to be a mother.' " And he has been over here 13 months and
it has floored him. That was four days ago. He hasn't slept or ate
since. I don't suppose I would either. The hell of it is he is such a
fine chap, about 38, has three other children as well. It makes me
boil too. And he is away over here. Maybe it is just as well because
I pity her when he gets his hands on her. Why do things like that
have to happen?

How are the kiddies darling? I don't know, but Murray is continually in my mind. He was so cute in Toronto and his pictures are
great. I keep continually trying to picture him.

Yes, Hazel, I'm afraid I will be quite grown up when I get back.
I've changed an awful lot, even to myself. I don't go out, and I don't
play any cards—that is, gamble (no desire)—and as far as drinking,
I've had the odd one and they have been few and far between. Went
to that party for the band in Seaford the other night, dance[d] all
night, had one glass of beer and a swell lunch and came home. And
that was my first evening out for months. The band was treated like
kings. I was invited by a young lady to go up for dinner today—it
is now 8 p.m. and I haven't been out yet. For an excuse I said, "no,
I'm sorry, but I have other arrangements." I was glad when she
didn't insist on some other day. She was nice and all that (met her

mother at the party), and [I] made it very clear that I was married, had two grand children, and she turned her charms elsewhere. I simply have no use for women. Maybe, I've past [*sic*] the menopause, not noticing it. Well darling, I love you and please don't worry about me—you will get me back just as I left you.

. . .

Bye-bye Mummy,

Love,
Daddy

⸙

Canadian Army Overseas
January 6th, 1942

Dear Mummy,

Received your cablegram this afternoon. It made me feel good
way down inside. Got one from the family too—thanks mummy.

Well, I've got a dilly of a cold. In fact, a wow. I felt terrible last
night, went to bed at five thirty and sweat pails of water it seemed,
but I feel much better today. This morning we took a bunch of
blankets to the cleaner, a truckload of them, and let me tell you
they sure clean them in a rush here. The machine they have is a
steam cleaner. The blankets, fifty at a time, are placed in a steel box
and the steam is turned on for one minute, and then they are taken
out and shook out, then through a dryer. That takes about ten minutes. For the same fifty, all we had to do was fold them and load
them back in the truck. It took about six hours to clean and dry
a little over a thousand. At that I was plenty tired and will be
soon be turning in, sleep is one thing I don't go short on.

I was just looking through my album and I enjoy every bit of it.
It makes me lonesome though, I miss my mummy an awful lot,
and those two kiddies of ours. Gee darling, it does make me awful
lonesome.

I understand there is more mail in again and parcels too. I hope we
get them tonight; if so, I'll be writing again tomorrow. How is your
health darling, any better? I do hope so.

Well be good,
love and kisses for you and the kiddies,
Daddy

☙

Canadian Army Overseas
January 7th, 1942


Dear Mummy,

Received the newspapers and your letter. I sure appreciate the papers. I never dreamt that I would ever see the day I'd be studiously looking over the *Lafleche Press* and *Prairie Optimist*—I sure do now. . . .

Received a note from Agnes McDonald telling me she has sent some cigarettes. Thank heavens for that because the only cigarettes I've received so far are the 300 from Mrs. Brunelle and they are all gone (owed so many and I am borrowing again from the other boys who always seem to have plenty). Do you know I've received only 300 cigs and a pound of tobacco in the last 3 months? I know darling it probably is hard on the finances at your end, but Lord knows how hard they are to get here and how rotten they are when we do get them—that is, the English smokes. So please Hazel, don't cut down on cigs you send me. The other folks probably say they are sending them and I can't believe they are being sunk because the other boys get theirs regularly. I owe six packages now, that is 120 cigs, so that is a big hole in the next 300 if I don't owe all of the 300 by then.

. . .

So you got my picture and it's gracing the radio. Sounds funny to have that word written by you because it is decidedly English, I hear it often here. I'm glad you like it because I wasn't so sure that I liked it myself. I'll be having others taken again soon.

So the kiddies had plenty of toys for Christmas. I'm glad. And I sure hope you had a good time Christmas too, and lots to eat other than beans. We did all right here Xmas day, and with all the Xmas parcels we haven't done too bad.

Well, I guess I'll close and look the papers over. I notice G-Bourg put on quite a splash over her boys, but I notice there are only about four or five overseas, nothing on Lafleche. We have nearly as many overseas as G-Bourg has enlisted.

Night-night Darling,
I love you,
Clarence

P.S. A big hug and a nose rub for Murray. And I suppose Rollie will soon be big enough just to want to shake hands.

Bye-bye, I miss you terribly Hazel, and hope 1942 is the end of this.

All of my love.

ↄ

Canadian Army Overseas
January 9th, 1942


Dearest Mummy,

How is everything today darling? Kiddies are fine are they? But I
suppose the weather is plenty cold and a lot of snow. I feel pretty
mean when I think of it all. I can just see you getting coal: the snow
knee deep and a cold wind whipping your hair into your eyes, and
the wind flapping your skirts, hands blue with cold, and the vapour
from your breath, practically gasping with cold, and the weight of
the pail, and it is all my fault. And that is only one of things you
have to do since I've joined up. I often think of all these things and
wonder how in the world I'll ever make it all up to you. One think
certain is, when I get back I'm certainly going to try mighty hard.

Once more my loving you and longing for you is not my imagination darling. I've been away over two years and I have had ample
time to think things out, analyze myself, my weak points and my
failings, and frankly in my candid opinion I don't think much of
myself and full realize what you had to put up with—just a long
streak of childishness, spoiled at that.

Well darling, I've got to go now, band practice. Did you get the
snaps of the band?

Take care of yourself mummy. And do the kiddies still talk about
their daddy?

I love you,
Clarence

[P.S.] Bye-bye, write often.

❧

Canadian Army England
January 14, 1942

Dear Mummy,

Got back off leave last night to be greeted by a raft of mail: seven letters from you dating as far back as November 14th (rather poor service), and a parcel of eats—peanut brittle, etc.—and was it ever good.

By the way, before I forget, got some snaps here, I am sending them on.

In all your letters you keep asking about whether I've received the
parcels and cablegrams. Yes, I've received everything darling as I
keep repeating in my letters. But, I haven't received the civvies yet,
I'm beginning to wonder if they weren't in that fire. And I haven't
received the Dec. cigs yet.

Before going any further, for some reason or other we have been
notified that a few bags of s.s.r. outgoing letters in the field post
office had been lost and recovered after a few days and sent on. Any
ones having mail in the post between Dec. 19 and Jan. 5th are the
mails that will be late going over. So, you may find more of my
letters taking longer to get over.

Well, Hedley and I went to Motherwell, Scotland, and we spent
our time visiting his people, a day here and a day there. We went to
Hamilton, Wishaw, Truan, Pearley [?]. Spent two days in Hamilton
about twenty miles from Glasgow; Hedley has an uncle there. We
went to two shows while there, then even went to Truan. Rather a
quaint old fishing town on the west coast. He has a cousin there
who is a fish packer, fairly well-to-do. We spent our time watching
the fishermen coming in with their catches. I've never seen so much
fish in my life. Tons and tons of it. From Truan we went to Motherwell and Wishaw, to adjoining towns and suburbs of Glasgow. Went
to a dance in the Playhouse in Glasgow, the largest dance floor on

the British Isles, to listen to Joe Loss and his band. Had a few dances, spent most of the time listening to the band and getting a few pointers, as Loss's band is rated the best over here, and they are good. After the dance we had an awful time to get home. . . .

. . .

Well, it is another day and I've been rereading all of your letters. So Rollie is giving you a lot of trouble and you are undecided as to whether you will send him to Gravelbourg or not? I'll admit you are having a lot of trouble, but Hazel, Rollie is just a baby practically yet and all children have to go through the lying age, some worse than others. The only thing is, if Rollie can't be made to tell the truth etc., don't rave at him. And you must never threaten him with any punishment unless you go through with it. Don't threaten, say nothing to him if he's apparently lying. Talk to him quietly as mother to son and gently say, "Rollie, you are not telling me the truth and it isn't nice." Hazel, if I were home I don't believe I'd spank Rollie unless he really had it coming. But one thing I would do is punish him otherwise by depriving him of some privilege. And no matter how much he hollered or cried I'd ignore him. . . . The fear of a licking will make any kid lie. Oh heavens, I should be home darling and help you. Yes, the kiddies probably do need a man's hand, but darling do your best.

. . .

As for answering your questions about our actions and possibilities, we can't Hazel, because the censors may get hold of it and just too bad for Clarence. So I'm being careful.

Anyway, you have nothing to worry about. I'll be alright and this will soon be over now darling. And I will be with you soon, where I belong.

All of my love,
Clarence

Canadian Army Overseas
January 19, 1942

Dear Mummy,

. . .

By the way, you will probably receive a letter from Miss Dorothy
Starbuck (don't worry, she is 49). As it happened one afternoon on
my previous leave with them, the conversation swung around to
the rationing of clothing and the subject was brought up that some
Canadian chaps had been giving their friends silk hose from Canada,
and as it was practically an impossibility to get them here, they
wanted to know if I would write home and ask to have some
sent over and they would give me any price.

I wanted to ask for them (like a sap, I practically promised that I
would), but I didn't write for any, so when I went back they asked
me about the hose, that is, Percy's girlfriend, and I was at a loss for
an excuse. So, I said Hazel wants to know for sure what and who
the hose are for and that you seemed pretty peeved at me over it all,
etc. As an explanation for no hose, I thought it would be good
enough, but Miss Starbuck, the busybody she is, must rectify our
misunderstanding because everything was above board and [she]
couldn't bear to think that she should cause any troubles between
you and I. So, she is writing you about what, Lord knows, nothing
that I need worry about, but if I didn't tell you what it was all about
you'd probably wonder what in creation is this all about. Hazel, I
believe as a diplomat I'm a flop. I promised I'd try and get some
hose sent over and didn't even write to Canada about them, and I'd
have to cook up a story like I did about you figuring it must be for
a girlfriend instead of owning up that I didn't write to have some
sent, and now they are going to clear up the situation for me, which
didn't exist. I hope I've made the situation clear enough, Hazel.

Well, my leave was nice and quiet. I got to Gravesend, or Starbuck's,
Monday afternoon at 3 o'clock. Went to a show at night; Tuesday,

I helped him in the office (Percy). I typed out statements all day.
Wednesday, I helped him splice rope. At that I believe I was more
hindrance than help because I was forever doing it wrong. Thursday,
Mrs. Starbuck, the old lady about 80, took me to the Coliseum in
London and we sat in the box overlooking the stage. It was "Jack
and the Beanstalk." [It] really was interesting. I'm enclosing one of
the programmes. I've never seen such swell scenery and acting in
my life. The show lasted four hours and every minute of it was
grand. One scene especially, I'll never forget. About twelve girls representing butterflies (and you should have seen the colour) were flying around over the audience up and down, tossing out flowers and
singing all in harmony. It was simply grand, all done with invisible
wires. How they could flutter around in all directions and not get
the wires all tangled is beyond me. All I can say [is] that the whole
pantomime was simply beyond description, it was grand. The Coliseum is the most famed theatre in the world, Hazel. It houses four
thousand people, so it certainly wasn't a small building. It was a
large horseshoe-shaped building, the audience sits in four tiers and
boxes on both sides of the stage. I was in a box just beside the stage,
just about head level to the actors, so I certainly had a ringside seat.

Friday, I read by the fire all day. I read the book "Western Union."
Went to a hospital ball at night—I was never so bored in my life.
Everybody but a few soldiers was in full dress, tails and cardboard
fronts. The mayor spoke, somebody else spoke, and somebody else
spoke. I danced one dance and then sat by the orchestra, which was
very good, and got a few pointers—so, the evening was of some value.

Saturday, we went out to Percy's girlfriend's mother's for a dinner;
and Sunday, I went to low mass in the morning and started back
for home Sunday. Stopped over in London for the night, went to
a show—Sonja Henie in "Happy Valley,"—and then went to bed,
and I had the devil's own time getting back to the hotel. First of all,
I got on the wrong underground train and had to walk about thirty
blocks in the blackout, and was it ever black. A thick fog, no lights
at all, and I didn't know where I was—no flashlight. I bumped into
umpteen hundred people. A good thing I did, because I could

always ask where I was and how to get to my hotel. The only way I could stay on the sidewalks was due to the cars which are allowed to travel with parking lights. And how many times did I excuse myself to lampposts, bump, crash . . . it took about two hours to get to the hotel. It really was quite funny this morning when I thought back about excusing myself to a post . . . I guess I'd better get me a flash-light in case I get out someplace like that again. Now I'm back in camp and rather glad of it.

Thanks for the tooth Rollie, it is quite cute. . . . Are you being good for Mummy? Did you tell Mummy a lie that made your tooth come out? Better be careful or they will all come out. Give Murray a great big hug for me.

. . .

Love and kisses Mummy,
Clarence

‿

ROLLIE'S NOTE: *My mother Hazel received many letters from Dorothy Starbuck. The following was the first. It was postmarked January 15, 1942.*

Dale Hill,
Southfleet,
Gravesend,
Kent

Dear Mrs. Bourassa,

I expect you will be surprised to get a letter from me, but Clarence is spending another leave with us and I thought you might like to hear how he is. Of course, I cannot tell you if he has altered, but I should not imagine he has much. He is fit, or he could not do the very hard training he has been doing, but the last time he was here his nerves seemed a bit on edge, just the fact of being so far away from you all, and the waiting, and the barrack life. But this time he is much better and is having a good rest from it all. My brother and I are a good deal older than he is; in fact, I think I am nearly his mother's age, and we lived through the last war, so understand things a bit. We shall always be pleased for him to spend his leave here if he cares to, and we are giving him the address of an uncle of ours who is living alone in Brighton—I think they will get on well together and be company for each other.

We hope to send him back safe and sound to you before very long, and that sometime in the not-too-distant future, he will be able to bring you to see us and the places he has visited. I think after this, our countries will be drawn nearer and it will be easier to get across the seas.

We have been looking over the church and some of the old houses in the village this afternoon, but I expect Clarence will tell you about that when he writes.

Hoping that you and your small sons are well, we have seen your photographs.

Yours truly,
Dorothy R. Starbuck

ᕖ

Canadian Army Overseas
January 20, 1942


Dearest Mummy,

Sent a wire today, I'm so worried about you not receiving any mail.
I can't bear to think that you are under the impression I'm getting
used to being away from you and neglecting to write.

I went through all the stores today to try and get a valentine, but
can't so far, and would like to send one now so that you get it for
Valentine's Day—it is getting rather late already.

. . .

We got the number "Yours" for the orchestra and is it ever swell,
and the other new one, "Tell Your Troubles to the Breeze." They
make me lonely, and believe it or not playing at dances, whenever
we come to a nice number such as these two, I always say to myself,
"To You, Hazel." It makes me feel good inside just to do that.

Went to a show in camp tonight: Carol Lombard, "In Name only."
Swell picture, and to think she was killed in a plane crash just a few
days ago, and for some reason the whole thing makes me feel terribly
lonely. Gee, Hazel, I miss you and your love terribly. Just the nearness
of you would make an awful difference, ease this terrible longing. Oh
darling, if I could only fold you into my arms and kiss your hair right
on the part. Sit by the fire these cold nights, side by side, hand in hand,
and the two kiddies at our feet. Oh, Hazel, at times this life becomes
unbearable. I pray and pray God, to get me home safe to you—oh, so
soon. Why, oh why, in heavens did I ever leave for the army? Lord
knows. I'm paying, and paying dearly, and I mean every word of this
darling. Now, please don't accuse me of failing you, etc. How could I
possibly, loving you the way I do? I keep busy at everything: I read a
lot (and, by the way, Hazel, could you send me the "Star Weekly"—

I mean, buy them and read them yourself, and then send them on to me, I like them), play plenty of music, anything to rush the time away.

Bye-bye, darling. Love and kisses, and hugs to the kiddies.

Love and kisses,
Clarence

ભ

Canadian Army Overseas
January 22, 1942

Dear Mummy,

. . . It was quite a letter, wasn't it darling? I do get awfully lonely
at times and maybe my letters get awful mushy. Well, it is the way
I feel and I meant every word of it.

I was just looking through my snap album and that one picture of
you standing by the house just after you got back from Toronto is
getting quite soiled, and it's the one I like best. A secret (don't tell
anyone)—if you got all the kisses I've implanted on it you wouldn't
wonder if Clarence really loves you or not.

I suppose you received my telegram saying I've received everything
including 4 airgraphs, my birthday cable, and the one at Christmas
too. Did you get mine at Xmas? I sent it on the 19th of December.
I enquired about airgraphs on this side and they are not being made,
so the reason for not receiving any. As for airmail, you once told
me it took as long as the ordinary route so I didn't bother sending
letters that way.

I'm going on dental parade in the morning. My gums are terribly
sore and bleed a lot, even with all the care I gave them. The teeth
are in fair shape but the gums are bad. Maybe they will pull them
this time, although I don't fancy the idea. I'll write again tomorrow
night and let you know.

We are in quite a layout here. Huts something like in Shilo, only
corrugated iron, and bullet-like barrels—that is, a round roof and
no facilities of any kind. Toilets out in the cold, no showers and
we bathe in tubs, and is the weather ever cold. A lot of snow, something new for this part of England. The country side is just like the
pictures on Xmas cards. The snow lays thick on the trees and over-
laps the eaves—nice, but decidedly miserable. We have one stove in

the centre of the of the hut, and six feet from it you might as well be outside. We have plenty of covers so we aren't cold in bed. Dick Nunn is having a bath at present and has the tub up against the stove and says he is freezing on one side and roasting on the other. I've my feet up against the stove myself. We are miles away from anywhere, so we sure hug the stove.

Well mummy, I've got to scrub up a little too, so here goes. May be chilly, but necessary about once a week.

How are the kiddies? Give them a big hug and kiss from daddy.

Take care of yourself,
love and kisses,
Daddy

☙

Canadian Army Overseas
January 23, 1942

Dearest Mummy,

Just came in from a show in our mess hut, "Rhythm on the River."
I enjoyed it real well and they sang your favourite piece, "Only Forever." Everything seems to remind you to me, I must be in love.

Well, I've been to the dentist and back and still have all my teeth,
and [was] advised to use salt instead of toothpaste for the next few
days to toughen up my gums. And had a couple of fillings replaced.
I'm glad, I was rather afraid I might lose a few teeth.

Well, we went into the dentist at Lewes, and in an open truck was
it ever cold and snowing a little. When we came back it was raining
buckets but much warmer. I got soaked, I hope I don't catch another cold. My clothes are all drying around the stove, yet lucky we
are supplied with two uniforms now or I would have had to miss
the show. It is still raining and all the snow has disappeared, everything is running water. What a country: winter one day, and the
rainy season the other.

Our orchestra leader hasn't come back off leave, we were all away
at the same time. He went up visiting friends in Glasgow and got
pleurisy and was taken to a hospital. And we have a dance to play
for on Wednesday (only five days), I hope he gets back on time or
I'll have to take over and Lord knows I have trouble enough playing
my part. We were asked to play for one tomorrow night and I
turned it down. Do you know I haven't seen any of the boys for
weeks, we are spread over such an area.

. . .

This is for Rollie. Hi there, Daddy's little man! Are you having lots
of fun playing in the snow? What are your pals' names? Does Mur-

ray get out much with you or is he too small for you? Do you play nice with him when you do? And Rollie, are you a good boy for Mummy? Sometimes she tells me you are naughty. That is not nice. Don't forget you have the nicest little Mummy in the world and the only one you will ever have. Better be nice to her because someday you won't have her anymore—then you'll be sorry. Be a good boy or Daddy will be cross when he comes home. Give Murray a nice big hug and a kiss for me.

. . .

Well be good and take care of yourself Mummy,

All of my love and kisses,
Clarence

☙

Canadian Army Overseas
January 24, 1942


Darling,

I've just finished my laundry so I am writing a note. I don't know
where to hang my clothes, it is still raining. Outside of rain, we
have rain apparently. I've my things hung all over the place: eight
hankies, two underwear shorts, three tops, two shirts, two towels,
five pair of socks—took me a couple of hours getting it cleaned.
Boiled all my hankies and white clothes. This hand-scrubbing
business don't seem to get things very white no matter how
much I scrub, so boiling does the trick.

Send plenty of writing paper Mummy, the stuff sure is hard to get
here outside of Salvation Army paper, and we have to keep asking
for it.

Do you know it is over a month since I've had something good
to eat. I mean something different, Canadian, for instance. So I
am sure looking forward to a parcel of peanut butter etc., etc. Even
tea, coffee, and sugar are very nice. I'm developing the tea habit too
darling, and I catch myself writing English expressions, leave alone
talking. I'll be quite the Englishman when I get back—tea drinking
and accent—how will you like that?

I understand we are due for another change of scenery; anything
would be better than this mudhole. It isn't to be very far away but
a better place, can't say anymore about that.

Bye-bye for now darling, I love you. How are the kiddies today?

All of my love and kisses,
Clarence

Canadian Army Overseas
February 4, 1942


Dear Mummy,

. . . I've been patiently waiting for almost a week. Got a letter from Dad then, and expected one from you the next day, but none till today and I understand we have lost a bunch as well. Received your parcel yesterday and the book. I like them, and I'll repeat in case the letter in which I mentioned it gets lost, buy the Star Weeklies and after you have read them send them on to me, comics and all.

Your letter . . . makes me awfully lonely and hungry. You mentioned bathing Murray, tucking him in, etc., and going different places to eat. Gosh all. Gee that makes me hungry when I think of hashes, stews, hash, stew, hash and stew and hash.

Went to a boxing contest last night in New Haven. All army boys fought and they were good. The heavyweights fight tomorrow night in Lewes so I'll go to that too . . . something different than blowing a horn or reading. Do you know Hazel, when I get back home I'm afraid I'll be a real stick in the mud. I don't care to go anyplace or do anything anymore, and when I have any Canadian eats I don't even go to the canteen.

. . .


Yes, the parcel was swell. And Rollie's cane was busted all in little pieces—it was good all the same. I like that peppermint candy. You ask if I received two of your Xmas parcel[s]. I did. I've received four airgraphs and your cables. Have you received mine? One at Xmas and another last week?

Yes darling, it is well over a year since we have seen each other. It has gone by so fast at that. But my it was a lonely year for me Hazel, and I do hope they don't last much longer. I love you Mummy. Oh, so much.

Received the Lafleche Press with my picture in it and all the others, but what a picture! I hope I don't actually look like that.

Take care of yourself darling, and tell Rollie that when Daddy gets back he might do something about that little sister he wants. Tell him that Daddy has the money to buy one.

Bye darling,
love,
Clarence

❧

Canadian Army Overseas
February 7, 1942


Dear Mummy,

So it is real cold there. Too bad the house has to be so cold—no
wonder Murray has croup.

. . .

I understand we have lost quite a lot of mail coming this way.
That probably explains why I haven't received the cigarettes sent
by the Lafleche Legion. Steve and James received theirs; as for the
others, I don't know, haven't seen them.

. . .

So, you folks in Canada, that is on the west coast, are getting nervous over Japan. Air raids, eh! Well, if they ever got mixed up in one
they'd certainly have reasons for being nervous. I'm glad you are in
a small town while these Japanese threats are in the wind. You are
as safe as a bug in a rug in Lafleche.

So, you have received notice re taxes and the house being up for
sale—I did leave you in a mess! I guess you'll have to pay something
on the taxes. Are they still charging you taxes while I'm in the services? I don't believe they can. Maybe with the house in your name
they can. See someone who would know, and, if necessary, to wade
[through] the taxes while I'm away. Sell the house to me, because
I do know that a person on active service is exempt from taxation.
Ask T.H. about it, he probably would know what to do. As for ar-
rears, I believe they can collect that. What do you think of the idea?
You could use the extra money?

So Murray is part Chinese is he? So he is starting to talk. He will
soon be asking questions about his old man pretty soon and all he

will have for a daddy is a picture till this is over. I'll bet he really is
cute. Is he much bigger than Rollie was at the same age? Lord,
but I do miss the kiddies. Is Rollie going to school?

. . .

We are going to broadcast again some time in the near future.
Our Orchestra is going to furnish the music, and again later on
twice this spring. I can't give you any definite date so you will have
to enquire from the CBC. Records will be taken and sent over to
Canada. If I can find out a definite date I'll wire mummy, so that
you can hear us. And I believe I'll have a chance to say something.

Boy, my throat is bothering me now. I'll go to the first aid post and
get a couple of aspirins and then roll in. My ears even ache. I guess
I'll see the doc in the morning.

So you are sending me a Valentine? That's nice, I'm sending one too.
Late, but as it is they were only put on the market a few days ago.
I hope you get it.

With it all Hazel, I love you, and give the kiddies a big hug
and a kiss for me—or has Rollie grown out of the kissing age?

Love,
Daddy

∽

Canadian Army Overseas
February 10, 1942


Dear Mummy,

Well, here I am again, feeling pretty punk, still have a sore throat.
Went in to see the M.O. and had my throat painted and got some
mouth wash, but it doesn't seem to help. I've stayed inside so much
this last week that I've decided to got out tonight even if I get pneumonia. So, I'm going to the boxing tournament in Lewes tonight.

How is the weather there now? I understand you have no more
official weather reports in Canada and that sugar is rationed. It
brings the war rather close to home doesn't it? I suppose everyone
is talking blackouts etc. in case the Japs try a raid. I'm sure glad
you are out in a small town, I know what happens when a city is
bombed. I've seen them and I've heard the sad stories.

Gosh, I'm hungry, supper is just about due and I could do with some
good old Canadian eats about now. Some mail has arrived dated the
9th of Jan. today, but none for me, maybe tomorrow. I'm always looking forward to your mail, that is about all I have to look forward to.

How are the kiddies? Is Murray's croup better? Must be by now as
it is over a month since you wrote about it. Did you get my letter
asking about taxes?

We are going to broadcast some time soon; that is, have records
made to send over to Canada. The orchestra is playing for the
broadcast on the sixteenth and the band on another broadcast
sometime in April, and I'll probably have a chance to say hello.
Supper is on, so bye darling, write soon. I need smokes.

All of my love,
Clarence

☙

Canadian Army Overseas
February 20, 1942

Hello Darling,

Well, the broadcast is over and was I ever nervous when I spoke to you through the mike. I forget what I said so it did no good for me to write it down. By the time I set my saxophone down and got to the mike I was so darned excited I couldn't think. I forgot I had a message written in my pocket, so when I was up to the mike I had to say something. Couldn't take time to look through my pockets for the note so I just let fly, and what did I say? I hope it was something appropriate because I do love you so.

I wasn't the least bit nervous playing the sax, and a good thing I wasn't, because I played lead, that is the solo parts, and if I would have got jittery it might have been worse. I dedicated "Tell Your Troubles to the Breeze" to you darling, but I understand the Padre made rather a mess of the singing. The words were there anyway mummy, and every note I blew was for you.

Well, [it's] after the broadcast, which was held in the Paris Theatre, London. What a theatre! I've never seen anything so classy in my life, and huge! Simply thousands of seats (no audience though), all deep chairs, cushioned arm rests, and, well, just like a chesterfield chair, all in a deep rich red, and ankle deep carpets also. Oh, yes, we broadcasted over the British Broadcasting Corporation first and then we made our record for Canada. After the Broadcasts we went to one of the swellest restaurants in London, the Criterion, and had a five course meal (I didn't have the least idea what to do with all the silverware, about eight deep on either side):

1st course was beer, and good beer for a change;
2nd—some sort of vegetable mixture, all diced;
3rd—soup;

THE SOUTH SASKATCHEWAN REGIMENT ORCHESTRA. FRONT ROW, FROM LEFT TO RIGHT: HEDLEY MUNRO, SAXOPHONE AND LEADER (FROM ESTEVAN, SASK.); DICK NUNN, SAXOPHONE (KENNEDY, SASK.); CLARENCE; AND [?] HOGAN, GUITAR (MOOSE JAW, SASK.). SECOND ROW, FROM LEFT TO RIGHT: ALBERT RUTZ, TROMBONE (CALGARY, ALBERTA); JOE HEINZ, TRUMPET (BIENFAIT, SASK.); AND WILF HONEYCHURCH, TRUMPET (CALGARY). BACK ROW: FRED PICKNEY, DRUMS (ESTEVAN, SASK.); AND ART BROCHER, BASS (MONTREAL, QUEBEC).

4th—meat, spuds, vegetables, pickles. And the meat was steak, first I've had in England, and all I could get of it too;
5th—raisin pie and whipped cream, side dish of cheddar cheese, etc. Latter, was swell.

After all this we went into the lounge for coffee and cigarettes— quite classy, eh! And all to the expense of the BBC for our services broadcasting a half hour. Then Jerry Wilmont, the Canadian correspondent who announces for the Canadians here, got nine rooms for the eighteen of us in the Gordon Mansion, a swell hotel in the heart of London. And in the evening he took us all to the Hammersmith Palais for a floor show and dance, and that was something, the best London provides. Two swell orchestras furnished the music, the show was dancing and singing (very good too), and I danced all evening. Jerry Wilmont acted as chaperone and acquainter. If any of us stood back he would come over with some girl on his arm and make you dance. I can remember only one girl's name. She was rather plain but expensively dressed and she insisted . . . her name was Rose Mary . . . and she talked ballet dancing and opera all evening and wanted to know about entertainment in Canada and what you looked like and my kiddies. I was rather glad to finish the dance and when I got Jerry I asked him what it was I just finished dancing with. He laughed and said, "Viscount Gage's daughter and she knows it." In all I had a good time for a change. Everyone was so friendly and said how we put on a good program, most of it bologna but they say the truth hurts. What do you think of our orchestra Hazel? Is it all right for a bunch of ham and eggers?

Received your letter . . . thought I had lost it. Sending some snaps darling, more in my next letter. I like to spread them out, I'm sure the mermaids aren't interested.

All of my love Mummy and big hug and kisses for the kiddies. And as for you, what I wouldn't do.

Bye-bye,
I love you,
Daddy

☙

Canadian Army Overseas
February 24, 1942


Dear Mummy,


. . .


The other night one of the s.s.r. boys, while being challenged by the
sentry, started being smart and wouldn't answer the sentry's calling
to halt and advance slowly to be recognized. Instead of doing that
he stayed halted and covered his face with his hands and did a dance
or something, and for his troubles the sentry fired and killed him instantly (shot through the heart). The sentry was exonerated and the
verdict of the court martial was, "Private Blanchard of the s.s.r.s met
his death from a shot fired by a sentry on duty. The deceased, failing
to comply with the sentry's challenge to advance and be recognized,
and making motions as if to hide his identity and charge the guard."
Really sad Hazel, because the chap killed was a swell kid and full of
devil, but his devilry went too far. As we are in a war zone in danger
of invasion at any time, the guards are jittery and are told to shoot
and ask questions after. But somebody had to do something like
what happened to drive home the fact that fooling around with the
sentry is dangerous. I can assure you that when a challenge of Halt!!!!
snaps at us now, we halt, and I don't mean maybe. The funeral was
today. The brass band furnished the music. The Colonel at the end
of the ceremony said just a few words. "Boys, you see what happened. This young man we've just buried, through his own foolishness brings grief to his loved ones and to the poor chap who was the
sentry, which I must say knew his duty. And in the future boys, respect the sentries. They have their duty to perform for our own safety.
So let's not have anything like this happen again." Just another one
of those things that do happen in the army.

Well Hazel, life still goes on. Here it is [the] usual monotonous
way: inspections by generals, route marches, diverse training stunts.
I'm so sick of it all, being hollered at, etc. Thank heavens for the

band and orchestra, it sure helps pass the time. We are to play for a dance Wednesday, another Friday, and the band concert in Lewes Saturday night. I do enjoy the musical part of this life, but I do get awful lonesome for home, you and the kiddies.

. . .

By the time you get this, spring will be around the corner and you will be looking forward to nice weather. I noticed the rhododendrons are ready to blossom here. They are so pretty and the weather is becoming much milder as the days grow longer. Yes, it will be nice here in a few weeks. I'm glad to see the nice weather and flowers, etc., but it does make me lonely. Darling, I love you and at times feel so alone.

Maybe I shouldn't have written in the mood I am, but I do miss you.

All my love,
Clarence

ɔ

Canadian Army Overseas
February 25, 1942


Hello Darling,

Received the kiddies parcel of candies and the two Valentines. I am ashamed of myself Hazel, because I didn't send any, although early in January I looked all around for nice valentines and couldn't find any of any sort. So, when they were on the market it was Feb. the 7th, too late then, so I didn't send any. Am I forgiven?

I just wrote last night and there really isn't an awful lot to write about more than weather, etc. Oh yes, I was out on a scheme today running up and down hills that were hills. I can run further uphill now than I could run on the level in peacetime, so I'm in good physical shape.

How are my little men? I keep looking at the last photos and it is too bad they are so blurred. You look swell darling, as far as the outline goes, but I can't distinguish the features. Anyway it's you and I love you.

Take care of yourself darling,

Love,
Daddy

[P.S.] Rollie, thanks for the Valentine, and give Murray a hug for his. Bye, be good little men. Did you hear daddy on the radio?

☙

Canadian Army Overseas
February 27, 1942


Hello Mummy,

. . .

Tomorrow, the s.s.r. band is to lead the war weapons parade in Lewes and play for a programme that night. And after that the orchestra is to play for an officers' dance in some big shot's home. So, I will have a lot to write about on Sunday.

How are the kiddies mummy? All fine, I hope. Rereading some of your letters I noticed your advice about going to church. I keep that up quite well Hazel. I haven't forgotten my religion or the numerous prayers for you and the boys. Well, I guess I will close for now.

Love and kisses to everyone, and an especially long kiss and hug darling.

Bye,
Daddy

෴

Canadian Army Overseas
March 5th, 1942


Darling,

Received three letters of yours today . . . and they were swell. I'm
afraid I'm very much in love with you Hazel—very, very much.
I'll answer your letters as I go and then give you all news if any.

You mention Canadian soldiers escorting prisoners back. That is
true enough darling, but the ones that are chosen for the job are
Canadians that have been over here two years or more, and there
are so many over here that one would have to be born with a horse-
shoe. Yesterday, 30 from our regiment left for Canada as instructors,
mostly NCOs whose health isn't any too good, and men that are too
old to stand the gaff. But I understand that the younger ones are to
be back in eight months. The older ones are to stay as instructors;
the younger ones will instruct a second S.S.R. battalion and come
back with them. Yes, they sure are lucky to get back, even for a day,
and they will be getting a few weeks leave. . . .

. . .


Yes, Hazel I think your idea of a larger place is good. The boys
are growing up and will need a room. And as to fixing up the shack
anymore, [it] is a waste of money.

Yes, received airmail letters, but they took five weeks, and the airgraphs take almost as long. I received the LifeSavers and the kiddies'
Valentines, yours too, but haven't received the parcel of the 21st yet.

. . .


So, the kiddies weren't feeling very good. And you say Murray
knows how to love and that he is really cute. Well, if I was ever to
get near you I'm afraid you would find Murray's love very mild.

. . .

So you wonder what I would like in parcels. Candy of all sorts,
cake (as far as cookies, they usually get busted all to hell), gum,
nuts, canned meats, peanut butter, butter, liquorice, bars, soap,
razor blades, tobacco, shaving lotions and cream, etc., etc.—hankies,
towels, socks, etc., etc., and a note saying you still love me. Is that a
large enough order? And the other parcels, make them cigarettes.

So Earl is a daddy and it is a daughter. I'd like a daughter myself,
and don't ever think I'm not going to try when I get [home]—
and it isn't going to be as long as you say. . . .

Did you hear our broadcast yet? I saw "Blossoms in the Dust"
here last week and thought it was very good.

So Rollie is beginning to look like his old man is he? Poor kid!
I wired you Xmas, didn't you get it? Another score to settle
with Adolph. Did you get the snaps I sent in my last letter?

Well Hazel, last Saturday we played for the war weapons procession
in Lewes. We marched along the main drag—thank heavens the
weather was grand. And the band concert that night went over
marvellously. As for the dance, it was an officers' dance, sedate and
formal. It was terrible trying to make a job of it, but we got by.
And since, we have been doing nothing much. As for me, I'm
fed up with it all and lonesome a lot of the time.

Well darling, I haven't much news, everything is quiet here and
I've no worries concerning myself, so don't you worry Hazel.

All of my love,
Clarence

P.S. Love and kisses darling.

Canadian Army Overseas
March 10, 1942


Hello Darling,

Received the parcel today that you mailed January 22nd. Takes
quite a long while doesn't it? Nevertheless, it was swell. The sugar
bag broke and got into everything, but I gathered most of it up.
And thanks for the soap because it sure is hard to get here. Those
chocolate puffs were swell, the first I've had since I left Canada.
Oh, yes, the grapefruit juice—what is the catch? Is it for a
hangover or is it because I like it? It was swell; that is, the parcel.

. . .

So Rollie is starting to visit the dentist? He will no doubt act up
after the dentist works on it. It will be good time to get him washing his teeth after every meal or he will have to go back to the
dentist. And he also has a bank account. I hope it increases and I
intend to help it increase plenty when I get back. He will have
use for it when he grows up, something I didn't have.

Well, here, things are awful quiet. You wouldn't think there
was a war on, only for what we read and hear.

Well, we are playing for a dance at Battle tomorrow night and
one at Heathfield on Friday and I'm going on a 48 hour pass to
Brighton Saturday, see a few shows and do a little skating. This
place out here is driving me nuts—mud, mud and mud.

A great big hug for Murray, and I suppose Rollie just wants to
shake hands now. Tell them Daddy thinks of them a lot.

Love and kisses darling,
Daddy

ᘓᘔ

Canadian Army Overseas
March 15th, 1942


Dear Mummy,

Received your letters . . . yesterday, and 300 cigs from the Canadian
Legion. Thank heavens for that, I was wondering if they had forgotten me as the other chaps received theirs around Christmas time.


. . .


I'll bet it is cute to hear the two little fellows playing and scolding
one another. And yes, Rollie will soon be going to school. It will be
rather lonely for you and Murray when he does. I think of my two
boys an awful lot and wonder how they are getting on. Of course I
do think of their mummy occasionally too, enough to make me not
want to go anywhere or do anything she wouldn't approve of, and
that is the truth darling.

I was going to get on a forty-eight-hour pass this weekend, but a
dance turned up Friday night for the officers at corps headquarters
and another for the artillery last night. So I didn't go on pass. The
dance at corps headquarters was a mucky-muck affair—generals,
brigadiers, colonels, etc.; and their lady friends. The ball room was
swell and what a floor, it looked like a mirror. And well, it was the
nicest room I've ever seen. Carved oak all over the place and the
ceiling was about forty feet up. Immense chandeliers all lit up.
Some lord's home, I can't remember the name. And as for the
dance last night, much more to our liking. Was for privates here
near Lewes and in just an ordinary dance hall. And quite noticeable,
everyone seemed to enjoy themselves while at the other dance
everyone seemed bored to death.


. . .

So the carnival turned out swell did it? That's great! I hope the
Legion keeps on sending smokes.

So your dad thinks you are quite lazy when you sleep past 8:30.
I think you are using some sense, because when the kiddies start
off to school you will have to be up earlier. And anyway darling, get
some sleep for me too. I always seem to be getting up in the middle
of the night, five-thirty now. I hope you had a good time at the
masquerade dance. I'll bet it was fun, you lucky punks, everything
here is so curtailed. Dances have to be over with by ten-thirty (cur-
few law), and the English people don't go in for anything like a carnival or anything like it.

Well bye-bye darling,
Take care of yourself, all of my love,
Clarence

[p.s] Did you get my Easter card? xxxooo I'm lonesome.

Canadian Army Overseas
March 17, 1942


Hello Mummy,

Received a parcel of eats from mother today and I'm sure going to
have a feed tonight. We have had a plenty miserable day of it today.
We were out in the hills watching a demonstration, and of course it
started to rain and still is. I got soaked to the hide and walked back
the small distance of six miles. I don't believe that this Army life is
much to my liking. I can think of much pleasanter things, such as
being home with you and the kiddies.

Well darling, it really is miserable tonight. The rain is simply pelting
down and we were in a mud hole as it was, so what is it going to be
like now that the rainy season has started? I suppose spring is in the
air in Lafleche—gardening and all that in full swing. Are you going
to put one in this year or will it be worthwhile?

The flowers are starting to bloom here. I noticed some of the crocuses
today, yellow ones. Everything will soon be a riot of colour, which is
sure nice to see to anyone from the prairies. You wouldn't believe it if
you saw the millions of flowers that are in bloom through the summer months here. I wish you were here darling. As it is, scenery and
all, I still say give me home, wife and kiddies any day.

The 17 of March, St. Patrick's, sure makes me lonely. I can still
remember the plays I was always in and we used to argue so much
over. Are they, or have they had, the annual St. Patrick's do again
this year? Who directed, since Nap isn't feeling so well? How are
the kiddies? Is Rollie a good boy? I keep continually trying to picture Murray, I'm missing the cutest stage of his life. Tell them
daddy thinks about them often.

Well darling, I really haven't an awful lot to write about, everyday is
just another day.

Bye-bye, are you getting more of my mail finally?

All of my love,
Clarence

&

Canadian Army Overseas
March 19, 1942


Hello Darling,

. . .


Just in case you don't get my previous letters, I received your
parcel and also Mother's. We were out on stretcher-bearing yesterday morning, carrying patients up and down hills, and boy, oh boy,
that is a tough job. Every muscle in my body is sore, I could hardly
get out of bed this morning.

Well darling, I guess I'll close. I really haven't anything to write
about, nothing happens. I'm fine, but do get awful lonesome.

All my love,
Daddy

☙

Canadian Army, England
March 25, 1942


Dear Hazel,

We have just received word that a large amount of our mail (Canadian) was lost through enemy action. Darned the luck. So no wonder I've been without mail. I was starting to get a little peeved and maybe some of my letters might have been a little sarcastic—I take a lot of it back now if they were unduly so.

Gosh, I hope to get something soon. I received one airmail letter from you since Jan. 15th, and I could most certainly do with smokes. And I do need underwear too, shorts and tops, something light. Tops, size 38, and short size 30 (for men)—if not procurable send 32s.

You should be getting another raise in your check soon, which ought to help some. How are you doing now, are you getting enough darling?

I sent you a birthday wire, did you get it on time? It seemed so empty when I sent it using numbers instead of writing it out. And one can say so little and has so much he wants to say, but it all boils down to this: I'm down right sick of all this, I want to go home to you and the kiddies. I'm plenty lonely at times.

How are the little fellows doing? Rollie still naughty? How is he doing at school? And Murray is growing a lot I suppose.

Well, take care of yourself, and a happy, happy birthday darling, and all my love. I wished I was there and hope to be next year at this time.

Your loving hubby,
Clarence

⌒

Canadian Army Overseas
March 26th, 1942


Dear Mummy,

Received letters . . . today. It seems funny to read all about bliz-
zards, the weather here has been swell. Flowers are starting to
bloom all over and we have had quite a lot of sun. The grass is
just like a carpet. Whenever I get a chance I lay out in the sun;
I've quite a tan already but Lord bless the schemes. We are out
continually now and heaven knows when they will let up. I'm
dog tired most of the time. We get in just long enough to read
our mail, clean up, and rush a few answering letters, and away on
some other jaunt through the country. Just in from one now and
going out again at midnight. I did a bunch of washing and read
your letters and am writing and I would like to get a little sleep
too. It's 8 p.m. now, so this will be short as we have to march
twelve miles before breakfast, which is to be at 4:30 a.m. So I'll
just skim an answer to your letters.

. . .

I agree Hazel, Lafleche is a thing or place of the past as far as I'm
concerned. There certainly isn't a thing there and frankly as soon as
you get away darling the better. I will like it, and thinking it over, as
far as you're concerned, make it Windsor [Hazel's brother, Earle,
lived in Windsor, Ontario].

So, Rollie can't figure out why I'm not home . . . poor tyke. I'll bet
he does miss his daddy, as poor a daddy as I've been.

I'm glad you are receiving more letters . . . I've all of yours so far.

. . .

Well, I guess I'll close, and in answer to your question about leaving Lafleche, I suggest you go out on the farm with your dad for awhile, save bills, etc., eats, lights, rent the house, sell furniture, pay what you wish on taxes and then sell the house and move to Windsor.

All of my love,
Daddy

P.S. The suggestion re: the farm. May be tough, but the quickest solution to getting ahead and therefore the quicker out of the dump. Love and kisses.

☙

April 4th, 1942

Dear Mummy,

Received [your] letters a few days back, but having been on schemes
Tuesday, Wednesday and Thursday, I've had plenty of time to read
and reread them. I've also received 300 Sweet Caps from you and a
parcel from Mother. I haven't received yours as yet, I suppose it will
pop up about Tuesday. I'm going on leave Wednesday and I believe
it is Glasgow and Newcastle this time, since I'm getting a free war-
rant. Kayo and I are going together, he is nice company. Anyway,
I'm sure glad to get away for a few days.

So you are surprised at me liking tea. Yes, I am becoming quite the
Englishman. Hope I don't acquire the accent, but wherever we go it
is inevitably tea that we must have. Coffee is practically a memory,
only for what we get from home, so no wonder we get to like tea—
frankly, it isn't bad.

. . .

Did you receive my Easter and birthday cable? I sent it on the 31st.
Your birthday darling, I didn't forget it either. And a happy birthday for Rollie too. This will be a little late but nevertheless I haven't
forgotten. Did you get my Easter card? Was it in time?

Yes, I received the book of Lifesavers, they were swell. And I received the parcel too, also the 300 cigs of February. . . .

Don't worry about Steve ever escorting prisoners back to Canada
in the near future. They have to be over here 2 years first, so that is
a good six months yet. He was turned down as an instructor to go
back to Canada, and re being smart, Steve can have his three hooks.
I'm having a decent time, no fuss and left alone, and when it comes
to action, if and when, he will notice what stripes mean and I hope
he can live up to it, but have my doubts.

As far as escorting prisoners go, privates or NCOs have the same chance (and if you are lucky enough). All everyone can do is keep their fingers crossed.

So Murray is quite the guy is he? I don't know what I'd give to see you all for even an hour. I'll be a complete stranger soon, it's soon two years since we've been together.

Well darling, whatever you do in Lafleche don't put any more money into anything but taxes. Get them cleaned up and sit tight, so that you can get away from that dump. And as I said in a previous letter don't you think it will help you save up if you can go out with your dad for a month or two and get on your feet. I don't care to even think of going back to Lafleche for reason of past, present and future. And the sooner you get away and get acquainted will help C.O.B. when he gets back for the purpose of getting a job. And do keep your eyes open when you get to Windsor, and maybe Earl can help plenty too. It would be swell if I could walk into a job when I get back. That may be assuming too much, but would rather be nice for everyone involved.

. . .

Well darling, bumming and all, I love you and will write a long letter re my leave as it goes by. So expect a long letter soon.

. . .

All my love,
Clarence

P.S. Received your letter re the broadcast you missed. Gosh, that is too bad darling. I wished you could of heard it. I meant everything I said and I do hope it will be rebroadcast.

☙

Canadian Army Overseas
April 6th, 1942

Dear Mummy,

Hello darling, just received your Easter telegram. Thank you mummy.
Today is Easter Monday and I was rather blue and the telegram came
along to make things brighter. Did you get the one I sent?

Well Hazel, tomorrow noon I'm going on leave. I'm going to tour
around this time—Glasgow, Paisley, Edinburgh, Motherwell, Newcastle—spend a day in each place and travel at night. I do hope the
weather will be decent.

Today I spent the day cleaning and pressing clothes and shining
buttons. No band practice or parades for the ones going on leave,
so I've got all cleaned up.

How are the kiddies? Keeping in the best I hope. And are you all
better I hope. This [is] pretty nice writing paper isn't it? Mother
sent it to me. The boys are all trying to borrow some, but no
chance, decent paper is hard to get.

The fellows want to iron on this table so I guess I'll have to quit.

Well, bye for now darling, have the CBC rebroadcast our
programme yet. Take care of yourself. What kind of a hat
did you get for Easter? Something outlandish?

Bye mummy, all my love,
Daddy

[P.S.] I'll make a diary of my leave and tell you all about what I see.
Love and kisses.

⁂

Canadian Army Overseas
April 8, 1942

Dearest Mummy,

Well, I'm sitting in the YMCA in London. Just had supper. Got here
about 2 p.m., went and saw the picture "Smilin' Through." Really
swell, have you seen it? Hazel, it was in Technicolor. Looking out
the window, I can see Piccadilly Circus, millions of people milling
around down there. Somehow London makes me wonder how so
many people in such a dirty looking place can exist. The buildings
are all old and of grey stone, winding streets, foggy, smoky, such a
rush, everyone seems on the run. Crowded homes and office buildings, the continual threat of an air raid. I'd feel like a rat in a trap if
I had to stay here much longer. A lot of the buildings have been
flattened to the ground and new modern flats and blocks are being
built, so probably after the war London will come out of it remod-
elled, it needs to be. Well, I'm catching the 9:35 train for Glasgow
from Euston Station here, I suppose it will be terribly crowded.
I hope not. When I get to Glasgow I'll tell you all about the trip.

April 10. Hello, this is Glasgow. I've got a room in the Overseas
Club with four other chaps, one from the air force and two others
from the artillery, all swell chaps. The air force chap is an American
from Miami and quite interesting. I didn't write any yesterday as our
train got [in] at 8 a.m. and I slept all day. It rained all day anyway. I
went to a variety show at night, good music and dancing, cost me . . .
about $1.00, but I had heard how good it was. Wasn't disappointed
either. After the show, I and the air force chap (his name was, or is,
Norman) had lunch in the canteen and proceeded to our room and
chatted to the wee hours this morning, we couldn't sleep. His work
was as a desk clerk in the Sunny Glade Hotel, Miami, and apparently has seen practically everyone of note in North America. He is
about 38, nice looking and quiet. This morning Norm and I went
on a tour through the Tennent Brewery, and after showing us
around they brought us a case of beer, or rather "Strong Ale"([that]
was the name). So we sat and chatted over that. Well, with all that

beer in us we did plenty of talking. In the afternoon we went out to a town named Stirling. It is a little early yet to see the scenery at its best, but Scotland and its ruggedness is really nice to see. . . . Norm just came in, it is 11 p.m. and still reasonably light out. We are on two hours fast time here and quite far north. Well, night-night darling, everyone in the room has so much to say and questions to ask that I'll have to quit. Love and kisses till tomorrow. Bye.

Hello, today is Saturday the 11th. The Overseas Club have what they call "Hospitality Hostesses" who undertake to keep the boys from overseas entertained, so they asked me this morning if I would like to tour the city with some of the boys so I agreed. This morning we went through Stewards jam factory, an enormous place and so clean. The work is done completely by women and I've never seen so many women in one place in my life. How they get along I don't know. The only men in the place work in the boiler rooms and that is about 20, and there must be all of two thousand women. Anyway, we were given tea and a sample of the jam they make with soda biscuits. This afternoon we are to tour the Clyde Docks where the Queen Mary was built and where other large well-known ships have been launched. And tonight, five [of] us are to go to the "Playhouse." I'll let you know all about the place in the morning. Tomorrow afternoon, we are going to the "Loch Lomond" for the afternoon. That is, Norm and I, he offers to pay the expenses. I've done fairly well, I've only spent a pound so far and [I have] three left. I'll just about make it. I'm getting low on smokes, I hope there will be some waiting for me when I get back.

Sunday morning. Well Hazel, I missed Mass this morning. Woke at ten-thirty, just had a wash and shave and [will] soon have dinner. We saw the big dry docks and moulds. So much to see and so little time to see them all. I'm still lost as to what it was all about, everything was so big. I believe it's raining, so it is. Norm is lying in bed and says we won't be going to Loch Lomond today, so as we were invited up to dinner and for the evening by one of the electric welders from the ship yards, a chap about forty, it being Sunday and nothing doing, it will be something.

Hello, just before turning in we went out for tea as they call it, a
nice home on the outskirts, and we had ham and eggs and canned
beans for supper. The best feed I've had since I've come to Glasgow.
The chap Norm and I [met] is Campbell Leitch. Met his wife who
is working in a munitions factory. We played rummy till about ten
and had lunch, and here I am. The Scotch people are really sociable.
Nighty-night, I'm half asleep now.

Hello, not much done today. I bought some orchestrations, these are
what I bought: "Stagecoach," "Jim," "If I Could Only Paint a Memory,"
"Lullaby Lagoon," "Intermezzo," "When Night is Thro," "Rustic Rhap-
sody." All nice numbers, and mostly sentimental tunes. As I was buying
them I kept thinking of what you would like. Now I'm near broke and
one more night here, so I'll go to a show tonight and back tomorrow.

Sorry, I didn't tell you about the "Playhouse." It was grand. It is a
dance palace or something with a floor show. In the centre of the
floor there is a large water fountain spraying rainbows of colour it
seems (light effects), and the fountain itself is of glass, transparent,
filled with goldfish—really a swell place, we got in for nothing. I
ordered tea and cakes for two as we sat watching the dancing, and
they charged six shillings for four small cup cakes and a pot of tea
for two. I got hooked for that, so we said if it cost that much to eat
let's at least get something for our money, let's go and have a dance.
We didn't know any women but Norm said, "Come on, they shouldn't
turn us down." But we couldn't get past the gates without a partner
or dancing tickets which would permit us to dance with the hostesses—jitney girls to me. At a shilling per ticket, I said no thank
you, and sarcastically remarked that I'd seen nicer dance halls in
Technicolor for a damned sight less and walked up into the balcony
and watched and listened to the orchestra. At least I can say I've
been in the nicest dance hall in Scotland and paid $1.50 for a 15
cent lunch. We had fun anyway. Well darling, I guess this will
be all. Tomorrow, I'm on my way back. I hope to get some mail.

Bye-bye, I guess I'll put this in an envelope and seal it, ready
to mail as soon as I get back.

All of my love,
Daddy

P.S. Have you heard our broadcast yet? I hope they do rebroadcast
it, I meant what I said. I'm lonesome and rather anxious to get back
with the boys, everybody is a stranger here. Bye Mummy, I love you.

ROLLIE'S NOTE: *One final message from Dad was included with the
letter above:*

April 15th

Hello,

I'm back, just got in. I'm dead tired, sat up in the train all night.
Got three of your letters, no smokes tho'—will have to bum some
more. Thanks for the letters. I'll post this and then answer yours
after a good sleep. Got a letter from mother too.

Bye for now,
love,
Clarence

❧

Canadian Army Overseas
April 17, 1942


Dear Mummy,

Heaven knows how I'm ever going to answer all the mail I've
received. Three letters from you, 1000 cigs (thanks a million), the
Toronto Star and a letter, Easter cards from you and the kiddies,
cards from O'Neills and two letters, two letters from Mother, one
from Camille [Clarence's youngest sister], one from Yvonne, one
from Elnora. I've been busy the last hour reading them and we are
going out on a seven-day scheme some time tonight. I've all my
equipment ready to jump into, my blankets rolled because we will
be sleeping under the stars. So it will be ten days before I can write
again, I suppose. But I'm going to bring my writing material along,
I may get a chance to write. I'll answer your letters first and the rest
can wait if I haven't time.

The cards were swell Mummy. I've got them in my treasure chest
(or that little cedar chest you gave me). I keep all my snaps and
things I value in it. I've still got that little aspirin box you sent with
the kisses in it and every time I open it I smile and think wouldn't
a real kiss be nice about now. One from you Hazel would be simply—well, I don't know how to put it into words—I ache all over
when I think of how much I miss you and love you.

So Murray counts up to six. Mother says he will be a much larger
boy than Rollie and that Rollie is going to be like me, poor kid.
As long as they are real healthy and apparently they are, especially
Murray, eating three plates of spuds.

. . .

So you are worried about the war; I'm not anymore. Things did
look bad, but what can you expect in the Far East? Hitler has to
[be] licked first and that is being done. As far as the Japs go at

present they are making headway, but that seems to be stopped
now—as long as we hold them, and take care as we hold them, and
take care of the Huns. As soon as Germany collapses, which will be
soon, Japan can hardly offer any opposition. What she got she took
easy, because munitions and supplies are all needed to beat Hitler's
ears back. And as soon as that is done and all the necessary munitions sent to the Far East it will soon be over. You wait and see,
and you won't wait long.

. . .

Well darling, all my love, and take care of yourselves. Has Rollie really decided on being a sign writer and mak[ing] his 3s like Daddy?
There is good money in it—if he shows tendencies that way encour-
age him along, it won't do him any harm.

Give them both a big hug and kiss from Daddy, and as far as you,
if I'd only get my arms about you Hazel you would then realise
how much I long for and love you.

Well darling, I want to try and write Mother a note before we
pull out, so bye-bye darling.

All my love,
Clarence

⁏

Canadian Army Overseas
April 22, 1942


Hello Mummy,

Well, here I am out on the scheme. We have sat around all day
and the weather feels pretty bad . . . not any too warm either. So
I'm having a grand and glorious miserable time. Slept comfortably
though. Last night swiped six blankets from the hospital truck and
it didn't rain for a wonder.

Yesterday afternoon we marched 17 miles and did my feet ever
get tired. I could hardly finish it off and I was sure glad to get here.
But tonight, we are to march all night. On top of being tired last
night and dying to lay down, I had to go around the 'B' company.
Company, I'm attached to [it] for the scheme). I had to go around
'B' Company with Major White and inspect the feet as I'm a first-
aider and tend to the blisters. And I saw some darned sore feet.
I taped and dressed blisters for three solid hours, finished the last
few with a flash[light]. Yes, I sure looked at plenty of feet and
didn't only see them either.

. . .

Did you get my Easter card and telegram? I received your cards and
your telegram, also the Easter parcels awhile back, also the 1000 cigs
just the other day. I wonder how much of my mail went down with
those 900 bags, some no doubt.

I'm writing in rather an awkward position sitting up against a tree
with my knees as a writing table, and my hands are getting cold.

Last night as I lay looking up through the trees the sky was
clear and my thoughts kept wandering back to our little house in
Lafleche. Then it would be about seven in the evening there, eleven
here. I kept wondering what you were doing—writing me, reading,

etc. I could just see you moving around the kitchen, picture your every little move and change of expression. I had a lump in my throat darling. I was wondering if you felt as lonely as I did, if you were longing for me as I long for you mummy—isn't life hell?

. . . as soon as I get back in from the scheme, just another six or seven days of misery, and then back to clean up for another. The next is to be 21 days and two hundred miles of marching as well as the manoeuvres. If I don't have flat feet after this it will be a wonder.

Take care of yourself darling. I'll close for now and if an opportunity comes along I'll write again.

Hugs and kisses to the kiddies,
all of my love darling,
Daddy

P.S. I'm awful hungry for something nice to eat. Bye-bye.

ᘒ

Canadian Army Overseas
April 26, 1942


Dear Mummy,

Well I'm back off the scheme and sure glad of it. It was the toughest I've ever been on. In the last five days of it, I got but six hours sleep, the last day I actually couldn't keep my eyes open. Thank heavens that is over—why I should I don't know—because there will be no end to schemes from now on. The wear and tear on a fellow is pretty hard. I'll be putting on years long before my time. My hair is quite grey, will soon be white over my ears. Do you think you will still like me with white hair? I believe in one of your letters you said you thought grey hair looked dignified, and in the same letter you told me to be careful and not lose it, to massage my scalp every day. My hair isn't thinning any darling, so I won't look too bad when I get home.

We got a bunch more new orchestrations and the nicest one of the lot in my estimation is "If I Could Paint a Memory." Have you ever heard it darling? It is really swell.

Gee, I expected to find some letters waiting for me after the scheme but no luck. I certainly look forward to your letters, and quite realize how you feel [if] my letters fail to come regularly. Well, I suppose I'll be getting a bunch of mail soon, including a parcel of eats I hope.

How are the kiddies keeping? Rollie much trouble? And is he getting to be quite the cartoonist? I get a kick out of his attempts at drawing and they are certainly not bad. And Murray, how is he doing? Big enough to get his way with Rollie now I suppose. I sure miss those little fellows. I keep trying to picture them as they are growing up, quite hopeless without snaps. Send the odd one darling.

Well darling, I believe I'll call this a letter. I'm "onesome" as Rollie would say. I miss and need you Mummy. And do I love you? I do.

Take care of yourself,
all of my love,
Clarence

శం

Canadian Army Overseas
April 27, 1942


Hello Mummy,

Here I am again and awful lonesome. A bunch of mail came and
none for me. It is disappointing, but I suppose the next mail will
do me justice. I'm awful blue tonight, the boys are all away but one.
I've had the sax out for awhile and played a bunch of sentimental
numbers and made myself feel worse. Gosh, it sounds lonely out-
doors as well. The wind sighing through the trees and so quiet in-
doors. Oh Hazel darling, to be with you again soon, oh, so soon.
At times I could go nuts. One would imagine a person would get
used to being away, I can't. I keep thinking of you, longing for you,
and there seems to be no end to this aching feeling. I hate being
alone. I want to be busy at something to sort of relieve the strain.
When I find myself alone as I am tonight I dwell on home, you,
and the kiddies. I must be in love to feel the way I do at times.
Oh, I hope this ends this year, indications point that way.

I guess maybe I had better stop all this sobbing, or I'll bore you
to death darling. Do you feel like this at times too mummy?

All of my love,
Clarence

❧

Canadian Army Overseas
April 29, 1942

Hello Darling,

Three cheers for our side. I've received two letters and the Star,
and a letter from you—feel much better.

Pretty nice writing paper, isn't this? Received it in one of Mother's
parcels. I could do with plenty [of] paper of the same kind or like it.
This stuff they call stationery here is going from bad to worse.

Thanks for the Star, it will keep one busy for a couple of evenings.
And your note don't sound so cheery, you ended up with, "I'm
bored to death."

So a lot of changes are taking place in Lafleche. The barber shop or
liquor store will make a swell drug store. Things must be looking up
for Adrien, and Bilodeau must be doing alright too, to be able to afford a bigger and better building for a post office, or is the Credit
Union the reason for the change?

Gosh, Lafleche must be getting dead. Everything I read about the
old burg mentions someone else joining up. Must only be grey
beards and cripples on the street these days.

Tell Rollie to draw a picture of his Daddy and to enclose it with
Mummy's next letter. And draw one of Murray too.

. . .

About that broadcast. Jerry Wilmont took all addresses of the
people we wished to have notified that we were broadcasting and
said that the BBC would let you know. If I had only known that
they wouldn't, I would have wired you. Next time anything like
that comes up I'll let you know myself, and if ever you get the

opportunity to say hello to me over the air, let me know yourself, don't leave it to the BBC, they have let us down once, that is enough.

. . .

You say I must be real good on the sax. To my surprise myself I'm doing all right playing lead sax. I'm getting a picture of the orchestra and will send it on to you—really snappy looking band, you wait and see.

Re the dancing all evening the night of the broadcast. I couldn't do much else as a party was arranged for us. All above board, nice people, etc., and dancing seemed to be the only thing to do. And as far as Rose Mary, I had forgotten of her. In fact, never gave the party at the dance another thought. As for her wanting to know what you looked like—"just feminine curiosity."

. . .

So Rollie and Murray get along quite well. Not all the time I bet. I can still remember the beatings I took from Bob one minute and playing together the next.

Well, bye darling, I haven't any news at all that amounts to anything. I love you and am a little lonely.

All of my love,
Clarence

☙

Canadian Army Overseas
April 30th, 1942

Dear Mummy,

Received another Star and this writing paper, thanks darling.
I've got reading for a few days and decent paper to write you with.

Well Hazel, you didn't enclose even a hello darling, but thanks for
it all the same. The Lafleche Press gave me all of the news.

Well, here we are on schemes and schemes and route marches, and
now that the nice weather is here we will be playing for inspection
on inspection and outdoor band concerts. For example, here is our
syllabus for the next ten days: today, that is this p.m., we are to play
for the inspection of the Canadian Army Services Corps inspection
by General McNaughton; tomorrow morning, battalion ceremonial
march; Sunday morning, church parade, and in the afternoon a
band concert in Firle Park; Monday a.m., inspection of the Canadian Armoured Corp by McNaughton; Tuesday and Wednesday,
scheme; Wednesday evening, band concert in Lewes; Thursday,
March Past in Seaford; Friday, March Past in New Haven. So
you see Hazel, we are kept plenty busy. I really don't mind,
it makes the long weeks fly by.

I don't believe I explained where Lewes is on the map. If you look
at any map of England you can find Brighton. Well, we are ten
miles northeast of Brighton and about five miles inland. That
should give you a good idea of where we are at.

I sat in a poker game last night darling [and] got fleeced proper.
I even owe a pound on my next pay. Not very profitable business,
so I guess I might just as well not play. . . .

The boys are just saying that more mail is in, so maybe parcels and
letters again I hope.

Well the whole s.s.r. has moved and to Firle now, mostly under canvas. Thank heavens we stay in huts, although the weather has been fair the last while. When it starts raining here, it rains. Now that all the boys are close together again I suppose we will see one another often. Do you know that the way we were before I didn't see any of the boys for weeks on end. I haven't seen Mickey for months, you would think he was in a different regiment.

Well bye for now darling, expect mail tomorrow.

All my love,
Clarence

⌘

Canadian Army Overseas
May 3rd, 1942


Dear Mummy,

Received your parcel of sugar, soup, razor blades, bars, cookies, shaving cream, and books. Thanks darling. The parcel was in fair shape, only for some of the sugar which got smeared with shaving cream—too bad. But it wasn't too bad, only about a dozen cubes were hurt anyway. Hazel when you send cube sugar put it into a tin or a separate box because it works through the parcel, and being square, chews the other articles in the parcel up—one worked into the shaving cream.

. . .

We played for the inspection Friday and what a day! We marched around and around a pasture rougher than the devil. Stepping into holes and trying to blow a horn don't work so well. When it was over my lips were puffed and sore from the horn jarring against them (felt as if someone hit me in the teeth). And another inspection tomorrow, hope it isn't on the same grounds.

Gee, the weather has been grand here Mummy. So mild, and flowers and sunshine, it would have been a swell day to roam around through the parks. Most of the boys went out; I stayed in, read and slept. I couldn't see any object in roaming around alone, and as I felt more or less lonely, so I let my mind roam around Lafleche till I went to sleep and now I'm finishing the day writing.

. . .

Hugs and kisses for the kiddies, and a long, long warm moist kiss for you darling.

All my love,
Clarence

☙

Canadian Army Overseas
May 5th, 1942


Dear Mummy,

Well, I'm rather in an uncomfortable position. I'm wearing my gas
mask, can't do much more than write. Having a few minutes before
we start out on a twenty-mile route march.

I suppose there will be more mail in today. Tuesdays, Thursdays,
and Saturdays are our mail days, so I'll be looking forward to a
letter or two when I get back.

We played for an inspection yesterday afternoon at Seaford and it
went over fine. The weather was ideal and warm, and as it happened
the s.s.r.s went on a scheme for the day. So, I got another break
being in the band. It won't be so hot tonight though because after
the route march we have to play a band concert in the park.

We haven't been playing for any dances lately—too many schemes,
etc., to be able to accept an engagement. We are asked often enough,
but have to refuse because if we accepted we would probably be on
a scheme and couldn't show up. But we do a lot of playing among
ourselves, which is a good pastime.

Have they rebroadcasted our programme yet? I understand they
were going to. I do hope you hear it.

How is your back behaving now? Back to normal? Gee, I hope
so mummy. I don't ever have anything wrong with me outside
of maybe a little cold or sore muscles from schemes, etc.

How are the kiddies? Is Rollie aching to start school or does
he want to stay home? When is he going to start, September?
I suppose Murray will be plenty lonely then.

Well, bye for now darling, the canteen is here and I'm rather hungry and have a penny or two left. I think I'll blow it on my tummy.

A few more days and it is Mother's Day.

This letter will be a little late, and mothers will be forgotten but I'm not forgetting darling. You are the mother of my children and I love you for it. And I love you for yourself. Darling, I miss you, and on Sunday for some reason or other I'm going to Communion for you Hazel.

I love you,
Clarence

࿏

Somewhere in the bush
May 8th, 1942


Dear Mummy,

Gee, I'm lonely darling. We are out on another scheme, seven days
of it. We left our huts at 7:30 this morning and marched out here.
We got here at noon, about twelve miles of a march. The sun has
been shining all day but there is a chilly wind and no matter where
we get the wind comes from all directions. As this is a scheme, we
are without blankets, just great coats. So I'm going to have a glori-
ously miserable long cold night. I'd really appreciate any old straw
stack tonight.

There is a little village close to us. I walked over after supper thinking I might go to a show, but I overestimated the town. A church,
a pub, a couple of stores and a few houses—a hundred yard walk
and I saw all there was to see, so came back and am now sitting up
against a tree. The boys have a small fire going and I'm reasonably
comfortable for the time being. But I am awfully lonely, I miss you
terribly darling. I miss a cozy home too and the kiddies. I sure got
more than I bargained for when I joined the Army. I love you
Mummy.

Received the April 4th Star yesterday darling, thanks. I enjoy
every little bit of them including The Lafleche Press. I see your
name on the top left corner . . . how is the town paper doing
anyway? Is Earl still editor?

I hope there is mail waiting for me when this scheme is over.

I'm with 'B' Company on this scheme; had quite a chat with Steve
this p.m. His conscience must be bothering him, he is talking turning over a new leaf. I saw Tom too, he doesn't say much, but Steve
likes to talk about his so-called conquests.

Well, I guess I'll close and walk around a bit and get the blood circulating properly.

Bye-bye Hazel, all of my love and kisses,
your lonely Daddy

P.S. Hello Rollie, are you a good boy? Do you do lots of work for Mummy? Bye-bye. Draw some more pictures for daddy. He will draw some for you too when he gets back to camp. Give Murray a big hug and kiss for me. Be a good boy, bye.

Oh Hazel, but I'm lonely—a big, big, long warm kiss.

છ

Canadian Army Overseas
May 12, 1942


Dear Mummy,

Well I'm still on this scheme and am I ever fed up. At least we
had a dry place to sleep in last night, not any too comfortable
as the springs are a cement floor.

Sunday we marched about sixteen miles. It started to rain about 4
p.m. and we had to find as dry a spot as we could to sleep. So I and
another stretcher-bearer, or bandsman, by the name of Rutz, went
to a farm and crawled into a cow barn and slept in the manger as
there were no cows. But Mr. Farmer let them in at four a.m. and
kicked us out. It was still raining and as it happens it was a good
thing the farmer kicked us out, because the company would have
moved out without us if we had stayed another hour. At 4:30 a.m.
we had breakfast (mush, bacon, and marmalade, and two half slices
of bread) and away we went. We marched eighteen miles and then
had dinner. We laid around in the sun all afternoon—can you
imagine lying around in the sun? We had supper and then into our
equipment and away. We had to retreat as we were acting as enemy.
About 11 p.m. it started raining again. Before we got through the
march we went back 26 miles, which made a total of 46 miles in
one day. And then had breakfast, as it was 5 a.m. when we got there.
So, we looked up some place dry and here I am. Have had a few
hours sleep and am quite dry at last. This is a garage on some big
shot's country home. The house is completely furnished, but no one
in it and it is all boarded up. Quite a swanky place, swell rock
gardens and orchards. The apple trees are in blossom and is it ever
pretty. We cleaned out the rhubarb patch and are to have rhubarb
stew for supper (something new to the army). As there is no one
here and the rhubarb was going to seed we plucked it all. Got about
two hundred pounds of it, enough for one serving apiece. As I was
strolling around I came onto a beautiful lily pond in the sunken
garden, and to my surprise it was full of goldfish. I spent an hour

feeding them bread crumbs. Yes, the place is lovely. Beautiful lawns, trees and flowers, even a Canadian maple, the first I've seen in this country. But it is still foggy and dull. I suppose nature has to be lavish to make up for the dampness here, it rains an awful lot.

Well the scheme will soon be over and no doubt I will get mail when I get back, so I'll probably write then again. . . .

One more day and this will be over. That 44 miles yesterday just about killed me and I feel as if I could do a little more sleeping. I can hardly keep my eyes open. I need a bath and a shave too, but will wait till I get back to camp.

So bye-bye mummy, I'm going to curl up in a corner because we will no doubt have to retreat again in a few hours. As we are the acting enemy we are supposed to be beat up proper and pushed into the Channel.

Hoping for mail soon.

All of my love and kisses,
Daddy

P.S. A big hug and kiss for the little men, bye.

❧

Canadian Army Overseas
May 14, 1942


Hello Mummy,

Back in camp and got a letter with the snaps. They are swell.
My but the kiddies are growing. Rollie is quite tall and Murray
is quite the boy now.

This is going to be short as we are moving to another camp near
Horsham or something like that. It is supposed to be a swell camp.
That will be a change to this hole.

We got back sooner than we expected as this move speeded things
up. We are packing in a devil of a rush. We leave in the morning.
My stuff is all over the place and I took time out to write a note in
case it is a few days, so this is going to be short.

Thanks again for the snaps and the letter, and don't worry about
this action business, there doesn't seem to be any sign of it. So bye
for now darling, I'll write as soon as we get settled in our new camp.

Bye, all my love,
Clarence

☙

Canadian Army Overseas
May 17th, 1942


Hello darling,

Well here we are in a new camp. Nice huts, swell showers, etc.,
and in what a place! It is a large park, Wakefield Park, acres and
acres of beautiful lawn, terraced, and millions of flowers. The rhododendrons are a riot of colour, bluebells like fields of flax I can't
believe, and you should see the drives. And what trees! The huts
are tucked away under oak trees. I rambled around a couple of
hours yesterday afternoon and looked and looked. As I sat on a
stone bridge gazing over the scenery I sure felt lonely. The sun was
shining in all its glory and the flowers all tended to make things
bright and gay, but I was lonely. I will always be till I'm with you
again, and wouldn't it just be heaven if you were here with me to
stroll around and enjoy this all together. A swell bunch of deviled
eggs, dill pickles, ham sandwiches, lemonade, icebox cookies, you
and this scenery all under one of these trees—oh Hazel, how I
miss you. And what the kiddies couldn't do in a place like this.

It isn't going to be for long as we are going away on some do or other
for the next few weeks. And as I understand there is to be no outgoing mail, so don't be surprised if mail stops for a while. After the do,
I'll probably have a diary to send home if we can't write while on this
scheme. After it is over we are to come back here for the summer,
rather a nice outlook even if it is miles away from any town.

Well, how are things anyway? I'm enclosing those negatives you
asked about, and if you enlarge one of them send me a copy too.
I think the pictures are not bad and [I] would like to see one on
a larger scale myself, and I would like to give it to the Starbucks.
I'm going there on my next leave.

I understand there may be mail in soon and I hope to get smokes
before we leave, which is Tuesday morning.

Bye-bye darling. How are you feeling now, fine?

All my love,
Clarence

P.S. Say Rollie, but you are getting to be quite the man. Nearly half as big as mummy. Are you a good boy for her? And as you are the only man of the family you gotta be good. Give Murray a hug for Daddy.

౬౨

Canadian Army Overseas
May 18th, 1942

Dear Mummy,

. . .

Well, I don't know if I'll have an awful lot of time. We are leaving
in the morning and I've still to pack and laundry to get in off the line.
I went to Communion yesterday and I prayed I get home soon, soon.

Received everything you have sent to date, nothing is missing.
I need 32 shorts and 36 tops, and maybe something to eat.

. . .

So conscription is working is it? . . . we will need the men.

I guess I'd better close, and thanks again darling. Re: house—don't
invest any too much money, Lafleche has nothing to offer in the
future.

All my love,
Clarence

⁊

Canadian Army Overseas
June 14, 1942


Dear Mummy,

Well here I am, fine and fit as a fiddle. These letters are all censored
and must be brief. I can't write about anything whatsoever so I'm
writing to let you know I've received the cigarettes and mother's
parcel of eats, but haven't received the underwear and I do need
them. I suppose they will be back in camp when we return.

Received six of your letters and will settle down to answering them
when we get back. Now we are quite busy. And some rather tough
training too, which necessitates all this secrecy. I'll tell you all
about it soon.

Bye-bye, take care of yourself,
love and kisses for the kiddies,
all my love,
Clarence

∽

Canadian Army Overseas
June 25, 1942


Hello Mummy,

Months it seems since I've written, and then it was just a note.
And I'm still in the same position, can't write any more than so
much. All I can say is that we are on special training. I'm tired
and anxious to get back to barrack life for a while.

I have received all your parcels, even the "Stars," nothing short so
far. Thanks for the smokes. I received them a few weeks back and
I would appreciate a letter saying more on the way. And have I ever
enjoyed your parcels. The eats come in just fine. We are under canvas and for hot water we heat that ourselves on open fires. So we
scrounged some lard, and potatoes being plentiful, we make French
fries practically every night. So with coffee, sugar, and the odd can
of meat, we can sure fix up quite an evening lunch thanks to my
parcels and the other boys' parcels as well. So don't weaken on the
parcels, they are swell.

The summer undies came just in the nick of time. The others
were just about all in, and your choice was swell.

How is everything darling? The kiddies are fine? Your letters are
always reassuring but between the time written and received a lot
can happen. So when I receive your letters I can hardly wait to
open them.

As for Rollie and G-bourg, get him started [in] school; home first,
and if things don't work out send him to G-bourg. Then I should
be home, the kiddies need me.

Well, I'll say bye for now,
all my love,
Clarence

[P.S.] Rollie, thanks for the drawings. Sometime when Daddy has a lot of time I'll draw for you. In the meantime, Mummy tells me you are pretty naughty. Is that nice now? Do be a good boy. You have the nicest mummy in the world and she is the only one you will ever have. Give Mummy and Murray a big hug and kiss for me, Daddy.

හ

Canadian Army Overseas
June 28th, 1942


Dear Mummy,

Received parcel you mailed on the 22 of May and everything was
in perfect order. The shaving cream leaked a bit (the top was a little
loose) but didn't harm anything. Now I have received everything
you have sent to date, but I am starting to look forward to more
cigarettes. It is a month since I've received any, and no word of
more.

Well darling it has been six weeks now since we have been on this
training and I'm about fed up. I hear so many rumours about
when we will be back to our barracks—I've sort of given up hope.

[At this point a portion of the letter was censored and a part of the
letter was cut out.]

I'm sitting on the edge of the sea and it sure is calm. I watch the
ships go by by the hour. The tide is coming in now, a few minutes
ago it was way out. Now I can't see the sand bars any more. I walk
along the seashore a lot in my spare moments and sit and watch
the breakwaters. It makes me lonely. The sea is lonesome in itself
it seems. It seems never satisfied, always restless. It does make me
lonely for home, you and the kiddies.

Well Hazel, I really haven't an awful lot to write about while
here, but you can expect a mile-long letter as soon as I get back.

Take care of yourself and write often. Your letters are changing
darling, or maybe it is my imagination.

All of my love,
Clarence

෨

Canadian Army Overseas
July 23rd, 1942


Hello Mummy,

Well here I am back in camp and life isn't too bad. Now, as to what
we were doing and have done, must remain in the past and forgotten, so I can't write anything about what we have been doing.

I got back last Wednesday and was immediately sent on leave. So I
went to Starbucks' and had a nice time. They took me to see "Maid
of the Mountains" (opera, if you please) and I really enjoyed it, at
the Coliseum in London. Outside of that I visited all their relatives,
and that kept me plenty busy. I had swell meals all of the time and
I never got up until 11 a.m. Never got to bed before midnight. Well
the leave is over and now I must apologize for not writing. The last
few weeks it was impossible. I wanted to, I kept getting your letters
regular and they made me awful lonely at times. I've got all the
"Stars" and I'm about six weeks behind with them, so I have
plenty of reading for a while.

Our wedding anniversary is soon and I'm sending a wire. Yes Hazel,
seven years, and I hope for many more, much happier than the ones
we did have. I'll make you happy darling. I love you so, and how
I mean that.

Gee, it has been a long time since I wrote and I feel so lonely
tonight. And I love you so much I could write pages of mush.

I'm fine but quite tired and glad to get back for a rest and a chance
to get caught up on my correspondence. You wrote so faithfully—I
love you for it darling. And I hope you weren't too disappointed in
getting so few letters in the last three months. Am I forgiven darling?

. . .

I'm as thin as a rake and [have] a wonderful tan due to a little work I suppose. I'm looking forward to some eats awful sudden.

How are the kiddies? According to your letters they are fine, but that is always six weeks news by the time I get your letters and I do worry a little. I don't want anything to happen to any of you.

Now Hazel, you aren't going short of anything to save a little are you? Don't darling, life is short and I believe if you made up your mind to save you would scrimp. Save when you can, but don't go short.

Do you get awful lonely for me as I do for you? Do you still love me as much as ever?

Bye-bye darling, I love you,
Clarence

P.S. I'll write every day for as long as it is possible.

☙

Canadian Army Overseas
July 24th, 1942

Hello Mummy,

Gee, it's nice to be able to sit down comfortably and write a letter
without rushing. I must tell you all about my leave with the Starbucks, but first of all I must thank you again for writing to me
so regularly. And thanks for the papers and parcels and cigs I
received, I have everything you have sent me to date.

We got back and I was given leave immediately and had just time
enough to catch the train or lose a day's leave, which I certainly did-
n't want to do after what we just went through. I got to Starbucks'
in the afternoon, and the first night I went to bed early. Stayed in
till 11 the next day—what a bed! . . . after sleeping on the ground
for two months it was grand. In fact, I didn't sleep so well the first
night. Not used to it I guess. But it didn't take me long to get used
to it. Friday, Mrs. Starbuck and Dorothy took me touring. We
spent the afternoon roaming around Leeds Castle (used as a hospital for the duration). It is an immense place and as old as the hills.
Solid gray rock, old and moss covered. The grounds were swell.
We got back at 10 p.m. and had supper. An English custom. I don't
know if I ever told you of the English eating habits. Breakfast when
you get up; dinner at noon; tea, 3:30 (quite a substantial meal); a
light lunch at 7; and a big meal called supper between 9 and 10. In
fact one seems to be eating all the time. And as it happens, while on
leave I ate and ate and enjoyed every bit. What a change it was to
army grub. Saturday afternoon I went to the show "Hot Spot," and
"How Green is My Valley"—both good pictures, but I was quite
lonely when I came out. I sort of wished I could get back to camp
and the boys. Do you know Hazel, when I think of home and the
kiddies I get awful lonely at times, and that is when I like to have
the boys around to talk to. . . . Saturday night we visited a cousin
of theirs [Starbucks]. Mrs. Tulk was the name. She owns a ladies
"ready-to-wear" shop, a nice home, [and has] one son who is in the

States with [the] Navy at present. We had supper there and played bridge 'til 2 a.m. I enjoyed it.

Sunday morning, I went to [?] in Gravesend, and then Percy and I went out to visit his girlfriend's people. That is, Mother and married sister, and now that didn't make me feel any better. They [have] two kiddies, a boy of six and a girl of three. I spent most of my time playing with the kiddies on the floor. The little fellow kept crawling up my back and having a whale of a time. We didn't leave there till the wee hours of the morning again. Between bridge and war gossip and Canada, the evening passed very quickly.

Monday, we went to see the light opera play "Maid of the Mountains," which took all of the day, and Tuesday, I was on my way back. So, the leave is over and I did enjoy it.

But what is a leave? It just leaves one feeling lonelier after seeing home life again and kiddies. Gee Mummy, if they would only call this mess off or let some of us go home once in a while. Something definite to look forward to. I don't know how in creation I stand this at times, this continual longing for home, wife and kiddies. It is enough to drive me nuts.

Have you heard the new number, a swell tune, "Perfidia"? I hear it on the radios quite often, it is very nice. I'm going to buy it for the orchestra.

We were issued with socks just now from the I.O.D.E. [Imperial Order Daughters of the Empire] of Montréal. I was getting rather low again—I've seven pair now. Sometimes on route marches I change socks as many as three times a day, so I need quite a few.

I'm out of toothpaste by the way, so in your next parcel include some tooth powder. In fact, I need shaving lotion and mustn't forget blades. I've enough shaving cream for a month or two yet. While I'm on the bum darling, send me a couple of towels and some hankies. And, of course, some eats and smokes. Am I getting worse darling? But we have such a time getting a lot of this here.

Well Hazel, I guess I'll close till tomorrow. All of my love.
A big hug and kisses for both kiddies.

Bye darling,
love,
Clarence

P.S. I'm lonesome mummy. It's raining here and quite chilly.
I'm going to bed and cuddle up in a ball—that makes me lonely too.
Bye. xxx

℘

Canadian Army Overseas
July 26, 1942


Hello Mummy,

Received two more Star Weekly's today (thanks a million), and, of course, the two letters enclosed, and I'm answering them at once.

Gee, it's nice to hear that you will have a swell garden. We don't get much of the likes here, no doubt the crops are coming good too. The farmers no doubt are pleased.

. . .

I'm sorry Hazel, damned sorry, that the rumor you heard about me is false. The only men returning home are the ones that are too old or medically unfit, and I'm neither, although I have quite a few grey hairs.

So you saw the picture "Smilin' Through." Swell wasn't it? And very touching in spots. I saw it in London six months ago.

Yes, I received the shorts. They are a little on the small side, and after they are washed I'm rather afraid to bend over—they may split all to the devil. So if you would send me a couple more bottoms or shorts size 32, and remember man size, not boys.

I'm enclosing a small photo of the orchestra and will send the en-largement later. What do you think of the boys? Quite the layout eh!

Well, bye-bye darling,
I love you,
Clarence

P.S. Are you a good boy Rollie? Better be, Daddy always finds out. Bye. Give Murray a big hug and kiss for me.

❧

Canadian Army Overseas
August 3rd, 1942

Hello Mummy,

Gosh, all my good intentions of writing everyday sure went
haywire; it is a week since I last wrote. I'm sorry mummy, but
we will blame the Army again.

Received your last Star Weekly. I did enjoy them so much, but it
really doesn't matter. There is another chap who gets it regular and
I've spoken to him about loaning it to me when he has finished
with it and it is OK.

Well Hazel, it will be our wedding anniversary in four days. Last
night as I lie in bed I was recalling it and it made me blue and lonely
and did something else to me. When I look back over the years I can
quite realize how at times and most of the time I hadn't grown up
and acted like a spoiled kid. Someone should have kicked the tar out
of me to open my eyes as to just how much I loved you and make
me realize just how much you mean to me. Now I know it and I am
suffering for it all. Little did I know how much I would suffer when
I joined the Army. I look forward to your letters and practically eat it
with my eyes. I love you Hazel, and do hope this is our last anniversary apart. I will try my best darling to make everything up to you.

Now, for what I've been doing since my last letter. We went out on
a four day scheme last week, and the first day I accumulated a swell
set of blisters on my heels, and marched and climbed all over the
countryside the next day suffering hell with my feet, and the blisters
broke and when I got in my socks were blood-soaked. When I went
in for treatment I was told to ride in the medical truck for the rest
of the scheme. That wasn't bad, but when we got back to this camp
I took the flu or something. No cold, but sore stomach, no appetite,
headache, and I am just beginning to feel normal again. So I certainly wasn't in any writing mood the last three days.

The last three have been spent in a camp under the trees in the mud and it has rained every day. And in fact, it is raining now in pails. Everything is simply running water. I'm sitting on the floor in the tent, the light is not too good, but it is dry for one thing as long as the tent doesn't leak. So you can see for yourself that this isn't just what you would call the comfortablest of camps. And I'm not forgetting how to skate as that is all we can do—is skate around from tent to tent and hope for a nicer day. And I understand we are to be here for a month or two, not a very pleasant outlook on life. We are getting ready for the Presentation of the Colours by some important personage of the Royal Family sometime in the next six weeks, so all we are doing now is band practice; and nights, orchestra practice, as we are far away from any large center the unit has to put on its own dances and entertainment for the boys. So, we should play for a couple of dances a week. I suppose you are wondering what the Presentation of Colours is. Well, I'm not so sure myself. It is quite an affair in the history of a unit and I'll write and tell you all about it when it is over. We played for the Presentation to the Saskatoon Light Infantry last summer, and I suppose it will be much the same for us. Plenty of ceremony anyway.

Well Mummy, I hope to get a letter, eats and smokes in the mail tonight. So do remember I like lots of letters if nothing else—of course, all helps.

Give the kiddies a big hug and a kiss from Daddy, and tell them Daddy looks at their pictures often, often. We can't buy any films here at all or I would have more snaps taken. Do include a film or two in a parcel once in a while (120).

I love you and I would send a wire for the 7th, but can't get to a telegraph office in time, so best I can do is say my intentions were good, and I certainly hadn't forgotten and I do hope you aren't too disappointed.

Gosh, it is miserable out. Thunder, lightening, and buckets of rain drumming down on the tent. Makes one wish he was with his wife and kiddies looking at it from a cozy room.

Bye-bye darling, I love you, and take care of yourself.
All of my love,
Clarence

P.S. The boys just told me that the Canadian Legion is putting
on a movie. I think I'll skate over. . . . All of my love and kisses.

❧

Canadian Army Overseas
August 4th, 1942


Hello Darling,

I just received your airmail letter—8 days, not bad eh? That's what
I call service. But darling, you mentioned our seventh anniversary
and expect a telegram. If I can get someone going on leave or something to send a cablegram for me I will. As I said in last night's letter,
I was a long way from any telegram office, so with scheme and dis-
tances the last ten days I haven't been able to get a telegram away.
I hadn't forgotten darling. I feel like a sap, a heel in other words,
but my intentions were good. There, I'm going to try and get a
cablegram away. Whatever, I love you just the same.

Mail in. I'm going to see what is for me. Smokes, I hope (getting
low), and eats and letters.

I've got a parcel of eats sent June 30th—no smokes or letters, unless
there is a letter in the parcel. Haven't opened it yet, but I'm hungry,
so you will have to excuse me for a minute. I could kiss you for the
parcel, thanks a million.

Gee, the parcel was grand—and film! Well darling, I'll get some pictures taken now and send them on. But no note or a letter, rather disappointing, but all the same everything was swell. Thanks a million.

I hear the orchestra warming up, so I'll have to close soon.

It was raining when I wrote yesterday, and it looks like rain again.
Mud, mud, and more mud, but I'm getting used to it . . . so, wet
now seems my element.

Well mummy, all of my love and kisses. Take care of yourself.

Your loving husband,
Clarence

P.S. I hope to spend the next anniversary with you, and those rumors about me coming home is just rumor. Nothing said or known here. Love.

&

Canadian Army Overseas
August 5th, 1942


Dear Mummy,

I was going to read the magazine you sent me and found this
paper in it so decided to write—the hint was quite broad.

I tried to get a cablegram away today, but no luck, and I'm too late
now and I believe I'll let it go for now. I'm sorry darling, but I
hadn't forgotten. Am I forgiven?

We had band practice all morning and all afternoon, probably orchestra practice in a few minutes, so I do get plenty of music. By the
way Hazel, what has happened to that old baritone sax? Still under
the bed is it? I may be glad to have it when this is all over, and maybe
able to play it now instead of just sputtering away with it as I used to.

It hasn't rained so far today, so it has been decent for a change.
But the day isn't done yet, I'd better touch wood.

We have another leave coming up soon and I'm broke just back
from one. So, I'll have to stay strictly to home. No shows, no canteen, so as to save about four pounds. Leaves cost money. One must
eat, sleep, and pay his way around, and I get plenty of the Army
without losing any of the leaves. The next one, I believe I'll go back
to Scotland, or maybe it will be Wales this time. Haven't been there
on my own yet, and I like traveling, so I really haven't decided yet.

I've spoken for a camera and will have those pictures taken as soon
as I get it. I do hope they turn out.

Well Mummy, in all your letters you tell me all about the kiddies etc.,
but I do like to hear about you too. Do you get lonely? Do you miss
me? And how are you physically? Fine, I hope. I really do want to
know all these things. Tell me something about yourself once in awhile.

I'll say bye-bye for now, and hope to get letters again soon.

I love you,
Clarence

P.S. Say Rollie, do you still remember what your daddy looks like or is it gradually becoming a memory? Mummy says you are getting to be quite the little man and are starting school. Are you a good boy for Mummy? Give Murray a hug and kiss for me and tell him Daddy can still remember his chin bites and wet kisses and him crawling over us in bed. Bye-bye.

છ

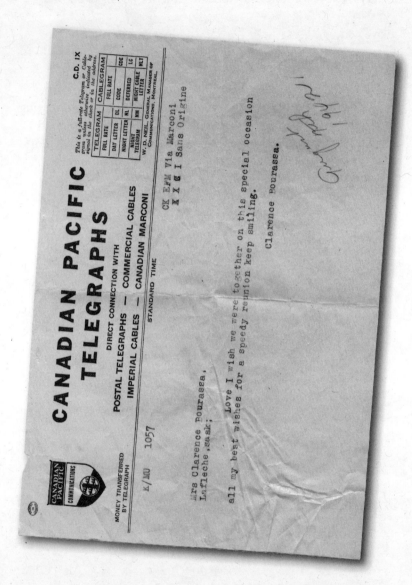

**CANADIAN PACIFIC TELEGRAPHS**

DIRECT CONNECTION WITH

POSTAL TELEGRAPHS — COMMERCIAL CABLES
IMPERIAL CABLES — CANADIAN MARCONI

STANDARD TIME

K/MU    1057

Mrs Clarence Bourassa,
Lafleche, Sask:

all my best wishes for a speedy reunion keep smiling.
Love I wish we were together on this special occasion

Clarence Bourassa.

CK EFM Via Marconi
X X & I Sans Origine

C.D. IX

This is a full-rate Telegram or Cablegram unless otherwise indicated by
signal in the check or in the address.

| TELEGRAM | | CABLEGRAM | |
|---|---|---|---|
| FULL RATE | | FULL RATE | |
| DAY LETTER | DL | CODE | CDE |
| NIGHT LETTER | NL | DEFERRED | LC |
| NIGHT TELEGRAM | NM | NIGHT CABLE LETTER | NLT |

W. D. NEIL, GENERAL MANAGER OF
COMMUNICATIONS, MONTREAL.

MONEY TRANSFERRED
BY TELEGRAPH

CANADIAN PACIFIC COMMUNICATIONS

**ROLLIE'S NOTE:** *My mother received the above telegraph from my father to commemorate their seventh wedding anniversary.*

*Airgraph*

Pte. Bourassa C.O.
L12541
B.H.Q., S.S.R.
C.A.O.
August 12th, 1942


Dear Hazel,

Just got back from another scheme to receive two of your letters
and one airmail letter, the second so far. Received just one set of
snaps, six of the kiddies and two of you. Congratulations, you
look swell darling.

So you have had the snap of Murray enlarged. The snap is grand,
must have developed well. The kiddies do look grand, makes
me quite lonely. I'm really missing the best of their lives.

You are worried about the parcels and smokes you have been
sending me. I've received everything but the July smokes,
even the shorts, etc.

I hope this gets through quickly, because I do intend using
these [airgraphs] a lot.

Lovingly,
Clarence


P.S. I didn't forget the seventh, have written.

☙

Canadian Army Overseas
August 13, 1942

Dear Mummy,

Did you get the airgraph? I hope they work good, as well as the
airmail from Canada.

Gosh, the pictures you sent are really grand, especially the ones of
you darling. Gee Hazel, they made me blue. Oh, if I could only get
the girl represented on those snaps into my arms—someday, and
not too far away I hope.

Yes Hazel, we no doubt are changing and in a lot ways. We will be
strangers, but there is the part of you in my heart that will never
change. Come what may, I do love you, and my thoughts are
constantly with you and the kiddies.

I haven't used the film you sent me yet as I had removed my mus-
tache and I remember you liked me better with it, so I'm cultivating
it again and it will only be a matter of a few more days and it will
be in full bloom.

There is a couple of guys just pestering the life out of me as I've
written a letter to Miss Dorothy Starbuck and left it sitting in front
of me and an addressed the envelope to you—they can't believe she
is only fifty.

I've just answered Starbucks' invitation to come up on a forty hour
pass and have accepted. I applied for a pass for next Wednesday,
and as I'm only a couple of hours away from a swell bed and eats,
why not go as often as I can.

By the time you get this Rollie will be started school. But how time
is flying, my little boy Rollie started school. I can't believe it, and
for some reason or other it leaves a little hurt somewhere inside.

Just starting his education. I hope to finish it off for him better than mine was finished off, and I hope to be able to give the boys a chance later on, something good. And Hazel, the boys must be proud of their daddy, and I mean that.

Haven't received the July smokes yet, and I will soon be out. Hope they get here in the next few days.

Take care of yourself Mummy, and I hope you are feeling better when you get this.

I love you,
Clarence

౭౩

*Airgraph*

Pte. Bourassa C.O.
L12541
B.H.Q., S.S.R.
C.A.O.
August 14th, 1942

Hello Darling,

Here I am again with an airgraph. I hope they are getting there
fine; your airmail letters come through as quick as seven days. That's
moving, for a letter to travel that distance in such a short time.

I've just been through all my mail and what a bum. So, I'm going
to clean it all out. I've half an apple box full of letters. I've been
reading old letters for the last two hours and enjoyed it, especially
yours. I read them in rotation and have come to the conclusion you
are definitely sick of Lafleche. And whatever you do about it darling
is entirely up to you and okay by me, as I certainly don't intend
returning there when this is all over.

How is everything? Are you feeling any better? And as for the kiddies, if they are as well as they look on the snaps they must be fine.
Give them a hug for me.

Take care of yourself.

All of my love,
Clarence

ᛩ

ROLLIE'S NOTE: *Prior to the August 19, 1942, raid on Dieppe, each man was asked to write a note to his next of kin. The notes were to be mailed in the event the soldier was killed; upon a safe return to England the notes were to be destroyed. The initial report was that Dad was missing and presumed dead, so my mother received this letter:*

My Dear Hazel,

Well, I hope you never receive this note because it can only mean the worst has happened. We are on our way to mix it a little with the Huns.

As the zero hour gets closer my thought[s] are constantly with you and the kiddies. And whatever happens darling take care of yourself and the kiddies, and as tough as it may be, keep that chin up.

Goodbye darling. If nothing else, I love you.

Your loving husband,
Clarence

ҫ૭

CANADIAN PACIFIC
TELEGRAPHS

DIRECT CONNECTION WITH

POSTAL TELEGRAPH-CABLE CO.

COMMERCIAL CABLES - - IMPERIAL CABLES

C.D. IX

*This is a full-rate Telegram or Cable-gram, unless otherwise indicated by signal in the check or in the address.*

| TELEGRAM | | CABLEGRAM | |
|---|---|---|---|
| FULL RATE | | FULL RATE | |
| DAY LETTER | DL | CODE | CDE |
| NIGHT LETTER | NL | DEFERRED | LC |
| NIGHT TELEGRAM | NM | NIGHT CABLE LETTER | NLT |

W. D. NEIL, GENERAL MANAGER OF
COMMUNICATIONS, MONTREAL.

MONEY TRANSFERRED
BY TELEGRAPH

STANDARD TIME

CK 28/25 DL  GB 2 ex

Ottawa, Ont. Aug. 21/42
726 PM

S MU 2153

Mrs Hazel G race Bourassa,
Lafleche, S ask,

private C larence Bourassa officially reported wounded in action
3368 sincerely regret in form you L-12541
multiple shrapnel wounds stop further information follows when
received.

Officer I/C Records,

# CANADIAN PACIFIC
# TELEGRAPHS

DIRECT CONNECTION WITH

POSTAL TELEGRAPH-CABLE CO.

COMMERCIAL CABLES - - IMPERIAL CABLES

STANDARD TIME

MONEY TRANSFERRED
BY TELEGRAPH

C.D. IX

This is a full-rate Telegram or Cablegram, unless otherwise indicated by
signal in the check or in the address.

| TELEGRAM | CABLEGRAM | |
|---|---|---|
| FULL RATE | FULL RATE | CDE |
| DAY LETTER | DL | CODE | LC |
| NIGHT LETTER | NL | DEFERRED | |
| NIGHT TELEGRAM | NM | NIGHT CABLE LETTER | NLT |

W. D. NEIL, GENERAL MANAGER OF
COMMUNICATIONS, MONTREAL.

Cable EFM Via Impl XOI

Great Britain, Aug 22/42

S MU 844

Mrs Clarence Bourassa,

Lafleche, Sask.

Injured and in hospital illness is not serious

all my love.

Clarence Bourassa

Canadian Army Overseas
August 25th, 1942


Dear Mummy,

I'm still in the hospital. Operated on last night and had 2 pieces of
a machine gun bullet removed from my chin, which went in at the
bottom of my right jaw and stopped on the front of my chin, and
removed from the inside so as not to scar my chin. And have I ever
got a sore face right now. Can't eat, smile, or talk, but allowed up
and around. I've been here nearly a week now and hope to get out
soon. Life is terribly monotonous here, just wounded.

Where did I get the wound? At Dieppe. As you must have read all
about it in the papers, so that can't be any military secret. On the
evacuation. After we did our job, all available space was needed for
casualties, badly wounded, so I had a two-hour swim out to the
ships and I was a rather frightened lad. Bullets snapping past and
hissing in the water all around me, my face bleeding quite freely.
When I was hauled aboard ship, I turned and looked back at
France and the intervening space of water and thanked the
Lord for seeing me through as well as he did.

Received the thousand cigarettes and papers and your letter of
the 18th of July. And the snaps simply were swell. I've received
everything. You ask about two lots of snaps and as far as the film
you sent me, I had taken two snaps and the film is still in the
camera back in camp. And as soon as I get back I'll finish it
up and have it developed and sent to you.

Mickey and Tom are back. Mickey without a scratch. As for Steve,
he is still missing. As for young Frankie James, I haven't heard a
thing, I believe he is alright. Due to censorship, I can say no more
darling about the raid, it was a good show. I saw the air force in action, and how. And no praise is too great for [the] British Navy.
They, and they alone, are responsible for the evacuation, and they

did a swell job. One of the Canadian nurses, a Mrs. Lefieve, asked to see the snaps and says you look like a girl of twenty. She couldn't believe you were 28, and as far as that goes I can't myself. Your pictures do look swell, and the kiddies, I am all taken up with. Murray, he looks grand. As for Rollie, he is soon going to be as tall as you are—going to be long and lanky like his daddy. I like their outfits, quite cute.

Where did you get the kittens? They are real nice. Black and white Angora I take it.

Supper is coming around so I'll say bye-bye for now. And take care of yourself darling, hope you enjoyed the dance.

All of my love,
Clarence

ROLLIE AND MURRAY WITH THEIR KITTENS, 1942.

*Airgraph*

Pte. Bourassa C.O.
L12541
B.H.Q., S.S.R.
C.A.O.
August 25th, 1942


Hello Darling,

Did you get my cablegram? I sent it as soon as I could after the raid.

I had a bullet removed from my chin last night and is my face ever sore. Outside of a few splinters of steel in my legs and arms, which will do me no harm, I'm fine and hope to be out of the hospital by the time you get this.

Thanks for the 1,000 cigs. I was out and if it hadn't been for Ancillary Services I would have been without. I took all I had left with me on the raid and, having to do a little swimming, got them all wet. A total loss, another score to settle with Fritzie.

I'm fine, none the worse. By the way, the snaps are swell. You're looking fine. Take care of yourself.

All of my love,
Clarence

෬

ROLLIE'S NOTE: *Dorothy Starbuck sees my father for the first time since Dieppe. A letter to my mother follows:*


Dale Hill,
Southfleet,
Gravesend,
Sept. 7th [1942]


Dear Hazel,

Just a line to tell you we have seen Clarence. He had a few hours' leave, just spent one night here. He is not disfigured at all. Has a slight scar where the shrapnel entered his face, but that will die out as it heals inside, and the doctor has made a fine job of removing it. Of course, he is feeling very weary and unhappy over the whole thing. I expect you have been feeling terribly anxious—we were too, because we guessed what was happening. We saw the airplanes going out all day. We sent a wire, but it took such a long time to find him that we did not hear for five days if he was safe or not. Then he wrote and we did not get the letter for 10 days, so we were very pleased to see him.

Hoping that you and the lads are well. We thought a lot about you when we could not hear anything of Clarence.

Yours truly,
Dorothy Starbuck

෴

*Airgraph*

Pte. Bourassa C.O.
L12541
B.H.Q., S.S.R.
C.A.O.
September 14, 1942


Dearest Hazel,

I've been a long time answering your letters and air mail. Just out of the hospital and spent two forty-eight-hour leaves with Starbucks and I really enjoyed the peace and quiet of their home. Did me a world of good.

Took the snaps of you and the kiddies with me and they thoroughly enjoyed them.

Send more cigarettes soon darling, I'm just about out. And a few eats would certainly hit the spot. I'm going to write an ordinary letter to answer all your mail.

I'm fine now, the only difference is a small scar on the right of my chin. My lower lip is quite numb and stiff yet, but that will clear up with time. My nerves were bad for a while, but that has all cleared up.

Yes, Steve is missing. Tough on Sarah and the kiddies. And if she uses her head she will be well taken care of by the government. Tom is fine, a few scars; Mickey didn't get a scratch. Frank James didn't get over.

All of my love,
Clarence

[P.S.] Hi Rollie, give Murray a hug for me.

છ

September 15, 1942

Hello Darling,

Now to answer all of your letters, which were all swell, and hurt me deep inside with you begging me to come home right away quick. I know for sure that you love me darling—and all your little suggestions as how I may get back. You mention pickles in one of your letters and I like pickles, but they are about as plentiful as fish in the Lafleche dam. Even after the raid I'm still in perfect health but very thin. Yes, I would give anything to get home for awhile, preferably for good, but I'm in the Army and apparently for the duration, so lets hope and pray it will soon be over.

Answering your letter of the 23rd of August: I was in bed in the hospital and I smiled when I read your letter—and how you must have been worried! But I wasn't bad. A bullet in the chin and a splinter from another in my lip, and six bits of shrapnel in my left leg, and a couple in my right arm, and I was terribly lucky to get away with only that. With fellows dropping around me like ten pins, it was terrible. Hazel, I always had a craving for excitement, I got enough in those few hours over there to do me four life times. I'm satisfied and ready to go home any time. Gosh, your letters do twist something deep inside, your pleas for me to come home. And, darling, I'm still classed A1, so still the Army for me, worst luck.

Re letters and the censors. One can hardly write about anything. Quite a few of the boys have been court-martialled for that reason and are spending a few months in the jug, so if at times my letters are short and [have] very little in them you will understand.

I started that film you sent me before we went on the raid. I had borrowed young Kohaly's camera and when I got back to camp, him being away and myself, the camera has mysteriously disappeared. So the two snaps I took and the balance of the film has gone west. I hope the camera has just been borrowed and will be returned, also the film—if not, the two snaps. So please darling, send more films. Enclose one in each parcel to ensure plenty of pictures. And parcels, I'm always hungry for something good.

So Carnahan and Davidson want you to work for them? If you ever do decide to go to work don't unless it is a real good thing. What I mean is a plenty good salary, something that will pay for the girl to keep house, see you to plenty of good clothes, a bank balance, and not too long hours—how's that? Otherwise, it isn't worth it.

Well, now for the time I was in the hospital. I slept the first day through and imagined I felt pretty well. After I got all washed up and had a good bath and the blood all cleared away, things didn't look too bad. A few bits of shrapnel in my legs and arms, which the doctors removed that day. And as for the chin, they waited a few days in case of infection and then removed it from the inside. In the meantime, I couldn't stay in bed. Terribly restless and jumpy, so I offered to help with the ward to keep busy and my mind occupied. So I started by carrying bottles, helping feed the chaps who were helpless, shave them, etc. So I was plenty busy for the time I was there. Couldn't sleep well [at] night. I'd kept getting nightmares: guns, shells, planes, bombs, etc. Many a time, I woke up in a cold sweat and couldn't sleep anymore. For awhile I thought my nerves were shot, but now I feel quite well and able to sleep for a change. Spent two 48-hour leaves with the Starbucks. They were sure worried about me after the raid. I got four telegrams asking about me. They are grand people Hazel, and treat [me] like a son and brother. I'm sure tickled to know them and I'm certainly welcome. I've my own room there, eat and sleep when and as long as I like. Dorothy Starbuck told me she wrote you since the raid to tell you I'm all right. Did you get that letter?

When I got back off the raid all I had on was a pair of shorts. I left everything in the drink so I landed in England with a blanket and barefooted and scared blue, and I don't mean maybe. I swam around in the water for over an hour and the Navy picked me up. Good old Navy! I was all in. And when the lead started slapping the water all around me, and the water shooting up in geysers all

around, I really wasn't frightened then, not a bit, just tired. And
after I got into safety and started to think things over I started to
get scared, and when the dive bombers came hurtling at our ship
through the air, time and time again, no more for me. Gad, that
was awful. How I came through? Your prayers and mine must have
been heard. So, no equipment and clothes. After the hospital I was
sent to the holding unit for a few days for re-equipping, and here
I am the same as before the raid.

Well Hazel, I guess I'd better close. Someday I'll tell you all about
my experience.

Give the kiddies a great big hug and kisses for me darling, and
as for you darling, I won't write it or this paper will start to burn.

I love you,
Clarence

CLARENCE SENT HOME A SMALL PIECE OF THE SHRAPNEL HE WAS HIT
WITH AT DIEPPE. THIS IS ONE OF THE FRAGMENTS THAT WAS REMOVED
FROM HIS CHIN; HE STATED HE LOST A LARGER PIECE.
ROLLIE HELD THIS PORTION FOR THE PHOTOGRAPH.

*Airgraph*

Pte. Bourassa C.O.
L12541
B.H.Q., S.S.R.
C.A.O.
September 17, 1942

Dear Hazel,

Received your airmail letter today sent on the 5th. That isn't bad service at all. Hope these get through as well.

So you are thinking of going out to the farm for a few days. As you say, it means a lot of work, but no doubt the change will be a welcome and as good as a rest. I'll bet Murray will enjoy that. Make sure and tell me how he got on with the pigs and stuff. I'd give anything to watch him romp around the farmyard. And how about Rollie? His first time away from Mummy for such a long time. I'm afraid O'Neills will have a lonesome kid on their hands. Rollie is lucky it will be only for a few weeks. And his Daddy now has been away nearly two years and he is still lonely for the same Mummy as Rollie is.

Yes, I received both lots of snaps and July's cigarettes. Hope you sent more since, as those are nearly gone. Do send plenty of smokes, will you?

So Rollie is off to school and comes back all boy, does he? I suppose if there is a mudhole in town he finds it and wades through it, mud and all. I'd give anything to gather that little tyke into my arms.

Well, take care of yourself darling,
love and kisses,
Daddy

☙

September 18, 1942

Hello Darling,

I'm on lines today so I am writing. Lines don't amount to very much work for me, but one must stick around.

Did you ever receive the post cards of the orchestra that I sent you awhile back. You have never mentioned it in any of your letters. The orchestra has had a few changes since the raid as Dick Nunn, Joe Heinz and Fred Pinkney didn't come back, and we also lost seven men in the brass band. We were lucky enough to replace the chaps in the orchestra and are playing a dance a week, but the band is totally disrupted as the seven aren't replaceable as yet. We are teaching green men now and it will be months before we are in any kind of shape at all to play as a band. I can't play my euphonium either, due to the wound I received in my chin, which made my lower lip awfully stiff and numb. And it will be a few weeks yet before I will be able to play, but the numbness and stiffness doesn't interfere with sax playing so I can enjoy myself that way.

How did Rollie behave for O'Neills? While you were on the farm I suppose he cried himself to sleep many a night, lonesome for his mummy and little brother, poor little tyke.

Tom Johnston is a full corporal since the do. As the companies lost practically all their NCOS there is room for all kind of promotions now, but I'm not looking for any. A private in action has to worry about himself and not a half dozen others and he can call his off-duty hours his own. So, I'm a confirmed private for the duration.

Oh yes, [I] remember that crack Uncle Jerry told you and you wrote me about. That I was still a private because I got into too much trouble. You can tell him for my sake, thanks, and how come I'm wearing a two-years good conduct stripe. Maybe he can explain that. (A good conduct stripe is worn reversed just above the cuff of the left sleeve.)

Well Hazel, I've got to help move a tent, so bye-bye, and all of my love.

Clarence

ROLLIE'S NOTE: *Dorothy Starbuck's letters brought a calming atmosphere to our home. Even though I was only six years old, the arrival of a letter from "Auntie Dorothy" was a happy event. Mom would read them to us and it made me feel my dad was okay and had someone looking after him. It is not until now, when reading her letters all these years later, that I can see and feel the compassion and wisdom that Dorothy had. It would have indeed been an honour and a privilege to have known her. This letter, sent September 23, 1942, shows what a wonderful person she was . . .*

Dale Hill,
Southfleet,
Gravesend,
Sept. 23rd [1942]


Dear Hazel,

It was very sweet of you to write to me as you did. You certainly need never feel jealous over Clarence. He could have all the girls he wanted if he wanted them—we get some laughs out of some of the silly daft things they do, but it gets a bit sickening at times. I jokingly said to him once that it was a good job he was married before he came over, but he answered quite seriously that he had not met anyone he would want to put in your place. And I think that after nearly 2 years it shows that all he wants is his own little wife and kiddies.

I did wish I could have packed him off to you when he came to us after he came out of the hospital. He was in a pretty bad way that night. He had been sleeping badly, having nightmares and living through all the horrors again. He was so tired he did not know what to do with himself, but he did not want to go to bed. I did kiss him that night, and talked to him as if he was his own small son. I smiled to myself about it afterwards, but I don't think he noticed it. He was too weary to bother. At any rate, he slept, and when he went back the next day we told him to apply for some more leave. They gave him another 48 hrs and when he turned up

two days after he was a different man. He said he had been on
light duty and had been sleeping well. They had had that Dieppe
raid hanging over their heads for some time; in fact, they had been
over before but did not land. And their nerves were all strung up
with hard training, so the break was bound to come afterwards—
especially, when they got back to camp and found so many empty
places. Of course, Clarence should never have gone into the Army.
He feels things too much, but I know you can't make them see
these things, they just think you are trying to put them off doing
what they want to do. And so they must learn by experience, and I
believe it forms their characters, although it is a pretty hard school.
My brother is just the same. I just let him go his own way now.
I think if you do they usually go yours in the end. . . . I think
Clarence has been through the worst of his trials; I don't think they
will send those men out again like that. Some of the others will
have to go next time, and I believe that he will come through all
right because we shall need men like him to carry on afterwards if
we are to have the new world we are all looking forward to—kind,
generous men with strong characters and deep religious convictions.
The trouble last time was that they tried to rebuild without God
and with all the good will in the world it was doomed to failure.
Of course, the churches were as much to blame over here. At any
rate, they had got bigoted and self-righteous, and there was too
much friction between them. I am not at all sure in my own mind
that God was not shut out of many of them. Men were trying to
run the churches their way and not God's way, but there seems a
different feeling about things this time.

Even on the radio, an airman speaking of the Battle of Britain
said the hand of God was in it and almost everyone is ready to
admit that the evacuation of Dunkirk was a miracle. The weather
was the chief factor, and only one hand can rule the weather. So,
let us pray that we shall learn by our own mistakes and so prevent
all this happening again.

We do not expect to see Clarence until October, then I think he
will go to Scotland for a few days first and finish his leave here.

He thinks he ought to show himself to the folks he knows there and so do I, but I will give him your message when I see him and write you after he has gone back.

Yours sincerely,
Dorothy

P.S. Yes, Clarence showed us the snaps. They are some of his most treasured possessions.

☙

*Airgraph*

Pte. Bourassa C.O.
L12541
B.H.Q., S.S.R.
C.A.O.
September 29, 1942


Dear Hazel,

Well at last here I am and I've been quite the busy guy. Starting up
a new band with green players means a lot of work for the fellows
that can play a little and the orchestra which is playing for at least
two dances a week. So, you can see I'm plenty busy and I like it.
I'm also doing the sign-writing for the regiment and I don't mind
that either. It all makes time fly.

I received 300 cigs from Mother and a parcel, as well as your two.
They are swell and just in time too. How about a tin of dill pickles
occasionally? And Hazel, I would like a pair of Oxfords, size 9 ½ . . .
we are allowed to wear them off parade now. Can you get me a pair,
something nice?

How did you get on at the farm? Was the work too hard? How did
Murray enjoy it? I'll be he had quite a time and I suppose Rollie
was lonely at O'Neill's. Dorothy Starbuck wrote me you had written her and she was quite pleased, and she thinks the same as I do,
and that is "you are swell." And she added the mystery touch, "of
course I can't tell you what we write about." Now what is this?

I've another leave coming soon and if I can scratch up enough
money I may go to Scotland again.

All of my love,
Clarence

[P.S.] If shoes are forthcoming, must have dress socks.

ↂ

*Airgraph*

Pte. Bourassa C.O.
L12541
B.H.Q., S.S.R.
C.A.O.
October 5, 1942

Dear Hazel,

Have you been receiving all my airmail letters? I've been using them exclusively, and the severe restrictions put on by the censors on all mail makes these as good as anything else because we can't write about anything anyway.

Received your two parcels. One from Mother, one from Yvonne. And 300 smokes from Mother, and waiting for yours now. Mine are getting low, or rather, Mother's are about all gone.

I've had a terrible cold and some fever the last week and haven't felt up to writing much, but I'm feeling better now and will make up for it. Tomorrow, I'll answer your last seven letters again.

How are the kiddies? In the best of health I hope. And you are back in town again. How are you feeling darling? Have all your little troubles cleared away?

As soon as Rollie is able to write, have him write a line or two. Bye-bye for now.

All of my love,
Clarence

☙

October 13, 1942

Hello Darling,

Gosh, but I've been poor writing this last while. Going through all the same old stuff again, nothing much to write about. I'm getting plenty disgusted with it all. I wonder if they will ever let me get back to Canada soon, even for a month. I do want to see you and the kiddies so bad. I lie by candlelight evenings, all in, looking at your pictures and the kiddies. Gee darling, knowing you seems to be a dream. We will have to start all over again when this is over. Getting acquainted, meeting the boys, but it will be fun. One thing I want [to] be able to do is fall in love again, because I'm in love with the girl I'm going to meet when they mark finis to this miserable chapter of our lives.

I wonder what you are doing tonight, thousands of miles away. Are you sitting by the radio lonely too, as I am? Yes Hazel, a cozy chair and you are at present my only wish—just to be with you. Life is hell, isn't it?

You once asked if we got anything playing for dances. A little mummy, but darned little, enough for a show or two, and our night's work is gone. But it is fun playing and keeps me busy. My favorite number now is "Starlight Serenade," and I received several compliments for the way I played it as a solo at the last dance. Some of the compliments were really flattering. To tell you the truth, at the time I played the number my thoughts were thousands of miles away—I was with you my darling. The tune of the piece must have lent itself to my feelings, so I must've outdone myself. In other words, it is my song to you. "Starlight Serenade," nice number isn't it? I've got my sax here (belongs to Dick Nunn who is a prisoner of war now, poor chap). But as someone else had to take his place in the band, I've borrowed it in exchange for the one I had, it is a much better sax. So here is "Starlight Serenade" for you Mummy. Am I going soft or just in love?

I've played it darling and I'm in no better mood. Some people may think a letter like this is mushy and that a chap my age should have outgrown such foolishness as they choose to call it. Well, I love you, miss you, and get terribly lonely, and it makes me feel better to pour my heart out to you Hazel. And as far as growing up, I never will as far as my love for you is concerned.

By the time you get this Xmas will be in your mind and another birthday of mine will have gone past. I'll have to write an airgraph tomorrow, how have they been getting through?

We are allowed to wear civvies now while on leave and I'm wondering if it would be asking too much to have you send me a pair of trousers and a nice windbreaker, a couple of dress shirts and a tie. Have you still got my shirts and ties and light socks. While I'm at it I might as well give you my measurements for the trousers: 34" leg, 30" waist, and 36" around the seat.

I hate to ask you to send these things but I would really enjoy the change, even if it is seven days of ninety. Make the trousers a nice striped grey with [the] windbreaker a pleasing contrast. Maybe the store still has my measurements. Order the stuff from Eaton's if necessary. The windbreaker, size thirty-eight (38), something neat; the trousers with 23" bottoms and cuff. That should complete my wardrobe and [it's] definitely unprocurable here. Wire me if you send the things. Am I forgiven for asking for these darling?

How is Rollie doing at school? I do keep wondering about him. Haven't heard a word from you in weeks. I guess I deserve that because I haven't written a terrible lot myself, but I certainly will do better now. As it was, mail restrictions were terrible immediately after Dieppe. And I just didn't care for our officers reading my letters. But things are back in the same old channels again. And as for a stranger, he doesn't know me and isn't interested in my family affairs or my mail as long as I leave the Army and its doings out of it.

Our brass band, as sadly depleted as it was, play[ed] for the inspection of the Canadian Minister of National Defense, Colonel Ralston, a few days ago, and the band is in the news reel. I hope they got a shot of all of us and that you see it. Have you ever heard that broadcast we made last spring?

Well take care of yourself Mummy,

All of my love,
Clarence

[p.s.] Rollie, how are you doing at school sonny? Do you like it and your schoolmates? Do you miss your mummy when you have to go to school? What does Murray do when you are away? Has he other little pals to play with?

Daddy still writes signs, and draws for the Army now, and it isn't near as much fun as when Daddy used to paint on the floor in the kitchen. Do you remember? It seems like a long time ago doesn't it? Daddy misses you a lot and Murray and Mummy too. And be a good boy for them, especially Mummy. You are the biggest man in the house now. Give Mummy a kiss for Daddy and Murray a hug for daddy. Bye-bye.

☙

ROLLIE'S NOTE: *Almost two months after Dieppe the following letters from the Department of National Defence arrived.*

Department of
National Defence (Army)
Ottawa, Canada
October 17, 1942

Mrs. Hazel Grace Bourassa,
Lafleche, Saskatchewan

*Re: No. L12541 Private Ovilla Bourassa*
The South Saskatchewan Regiment (C.A.)

Dear Madam:

I am directed to advise that information has now been received
by mail from Overseas to the effect that your husband, the soldier
marginally named, was admitted to No. 1 General Hospital the
20th day of August 1942, the casualty being described as "multiple
shrapnel wounds."

On receipt of further information respecting Private Bourassa,
you will be immediately advised.

Yours truly,

G. Robertson, Lieut.
For (W.E.L. Coleman), Lt.-Col.,
Officer i/c Records,
for Adjutant-General.

☙

Department of
National Defence (Army)
Ottawa, Canada
October 26, 1942


Mrs. Hazel Grace Bourassa,
Lafleche, Saskatchewan

*Re: No. L12541 Private Ovilla Bourassa*
The South Saskatchewan Regiment (C.A.)

Dear Madam:

I am pleased to advise that information has now been received
by mail from Overseas to the effect that your husband, the soldier
marginally named, was discharged from No. 1 General Hospital on
the 29th day of August 1942.

Yours truly,

G. Robertson, Lieut.
For (W.E.L. Coleman), Lt.-Col.,
Officer i/c Records,
for Adjutant-General.

❧

November 1st, 1942

Hello Darling,

At last here I am. I was really peeved for about a month—not a note, letter, or parcel. I was always waiting for letters, especially smokes, none came till today and I've been out for two weeks. I've spent two shillings a day to keep in smokes. I had understood you sent me 1000 in August; well, I didn't get them, and I didn't get a single parcel. Mail has been coming in in gobs and Clarence got nothing. Anyway, thanks for the 300 today as I'm going on leave this week. I'm going to Starbucks' again, and the smokes will certainly help. This may sound rather hard, but darling if you could only realize how we depend on smokes and eats from Canada. Please darling, do send plenty of smokes regardless to what others say they are going to do because nine times out of ten they are just talking so it seems to prove.

Did you get my letter regarding civvies? If you can send them to me do. I'm no bigger than I was at home. . . . I need socks, too, coloured shirts, oxfords (brown), trousers, and a windbreaker. My measurements will be in the store I believe. . . . it would be nice to get out of the khaki a few days every three months. Can you send them to me? Do, if it doesn't make you too short on anything else. Only if you can see your way clear.

Well darling, I've found out something about what the government will do after the war. As for us, if I can't get work immediately the government will give us $13 a week for 52 weeks or the equivalent to assist one in getting started in something, and a small allowance for clothing, $35 I believe. That is something anyway.

Well darling, this is rather a rough letter financially as far as you are concerned, but just the same darling, as mean as it may read I still love you and how. Even if I haven't heard for a month. I was pretty peeved, but I'll probably get a bunch all of a sudden. Are you still working for Davidson?

Yes, Steve is a prisoner of war. Tough in a way. I do hope the boys aren't being treated too rough over there.

I see my picture in the Regina Leader, not a bad picture. If I say so myself, rather flattering.

How are the kiddies Mummy? Fine, I hope. How is Rollie doing in school? It must be getting close to snow by now. Oh yes, my birthday is on Thursday—29 darling—time does fly doesn't it? And a few more weeks and Christmas. I'll have to get a bunch of Xmas cards and my photos taken for you darling. I'll do all that while I'm on leave. Thursday morning I'm going to Communion if at all possible, all to celebrate my birthday, and [to] thank the Lord [for] how lucky I am being able to write you and still able to carry on. I've decided to write you a letter telling you all about Dieppe. I'll do that as soon as I can get another of these forms [airmail form]. We are allowed one a week, but I may get someone else's.

Well darling, we are in a decent camp now (no canvas), and now I'll be writing a couple of times a week, that is a promise. In the other camp we had to sit on the tent floor to write, so no one did much writing.

Love and kiss Mummy,
Daddy

P.S. A hug and a kiss for both boys.

☙

November 5th, 1942

Dear Mummy,

Today I am 29 and not celebrating. As it is (now 10 a.m.) I just got up. I was inoculated and vaccinated yesterday, so I got 24 hrs excuse duty, therefore the reason for not being up any earlier. I feel rather dopey due to the inoculation and my arm is quite sore, but that only lasts a day or two.

Tomorrow I go on leave. So, I washed my hair this morning and is it ever raining out in buckets. Thanks to the new camp, it can rain all it wants.

Received a telegram from the Starbucks wishing me all the best on my birthday. Gosh, they are swell people Hazel. I sure thank my lucky stars that I met them. Makes my leaves just swell. They don't seem to be able to do enough for me, what a grand change to the Army.

My lip and chin are still numb from my wound. It doesn't interfere much, but certainly a funny feeling. Just like a piece of shoe leather, and I've got a dimple now whenever I smile.

Sent out all my Christmas cards last night. I shouldn't say all, because I didn't send you one for the simple reason I couldn't get a good enough one for you which I will get yet while on leave. I sent out 20 cards: to all uncles, aunts, brothers, sisters, and any one else who was good enough to write me while over here.

I suppose winter is on the door step back home. What I wouldn't give for the nip of Canadian frost and the crunch of snow under-foot instead of this slush, mud, and penetrating damp chill, and for a nice cozy room with you and the kiddies to put in the long wintry evenings. Then I would be happy. I definitely do want to come home now that I've had my taste of war. Re this taste of war, I am writing you through ordinary channels telling you all about it.

404    ONE FAMILY'S WAR

How are the kiddies? Rollie still likes his school does he? And how
is he doing? Give them a big hug for me.

All my love,
Clarence

P.S. What I would not have given to hear you say as I woke up this
morning, "Happy Birthday Daddy."

ↄ

November 17, 1942

Dear Mummy,

Just got back off leave to receive your parcel of eats of October 4th and three letters and an airmail (no smokes). Thanks all the same and thanks for the smokes you are sending according to your letters: 300 November 30th, 1000 Oct. 6th and 1000 Oct. 24. That is swell. I've been out the last two days and I'm borrowing on the strength of the above. Thanks for the shoes on the way, and as for the civvies I asked you for, forget about it, it is not worth [it], can't wear them often enough.

Well, I went up to Glasgow for two days and had another look around. Visited Miss Banks in the Sanitarium near Glasgow last Tuesday afternoon. You can tell Jack that she is looking well but is still not allowed out of bed. I guess she was in bad shape when she went in. She asked all about the Banks and you and the kiddies and she says that when she gets out of the San and the war is over she is going to Canada to a drier climate. Now don't get any ideas about Miss Helen Banks. I still write to her father and I know her, so when I was that close to where she was I considered it a nice gesture to drop in and say hello. She hasn't seen her Dad or anyone she knows for nine months. Must be hell to be locked up like that. Then I came back to Gravesend to Starbucks' and had a swell time. Yes, they sure are grand people Hazel. I'm glad you are corresponding with Dorothy. They met me in London and took me to an opera, "Wild Rose." And swell show it was too. I don't know how I will ever make up to them all they do for me.

I'll bet the kids were cute Halloween. Gosh Mummy, you don't half realize how lonely I do get for home. It hurts, and how it hurts. Mummy, I love you and need you, and thank heavens for the way things are turning. The end of this is gradually coming in sight, which will never be too soon for me.

Received an airgraph from Bob [Clarence's brother], the first I've received from him since I've been over and I'm answering tonight.

You asked about drinking. Hazel, frankly, the drinking I do don't amount to much. I have never so much as had a glow on over here. I don't mind a glass of Old Ale occasionally, but as to getting tight on it, I believe that is impossible. As for the hard liquor, it is terrible. And as for the price, it is prohibitive to a private soldier. So don't worry darling, I'm practically a teetotaller. Excuse [me] for a minute, the boys have pooled their parcels and we are going to have a feed. Thanks for the Klik, it is included in the menu.

While on leave I tried to get [a] photo taken and couldn't get it done. Had to have an appointment, and my goodness, what a price. At any rate I'm going to get it taken some how. Oh say, I sent you an Xmas card while on leave, and darling I didn't sign it. I thought of it after I mailed it, I'm sorry darling.

Well, I've lost my pen. This is a borrowed one and I'm sorry but I must ask you to send me another set of the same as the Legion gave us, they were swell.

Well bye-bye, all my love,
Daddy

ᴄᴐ

*Letter from Dorothy Starbuck.*

Dale Hill,
Southfleet,
Gravesend,
Nov. 18th, [1942]


Dear Hazel,

I received your letter dated Oct. 15th this morning. Don't worry
too much about not seeing Clarence again; he used to feel like that
when he first came to us and used to talk about not coming back
again, but this time he was planning to get to you somehow as soon
as hostilities cease, and wondering if they were not allowed to come
back if you would be able to come to him, which I think is a much
more healthy attitude. Anyway, just be prepared to give him all the
love you can. You are the only person that can do that, and in the
meanwhile we will do what we can for him.

Wishing you the best Christmas under the circumstances. Clarence
does not expect to get leave until February, but if he should get
Christmas he knows he can come here. We shall be very quiet as
my mother is too old to stand too much noise. But I don't think
he minds that. He says they get too much racket in camp. You
would have laughed if you had seen him last week in a pair of
Percy's trousers too large for him, pressing his uniform and
playing with the cats. But it all takes his mind off war.

Yours sincerely,
Dorothy

☙

ROLLIE'S NOTE: *We finally hear what Dad really went through at Dieppe.*

November 18, 1942

Hello Hazel,

In quite a few of your letters you accuse me of saying very little about Dieppe and insist on more. So, I've decided to write and tell you all I consider I am able to write about. I'll deal with the boys of the hometown first.

As for Steve, I didn't see him after we left the ships. And Tom, not till after I got out of the hospital. Yes, Steve is a prisoner of war and was wounded. Mickey Faille didn't get a scratch. Frank James was in the hospital at the time of the raid, and as for me here goes.

One nice sunny afternoon we were told to get ready for a scheme. We got on the trucks and away. The first thing I knew, we were aboard a ship and heading out to sea. No one knew what was up, and an officer came down to our deck and told us quietly we were going to France. I don't know just how I felt. All tight inside—so, finally it had come. We were going into action. I couldn't sleep, so sat around chatting, and then went up to the stores where I met Steve. We both wrote a farewell letter, which was to be destroyed if we came out of the raid. It was a hard letter to write. When we were through, both of us seemed tongue-tied and all we did was shake hands and wish one another the best. I went back down below and tried to get a little sleep. I finally dosed off to be rudely awakened from a dreamless sleep to hear, "get into your equipment, make sure you have everything." Everybody was grimly checking ammunition, grenades, and equipment. We knew it was a tough assignment we had. After a few restless minutes the order came through, "to your boat stations and prepare to leave ship." We did everything very quietly. Everyone seemed to be on tip-toes. The boats were lowered and the motors were started and away we went. It was still pitch dark. The sea very calm, just a pleasant sleep-inducing roll. I sat crouched in the rear of the assault boat with a stretcher across my knees, and to my surprise I had to be awakened before we landed. With it all I went to sleep, thank heavens for that. The trip into France was quickly over. When I got complete control of my senses it was just breaking dawn, and we were still quite away from the coast. A few more minutes and the word came back, "prepare to land." Then the scrape of gravel on the bottom of the boat and the clatter of the landing door dropping down, and the rush of men from hundreds of boats over the beach raised an awful din. I rushed up over the beach with rifle and stretcher till I came to a wall of concrete (sea wall) about eight ft. high that ran along the beach. Some men were up the walls getting away barbed wire. Thousands of men were along this wall. Not a shot was fired at us till we were all under cover, and most of us were over the wall in among buildings. And then all hell broke loose. The ground seemed to heave and the air was just loaded with pressure that seemed to want to cave me in. Frankly, I wasn't the least scared, I was too busy trying to keep up with company headquarters with the stretcher. Finally, we came to a stop. Our boys had taken a few buildings and were bringing in prisoners, and we hadn't a casualty yet. Our machine guns spitting lead and fire for hundreds of yards around us, everything seemed in our favour, not much opposition to speak of, and then crash, boom—all hell broke loose. The German mortars and artillery opened up on us and then things weren't so funny. I was standing back of a building and a bomb landed on the roof and blew a big hole in it. I was standing underneath the eaves, and slate shingles started to come down by the thousand, a brick or two, and they all seemed to land on my head. Thanks to the steel helmet I just got drove to my knees; otherwise, I would have got knocked flat. Even with all this hell busted loose the men kept their heads and went about their work grimly, never a word was said. All this time us stretcher-bearers were waiting for calls and we got plenty of them. I finally threw my rifle away; that is, I left it at the R.A.P. [Regimental Aid Post], and got busy carrying. And what messes we had in the stretcher. At times, it wasn't nowhere near pleasant to rush across open spaces with a man on the stretcher and bullets making the air crackle and gravel dance around our feet. Time and time again we went out under the same circumstances. It was gradually getting me. My mouth was dry, and many times as we came back in sweating and covered with casualties' blood, I didn't think I could go out again. Then out of nowhere, "stretcher-bearers, stretcher-bearers." Up we would go regardless of what the danger may be. Away we would go like frightened rabbits ducking behind anything we could hide behind, until we found whoever was hurt. Coming back wasn't never pleasant by any means, encumbered with the casualty and the air full of lead. This kept on and on and I was so tired my will and guardian angel was all that kept me going. Finally word came along, "we will evacuate at such and such a time, from the same place we landed." So we started carrying all the casualties down to the protection of the same sea wall we had to scale coming in. We lined all the casualties side by side safe from everything but the air, and relatively safe there too, as our own planes were up there by the thousands it seemed.

The boats started coming into the teeth of it all. They came through a wall of lead and fire, not a one turned back. Some sank, but on they came. And then the rush down the beach under continual fire. I can't quite recollect all that actually happened. All I know is men fell all around, dragging some back under cover, helping others into boats, and still we had stretcher casualties still to carry out. Well, they were eventually all boarded and more and more laying on the beach to be picked up. It seemed ages before we were told to hit out for ourselves. All the stretcher-bearers were still intact by some miracle, and away I went like a deer down the beach to the only boat loading. The rest were all heading out to sea with mangled and limping men. I made the boat all right, and it was stuck on a sand bar, and we had to stand in water to our waists—pushing, cursing, sweating—trying to get the boat afloat. All this time the Huns up on the cliffs were having a field day picking us off like clay pigeons. After ages the boat slipped off the bar and I started to clamber on. And smack, down I went underwater, and came up dizzy as a coon. The boat was just slipping by me. I made a grab for a rope and someone hauled me up. I no sooner got in under cover and the boat started to sink and I still had all my clothes and equipment on and my face was just spurting blood. The boat was going down and down, and what a scramble to get out.

We were in deep water then and I had an awful time shedding the ammunition; that is, my pouches were full and pack [too]. It would be impossible to swim with that weight. The boat was just about gone when finally I got clear and dove into the water with my uniform and shoes on and found I couldn't swim very far with that on. I dropped my tunic and then tried taking my shoes off. A submarine has nothing on me—I was underwater for hours it seemed trying to untie my laces. I'd come up and gasp for air, and I'd reach for the shoelace again and down I'd go. I finally got them untied, and then to get them off, that seemed just as hard. The shoes would insist on sticking to my socks. Finally, they came free and I got my senses gathered together. No use getting rattled, I thought, if I ever expected to get out alive. So, I took stock. I could see heads bobbing around in the water, and the ships out about two miles away fighting a duel with German dive bombers. Regardless of the Huns' incessant attacks and bombings, they represented safety. The water was just sizzling and snapping with bullets from the cliffs. Some Huns I'll bet were betting who would hit me first. Thank heavens they were poor shots. I finally swam out of rifle range and safe from that, but I was getting awful tired and my left leg seemed awful stiff and sore and the ships were still as far away. An assault boat was coming towards shore, so I started frantically swimming toward it as it was gathering up swimmers. I was just getting within shouting distance and away it went leaving me and others still swimming. I was frantic and practically despairing of ever seeing English shores again. Looking the other way, another boat was coming up towards me and picked me out of the water. They tossed me a rope and started to drag me up, but I hadn't enough strength to hang on to the rope, so I had to loop it under my arms to unceremoniously be dragged aboard. I hit the deck like a sack of spuds and just lay there. I was practically exhausted, half full of water, and sick to my stomach. I really didn't come to my senses till someone was helping me aboard a destroyer, and then I had a stiff drink of rum. That just about polished me off, but when it got working I began to feel much better. Someone was pulling off my trousers and another bandaging my chin, and I had a look at my left leg. It was bleeding slowly from a half dozen small wounds along the inside of my shin bone, and my right arm was bleeding a little too, but the

only thing more than a scratch was my chin, and that wasn't bad. So,
I felt pretty good about it all, relatively safe, but still the airplanes to
contend with. All I can say is thanks to the good old navy or I would-
n't be here. They stayed within reach through hell and lost many men
as well as a few ships to get us safely away, which they did very well
within reason. From there on it was just to get to a hospital and get
properly patched up. And now here I am as safe and sound as ever,
but more in love with a little girl back in Lafleche who was continually in my thoughts through the thick and thin of it. Let me tell
you, many a time on that terrible day your name was on my lips.
I seemed to draw courage from the thought of you.

Now, I've had my taste of fire and lead and I am now willing to go
home. I couldn't stand another thing like that, and anything like that
will never happen again. Experience is a grand teacher, even to generals.

As I reread this I feel as if I shouldn't send it to you. It is too gruesome, but you insist, and you will probably wish you had never received it. That is what a soldier has to go through to hold up rights
of humanity, and by God we are doing it. Finally, the war is turning
in our favour. Now, to finish the Huns off.

Our big battle is over darling, we won't be given assignments anywhere near that again, so don't worry about me. I got through that
so my chances are practically 100% of getting back safe and sound.

. . .

Listen Hazel, if the others want to hear about the raid you read this
to them. I don't care to dwell on it any longer.

Give the kiddies a hug and a kiss for me, and thanks for the snaps
of the O'Niells and friends and Murray. The one with you in [it] is
the most important, you look swell.

All my love,
Daddy

☙

Canadian Army Overseas
November 22, 1942


Hello Mummy,

How is everything darling? Are you well and is everything OK as
they should be? How are the kiddies? I keep looking at all my snaps
and really scrutinizing them looking for changes in the family, and
I must admit I have a darned nice wife and two grand kiddies. As I
lay in bed last night I kept wondering what the kiddies looked like
now and how I should act when I come home. Rollie will be too
big to make a fuss over, so I'll probably have to shake hands with
him as man to man. And if I don't hurry up Murray will be the
same. I'm really tired of all this darling. It is over two years since
I've seen you darling, and that is a long time to be away from the
one you love. How I've stood it I can't say. At times it is practically
unbearable. Thank heavens I'm in the orchestra and band, it sure
makes a difference. Time goes much faster. There is always something doing: a concert to play for and the dances. Do you know
that when I am feeling low I pick up a sax and play away for hours.
The boys are beginning to see through it—"Clarence has a fit of
the blues," they say.

I'm still the battalion sign writer too, and I've certainly improved
on my work. I can write a nice sign now Hazel, without effort.
Of course, I get a lot of it to do and practice makes perfect. Who
knows, but that my ability with a brush may stand me in good
stead some day.

I lost a filling yesterday so that means the dentist tomorrow. Gosh,
I spend a lot of time in the chair. My teeth never ache or anything
like it, my mouth is healthy thanks to the dentist's efforts. As long
as I'm in the band and my teeth are fair they will not take them out.
I'm going to complain anyway when I'm in the dentist's tomorrow,
my teeth are all fillings and maybe [I'll] get them taken out.

We played for a dance for the Cameron officers Friday night. It was a swell dance as far as we were concerned. The orchestra was complimented a hundred times if once, and we may broadcast again soon. When and if, I will wire. I hope we do, you haven't heard us yet have you? We have about eighteen dances to play for between now and the first of the year. Not bad, eh? It's too bad we couldn't get decent pay out of it. We make enough to clear our expenses and that is all, but it's fun.

There was an officer of the Montreal Fusiliers in to see me, I went to college with him. He has been over only two months and is thoroughly disgusted as we all were, till we just made up our minds we had to take it. His name is Maurice Chevalier and wants me to spend my next leave with him; that is, we would go someplace together. He was just married a month before sailing and misses his wife terribly. He was telling me all about it and how he didn't dance or drink and there wasn't much else to do. He said he'd been going nuts—so Hazel, that is England. So no wonder I'm all taken up with the orchestra.

Well darling, I'll say bye for now. And take care of yourself for Daddy, this job shows signs of finishing up.

All of my love,
Clarence

P.S. Big hug and kiss for the kiddies.

☙

Canadian Army Overseas
November 29, 1942


Dear Mummy,

Received three airmail letters from you and you ask if I received your cablegram while in the hospital. I thought I had acknowledged that before. I did darling, and it sure was welcome.

Thanks a million darling—received the 1000 cigs of the 6 of October, the bars, the little cheese box, the shoes, socks, and paper. The shoes fit swell and are real nice. I've everything you say you have sent except the 1000 smokes of October 24, which will be in the next mail. Thanks again, Hazel.

You mention something must be wrong, me not receiving your l etters. I'm sorry I said that darling, but that is the way mail comes to us. Nothing for a spell, and then by the hundreds. I am getting your mail alright, but I do get impatient at times when I've got to wait weeks.

Re the civvies, your plan would be swell darling. Dark coat and grey trousers would be nice. Maybe taking the expense into consideration, I shouldn't ask you to send them, especially after asking for a pen and pencil again.

We played for three dances this weekend: Thursday at Bognor Regis (on sea, south coast); Friday, in Pullborough, Sussex; and, Saturday, here for the sergeants' dance. So this afternoon I had a good sleep. I was getting kind of tired, three nights in a row.

. . .

Funny you asking if the Starbucks are very English. As it happens they are English and live in England, but darned nice people. Of course, they have quite an English accent, but not Cockney, not as exaggerated as you hear in shows, but noticeably English, concise.

I'll bet Dorothy will be glad to get to those stockings. I understand that they are as scarce as hen's teeth here. Thanks for doing it darling, one can't do enough for that kind of people, they are so darned nice in every way.

So you want news about the boys over here. I'm afraid I can't help much. I don't see them very often. Tom is at school, now a full corporal; Mickey is a full corporal in the anti-tank platoon; Frank James and I are still happy privates—that's all I can say, and if anything does happen I'll let you know. And as for news, when you get that letter re: Dieppe, you will have plenty. Twenty-six days and Xmas. I'm afraid I'm going to be lonely again like last winter. Still I don't know, as we are to play for dances Xmas Eve, Xmas night and Boxing night. So, I'll be probably busy enough not to be blue. As for being lonely, I always will be till I'm back with you and the kiddies.

I'll bet the Lafleche people do plenty of kicking on three gals [gallons of gasoline] a week. In this country, no gas for anyone but business and services. . . .

I've had that film taken today, but not sent in, yet sometime this week.

Bye-bye darling, love and kisses to the kiddies. As for you, this paper won't take it.

All of my love,
Clarence

꿈

Canadian Army England
December 13, 1942

Hello Darling,

Exactly two years ago today I walked down Toronto's icy streets
early in the morning, walking practically out of your life. Every
time I think of it I feel that lump come up in my throat. How I
longed to turn back. I must confess I sure had tears in my eyes.
And I don't ever intend to go through anything like that again.

. . .

Did you get the parcel of postcards, dad's photo, the orchestra's and
etcs? I sent them a couple of weeks ago.

Also received some letters two months old. Got sidetracked somewhere I suppose. They were swell anyway, and thanks for the birthday cards and also the Xmas card.

Haven't received [the] parcel with Xmas cake yet, so I'm looking
forward to that in the next mail.

How are the kiddies? Fine, no doubt, and I suppose really enjoying
the snow. We are enjoying the mud, as awful as it is. We would go
silly without it now, day in and day out—great stuff!

How is your health Mummy? Are you taking good care of yourself?
Is everything alright? I'm fine, still playing for dances, and I am still
painting, becoming quite the artist. I made an oil painting of our
regimental badge, the deer and all, which turned out grand. I am
receiving no end of compliments about it; it is for the officers' mess.

. . .

I'll be going on leave again in January. Going with Hedley Munro, our orchestra leader, visiting his people in Scotland. So, I'm going no place at all these days, hoarding every penny I can get my hands on.

Hope you enjoyed your Xmas darling, did the kiddies get many toys?

You asked me to have my photo taken for a Xmas present, but I didn't darling, but I will when I can. Next leave, I hope. And you will be getting it the quickest way I can send it.

Well, take care of yourself Mummy and don't have too many nightmares over me. Just nice dreams. I dream of you at times too darling, but have had no nightmares. And all I wish is that the dreams were realities.

All of my love,
Daddy

❧

Canadian Army England
December 19, 1942

Hello Mummy,

Received Xmas parcel of eats. The other will follow tomorrow or
next day, and I've received seven of your letters dating as far back as
October 29th, and I can't understand why you haven't been receiving my mail because I do write at least once a week. And, lately, I've
been using the blue air mail forms, which according to your letters
take as much as six weeks to get there. So, it can't be any faster than
the ordinary. . . .

I've received your cables, birthday cards, Xmas cards, all the cigarettes you have sent to date. Thanks a million. I've been well supplied lately, and hope to be from now on.

I've got so darned many letters to answer and I don't seem to have
time anymore. Between Orchestra practices and dances I'm really
busy. We have eleven dances to play for between now and the 4th of
January, so my letter writing will slip a little further back, but after
that I presume I will have all kinds of time.

I'm sorry about my photo mummy, and all I sent you was a cable
for Xmas. I looked around for something nice to send; anything
decent is a way out of my financial reaches. Gosh Hazel, I hope you
don't think I'm forgetting or don't care, because I'm not forgetting
and do care.

Just had an argument with Hedley our band leader about practice,
etc., etc. and etc. I told him writing you was more important and,
furthermore, just because of the band I'm not taking proper care
of my writing. We had quite a set to and I've practically told him
to shove the orchestra. Anyway, he is away pretty sore and I'm not
in any too good a mood myself.

How are the kiddies? I've their snaps in front of me and that reminds me I've a film being developed. Should have them soon, and I've three other films to take too. So, you will be getting a lot of snaps soon.

I'll be going on leave on the 4th of Jan., not sure where yet.

All of my love,
Daddy

[P.S.] Give the boys a big hug for me and thank Rollie for the paintings.

Bye-bye, love.

და

December 25th, 1942
Xmas Day


A Merry Christmas Darling,

I promised to write yesterday, but between parades and getting
ready for midnight mass, which was eighteen miles away, I didn't
get time. Received a wire from Wilfred Morrissette, what a surprise.

Yes Hazel, it is Xmas. Had dill pickles and Xmas cake of yours with
our dinner, which was turkey, ham, dressing, apples, gravy, mashed
spuds, all very good, but something was lacking. No home feeling
to it at all, everyone seemed so quiet. Oh heavens, when, when am
I going to have a human being's Xmas again? The boys are nearly all
out and I and a chap named Haugen [?] are all alone in the hut, it is
3 p.m. Gosh mummy, I can just see you and the kiddies going to
Mother's all smiles. Were there many at Mother's for dinner or
supper? Did Bob get home? Lucky punk, still in Canada.

Gee, it's lonesome here. I think I'll go out for a stroll. The weather
is swell, a little cloudy. If I stay sitting around like this I'll start
crying or something. Mustn't let that happen, I feel as if I could.

I think I'll walk down to the village after a bit and have a cup of tea.
I could even do with a beer today, but everything is closed today, so
another temptation gone west.

We have to play for five dances next week. New Year's we are
playing in the Regent at Brighton, one of England's swellest dance
palaces. So, we will be plenty busy, and I won't be able to write until
the first, and then I go on leave the 4th of Jan.

A merry, merry Xmas Mummy. I'm going out now. Haugen says
let's go to the tea room downtown. He feels like I do I guess. I'll
continue this later. In the meantime I hope you are enjoying every
little minute of the day, thinking of me once in a while. . . .

Well bye darling, I love you.
Hello Mummy,

Xmas is nearly over. It is eleven p.m. and I've been out for supper. While we were having tea at the "tea shop," as they call a cafe here, a Mr. Tear invited Haugen and I out for dinner, that is, at 9 p.m. In fact, he asked us in for an Xmas drink and as we had nothing special to do asked us to stay for dinner. It was a real good supper (as I call it), roasted goose and all the Xmas trimmings, and old English plum pudding, on which they pour brandy and then set it alight and then serve. I really enjoyed the evening. We played bridge from five in the afternoon till supper time. They are quite an elderly couple, and as their sons were overseas, they thought it would be nice to [have] a couple of us in and hoped that their sons would be luck[y] enough to have a nice meal today as they are in Libya. Yes, I really appreciated their hospitality and we are invited in for New Year dinner, which we had to turn down as we are to play in Brighton New Year's Eve and [are] not likely to [be] back. They said it was too bad, but anytime we felt like dropping in to certainly do so, which no doubt I will as they are very nice people and live quite close, about a ten-minute walk.

Yes Hazel, Xmas is nearly over and I've been quite lonely. Even with the nice evening, everything so quiet and peaceful at Tears,' the homey feeling made me quite blue. And Hazel how I pray and hope this is my last Xmas here. I want to get home so bad. You, the kiddies, no one, has the slightest idea how terribly lonely I do get.

26th tomorrow, we play for a dance at Billinghurst. Monday night at Petworth, Tuesday for the officers here, Wednesday at Horsham, and New Year's Eve Brighton. And Saturday night at Kirdford, so we are busy.

Well Mummy, I hope you have had a better Xmas than I and missed me a little. You have the kiddies as a consolation, I haven't a thing, just memories. Bye-bye.

I do love you, even the lump in my throat loves you, Hazel. Thanks
for the box of kisses, I'll take one now as I certainly need it.

All of me,
Daddy

∾

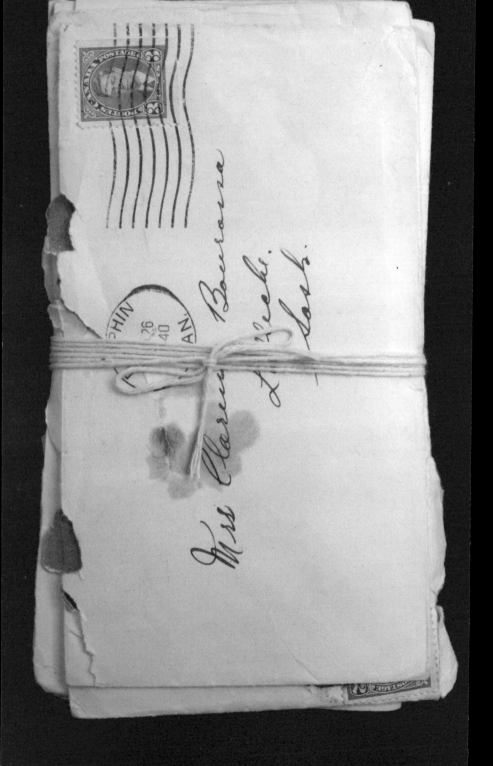

# LETTERS 1943

Canadian Army England
January 17, 1943


Hello Darling,

Sunday, and the weather is grand for a change. The band played
on church parade this morning and we had a march past for the
brigadier, and did we have a civilian audience! Church parade was
held in the village church and the whole place was out to watch us
march and the band play. On the way back, the band came up in
the rear of the battalion; one little fellow was running along beside
me, about 3 years old and quite talkative and cute. I picked him up
and let him try to play my instrument as we weren't playing anymore. I hugged the little fellow. He was so cute and reminded me
so much of the kiddies at home. I've had a lump in my throat ever
since. The little fellow said his daddy was gone to shoot "Musini"
and then he was coming home.

I hope you get [the last letter] as it has the snaps in it. Or maybe
you will get this letter first. I've another film in the camera now
and will take a few snaps this afternoon in the village.

Some of the boys are having a heated argument over a flashlight.
May prove exciting yet, the language is quite strong. No, nothing
doing, one of them walked out. Things may quieten down.

How is Rollie doing? Just as hard to handle as when I was a kid?
Yes, I should be home Mummy and help, it must be hard.

. . .

Well, if I want to catch any of the sunshine for pictures, maybe
I had better get started.

Well darling, take care of yourself. And I miss you and keep thinking of you and I still love you all over. And re that new nightie that

you're going to save for when I get home, it will be just like the new nightie on our honeymoon. And Hazel, I'll be so glad to see you that what you have on will make very little difference. I love you not your clothes, although you do look swell as the snap of you proves when you are all dressed up.

Bye-bye, love,
Daddy

Canadian Army Overseas
January 20th, 1943


Dear Mummy,

Received your airmail letter . . . last night. Having an orchestra
practice, then I'm answering it this morning (7 a.m.), and it is
raining buckets.

. . .


I saw Mickey yesterday, he is a full corporal now and will probably
be a sergeant soon in the anti-tank platoon. He isn't fussy, he says,
more work and a hell of a dangerous job. Yes, I often have thought
of going back to a company and taking stripes, but there is a lot of
other angles to it. The Army has nothing to offer me as a future, so
why stick my chin out any further. Life is too short and I've too
much to live for. I've seen and witnessed the responsibilities of NCOs
in action, and most of our missing and casualties from Dieppe had
stripes. When and if we are ever in action again I'll have all the responsibilities I care for getting my job done and keeping a whole
skin without having to nurse along another ten or twelve men.
I've other responsibilities for when this is all over—you and the
kiddies—responsibilities that I'm aching to take over.

Well Mummy, it is getting near work time so I'll be ambling along.
All of my love and a big hug and kiss for the boys.

I miss you an awful, awful lot darling.

Love,
Daddy

☙

Canadian Army Overseas
January 21, 1943


Dear Mummy,

Received everything except December cigarettes. The civvies are
swell. The trousers are in good shape (having the tailor fix the cuffs),
and sweater is grand. Also received a parcel from Aunt Florence,
two nice long letters from you (Dec. 19 and 21st), a letter from Jim
Hooker, and one from Mother. Rather a nice lot of mail for a change.

You ask about what and where I'm going to stay after this is over.
Hazel, that is something I've thought and thought [about]. I really
don't know what to do. I'll just have to look around somewhere,
and it will not be Lafleche (only as a last resort). What I really want
to do is start up in business myself. My dream is a nice neat grocery
store. Boy, oh boy, someday, and I don't mean maybe. I'll get the
money, beg, borrow or steal. Painting I like as a hobby and it will
no doubt stand me in good stead getting work, but I still want a
store. It seems to be in my blood. A thousand would swing it and
the rest would be up to me, and I will watch my p's and q's. The
truth is my ambitions reach a little further, but I would rather
keep that to myself.

Thanks for the clippings, I do enjoy them, but The Lafleche Press is
so full of strange names. Must be a lot of people moving around.

. . .

You asked about Steve being wounded. He was hit through the
right chest high up just below the collar bone. That is all I know
besides him being a prisoner. That is what I dislike about this war,
this retaliation by shackling prisoners. As you ask about going into
action again, there is no doubt about the Canadians being in it
again. There was only a few of us at Dieppe, the others will no
doubt get a taste of it. As for our division, we will be a reserve I

think, but one never knows—I'm still in the Army! What is more, we will never be in anything like Dieppe again.

. . .

It was nice to read that you will soon be in the clear and able to breathe freely. That is really nice to hear Mummy.

. . .

Well darling, I've got to answer Mother's letter and Jim's, so I'll have to close for now.

Thanks for everything darling. I miss you and the things you write me about the kiddies make me lonesome, but I like it all.

All my love,
Daddy

ℰℐ

Canadian Army England
January 31st, 1943


Hello Mummy,

I haven't heard a word from Canada the last couple of mails.
Maybe I am due for a long wait, with all my letters being saved up
so kindly by our postmaster and sent all at once, and some mail
going over being sunk. So heaven only knows how much of my
mail you will actually get.

I'm working in the pay office for the time being, book work. Simple,
pleasant and clean work. I really am enjoying it and hope to get it
permanently if at all possible. There isn't a vacancy yet but one is
expected soon, and I'm pulling all the wires I can in case there
does happen to be a chance.

When I read your letters and read you are hoping upon hope that
I get sent home etc., and the surprises you would like to get etc.,
makes [me] hope upon hope myself there was a slight chance—
one in a million that I might as an escort to prisoners of war. I put
in my application and like many others it was rejected, because of
not sufficient compassionate grounds to even consider it. The ones
that will be going are those who have filed for divorces or are having
trouble of some sort that requires their presence there. As [it is] we
aren't after a divorce, [are] on good terms, in good health, family
fine, business affairs none. And the fact I was a father etc., didn't
make any difference. My application was just ignored. So, I guess
I'll be seeing this over on this side and may that be soon.

The orchestra is still on the go, a few dances, a lot of punk weather,
and all kinds of rumours, etc. And the Army life carries on as per
usual. So per usual that I'm gradually going nuts. And I still get awful
lonely even after being away two years. They say one can [get] used to
anything in this world, whoever thought that one up better think
again. "Getting used to" and "having to" are two different things.

March the 30th [31st], soon now, so a happy birthday darling, and may we celebrate the next together. I'm still without a photo for your birthday and if I don't get some place soon it will have to be too late for your birthday.

I'm out of smokes, writing paper getting low, still borrowing pens. I like sauerkraut, pickles, peanut butter, etc., etc., so I'm looking forward to the next mail. An awful bum, eh, Mummy?

Goodnight darling, a big hug and a kiss for the kiddies. As for you, this isn't asbestos I'm writing on.

Anyway, all of my love,
Clarence

P.S. X ← right here.

෴

Canadian Army England
February 1st, 1943

Dear Hazel,

Received your airmail letter tonight, sure was glad to get it. First
letter in two weeks. You again mention not getting my mail and
that I write so seldom. I will admit I do slack off occasionally, but
I do write often. . . .

I'm in the pay office now. It is quiet here, not a sound except for
the steady drum of rain on the roof.

Gosh, I was surprised to hear that Davidson has cancer. In all probability he will never be in the office again. Who will take over the job?

So, the kiddies haven't been too well. By the time you get this I
hope they are fine and the weather is fine and spring well on its way.
It must be terribly unhandy and worrying to you with the kiddies
as no doc for miles. I do hope nothing happens. I do worry that
something serious might happen, and me over here. Oh, if this
would only finish up.

. . .

Gee, I'm anxious for summer to come around. This weather is terrible. Do you know what I saw this morning? Primroses in bloom.
So maybe it will be an early spring.

. . .

Gosh, with all the deaths and enlistments, Lafleche must be full of
strangers. Or there is no one left except a few grass widows and old
cripples.

Sometime when you send me a parcel send me a couple of serviceable pocket combs. And I need shirts again, size 32, "men's measurements." The others were a little small and I've split them all to the devil.

I've a thousand letters to write it seems and never seem to be able to get caught up. I still owe quite a few, but yours come first. I think I'll answer Jimmy Hooker's tonight.

Bye-bye darling, don't forget to keep my side of the bed warm.

All of my love,
Clarence

p.s. Because I won't keep it warm when I get there, not the first few weeks anyway. Soon I hope, bye.

℀

Canadian Army Overseas
February 9th, 1943

Dear Mummy,

Received your letter of the 12th of Jan. today, also one from Bill
Metcalf, Mother, and one from Yvonne.

Yes, I'm still working in the pay office, and I like it real well. Of
course I still get the odd sign to write for the regiment, and when
I actually think things over I'd much prefer to have this job steady
and I do hope I do. It is clean work and dry. The paymaster wants
to get me in steady and hopes to soon as the pay sergeant may leave.

Gosh, things must be getting fairly tough back in Canada. I never
did expect to see rationing there, especially meats and the likes. I
still can't understand it. And no doubt with all this extra on goods
they certainly must be getting expensive. It makes one wonder what
wars can possibly be of any good. Everyone feels the strain all the
way down the line. (Gosh, I've got a toothache playing hell right
now.) We in the Army get plenty to eat of something or other;
don't have to worry much about clothes.

Gee, this tooth is raising hell. No cavity, just a filling gone wrong.
Will have to see the dentist in the morning.

. . .

That was cute of Murray. I hope he likes his daddy when he sees
him for the first time. Rollie, you say, doesn't give him a chance to
forget about me. Good boy, Rollie!

Well Hazel, I can't concentrate on a thing. This tooth is raising hell,
so I know how you have been feeling with your teeth.

Bye-bye for now, will call this a letter and write again tomorrow.

Bye-bye, all my love,
Daddy

P.S. If I could have only been home those cold, cold nights for you to cuddle up to. I certainly wouldn't mind. Oh darling, at times I go nearly nuts with longing.

A big, big kiss.

ᏉᏏ

Canadian Army Overseas
February 15, 1943


Dear Hazel,

Believe it or not [this] is typed. I'm supposed to do a lot of practicing on this, because if I get into the pay office steady I will have a
lot of typing to do.

Received the parcel you sent me the earlier part of January. Was
it ever swell. And did the raspberries ever hit the spot. In short,
everything in the parcel was simply swell.

With it all, I'm out of smokes. Could do with a bunch any time
now as I owe 300 (not so good). The three hundred you sent in
Jan. won't go terribly far. Do send plenty of cigarettes darling.

Did you ever receive the snaps I sent you about a month back? I've
another film in being developed now and will send them on later;
also, all the negatives I have, split up of course—in case, just in case.

Received a parcel of books from Dorothy Starbuck this afternoon.
They send me two or three every month, and always good ones too.
Hazel, they are the grandest people I've ever met and it would sure
be nice if we could come back after the war and visit with them.
You would really enjoy the scenery here and their company, but all
this is wishful thinking. At that Hazel, someday I hope to take you
on a nice trip—a brand new honeymoon. What say, is it a go?

Thanks for the papers. I read the write-up and I can't say that I am
any too pleased having it in the paper. It may seem as if I was blowing my horn. The fact of it is I didn't exaggerate. That was Dieppe
in all its glory.

You mention Rollie going to the kindergarten. I don't know if I
agree. Of course, I don't know just how bad he really is. I should be

home and look after the little fellows. No doubt Rollie is getting
a little big to handle. Raising, financing, keeping house, working,
is a big job in any language, too big for any one person.

We played for a dance on Saturday and what a mess it turned out
to be. Hedley, the leader, the second sax player, the pianist—all got
tighter than drums. It wouldn't have been too bad if they would
have stayed away and let the rest of us struggle through. Nothing
doing, but they must play and play. They did, and how my ears are
still burning. From the compliments we received for the performance, the outcome of it all is that if anyone is at all under the influence of liquor I absolutely refuse to play. At least, I won't have to
take the ribbing I have since.

I still haven't been able to get my photo taken. You will be probably
thinking I don't want to. I've been in several studios, they all have
the same story, "sorry, we do not have the necessary material, but if
you care to, we will take your name and advise you when to come
and have your photo taken." Very nice of them. Of course, being in
the Army we never know where we will be tomorrow. I told them
that, which didn't seem to do any good. This is their answer: "we
understand it does make it hard for the troops, but that is what war
does." I've left my name at no end of places just in case. Whenever
I see [a] studio I walk in and try. No luck yet, but one of these days.

Yesterday was Valentine's Day and I didn't send you one. My apolo-
gies darling, I thought of it a month back, but none were available
at the time. So, it just slipped my mind till too late. Am I forgiven?

Give the kiddies a big hug and a kiss for daddy.

As for mummy, all of my love and a long, long kiss,
Daddy

☙

Canadian Army Overseas
February 16, 1943

Hello Mummy,

Here I am again with the typewriter. Just through work and Cale is fixing up a lunch: cocoa, toast, Spork, and cheese, thanks to your last parcel. Sounds good doesn't it? And at this time of the night not bad, as it will soon be midnight. Yesterday, being pay day, means a lot of work in the pay office for a day or two, and I don't mind at all.

Some Canadian mail came in today but nothing for C.O.B. Maybe tomorrow. Cigs, I hope. Another thing I am in dire need of is underwear, shorts size 30, made for men. The last ones you sent me were rather on the small side, must have been for boys. At any rate it sure didn't take me long to bust the seat out of them. And I could also do with a few hankies every now and then. I can't say what happens to them, but they all seem to disappear into thin air, or someone needs them worse than I. I've only about six left, and with all the colds I get I find six rather too few. And probably by the time yours get here I won't have any but borrowed ones.

Well the lunch is all gone darling. Sorry, didn't keep any for you. It was good, thanks again darling. It is now twelve-thirty. I should be going to bed but I think I'll struggle along with this for a while yet. The sheet is quite long, but here goes.

Friday, I go out on the Bisley Ranges with the s.s.r. team. It [is] supposed to be an honor representing the s.s.r., it is to be a Corps meet—I hope they aren't depending too much on my ability. I did qualify once as a first class shot; that must have been an accident and I don't suppose that will happen again.

Did you ever get a raise on your monthly cheque yet? There has been an awful lot of talk about a raise for the Canadian Forces, which we haven't seen yet. It was supposed to start the first of the year. Has there been any changes for the better on your income?

Cale is getting ready for bed; I guess that means I'm to vacate the premises pretty sudden as I don't sleep in the pay office and I'm sure he can't sleep to the tune I play on this thing. How am I doing anyway? Not bad for such a short time and I'm not too slow either. This takes me about thirty minutes. I probably wouldn't make much by the job now. I do wish that I had learned typing when you offered to teach me.

Yes Hazel, I wouldn't mind having you leaning over my shoulder right now correcting my mistakes. Now, I don't know whether you would have any typing mistakes to correct, because I would be doing a different kind of typing the first few days when I do get home.

Well nighty-night darling, a great big hug and a long kiss—a honeymoon one (must I explain?).

All my love,
Clarence

Canadian Army Overseas
February 27, 1943

Dear Hazel,

Received your letter and I must thank you for all the parcels sent since the fifteenth of January. Especially cigarettes, which I have been out of for some time. And as it happens, we are going out. A 30-day or more maneuovre, which will be starting in a day or two. I have no smokes and, apparently, no hope of any. And if Wilfred's gets here, it won't do any good because no parcels will be delivered while we are away.

You seem to forget I'm in the infantry and forever moving about. We don't get the time to write as often as artillery or air force, who are usually stationed in one place for months on end. And I still don't understand how you come to get only three letters in five months. I've been checking back on your letters and you haven't received more than three letters since November; at least, that is all you have mentioned. And I know I have written oftener than that—a good deal oftener. I've always had a decent reason when I didn't write often, and this continual ranting in your letters is getting under my skin. I'll admit it is disappointing not getting any mail. I've received everything you have sent, nothing missing whatsoever to date.

. . .

How are the kiddies? I'll be sending more snaps one of these days.

. . .

Yes, the orchestra is still going. We are playing for a dance tonight, so I won't be writing tonight. I'm writing now, because I've time and I'm in the pay office, a place where one can write. As for the schemes, I don't know if I will get time or if letters will be allowed out. It is to be a security scheme—if I can I will write. . . .

. . .

All my love,
Daddy

Canadian Army Overseas
March 6th, 1943


Hello Mummy,

I guess your threat holds good, when you said you weren't going to
write anymore if you didn't hear from [me]. Apparently, I'm losing
a lot of letters.

I'm now sitting in the pay truck out on a scheme. We have been out
for eight days and by all appearances for quite awhile yet. And is it
ever chilly and damp. No rain so far, thank heavens. I'm just about
all in and feeling lousy. I've only been able to wash my face and
hands so far (and sleeping on the ground too), so I really am grimy.
We are on the move most of the time, and whenever we do stop out
comes the files, typewriter, etc., and to work. So, this is really the
first chance I've had to write to anyone. I suppose you know what
it is like writing and typing when your fingers are cold. I've had a
week of it. When I'd walk over to a fire to warm my hands my fin-
gernails would start to sting. It has been quite miserable but I'm
thankful I'm pushing a pen for a change and not marching cross
country with seventy pounds harnessed onto me. It is much easier
on the feet and back, and nights I know where I'll be sleeping and
quite comfortable, even if it is under the stars. Oh darling, for that
nice bed of ours and you and the kiddies. Something stable and
sound. That is really something nice to look forward to. I do get
quite impatient at times. It has been such a long time already. I love
you, I love you Hazel, you have made me a little sore lately, but you
no doubt have reason. Maybe I'm not writing as often as I should.
I'm sorry Mummy. Am I forgiven? But don't forget to send smokes.
We are out on a scheme and I'm out of smokes—they sure don't
mix. I'm a perfect nuisance trying to buy, borrow, or bum smokes.

The 31st of this month is your birthday; I'm sending a wire as soon
as we get back off this do.

Outside of being tired and dirty, I'm in the pink and able to make a promise to write again in a day or two. And I hope my hands are a little warmer then.

How are the kiddies? Are you still working? Have you been receiving any more of my letters? Did you get the snaps? Mickey Faille married an English girl about a month ago; I don't know if Kay knows. I asked him about it and he said to leave that [to] him. He would rather tell her himself. In case Kay hasn't heard, don't tell her as Mickey would probably shoot me. By the way, Mickey is a sergeant now. All since the Dieppe do, doing quite well for himself.

Well Hazel, I'll say bye for now as it's long past sunset and I can hardly see to write.

So, all of my love, and kisses,
Daddy

P.S. Ruined a film of snaps I had taken on this scheme. As I was taking the film out it slipped out of my hands and unrolled. I tried to save it but I'm afraid light got at it. I'm going to send it in, in case some of the snaps may still be good. Give the kiddies a big hug and kiss from their daddy. Gosh, I'm lonely tonight darling. It is still only about seven-thirty and I'll soon be rolled in. Last night, as I lie looking up at the stars I could see the Big Dipper and waved a kiss to it to be taken to you. So, if you haven't received it, go out and look for the Big Dipper and take a look at it and think of me. Bye-bye darling, love and kisses. Bye, write often.

∽

Still on the Scheme
March 10, 1943


Dear Mummy,

I'm going to have fun trying to write this. We are on the move
and the only chance I have to write is when we stop for traffic.

A large Canadian mail came in today, but my name was conspicuous
in its absence. I suppose I'm getting my just desserts. I'll just have to
write oftener before I can expect any more mail, smokes, or parcels.

It isn't too uncomfortable on the scheme—this is the 10th day.
I'm getting plenty of sleep and eats, the nicest time I've had yet on
a scheme. So, I didn't do bad going into the pay office even if there
is a lot of work to it and sometimes quite long hours.

I've been rereading your last few letters and you are definitely plenty
sore at me. It hurts darling, and I don't like your accusations. Of
course you are a long ways away and an imagination can do wonders,
especially when one looks around and sees what is going on. It does
make one lose faith in human nature . . . you have only my letters to
believe, and words can be written easily. If repeating will do any good,
I will. You needn't worry Mummy, even after this long a separation
I still love you and I am the same as when I left you, except for a few
gray hairs and three years in age. As for other women, no change
whatever. (We're moving . . . we have stopped for a minute.) Anyway,
as I was saying, as for other women, Hazel, none whatsoever. Not
interested, and the above is not just written words, I mean it.

How are the kiddies? It is a month since I've heard from you and
I'm beginning to worry a little.

There doesn't seem to be much chance to write a descent letter,
so I will close with all my love and kisses darling.

Please write,
Daddy

☙

*Letter from Dorothy Starbuck.*

Dale Hill,
Southfleet,
Gravesend
March 10th, [1943]


Dear Hazel,

We received a short note from Clarence last week saying that they
were going on extensive manoeuvres, and he hoped to get leave
when he returned. After that, well, we can only leave him in God's
hands. But I am hoping that now he is in the Pay Office he will
not go into the front line. Last week, a miracle happened in [cen-
sored]. There were a lot of soldiers stationed in a [censored] and
houses around it, because the barracks were full and they were
moved out on the Wednesday. That night, we had an air raid and
[censored] got a direct hit and the surrounding homes were damaged. Probably, if the weather had been suitable we would have
had it the night before as it was undoubtedly a reprisal raid on
London after our attack on Berlin.


. . .


I have always felt that our casualties would not be too heavy.
I believe we are destined to crush this slavery and our men will be
needed afterwards to carry on the work, and we must give them all
the help and encouragement we can. This is our testing time—it
will either strengthen or weaken our characters. We are naturally an
easygoing people with a sort of live and let live policy. So, we had to
see the horrors to make us indignant enough to raise ourselves to
crush this evil thing.

Well Hazel, I do feel for you dear. You are so far from Clarence. But
believe me for the children's sake it is better so. I think you are seldom out of his thoughts. When he writes, it is always, "I have had

letters or parcels from Hazel," or "have you heard from Hazel?"
Or, "have you written to Hazel?" And, one day when he was here,
he was reckoning up what the time would be over home and what
you were likely to be doing. They say that absence makes the heart
grow fonder—I believe it. . . . I will write as soon as I have seen
Clarence. Good-bye my dear and may God bless you both.

Yours truly,
Dorothy

☙

Still on the Scheme
March 11, 1943

Hello Mummy,

More mail came in today and still none for c.o.b. It made me awfully lonesome. We only get a mail in every twenty days. No matter
how mad you may be, even a bawling out would be welcome now.

Today, we are parked near a little village, and a couple of little fellows were playing around the trucks all day. This evening they were
playing with an old tennis ball and a couple of us started playing
with them. One little fellow had a cast half way to his knee; it was
pitiful to see him running around limping. He got a machine gun
bullet through his ankle by a hit-and-run raid made on the village
by Germans. He was the only one hit; this happened in January. I
suppose he will always have a deformed foot. He is only seven now
and reminded me so much of Rollie as he was quite fair-haired and
awful talkative. He sat on my lap till after it got too dark to play
ball anymore. And did he ever ask a bunch of questions, such as
did we have trees in Canada, cows etc.? I really enjoyed talking to
the little fellow. I gave him a couple of hugs as he made me so
lonely for home and our boys.

I'm sitting in the pay truck now and we have the trouble light on—
so the reason for writing so late. I'm to go on guard in a few minutes—ten o'clock to be exact—only for an hour, so that won't be
too bad.

My hair is getting awfully grey darling. Everybody tells me about it.
Some call me the "silver-haired daddy"—and me, only twenty-nine.
But my hair isn't thinning any, that is something. You will hardly
recognize me when I get home, in more ways than one—mostly
the habit I've acquired of staying home and not drinking. In fact,
it surprises me when I look back four or five years; maybe, I've
finally grown up.

Gosh, we have been lucky on this do so far—11 days and no rain.
I hope this keeps up till the scheme is over. The winter here was
swell this year. No snow whatsoever and very little frost. The fruit
trees are breaking out in bloom, the crocuses and mayflowers are
all out, primroses are out too. When the sun is shining England is
beautiful. With it all, give me Canada, home, you and the boys.
Darling, that is all I ask for now, and pray, God, that is soon. I've
got all the war and adventure I want. This wanderlust I've had is all
worn out. I want to settle down to a normal happy life. I'm simply
sick of all of this, I've got enough. In this case enough is too much.

Well, I guess I'll close now darling and I hope to hear from you
soon.

All of my love,
Daddy

∽

Canadian Army Overseas
March 14, 1943


Dear Hazel,

I'm typing this as we are back in camp again. The scheme was
the longest I've ever been on and I sure was glad to get back into
a camp with a bath tub in it and get cleaned up. You should have
seen the ring I left around the tub. The fact is I was filthy too.
Weeks of rolling around in the dirt, sleeping outside, and the blankets weren't any too clean when the scheme finished up. I shook
mine out today and you would have thought by the amount of
dust flying around that I was cleaning out a vacuum cleaner.

There is supposed to be a lot of Canadian mail in so I should get
something surely this time and pray to gosh it is cigarettes. Is it
Mummy?

We got back yesterday noon. We weren't back in camp an hour
when Mr. Tear phoned me and said he heard we had came back
and was inviting me out for dinner on Sunday (today), which I
gladly accepted, and it was darned good meal. Rabbit pie, mashed
potatoes, pickled beets, Brussels sprouts, apple pie, and tea—not bad
for a change. I told you of these people before in one of my letters;
in case it went astray, too, I'll repeat how I came to meet them. It
was Christmas Day. Having no place to go in particular, we were
strolling around the village and a gentleman spoke to us and eventually invited us out to a Christmas supper. So, I have been invited
out several times. They have boys in the services and hope that some
mother [would] welcome their boys to a good meal occasionally.

Well, here I am again; I am really supposed to be working. We just
got through pay parade and there is no end of work, but I just have
to write and say that I didn't so much as get a letter in this last mail
and there was an awful lot of it too. Gee Hazel, that hurt. I hope
you are getting my mail now and are writing occasionally. . . .

This letter is in its second day so I had better get to work and get it finished. Do you know since we went out on the scheme I've lost track of the number of letters I've written to you this year. I believe that this should be about letter 18; let's call it that and go from there.

I suppose the weather back home is swell now and the snow is all gone. Do you know that we didn't have a bit of snow here this winter, and, lately, that is the last fifteen days, have been simply grand—sunny and warm. You should see the flowers right now, no end of them. Yes, it is beautiful, but still darned long way from home. And I still miss you as much as ever and I am still praying that this will all be over soon.

I'm hoping to hear from you soon, awful soon darling. And to make sure I hear often I'm going to write real often.

All my love,
Daddy

p.s. Say Rollie, are you a good boy for Mummy? She tells me you are pretty naughty at times. You are too big now to be a bad boy, and as I said before she is the nicest Mummy you will ever have so be good. Give Murray a big kiss and a hug for Daddy. Bye-bye, and give Mummy a long kiss for me, you lucky guy.

☙

*Letter from Dorothy Starbuck.*

Dale Hill,
Southfleet,
Gravesend
March 19th, [1943]


Dear Hazel,

Clarence has just got back from a hurried 48 hrs leave. He rang up
about 9 o'clock on Wednesday evening to say he was in Gravesend.
He and I spent the day in London and went to a store yesterday, and
this morning at 7 o'clock he went back. He is looking a lot better
than he did. His present job suits him. He has plenty to concentrate
on, so does not have so much time to think. But he was fretting a bit
because he said he had written you a rather snuffy letter as he had
not received any mail for a time. I told him I expected it had got
hung up and he would get it all in a bunch. Don't take too much
notice if he seems snuffy, he is a bit on edge. They have got this
Western Front idea hanging over their heads and they are all keyed
up. I was glad to see him for a few hours. I think it helps a bit to talk
things over. . . . It is a pity he feels things so deeply. Those people
are always difficult for most folk to understand. I have a girl in my
Guide company like it. She has a stepmother, and being only 14 is
just at a difficult age and hides her feelings behind a screen of
bravado, and in consequence comes up against most people. But
those people always interest me. They always have so much character
when you can get at it. . . . He had got that idea into his head, that
many of them do, that they probably would not survive the war and
would never go back anyway. Well, that is fatal[istic], but I am glad
to say that he has quite gotten over that and is just longing to get
back home. And that to my mind is much more healthy. . . .

We can only leave things in God's hands. . . .

All my love,
Dorothy

❧

Canadian Army Overseas
March 27, 1943

Dear Mummy,

It is simply a grand day out and here I am writing letters to my wife. I believe it is proper at that when one is lonely. It would really be swell if you and I could go for a stroll over the countryside this afternoon instead of me alone or with some other chap who hasn't any more to do than just that.

Did you get my birthday wire? Only three, or is it four, more days till you're twenty-nine. What are you going to do to celebrate the day? Whatever it is, I wish I were there to help celebrating; more so, if it was to be just a quiet afternoon together. Do you know I frankly believe I am still in love with a girl by the name of Hazel. Anyway, I spend an awful lot of time thinking about her. Some people call it mooning, and here I am thinking I had grown up.

We played for an officers' dance at the Royal Hamilton Light Infantry Regiment. We got back at 3:30 this morning as it was quite a distance away. We were once again complimented on our performance. We have a bunch of new numbers which may be old ones to you folks back home. Sometimes the new numbers over here were on the air in America for weeks. So here they are: "I Got a Gal in Kalamazoo," "Dearly Beloved" (a swell number if you ask me; I've dedicated it to you while it is still among the song hits of the day), "My Devotion" (another swell one), "Massachusetts," "920 Special," "Someday Marie," etc., etc. In all, we have a repertoire of a hundred and thirty-six reasonably new numbers. Of course, some old favorites such as, "In the Mood," "Sheik of Araby," "Just Molly and Me," and the one you once thought was very nice, "Yours," [and] "Darktown Strutters' Ball," "Sugar Blues," and so on. I wish you could hear our band. You [wouldn't] believe for a minute that I was playing lead sax unless you were told or had seen [it]. I've really surprised myself. Our leader is to thank for that; he took hold of a bunch of us and taught us how. And the boys all went to work and the results are sure showing themselves now.

I suppose that now being Lent there are no dances around. What have you for music around Lafleche right now? Are there any decent orchestras around since the McPeek's band broke up?

Well darling, it is being a long wait for mail. I'm still waiting for a letter from you, any kind—a bawling out, anything as long as it is from you with news of yourself and the kiddies. Darn that Hitler guy anyway; my name was on the list of parcels lost—cigarettes it is stated. As for other mail there was no mention, but no doubt plenty of mail is going down with this all-out submarine warfare. So Hazel, I apologize for some pretty mean letters I've written. Just lay the blame on Fritzie, and that is another score to be settled. Do send plenty of smokes darling, so that I can build up a little reserve in case something like this should happen again. I've been out of smokes over a month.

Bye-bye darling,
all my love,
Clarence

∽

*Canadian Pacific Telegraphs*

GREAT BRITAIN

MRS. CLARENCE BOURASSA,
LAFLECHE, SASK.

LOVING BIRTHDAY GREETINGS MY THOUGHTS ARE WITH YOU,
LOVE AND KISSES.

CLARENCE BOURASSA

෨

Canadian Army England
April 14th, 1943


Hello Darling,

I'm late answering your letters but we have been quite busy: with
this new rate of pay, making up wills for the regiment, etc. And
April, being the new year for the pay office, we are working every
night and the sergeant is on leave at present, which makes it much
worse. And when he gets back I expect to get my leave, which will
be about the 19th. And if I don't get some letters answered, it will
be May before I can do any writing.

Gee, your last letters are long-winded. Did the heart good after
such a long wait. I was afraid you had forgotten about me.

So, my letters are getting through are they? So, now I should get letters, nice letters, not bawling outs. I'll admit I do not write any too
often, but it isn't because I've other interests or anything of the sort.
As it is now, being in the pay office I have very little time to myself.
I'm beginning to wonder if it is such a good thing. In some ways, yes;
in others, no. There is no end of work and we are continually rushing.

. . .

Yes, I did like your Xmas cake. I've learned to like a lot of things
I didn't care for at one time because good eats are so rare. The national diet in England isn't too elaborate, rather plain, but plentiful
fruit cakes and the likes are but pleasant memories to most.

I didn't kiss a girl New Year's night, evening, or day. I moped about
between playing for dances, and if I remember correctly I was
rather quite lonely.

So, you do hope I love you, because when this is over and I'm back
we will have quite a time adjusting ourselves to one another. There

may be some changes in both of us, but as you say we have learned how to give and take a little more. So, I don't think it will be terribly bad darling, and as for the necessary love, I think I have enough to stand practically anything. All I want is to be near you, with you, you in my arms. Oh, everything, anything, just to be home.

I haven't received the pen yet. I'm still using the prehistoric ones. There has been a lot of losses at sea. I hope the pen doesn't go down. I could sure do with one in the pay office.

You ask for the negatives of the snaps I've sent home. I've got them out, so here they go. I should have sent them on long ago.

So, rationing is getting tough over there too now. I suppose coffee, as you say, is hard to get. As for here, it is an impossibility. They have some kind of an extract, a cross between Postum and _____ [Clarence left a blank], awful rubbish. I'd sooner drink tea, which we do get a lot of here. I've learned how to drink tea, practically an Englishman now: tea in the forenoon, in the afternoon, and evening, and at my meals.

As for the orchestra, it does take up a lot of time. Too much, it interferes with my work now and takes up altogether too many evenings . . . I'll admit, it does curtail my writing you as it does to the others. I've quit orchestra practices to get my work caught up and a few evenings to myself and maybe write a letter or two.

. . .

So, Rollie is still naughty? He should soon outgrow a lot of those tricks, but as you say he has a bad temper but a good heart and usually is sorry after he causes anyone pain. That is a good sign. I was a little worried that maybe he might be a little mean. As for me being a psychologist, I need to be looked over by a good psychologist and have him figure me out. No doubt if one did, I'd wind up in a psychopathic ward. When I stop to think of me joining up, leaving so much behind, I must be nuts.

Well darling, I wish I was with you to absorb some of that love you claim you have so much of, and if it keeps boys from going wrong, how about this boy? I'm a long ways away and I think that it is the fact I love you and that you love me that keeps me on the straight and narrow as to other women.

As for passes made at me, I must be stupid or certainly not interested, because I never notice anything like that. As if you would believe that—nevertheless it is so.

Well, bye-bye for now darling, I'll answer [your letter] tomorrow.

All of my love,
Daddy

ᴄ∽

Canadian Army Overseas
April 15th, 1943


Dear Mummy,

Just a few lines in answer to your letters before we start paying.

I'm going on leave Monday and I'm going to Starbucks.' I've written and asked them to make an appointment to get my photo taken. I hope they have. I've borrowed three pounds for my leave to make sure I have enough for the photo.

So, I'm irresponsible and don't know the value of money, etc, etc.—so some of your kind friends have told you. I'll admit I've left no other impressions behind than just that—and I would like to surprise them all! I've seen all my failings and know my weaknesses and have my mind made up as to what I am going to do and how I am going to go about it, and all I will need is a few hundred dollars, your love and confidence, and my resolution to make good for you and the kiddies and our future. It will be a tough battle for awhile. We won't be millionaires, but we will acquire security and a good living, which is about all one can ask for after this mess will be all over. I'm still young and the world is hard, and to my knowledge to face anything hard one must be hard and use hard methods to get a footing and then push like hell—and what I mean is I'm sure going to push.

Gosh, I was surprised to hear about Grandma and, nonetheless, to hear Grandpa was back in Lafleche. The next thing I will hear is that he has passed away also. I really would like to see Grandpa again, but according to your letter there doesn't seem to be much hope.

Yes, I received the "Luckies" [Lucky Strike cigarettes] with the civvies, and they were good. And as for Dorothy's stocking size, 10 would be the size, as she is a big woman and I noticed her feet are quite large. Anyway, she was sure tickled with the ones she did get.

So, you have had the flu too. Is it a worldwide epidemic? There was a lot of it about in England including jaundice and measles. Have our boys had the measles yet?

Well, here is the paymaster and the necessary funds, so I'll have to close.

Take care of yourself darling and all of my love. All that I can squeeze on paper for the time being and I do hope to get home soon.

All and all of my love and kisses, a big hug for the boys. And as for Easter greetings darling, Easter cards are unprocurable as yet. And I'll be at Starbucks' for Easter, so it won't be too bad—a good meal, pleasant people, a nice home.

I love you,
Clarence

༄

Canadian Army Overseas
April 19, 1943


Dear Mummy,

Well today is the [day] I go on leave. I'm not terribly rich but
will make out somehow. And I'm glad to get away, because we have
been terribly busy lately, working nights till all hours. And I'm sure
looking forward to a nice bed, white sheets, lots of sleep and swell
meals, all which I'm sure to get at Starbucks.' And the weather is
grand; I hope it keeps up. And I'm going to wear my civvies.

I just received four more of your letters; the sergeant just handed
them to me. Excuse me for a second. And if I have time before the
paymaster gets back from field cash I'll try and answer them before
going on leave.

So McLachlan has taken over the secretary's job and he is your
new boss. I imagine he would be a nice chap to work for.

Gee, I can't make out just what you are going to do about quitting
your job. In one letter you say you are going to work till the end
of the week, and in the next you will be working for a month yet.
Can't they make up their minds? I'll bet you will be glad when it is
all over and you have a little time to yourself. As you say, there can't
be much in it as your expenses are higher, girl, etc. etc. Don't you
ever get tired darling? I'd much sooner you weren't working.

. . .

Do you know with it all you are a lucky girl. You have the two little
fellows for consolation; I'll bet they are cute. I'm forever wondering
about Murray. According to you he is just it, and a great bunch of
company. I miss those juvenile hugs and kisses terribly—some day
soon I hope. Just in time! The paymaster just drove up. So, bye-bye
for a few days. All my love and kisses darling.

Well darling I'm on my way; I'll have the Sgt. post this for me.
Wish you were at the other end when I get there.

All my love,
Daddy

⁊

*Postcard*

April 30th, [1943]

Dear Hazel,

Thank you. I've just come back from a leave at Starbucks. Had a
nice time and the cigarettes were certainly on the spot when I got
back. Writing a letter.

Love,
Clarence

⁊

Canadian Army England
May 1st, 1943

Dear Mummy,

Well, I've had my leave and had a grand time, but still haven't had a photo taken. They just simply can't do it, supplies are terribly short.

Thank you darling, I'm using the pen you sent me. It is grand. The shorts were swell, the hankies quite the splash of colour, but certainly welcome. Also received writing paper and envelope[s], biscuits and bars, gum, razor blades, all swell. And thanks for the smokes (300). I mailed the card that was enclosed with them. Received a parcel from Mother with sauerkraut and sausage and eggs, which were still fresh. Frankly when I broke one open to fry last night I had my gas mask handy. But to my surprise, they didn't smell at all and did they ever taste good. And fried in dairy butter, just simply swell. Also received four letters of yours which I will attempt to answer now.

Thanks for the Easter card darling, I didn't send one; in fact, haven't seen any for sale yet. I did look all over a month ago and they weren't out yet, and I haven't noticed any since.

Before answering your letters I'll write about my leave. I got to the Starbucks' Monday evening; they were waiting at the station. We drove out to their place and had a swell supper then we sat and chatted about Canada. I had all the snaps of you and the kiddies, which took up an hour, and then I was shown to my room, "Clarence's room." And did I enjoy the bed. It is a honeymooner's dream. Big and as soft as a pillow, [but] the change was too much I didn't sleep any too well. In the morning, Dorothy woke me up with my breakfast on a tray . . . and then I went into Gravesend to shop and spent the afternoon watching the shipping going up and down the Thames. Big boats, small, all kinds from battleships to tow boats. That evening we went to the local pub. Percy and I had a few light ales and played

darts and dominoes till nine o'clock and then home to supper
and bed. Slept well from then every night till the end of my leave.
Wednesday, we went into London. Dorothy, Mrs. Starbuck and I
went to His Majesty's Theatre and saw the "Merry Widow," a revival,
very good too. We got home about 8, had supper, and then Percy and
I started a 3000-piece jigsaw puzzle. We worked on it till two a.m.
and got about seventy pieces together. We worked on it every day for
awhile, and according to Dorothy's letter today, Percy is still working
on it. In the daytime, I'd lay around the garden. Went to Seven Oaks
on Friday, "Good Friday," didn't go to church, but did go on Sunday
to St. Mary's in Gravesend. (Haven't made my Easter duties yet, will
do so next Sunday.) St. Mary's is an immense place, all marble and
stained glass—a church if there ever was one. Went to Mrs. Tulk's
with Percy on Monday, and Tuesday night her husband was killed in
an air raid. Her son was home (a lieutenant in the Navy just back
from New York). We spent the evenings playing bridge and rummy,
so that was about the extent of my leave. A few drinks, not enough to
even feel it at one time, and I've come back satisfied with my leave.
Had a grand loaf and a grand home for nine days.

. . .

Yes, we are quite near London, an hour or so by train. That is about
all I can tell you darling, except that I've only been there about ten
times since I've been in England. Quite an interesting place. I still
can't find out where I'm at when I am there—a proper jigsaw puzzle
with half the pieces missing.

Haven't heard either of the pieces you mention in one of your letters. They read good—rather on the sentimental side—I'd no doubt
would like them.

So, you don't think much of the pen I'm writing with. It works fine.
The nib is a little too pliable, but one can get used to that, and it is
a good pen.

. . .

Yes Hazel, it would be nice if I get home, but no matter what I can think of I can't figure anything out that would help. I'm in good health—reason number one for staying here. Secondly, no compassionate reasons for applying for a furlough to Canada. I guess we will just have to pray and wait for the end of this.

. . .

. . . I am your husband and in no danger of being seduced, vamped, or Shanghaied by any other woman. As for Marvin Black, if he thinks the women over here are grand, his taste is all in his mouth. Anyway, they are Englishwomen. Could you imagine a Canadian having to listen to that awful accent for the duration of his life? Heavens, how some of them can stomach it, I don't know. And you are still playing solo fiddle Mummy; I like your style and your touch.

So Murray needs his tonsils out. That's too bad. But if need be, I guess they must come out while he is young. So, now is as good as any other time. And he will be alright being as healthy and strong as you say he is.

Thank Rollie for his drawings. He certainly isn't doing bad for a young fellow is he. Seven now, isn't it? Well, what can one expect with a mummy like he has got.

I'll say bye-bye for now. We are playing for a dance in the village hall in a few minutes, and one in the officers' mess next Saturday.

Take care of yourself darling and say hello to Mr. Davidson for me.

All of my love,
Daddy

p.s. Give the kiddies a long hug and a kiss for me darling.

❧

Canadian Army England
May 6th, 1943

Dear Mummy,

Received your letter and of course with the two letters enclosed.
I've seen Mickey since but didn't say a thing to him as I don't know
the circumstances and don't want to stick my neck out. As I said in
a previous letter it was a surprise to me and I don't quite understand
what it is all about. The fact remains, he is married. It no doubt is
an awful shock to Kay. I really figured those two would marry
eventually, but I guess I was mistaken. To tell you the truth I am
disappointed in Mickey. And what is more I can't for the world
understand why he didn't let Kay know. The truth is Hazel, I can't
figure it out at all. It is all a mystery to me, and he hasn't said any
more than that he loved this girl, which I took with a grain of salt.

. . .

You wish you could talk to me. And don't I wish you could. And
whatever you'd have to say, you would have to say it fast, because
if I ever got you into my arms talking would come later.

Did you enjoy your trip to the city? Or was Rollie too many for you.
Boy, he is really coming on. You can't imagine what a queer feeling I
had when I read his note. I'm losing my boys—"baby boys" no
more. They will soon be all grown up.

. . .

All my love,
Daddy

P.S. I understand a lot of our letters going to Canada have been lost
through enemy action. Darn the luck, I hope it didn't catch any of
mine; it probably will catch about two weeks of them.

ᘓ

Canadian Army Overseas
May 10, 1943

Dear Mummy,

Received a letter from Aunt Agnes. I was really surprised and
hurried an answer. She gave me Howard Sewell's address, so I
wrote him, and Raymond Belcourt too, to try and arrange a
meeting some place. It will be nice to see fresh Lafleche faces.

We played for our officers' mess dance last night, or rather Saturday
night. It was a nice dance, well organized, and they seemed to be
enjoying themselves, some of them very much. A confession, I had
three drinks of Scotch whisky during the evening, between 9 and
2 a.m. Very conservative, and it was the first in a long time. There
were a lot of Canadian nurses there, being 'Sisters' as they are called.
Ranking as lieutenants, we privates didn't speak to them. So, I can't
say anymore about them, where they were from, etc.

Sunday, I went for a walk through the apple orchards. The weather
was simply grand (Oh, excuse me, three soldiers: a chap by the
name of Martin from Radville, and a boy by the name of Cowan
from Estevan). We walked miles, missed our supper, but thanks to
Canadian parcels I had a good supper: poached eggs on toast with
good Canadian coffee.

Well, the paymaster just came in and there is work to do so I will
have to close soon.

Yes Hazel, I would enjoy a walk down the tracks on a sunny afternoon and gather crocuses. I believe I could really enjoy that. The
scenery here is very nice I'll admit, but something is missing, and
that is you. Everything seems so empty.

So, you are going to wait and see how much I love you when I get
back. And it is going to be more than you bargained for, or can you

stand an overdose of love? I can, as I've been nearly three years without, and I've quite a surplus stored up too. Oh, when in heavens is
it going to be? I get so impatient.

Really darling, I must close. Take care of yourself.

All my love,
Clarence

❧

Canadian Army England
May 18, 1943


Dear Mummy,

Received your airmail letter of the 6 of May yesterday. That is fairly
good time. And I've also received the 1000 cigs you and Mother
sent, "thank you." Oh darling, it is nice to have enough cigarettes to
do a few days, and if the others keep coming as you say, my smoke
worries should be over.


. . .


What is this unemployment insurance you write about, and that
you were reported about, and why the inspector? Speaking of gray
hair, I've plenty of it too. Not terribly noticeable till you [are] fairly
close, especially over the ears. In fact, it is pretty well all through my
hair now, it must be hereditary. You once said gray hair made one
look dignified; I hope you still think so because I'll soon be a silver-
haired daddy.

The paymaster and sergeant are on a scheme for a couple of days, so
I'm the big shot in the office for a few hours and I'm not too fussy.
All alone and plenty to do. But being my own boss I've taken out a
little time to do more important business and this is it.

We played for three dances last week—Wednesday, Friday, and
Saturday—and on Sunday we played for two Home Guard march
pasts. So, we had plenty of music last week, and I understand we
are to play for three more this week—Thursday, Friday and Saturday. As most of the dances are over at midnight [at] the latest, we
don't go too short on sleep. So, it isn't doing me any harm. And
as it is a standing regulation no drinks when we are playing, you
needn't worry about me getting tight and meeting up with some
English dame. Anyway, I'm too busy playing to be bothered,
and in love with my wife, which does make a difference.

Well darling, I'll close now. I've still a little to do before morning and I don't want to be too late to bed. So bye-bye darling and thanks for the smokes. Could do with a few more eats soon, and, Hazel, don't bother sending cookies anymore as they get here all smashed. Send honey, canned things and a bit of candy too, writing material, etc.

Give the kiddies a big hug and kiss for me.

All of my love mummy,
Clarence

P.S. This is a swell pen once you get used to it. Thanks to you.

⌘

Canadian Army England
May 21, 1943


Dear Mummy,

As I've pretty well caught up with my work and the paymaster is
out, the weather is simply grand and I feel a little blue, so this may
help out.

We played for a dance last night and were home in bed at twelve-
thirty, so that is not too bad. The camp is awful quiet as companies
are all out on some scheme or other, the only noise is the continual
drone of fighters and bombers going over. We have that noise all the
time, night and day, weeks on end. It is something that one gets
used to and never notices. I can remember when a lone plane used
to fly over Lafleche and everyone and their dog would be out gap-
ing away. In fact, now we see many more planes than we do cars.

The brass band is still on the go and I'm rather afraid that they aren't
very much in favour of my playing, or rather, working in the Pay Office. I've heard rumours that the bandmaster is trying to get me back
as a stretcher-bearer. That would be disappointing, and the pay office
has all kids of possibilities that I would like to take advantage of.

The war news are certainly good and I hope they stay that way,
and in fact get better. I wonder what is next now that the Africa
mess is all cleared up. Whatever it is I hope they get at it soon and
get this over with. I'm ready to go home anytime. As for staying in
the Army after the war I don't even care to think of it. These chaps
that you say are considering it, are still in Canada and have just seen
the best side of the Army. Give them a taste of what our regiment
has went through and what we have to put up with, and I believe
they soon would change their tune.

I understand there is a big Canadian mail in, so in a day or two I
expect to get a half a dozen of your letters. I could do with one now.

Well darling, I suppose I should maybe do a little of something or other, a little more work than what the paymaster left for me to do—sort of make myself indispensable in the event of an attempt to have me taken back to the stretcher-bearers.

Well darling, I'll close now, sending the boys a big hug and a kiss. As for you—my, my!

All of my love,
Clarence

℘

Canadian Army Overseas
June 1, 1943


Dear Mummy,

Received two airmail letters from you in the last week and I haven't written very often lately either. This Pay Office job sure keeps me humping. I have never worked so steady and such long hours in my life. Nevertheless, I like it, and I do work real hard at it so as to make it permanent if at all possible. It was rather hard at first and I'm afraid I seemed quite stupid to the paymaster—so many legal forms and letters—and he would always refer me to some regulation such as A.A. Sec. (15) under paragraph 40 and so on at first. I was completely lost, but now I am beginning to see the light. And I do ask an awful lot of questions if I'm not too sure. At any rate, I haven't made any serious mistakes so far. If I have, they haven't caught up to me yet. The pay Sgt. is on leave and I've all the correspondence to look after as well as my usual work, and all routine which was the Sgt.'s work, so the reason for the typing.

Thanks for the nice kiss imprinted on top of your last air letter.

Received the Easter parcels which were grand. Thanks a million. Received the smokes which were certainly welcome, shorts, and hankies, and I've written Wilfred thanking him for the smokes and the wire. Excuse me for a few minutes darling. The water I put on the hot plate is boiling. I'm going to wash my hair and then finish this off while it is drying. (The water is damned hot and I've got my hair full of soap.)

Well, that is all done and I feel very much better, and a good deal lighter at any rate. The only thing I did not like was having to rinse my hair myself. Would have been much nicer to have you do it, and I'd probably have my arm around your waist while you were doing it, and make you spill water all over the floor as well as on my head, which would make you a little sore—getting your nice clean floor all wet—but I would not let you stay mad. I'd kiss a smile back into your eyes even if you were giving me the very devil. Yes darling, my one and only desire is to get back to you and the kiddies, 'specially you. I do miss you an awful lot and I believe in much the same ways you miss me. It is hell isn't it? All these long solitary evenings, the weather swell and inviting, and still one is lonely. Yes, I remember the promises we made at the altar, "to love and to cherish until, etc." Yes Hazel, I've been away three years nearly and I've still to meet any other woman that comes anywhere near you in my estimation. I've been true to you so far and intend on doing so. In fact, I simply am too much taken up with [the] wife I left behind to even consider any other woman. So, you needn't worry about that. I do believe I have become a little more sensible since I've joined up, and quite realized all I have missed and messed up in our lives. When I get back, I certainly intend to make up a lot to you darling. As you say, we will no doubt be practically strangers, but it will be fun falling in love all over again with my wife. After this long wait I should have a plenty large reserve of it stored away for the day I do get home (you are going to get snowed under with kisses).

Gee darling, some of your last letters are awfully blue. Don't leave it get you down, girl. This will be just another incident in our lives as hard as it may seem now. I think it has done me a world of good; I do realize how much I do love you.

Tom Johnston left for Canada today as a prisoner of war escort. I wonder what compassionate reasons he used to be chosen. I asked him outright, but he wouldn't say. Has he been having trouble with Pearl? Or is she stepping out?

I was speaking to Mickey tonight, and do you know that he never did know how much Kay cared for him, and that he gave her plenty of opportunities to assert herself. He feels quite bad that she has taken it the way she has. I haven't met his wife, so I really can't say much.

Am I ever flattered a young lady that I had seen standing around the orchestra at a few dances is awful disappointed that I'm married.

So, one of the boys was telling me she said, "it seems that all the nice Canadians were picked off by the girls in Canada." Now don't go worrying your pretty head over it, because the English girls just simply fall all over the single Canadians—a nice income to what the soldiers' wives get from the British government.

Well darling, this page is about done, so I'll say night-night. Give the kiddies a hug for me.

I'll send another of these tomorrow.

All of my love,
Daddy

℘

Canadian Army England
June 15, 1943

Hello Darling,

At last I've got around to writing. I owe you about a dozen letters
and I simply don't seem to be able to find any time at all. I'm cooped
up all day, and at night I go to a camp show or for a walk if we don't
happen to be playing for a dance or having orchestra practice. I'm
sorry darling, but I will do better. I just long for your letters and am
disappointed when I don't hear. Why should I expect to? I write so
little myself, but I'm still selfish when it comes to hearing from you.

I've received everything you ask about in your telegram: parcels,
smokes—good work darling, keep it up.

. . .

No Hazel, I don't worry unnecessarily about you and the kiddies. I
trust and believe in you and know that the kiddies are fine and in
darned good hands. I wouldn't mind being in your hands myself right
now. You keep asking about my plans re: post war. . . . I've been doing
an awful lot of thinking and as we have no connections elsewhere it is
rather hard to plan. If I had the least idea of what I could find to do for
a living elsewhere, I most certainly wouldn't consider Lafleche. The best
I can say to suit your plans would be for me to stay in the east and rus-
tle myself a job. As for courses, etc., it seems terribly hard to get into
any of them. My age is against me for one thing, but I haven't given up
yet. I'm going to see someone about [it] at once, again.

I've had fresh strawberries for the first time since we left Canada.
I paid four shillings for a basket, about a pint. I couldn't resist them
and were they ever good. Fresh off the plants and nearly as large as
hen eggs. Have you had many yet?

Writing again tomorrow.

All my love and kisses,
Clarence

Canadian Army England
June 17, 1943

Dear Hazel,

Thank you, received a thousand cigarettes mailed from the company May 7. Keep up the work; I may then create a surplus in case of a move or losses.

The paymaster is away on leave, just Cale, the Sgt. and I in the office. We are getting our work done in half the time as we haven't got him puttering around. The brass band is in full swing again, twenty-eight of us, getting ready for the Presentation of Colours. Yesterday, the band was out for the brigade sports meet—the s.s.r.s won the meet by the skin of their teeth.

Now, I'm as busy as ever. On top of everything else I have to attend band practices every afternoon, but I really don't mind, it makes time fly. Yes, I'm wishing my life away because I do want to get home as soon as possible. So, the more I can do to make time fly, the better I like it. I'd go nuts if I hadn't plenty to do.

How are these letters getting through? Yours come through in good time—ten days. If mine do half as well I'll be satisfied.

Yes, the war news are good and soon the whole thing will be in dead earnest to finish old Hitler up. It has taken a long time but gradually we are getting there. By the amount of planes that keep flying east overhead, Germany is taking an awful pounding. They should soon be on their knees.

I need razor blades darling; and underwear, tops, size 38, something light, and light socks too. Do you mind my asking?

So, the two kiddies are having their tonsils removed. If it must be done it must be, and all the better when they are young. I've been lucky myself, I've never had a thing wrong with me yet. I'm still in A1 condition, the last medical I had. So, I guess it is still the Army for me till this is over.

Has Tom Johnston got home yet? He left twenty days ago. I'd like to hear the line of bull he will be pitching The Lafleche Press. . . .

So Dad doesn't like your working does he? I wonder why? And what is more, I wonder if he is going to lend a helping hand when this is all over or is his letters just words?

Well darling, I guess I'd better do some work and not have it pile up; I've got to go to Band practice after dinner.

Yes, I would like to feel your arm crawling around my waist in the night, they are long and lonely at times.

All of my love,
Clarence

[P.S.] Give the kiddies a kiss and hug for me.

℘

Canadian Army Overseas
June 18, 1943


Dear Mummy,

This is supposed to look like I'm working. I hope you don't mind
me stealing a few minutes of Army time.

Last night we had an orchestra practice to try out two new players
who were taken on strength yesterday. They have been in England
only two weeks the lucky punks, or should one say the unlucky
punks. One of them is a sax player and not bad either. If he is good
enough, as he plays clarinet too, we are going to leave him take
over the sax lead and I will play the tenor sax as I can't play clarinet.
I must say I would like that as the tenor sax is the nicest instrument to play in the band and one doesn't have to double on some
other instrument. And the chap we had playing the tenor was
pretty rough. He played too loud and more or less spoiled the sax
section. As he is a trumpet player, he will take over the second
trumpet spots and be in his glory. He is a hot trumpet player, and
second trumpet is the hot spot in an orchestra. So, our band is getting bigger and better, which won't be bad. All indications are that
we won't be seeing any action for quite awhile, or even making a
move to any other camp. So, we will no doubt be playing for a lot
of dances. You once mentioned buying me a new sax after this over,
which would be nice—thanks darling. As it is I'm getting sort of
tired of so much music and no doubt won't want to see a sax for a
long time. Anyway, when I'm home I would be wanting to dance
instead of playing as I would have someone to dance with, my
best girl, so what would I want with a sax.

Has Tom Johnston got home yet? He said he would drop in and see
you and give you some first-hand news about your hubby, his condition, battle scars, which have practically disappeared now. He was
in to see me before he left and asked if I had any special message for
you and I said simply [to] tell her, "if it could only be me instead of

Tom." Yes, I'm lucky compared to some of the Dieppe chaps, all
that is left of the scars is a new dimple on the side of my chin and
few blue welts on my legs that are gradually fading away. So, you
will be getting me back in better shape than when I left.

You mentioned Toronto in your last letter, I will never forget
Toronto. It brought us closer together than anything that has happened in our lives. It wasn't a long reunion, but swell. It reminds
me of the song, "That Lovely Weekend." Do you know the words,
they sort of fit in too?

Tell the folks that I haven't forgotten all about them. And as you
have priority and my time is more or less curtailed, I haven't the
time to write as often as I used to. You are the only person I've written to in the last month. I owe everybody else a couple of letters,
and tell them I expect to get caught up soon.

You haven't mentioned Rollie's progress in school in any of your re-
cent letters. Is he still doing fine? Not in grade six yet or anything
like it is he? He should be a smart kid, taking his Mother into
consideration.

So you have a hundred dollars in bonds now. Good work darling,
that should help considerably when I get back. And it would be
nice if we or you could pile another dozen more onto that. One
never knows how bad we will need a few dollars after this over.
It would certainly be swell if we could start up a nice little store
someplace. I don't know why I insist on a store, but I guess it
is in my blood.

Yes, it would be nice to start up someplace new. I've thought of one
hundred and one places, even Innisfail [Alberta] where Uncle Joe is.
Someplace where one needn't depend on only farming. Someplace
where there is farming, lumbering, mining, etc. Someplace where if
one or the other has a bad year there is still something coming into
the district. In a place like that, if a person is ever going to make
good, he should there.

I'm alone in the office this morning as the Sgt. is away on some sort of scheme and left a lot to do behind. So, I had better get started or I'll catch the devil.

I'm having a hard time to save up enough money to go on leave next month. Every time I turn around, go to a show or something, I spend ten shillings. Everything is darned expensive. Broke or not, I'm taking my leave. This Army routine is enough to drive one nuts. Now I know why the Army give[s] so many leaves: to keep the men from going stale.

Well darling, I'll say bye-bye for now and will write again this weekend. As you said in your last letter, "lots of hugs and kisses until I write again." So, take care of yourself darling.

All of my love and great big KISS,
Daddy

☙

Canadian Army Overseas
June 21, 1943


Dear Mummy,

Well here I am again. I do hope these are getting through in decent
time. I should be getting an answer to the first one I've sent soon.

Yesterday, Sunday, I took the paymaster's portable radio and went
out into the country with a lunch that we made up from parcels
Cale received from home, and a few radishes, hard boiled eggs that
we paid 3s a dozen for from a farmer near camp (75 cents a dozen),
some green onions, Spam sandwiches, and fruit cake, hot coffee in a
thermos jug. With a couple of blankets, Cale (Pay Sgt.) and I spent
a nice lazy Sunday afternoon out on the lawn in the park. As we
lay basking in the warm afternoon sun we talked of home. . . . Yes
Hazel, England and its scenery make it ideal picnicking, but not
so good when one is alone—it made me feel awfully lonely.

In a week or two I expect to be on leave again, back to the same
place, Starbucks.' And it will be cherry season too. Gravesend is
in the cherry district so I sure will get my fill of cherries. All kinds:
Bings, Royal Annes, Lamberts, etc. I was there last year at the same
time, and cherries day and day out. I ate them till I didn't care if
I ever saw a cherry again—they were all over the place.

This time they tell me they are going to take me out on the Thames
estuary fishing. So, I should really enjoy my leave this time.

I was speaking to Mickey for a while last night. He dropped in to
listen to the news. We had quite a chat. He mentioned Kay, so I hit
him up about it all and he didn't have to get married. He says he
loves this girl. I haven't seen her myself yet; I understand she is no
beauty contest winner, but very nice. Mickey felt kind of bad about
the way Kay took it and, of course, blamed himself a little for not
having told her.

The radio is on and an orchestra is playing "I've Heard that Song Before." Rather nice; in fact, darn nice. I think I'll order it right now for the orchestra. Another 4s gone west for music; that is the price of orchestrations on this side.

. . .

I was inoculated for tetanus Friday and my arm is still swollen. I was also vaccinated for small pox and that is showing signs of taking, so I may have fun yet if it makes me as sick as it does some of the boys.

Say darling, I've lost a pair of those shorts you sent me a few weeks back. They were lost by the laundry and they paid me 3s for them, which didn't help much. I can't wear the 3s and we can't buy anything like them in this country. So would you mind sending me more of the same, they were swell. While I'm at it I may as well put in my order. Things that are always welcome are shaving material, toothpaste, shaving lotion (which I believe is forbidden), talc, and I could do with a couple of pair of light socks, light tan shoe polish—it's always the same old story, isn't it darling? Send this, send that, and that, but what I ask for is usually not procurable to the troops—our Army kit is supposed to be ample. Smokes, eats, and decent underwear and shaving material are certainly always welcomed by this guy.

Say Rollie, how are you doing anyway? Are you nearly as big as mummy yet? Are you being a good boy for her or do you do things to make her mad? Do you do as she tells you? You don't get mad anymore like you used to, do you? And are you nice to Murray? Someday Daddy is coming home, and if Mummy tells me you have been bad I don't think Daddy is going to like you so much. Sometimes Mummy tells me in her letters that you have been bad, why? Rollie, Daddy thinks you have the nicest Mummy in the world, and when you are bad it makes her feel bad, and that makes Daddy mad at you for making Mummy feel bad. You are getting to be a big boy now Rollie, so act like a big boy and be good. Bye-bye, give Mummy and Murray a big hug and kiss for me.

Well Hazel, this looks like the end of the page so I must call this it. Take care of yourself and don't let gossip get you down.

All of my love,
Clarence

෴

Canadian Army Overseas
June 23, 1943

Dear Mummy,

Received your letter . . . in answer to one of my airmail letters,
which took 8 days to get to you. Boy, that is what I call service, and
[I] will use more of these seeing that they get over in such good time.

Hold on, that compliment of yours saying that I might be better
than you is a little far-fetched. You should see the system I use on
the typewriter! And please note the mistakes—letters in the wrong
places—but one thing I can say is, mistakes and all, I sure can crawl
all over these keys even with the punch and hunt system.

Yes Hazel, I would certainly like to have a store of our own. Have
you any idea where we can raise a thousand bucks? It would take all
of that to set up with a decent stock of groceries, and then it would
be entirely up to me to increase our capital. Groceries and gents'
furnishings are my dream darling—do I sound foolish? Don't you
think we could make a go of it?

. . .

Gee darling, the scenery here is simply grand. So green, no end of
flowers and beautiful lawns, and I spend most of my spare moments
strolling over the countryside and through orchards. I've never ate
so many strawberries in my life. Gooseberries are on now, so are
black currants and red currants. The cherries will be starting soon
too and the apple trees are just simply loaded with fruit. The heavi-
est crop of fruit in years, so the growers say, and no sugar to pre-
serve with. Yes Hazel, to us prairie chaps England is beautiful. We
will no doubt miss it a bit after the being stationed in Sussex for
three years, the nicest county in England. But give me Canada—the
wind-swept prairies any day—with you and the kiddies. The only
thing I would like to do someday is to bring you and the kiddies

over here for a trip. I'm positive you will say the same as I am: it is beautiful, especially at this time of year.

. . .

So, Rollie has to have his teeth straightened. Yes, it would be a good idea. Teeth can be a wonderful asset if they are nice and straight. And if they happen to be crooked, I understand that they are easily straightened when they are young. It will be more or less a nuisance for Rollie, it probably means wire braces all over his front teeth.

Have you seen Tom Johnston yet? I would like to hear the line he is stringing to the people of Lafleche. I'll bet there will be some glowing accounts of daring and heroism flying around for the next few days after he gets there.

It is just about Lafleche sports time. What did they have this year? A baseball tournament with big prizes? Or just a picnic, more or less, with a dance at night? Do you know it would be fun to play for a dance in Lafleche with our dance band. I'll bet we would be as good if not better than anything they have ever had play in Lafleche, not because I'm in the band, but the other boys sure are good.

Well darling, I've a little work to do so I guess maybe I had better do something about it. So, I will say bye-bye for now, and take care of yourself.

All of my love and kisses,
Daddy

‹›

Canadian Army Overseas
July 4, 1943


Dear Mummy,

Received an air letter of yours on the second, that you mailed June 26. Not bad time if you ask me. And thanks for the kiss imprinted at the top. Sorry, I haven't any lipstick here or you could see where I stamped one myself in the same place.

. . .

So, Murray is going to come into my bed every morning after I get home and kiss me and love me all over, is he? I sure won't mind either Hazel. I often think of his chubby little arms wrapped around my neck. I do miss my two little men, and if I don't hurry home they will be big enough to beat me up for enlisting and leaving you to face the world with two little boys all alone.

As for what I'm going to do after the war will depend a lot on circumstances darling—money, opportunities, etc. I'm not frightfully keen on Lafleche myself. . . . I'm beginning to be quite the tea drinker, just like a Limey: tea in the forenoon, tea in the afternoon, tea in the evening, just like any other Englishman. So, don't be surprised if I ask for a cup of tea in the forenoons or afternoons when I get home.

I haven't received the eats you sent in May or any cigarettes either, and there has been a lot of mail in too, later than the first of June. As the mails come in, in any order as to dates, I will probably get them any day now. And the parcel of eats will certainly be welcome as I haven't received any eats from home for a long time now. And some evenings after supper, not so good, I could have done with something nice and have went to bed a little hungry.

I've received the snaps alright and thought I had mentioned in a previous letter, but maybe I forgot to mention it.

Boy life sounds inviting for after I get home. BOY-OH-BOY, do I
want to get home. So, I'm going to get loved so much that I will be
all in when you take me anywhere. "Loved right up to the ears," as
you put it. You better be careful that the shoe isn't on the other foot,
because I had intentions myself. There is going to be quite a love-
making competition in the C.O. Bourassa home when I get there.
M-m-m-m-m, should be quite interesting. Gee darling, I can
hardly wait, and I do hope that the competition starts soon.

. . .

Bye darling, all my love,
Daddy

ROLLIE'S NOTE: *The regular flow of letters from Dad suddenly stopped, but after a couple of weeks letters from Dorothy began to arrive on a regular basis. Some were mini-updates as to what might be happening at the time.*

*Letter from Dorothy Starbuck.*

Dale Hill,
Southfleet,
Gravesend
July 12th, [1943]


Dear Hazel,

Received your letter on the 9th. We have been expecting Clarence on leave. He wrote at the end of June and said that he would be seeing us early in July. He did not know when, as the paymaster was on leave, and we have not heard a sound of him since. Now since the invasion of Sicily, I am very much afraid he has been sent there. It would be strange if that is so, because he was due to come on leave the day they went to Dieppe. Another strange thing is that the day [before] he went back on his Easter leave we were coming back on the bus from a neighbouring town, when Mother said we would go there again on his next leave, and Clarence turned to me and said, "I have a long journey to go before then." I did not take any notice at the time, but it gave one a clue to what was on his mind. And in the morning when he went back I said, "Clarence, I am not going to say good-bye. Good morning, or anything else you like, but not good-bye." I did the same thing on the leave before Dieppe. That time, I saw him off in London and he was inclined to smile because I refused to say good-bye. But, this time, he took it quite seriously and said, "no, don't, I don't want to say good-bye." Well, by the time you get this letter I expect we shall both know where he is. I am thankful to hear on the radio that the landing was a success and that so far our casualties have been light. I pray they may continue to be so. I shall continue to write to Clarence; the post office will sort them out and send them on—they may be delayed or even lost, but I think it will help if he only gets a few.

. . .

I will close now and will write again as soon as I get news, but I expect you will get it first. In the meanwhile, do not worry too much. Clarence is in God's care and perhaps this will bring things to a quicker end.

All my love,
Dorothy

p.s. [July 15th] Did not post this at once as my brother said I was taking too much for granted. But, three more days have passed and we have had no news, so decided to post it today.

෴

*Letter from Dorothy Starbuck.*

Dale Hill,
Southfleet,
Gravesend
July 17th, [1943]


Dear Hazel,

Received your letter yesterday, I will answer it later. I am just writing this to tell you that my brother met a Canadian soldier yesterday; of course, he could not say where any of the regiments were, but he did say that all leave and letter-writing had been stopped. So, that probably accounts for us not hearing from Clarence. I do not know if that stands for home letters as well, but you will understand if you do not get any.

Don't worry too much. I will write soon and directly [if] I get any news.

All my love,
Dorothy

☙

*Letter from Dorothy Starbuck.*

Dale Hill,
Southfleet,
Gravesend
July 18th, [1943]


Dear Hazel,

I am going to try to answer your letter, but first, I see by our paper
that Clarence's regiment and one of the others who were at Dieppe
have been presented with their Colours by the King this week, so
[likely] they are still in this country.

. . .

As for Clarence getting involved with other women, I don't think
you need have any fears. He is very good-looking and he only has to
smile to get plenty of them throwing themselves at [him], but it sick-
ens him. We talked it out the last time he was here. He said, "I tell
them all I am married. And it took me 5 years to persuade Hazel to
marry me; do you think I am going to throw all that up for a lot of
silly scatterbrains." The only thing that really worried him was that
some of them were quite young and he was afraid they would get
hurt. I told him that he could not possibly go through life without
coming in contact or speaking to women, and if when they knew he
was married and they continued to be silly, I should have a straight
talk with them and tell them he had you and the boys to think of and
he had no intentions of breaking his vows to you. If, after that, they
got hurt, they would have to get over it. A lot of it is hero-worship.
They get the same sort of passions for film stars, but in that case the
stars don't have to put up with their silliness. I heard the other day of
a young American soldier who said he was almost afraid to speak to a
girl in this country—they took him the wrong way. We have not had
the mixed schools and colleges in this country that you have had in
Canada or the States—that may account for some of it.

. . .

Don't worry more than you can help. I will write again as soon as I get news.

All my love,
Dorothy

☙

ROLLIE'S NOTE: *And then a letter from my father, dated July 23, arrived.*

Canadian Army England
July 23, 1943

Dear Mummy,

It has been nearly a month since I have written. I'm sorry darling, but couldn't do very much about it. As it happened we were taken to a drill camp to prepare for the Presentation of Colors, which were presented by the King accompanied by the Queen. It was a grand ceremony. I was in the band, moving pictures were taken of the Presentation, so you may see us, even me, on some news reel in the near future. The Presentation took two weeks and then all our mails were froze on account of the Sicilian campaign, so I didn't write then. When we got back to camp—to the Pay Office! And I've simply stopped all work to get this letter written or you will be starting divorce proceedings. But, I have been terribly busy as this is the time of year we change pay books. That is once every six months, and this is it. We will be at it for another two weeks yet.

Am I ever tired too. Night in and night out, never to bed before 1 a.m. The reason for there being so much work is that the paymaster is in the hospital with pneumonia and the two of us are caught at the busiest time of the year. But I'm not kicking, because when this rush is over it will be four or five months of fairly easy time. By the way, I resent that crack Tom made about me having picked off a soft job. In all appearances it is. But you know what office work is like. And the hours at times are terrible. I spend many an evening pushing a pencil. Not terribly sweat-raising, but still it can be darned tiring.

Received 1000 smokes you sent the 1st of June today, thanks a million. I also received 11 letters from you since I have last written. I'm so far behind darling that I don't ever hope to get caught up. But I will write oftener from now on. I received a photo of Elnora's two kiddies yesterday; my, but they have grown—I was comparing them with snaps I have.

GOOD NEWS DARLING! I've finally had my photo taken and am going to get them on Saturday. And if they turn out real good I'm going to have a large one made up. I'm just having postcard size made up now as they do not make proofs any more. And what a price too. About three bucks for three postcard-size pictures, but they are guaranteed to be satisfactory. They had better be or I'll certainly demand my money back. I'll send it on to you and you should get it in a month's time.

As I reread your letters I feel like a heel. You keep asking me to keep up the good work and write often, and this lapse has to happen. Am I forgiven? I'm rather afraid to read the next few letters I will be getting of yours, and I won't blame you at all if you bawl the hell out of me.

Thank you for the grand letter Rollie. You are getting to be quite the big boy, eh! Writing all by yourself and good too. Write often, won't you my little man? Are you being a good boy for Mummy? Give her a big kiss for me and tell Murray to scratch a few lines to his daddy too. Do you think you will remember what your daddy looks like when he comes back? I went away a long, long time ago. I wish I could have been to Communion with you the day you made your first. Go to Communion again soon, and pray that your daddy comes home soon. He get awfully lonesome at times; he misses his Mummy and two boys.

Thanks for the nice big kisses on the letters Mummy, you can't imagine what they do to me a way down inside. And thank you for the threat that you are going to love me so much that I won't be able to do anything else. Sounds darned interesting and you will find that I am a willing victim. And don't forget that maybe I've quite a bunch of love all stored up too. So, we should have quite a glorious honeymoon all over again. Gee darling, when, oh when, is it going to be? By the news, we shouldn't be long now, at least for a while. I frankly believe we will see the end of the European side of the war in the next year, and then surely we can get home for a while at least. Heaven knows we have been away long enough.

I've received all the snaps you speak of in your letters. I'm short the parcel in which you enclosed two snaps; I suppose they will come along one of these days as there has been no loss of mail lately.

I am really supposed to be working, although it is nearly midnight. I don't think I will do much more tonight, I'm darned good and tired. As today was payday to boot, we are paying ahead so as not to get too far back on the change of books.

Jerry Wilmont is coming on the air in a minute, so excuse me, it is Canadian news and we can sure eat that up.

Well, bye-bye darling, I will write you a decent letter sometime soon, maybe tomorrow if I can possibly squeeze in the time and not catch hell. Oh, nuts! I'll write tomorrow. A person must be entitled to a little time, but I've sort of developed a funny trait; as long as there is work to be done I can't leave it alone till it is done.

All my love,
Daddy

એ

Canadian Army Overseas
August 6, 1943


Dear Mummy,

Thanks for the parcel. Socks were swell, same for the tops. Could
do with a pair or two of shorts as well. Thank Mother for her parcel
too. It was swell. Good old Canadian coffee for a change. I'll drop
her a line as soon as I'm through with this letter.

I haven't been living up to my promise of writing oftener as we have
been terribly busy, even through Saturday and Sunday this last week.
We have a new paymaster now, just got here today. And to all appearances he is going to be nice to work for. Anyway, the first impression is good. And now that we have pretty well got out from
under, I definitely will make up for not writing so often.

The photos I had taken didn't turn out so good so I had them re-
taken and got them today. Not too bad and I am sending you one
ordinary mail as a wedding anniversary gift. Got your telegram this
evening; did you get mine? I sent it Monday. As busy as we have
been I hadn't forgotten that I married the nicest little girl in the
world and hurried to send a wire. Even at times when it seems as
if I have forgotten about you by not writing as often as one might
think I should, don't worry darling, there is some reason for it, because I do love you and I realize how much too. Ever to the extent
of feeling a little jealous at times when I read your letters and see
different names mentioned, especially when you use their Christian
names. I know it is silly, but it must mean that I do care.

I got quite a kick out of Tom's stories and I still can't for the life
of me figure what grounds he used for getting back to Canada.

By the way, excuse typing, as I still use the punch-and-hunt system,
and it is late so I am simply banging away here as fast as I can spot
the keys. And I've been typing all afternoon and evening and the

keys all seem to run together at times. I should settle down to learning how to handle this thing properly—I don't know where I'd find the time! As it is, I can hardly find time to write anyone and I owe literally hundreds of letters, even [to] Uncle Jerry.

As soon as we are all caught up I expect to get my leave and have just written Dorothy to be expecting me on or about the 15th. She writes me every week and I hadn't written to her in four weeks, that is how bad things are.

The radio is giving out some sweet sentimental music. They are playing "Black Magic"; pretty nice, isn't it? The number that I really like is, "Don't Get Around Much Anymore"—we just got it for the orchestra—there are no end of nice numbers out now. I hate to tell you what is considered new over here as you likely have heard them months ago. Such as, "I've Heard That Song Before," "Johnny Zero," etc. etc.—all good numbers though. Do you remember when you told me in a letter that you liked "Yours." Well darling, we still play that at every dance [we] play for, and I honestly always whisper to myself, "to you Mummy."

Well darling, I'll close now saying I'm fine, and I do hope the kiddies and yourself are the same. Give them a big hug and a kiss for me.

All of my love and kisses,
Daddy

☙

*Canadian Pacific Telegraphs*

GREAT BRITAIN

MRS. C.O. BOURASSA,
LAFLECHE SASK:

YOU ARE MORE THAN EVER IN MY THOUGHTS AT THIS TIME
HAPPY ANNIVERSARY BEST LOVE FROM DADDY.

CLARENCE BOURASSA

ↄ

HAZEL AND CLARENCE'S WEDDING PHOTOGRAPH.
THEY WERE MARRIED AUGUST 7, 1935.

Canadian Army Overseas
August 24, 1943


Dear Hazel,

. . .

Well darling, in answer to your final question, you are still, and will remain, the one and only in my life, and you are most certainly forgiven for that one nasty letter. I will admit that being so far apart, our imaginations, with a little suggestion here and there, will run away with us. To be honest darling, at times I do wonder myself, and my imagination does try to get away on me occasionally. When I feel in that kind of a mood, I don't write to you in case I say something I may be sorry for. A letter can be misunderstood, and being so far apart, and explanations so long in getting back and forth, irreparable damage can be done.

So, you would like something nice, something you can wear as an Xmas present. Funny, it should happen, but I spent the last few hours of my leave running from store to store in Gravesend to buy you something like that. And I've come to the conclusion that England is at war in earnest, because the jewellery stores have very poor stocks, mostly pre-war goods. And, my, what a price they want for anything decent. So, I had to come away empty-handed. What I would have liked I couldn't afford, and what I could afford, I wouldn't think of sending to anyone I thought anything of.

Did you get my photo yet? I sent one to Mother too. I also gave one to Starbucks. They thought it was real nice, I hope you think so too.

You keep asking the same question. When are you coming home? You know very well that I will as soon as I can. And please darling, stop this worrying about me. I'm fine and will remain so long after I get back to you. As to the date, your guess is as good as mine. In the meantime, let us trust in God that it will be soon, and darling, don't please, don't get sick. Your last letter worries me. You talk as if you are not any too well. Darned it all, I should be with you where I belong and see that you take care of yourself the way you should.

All of my love,
Clarence

[p.s.]. . .When I say I love you it isn't just scribbled words darling. Take care of yourself, and tell Yvonne I received her airgraph and will answer as soon as I can. I owe so many letters and just simply don't find the time to write too many. Yours have priority, and they are scarce enough aren't they? A big long hug and a kiss, Daddy.

෴

*Letter from Dorothy Starbuck.*

Dale Hill,
Southfleet,
Gravesend
Aug. 25th, [1943]


Dear Hazel,

At last I have settled down to write to you. I should have done it
before, but these days one seems to be living on top of a volcano. Well,
Clarence came for a few days last week. He only got five days instead
of nine, so with the travelling was only here three whole days. He came
on the Sunday evening and went back just after noon on Thursday. He
had to leave our telephone number, so the consequence was he sat
nearly on top of the phone in case he might be recalled. As you may
imagine he was pretty well strung up. But he had a good rest and his
nerves were much steadier when he left. I think when all the men are
together they get all sorts of rumours and work each other up. Anyway,
Clarence has left his civvie clothes and a few odds and ends he did not
want to lose here. So, we will look after them until he needs them again.
If he comes back this way he can take them with him, or if he comes
straight home without calling this way again we can send them home.

Clarence has had a beautiful photograph taken. He sent one off to
you and one to his mother while he was here. I hope you get it, I
am sure you will be pleased. He gave us one and my mother has
put it in a frame. She likes to show people what a nice-looking
young man comes to stay with us. She is getting old and a bit
childish, but it keeps her amused.

We saw the latest snaps of you and the boys—how they do grow. It
looks funny to us to see a boy in long trousers; our boys keep in
short knickers until they are 14. I am sure that is a lot of Clarence's
trouble—being so far away from you and the children. He went
with Percy the other evening to see some friends and there was a
baby about 18 months old there. Percy said they saw him bathed

and Clarence played with him and he came home quite cheered up. It is not natural for a man to be away from his family so long; we try to do the best we can for him, but I often feel it only makes him more homesick. Last Monday when he was having his breakfast he said he thought things should be settled down enough for him to get home in about 18 months time. I said, "Well, lad, we shall miss you, but for your own sake I hope you do." The tears came into his eyes and he said he was going to Gravesend to find Percy. Well, things seem to be moving rapidly now and I hope for all the boys it will soon be over. Our village seems nearly empty of young men now; as soon as they are 18 they are called up, and the girls, too, for that matter—but a lot of them are working on the farms or near, so that they get home at night.

Well dear, I don't think I have any more news just now. I will write again when things are more settled or I have any more news.

With all my love,
Dorothy

∽

THE PHOTOGRAPH DOROTHY DESCRIBED ABOVE. THE STARBUCKS WOULD LATER HAVE AN ARTIST PRODUCE A PAINTED PORTRAIT BASED UPON IT.

Canadian Army England
August 27, 1943

Hello Darling,

Gee, it's late. We are on a scheme and I'm tired. Worked like a nig-
ger all day. I'm Casualty Clerk now, and work both in the Orderly
Room and Pay Office. I'm on the dead run all day lately, mostly because I'm not sure of my work yet. A lot of it is still as clear as mud
to me, but I'm getting there, and there is a possibility of a little
more pay, which I intend to turn over to you if I ever get it. A
couple of dollars or so, not a lot, but will pay for my smokes.
That's a little help anyway.

When I think of my last letter, I wonder if maybe I wasn't a little
too short. The trouble is I've been pushing a pen and figuring so
much the last few weeks and working rather hard, that I'm inclined
to be cranky at times. Especially, when you tell me off for not writing. I'll admit I don't write as often as I used to, but I really am
quite busy now. But I won't always be. I'll write as often as I can
Hazel, and I'll at least write once a week. If I don't hear from you
every week, I begin to fret and worry myself.

Haven't you received my telegram yet? I sent it, or had our postal
clerk take it, on the 3rd of Aug. You should have it in a couple of
days. I should have sent it about the 27 of July to make sure.

Percy Starbuck offered me a job here in England when I was on
leave, a job after the war. He didn't promise anything, just casually
mentioned it. I laughed and thanked him all the same. No, I've had
enough of England long ago. It is to me nothing but loneliness for
Canada, which means you and the kiddies, and the sooner I get
back the better.

Yes darling, I often wonder why you worry about me coming back
to you. Will I still love you, will I be decent, etc., etc. As for loving

you, I do, and I will, and as for being decent, well now, if I love [you] I can't help but be where you are concerned. And for an added incentive, I've two boys.

Gee darling, I owe so many letters I'm ashamed of myself, but I just haven't the time to write to them: Yvonne, Min, Delores, Bob, etc., etc. Tell them I'll write as soon as I can. At present, we are allowed two letters a week, and you have my quota this week. Of course, that is only for the duration of this exercise—a security test.

The band and orchestra have been put on the shelf for the time being, and quite possibly for good. I can't say that I mind much as yet; anyway, at present, I haven't time.

Well darling, take care of yourself please and don't worry about me.

I love you,
Clarence

P.S. Give the kiddies a big hug and a kiss for me, and tell Rollie if he don't mind to scribble a word or two to his daddy.

&

Canadian Army Overseas
September 19, 1943


Dear Mummy,

Well, I believe it is certainly about time I answered a lot of your letters, which have been coming through very regularly—thank you
darling. Yes, I have not written for three weeks. I am sorry darling,
but there is nothing I can say but that I honestly have been terribly
busy as there has been some changes made in my line of work, and
I just simply had to buckle down and learn how to do it or some
one else was going to take over my job. And believe you me, I spent
many a long night going [over] things over and over again till I had
them right. I'm in charge of records now as well as doing the same
work I was doing in the Pay Office, so I've had many a headache
over nominal rolls, strength states, ration states, etc. But, now I've
learned how to do things, I will find more time to breathe and write
letters. I think of how I used to shirk hard jobs. Now that I have
one, I seem to stick to it till I have mastered it and look for more.
I like it, though, as it sure makes time fly.

So, you finally received my photo. I don't like that crack about the
wave. My hair has been like that ever since we have been in England. And don't talk to the darned thing too much darling; after all
it is just a picture, and it is very flattering as well if you ask me.
And it doesn't show any grey hair, which I have plenty of.

Received a thousand smokes the other day, thank you. You have
written about a box of chocolates; I haven't received those as yet,
and I am really looking forward to them. (Excuse the odd word
dropped out, I'm trying to speed up my typing as I am to go on
a trade test sometime this week. Typing is the test I'm the most
afraid of, but they are not very exacting as you only have to type
ten words a minute for a pass mark. So, I shouldn't have too
much trouble. . . . )

So, the kiddies have had their tonsils out. I suppose that by now they have completely recovered. It must have been quite an ordeal for you. I hope they were not too sick. Give them a great big hug for me. So, Rollie thought our home was nice after being away for only a couple of days. So, you can imagine what it will mean to me to get back. I do hope things continue in our favour for the next few months, and probably I will be home before another year is up. Yes, this is my fourth Xmas away from you darling . . . I can't really believe it has actually been that long, and I hope that the next few months go by just as fast.

. . .

So, Toronto is the place you have picked for us after the war. I don't think I'd mind myself as I have some very nice memories of the place. The only snag is what will I do for a living in a place like it. We don't know anyone and no one gives a damn, which for that matter is the same even in Lafleche. Nevertheless, I'm going to try for a job some place out east. If we only had a few dollars we could start up some-place on our own, which would suit us down to the ground.

As for an Xmas present for the Starbucks, I haven't the least idea what they would like as they are considerably older than me and their taste[s] are very simple. Could you make it hose again? I be-lieve Dorothy was thrilled with [the] last you sent her. I imagine about 10½ are her size as she is a big woman.

Thanks for the nice big kiss that started out your last letter. My what nice lips you have Mummy. I'd sure like to smear your lipstick all over your face with my lips. As for being unconscious after I get home, I don't know about that. I've had a long spell without women so no doubt will be able to take all you can and maybe hand out a little on my own. All I can say darling, I'm game and willing, and it will certainly not be too soon when I do get there.

Well darling, I guess I had better close as someone just came in with a marriage certificate and wants me to make out an application for dependant's allowance for his wife of a day or two. So bye-bye for now, will write again in a day or two, as soon as I can.

All of my love and kisses. Sorry, I don't use lipstick or you would see where I'm sending you one too.

Take care of yourself,
love,
Clarence

෴

*Letter from Dorothy Starbuck.*

Dale Hill
Southfleet
Gravesend
Sept. 25th, [1943]


Dear Hazel,

I received your letter dated August 19th this morning. I am not surprised you are suffering from nerves. I think we all are more or less,
it is a kind of war weariness. Do not worry yourself about the expense of having Clarence here, our business is doing very well just
now. And if coming here for a bit helps to make life easier for him
it is money well spent, because if his nerves get too frayed it will
cost more in time and money later on to mend them.

I don't expect Clarence does answer when you ask if he is likely to
go into action again, because he cannot truthfully say he won't. And
I expect he knows it will upset you if he says he will. Well, we do
think he will see more action, but my brother says that he does not
think he will be sent out at once. Even if the Regiment go, because
of his work they are not likely to send all the records of the Regiment into the front line in case they get lost. They will wait until
they are established and then send them over to a reasonably safe
place. I am telling you this because I think if you know how
things are you worry less.

Yes, Clarence was going back from his very short leave the day
you wrote. We have had one letter from him since and he said
something about being on a scheme. We know they have had large-
scale exercises, so I suppose they have been on them. That was why
his leave was cut short, but when he was here he was not sure if it
would be the real thing or not. So, [he] was all keyed up and told
one he was pretty sure it was the last leave he was likely to spend
on this side. . . .

Well dear, I must close now, do take care of yourself. I will do what I can for Clarence and I hope [to] send him back whole in mind and body. We can only pray that the time will not be long.

All my love,
Dorothy

౿

Canadian Army Overseas
October 5, 1943

Dear Mummy,

At times I suppose you wonder what in the devil keeps me from
writing oftener. Well, the truth is I have darned little time to myself
anymore. This is a desk job alright, and how. I work most every
night, time sure does fly too. I don't realize that you are waiting for
a letter till I get one from you and then I'm ashamed of myself. And
I continually keep promising that I will write oftener. Please don't
get peeved with me darling, even if it does seem that I do not write
as often as I could, because I would like to, as I certainly look forward to your letters. And I'm rather afraid that some time or other
you might get peeved and not write as often as you have been doing.

Received an air letter from you yesterday. It was swell and it made
me feel much better as I was a little worried about the way the operation [the tonsillectomy] reacted on Murray. So both the boys are
themselves again. Apparently, real boys, as you say that they are still
hard to handle. In one way that is a good sign, they must be healthy.
Yes, I quite realize I should be home with, and help look after, those
little tykes.

You mentioned sending different parcels. All I have received in
the past few months are smokes darling, and I could do with a few
razor blades, etc. Something I seem to fancy lately is Niblets, are
they still procurable? I do miss those parcels of eats and I am certainly looking forward to Xmas parcels.

It was nice of you to send Dorothy a pair of stockings, they are so
darned good to me. In her last letter she said she was getting my
room ready for my next leave and that she was expecting me soon.

There go the air-raid warnings. We are down on the coast again. A
very nice town, a lot of theatres, and I haven't even got time to take

in the odd picture. As for the orchestra, I've given it up. I just can't make ends meet. I can hear planes overhead, probably our own.

Well darling, I have to write a letter to the Starbucks tonight so this will have to do as a letter. And tomorrow we go out on a scheme—six days of misery—and the weather isn't any too nice. I'll probably be cursing the day I ever joined the Army about this time tomorrow night, sleeping out under the clouds. All I hope is that it don't rain. The weather can be so nice at times, and others darned miserable.

Yes, what I wouldn't give to wrap my arms around you darling and cuddle you up real close. I'd kiss you till [you] hollered for mercy. Don't think I won't when I do [get] a hold of you. As you say, I'd better come in the best of health. Now that goes for you too as well. Must I say it? You know, just boy-oh-boy!

The next thousand cigs you send darling, send MacDonald blends, they would be nice for a change. After that, make them Sweet Caps as they are always good.

As for what I will be doing after the war, I really haven't made up my mind yet, because I haven't anything definite to go to—a job in the East would be nice.

Well darling, I'll say night-night. Give the kiddies a big hug for me.

All of my love,
Daddy

❧

Canadian Army Overseas
October 19, 1943


Dear Mummy,

At long last here I am. Your letter of today sure woke me up. Yes, it does only take a few minutes to write a letter. I've just had supper and before I start in to work I must write or you will disown me. . . .

So, the old town is still as dead as ever. And I suppose as gossipy as ever. That accident young Crooks had must have been quite the choice bit for the tongue-waggers. You didn't say who the girl was that got hurt, and how did she do.

Gee, I've been busy darling, and at times not doing so well. I seem to have developed a stubbornness I didn't know I had. I'll have to keep it under control or I'll find myself back on parade one of these days. I do get into the darndest arguments with the Sgt., and I just won't give in or knuckle down to him as a private should, which sure seems to burn him up as I'm in charge of records. And at times I don't seem to see things with his eyes, and then all hell busts loose in the Orderly Room. I must have crossed him up sometime or other because he sure seems to enjoy picking my work to pieces. Instead of saying, "yes, Sgt.," I usually come out with something like, "to hell you shot a bear," and away we go at it again. As long as my records are correct I'll be damned if he will ever make a yes-man out of me.

How are the kiddies Mummy? Fine, I hope. And by the way, thanks for the birthday cards, they are sure swell. Yes darling, one or two more weeks and I'll be thirty. If this war don't ever end I'll have grandchildren before I get back. Gee, your letter was blue in spots darling. I should be home near you where I belong, do all those lit-tle things you have to do now, such as puttying windows and the likes. And most of all, and what I miss most is, to cuddle you these long cold evenings. Just to be with you Mummy seems to be my sole ambition—soon, I hope.

I suppose winter is just around the corner over there. We are starting to get the rains now. It has been terrible out today, the sea is sure rough. If you could only hear the roar of the waves crashing against the breakwater. It is an awful lonely noise, makes me lonesome. Do you remember all of Rollie's little sayings? Can't say I remember any of Murray's as he wasn't talking before I left. I missed all of that, and his cutest age too. Darned the luck. I sure put my foot in it when I joined up. It is just simply gone by. What I wouldn't give to see those two little boys of mine, to see what they look like, pick them up in my arms, hug and kiss them. As it is, I suppose they will have outgrown the kissing stage and will be shaking my hand when I do get home. Or slapping me on the back and saying, "Hi-ya, Pop."

I started this last night, and couldn't finish.

I'm back in the orchestra again as they claim they could not possibly keep on without me. Rather flattering, if you ask me. As we are back on the coast again and there is no end of dance halls, the orchestra is certainly in demand.

. . .

Yes, Xmas is getting close once again. The third in this country. I hope I can get up to Starbucks' for a good Xmas dinner; I got a letter from them today asking me to come up then and try to arrange my leave for then.

We are playing for the regimental dance tonight and we have four dances next week. So, that is something else again to take up my time. I really am kept awfully busy and time does fly. The first I will know is that [this] will all be over and I'll be on my way home. That is the day I'm certainly praying for, to get back to you and the kiddies.

Well darling, it's soon time to go and I have to shave. So bye-bye for now, and I will write again on Sunday when I won't have to rush through a letter.

Take care of yourself and give the kiddies a big hug for me. Bye Mummy.

All of my love,
Clarence

P.S. Oh, I miss you mummy, so much, in more ways than one. A big, big kiss.

ℰᴐ

Canadian Army Overseas
October 28, 1943


Dear Mummy,

I got a surprise today—a box of Smiles'n Chuckles. I have not
opened them yet; I'm going to wait till next Friday, my birthday, and
have a treat. I'm sure have a time of it to keep away from them, even
the box is awfully inviting. And another surprise, two swell Xmas
cards, rather early, but swell all the same. You mailed them on the sixteenth and they got here on the twenty-seventh, 11 days and not airmail either. Not bad I say. But where in heavens is the cigarettes? I do
hope to get a few soon. There is two-thousand of them somewhere in
the mail waiting to be delivered and I sure could do with them.
Thanks for the air-letter, which I received the day before yesterday.

There is to be a big Canadian celebration here on the eleventh of
November, and our brass band is to lead the military parade. So tomorrow, we start rehearsals. It is about time, as I haven't blown the
euphonium for two months at least and I am plenty rusty.

. . .

Well darling, I'm still as busy as ever but in the pink. I haven't had
so much as a cold in the last six months. Doing alright, aren't I? I'm
looking forward to another leave again soon. I was hoping to get
away for my birthday. No chance though, as there are some of the
boys who haven't had their third leave yet and this next one will my
fourth—my quota for this year. I got beat out of a leave last year and
I'm going to see that I get them all this year. Outside of mail, our
leaves are the only other pleasure we have on this side of the pond.

. . .

There is only Mickey Faille and I left in the regiment at present. Frank
James was struck off strength yesterday to the reinforcement unit. . . .

Tomorrow is pay day, more headaches for us, and an awful lot of noise tomorrow night, as all pay nights are. Some of the boys don't seem to be able to stand prosperity and proceed to paint the town red every pay night.

When in creation am I ever going to get back to you and the kiddies darling? Thirty-years-old next week, children big enough to beat me up, practically strangers to me, my hair is getting quite gray. It all boils down to this: if I don't hurry home, I'll be getting my old age pension first.

How are the kiddies Mummy? In the best of health I hope. Give them a big kiss and a hug for me. Say Rollie, you should be here with me. There is a great big playground for kiddies. Merry-go-rounds, all kinds of swings, a roller skating rink, little cars with real engines in them to play with—you should see all the little fellows your age driving them all over the grounds having a whale of a time.

Yes Hazel, this is the ideal town for kiddies. Purely residential and chuck-full of evacuee children. I see no end of them, all ages, and they remind me so much of our little men. Oh, please God, send me home soon.

I haven't got that raise in pay yet; in fact, haven't had a [chance] to try the test yet. The raise won't amount to much, but it is there to get and I suppose you could do with a couple of extra dollars at that [to] help pay for my smokes. Whatever happens to the cigs you send, don't stop sending them, as most of them get through.

. . . in the meantime, all of my love, and kisses [to] no end. Oh, for the feel of you in my arms again.

I love you,
Clarence

⁊

Canadian Army England
November 8, 1943

Hello Darling,

Thanks for the telegram, it got here on the fourth. Well Friday, I opened up that box of chocolates and were they ever good. Still quite a few left. As I consider them as a birthday present I offered a sample or two, but am hoarding the rest for as long as I can.

Received September's cigarettes today. They were rather long in getting here but nevertheless they were all the better as I've been smoking anything I could get as I've been out over three weeks.

We are on the coast again. Evenings, I walk to the canteen, down [to] the waterfront for a cup of coffee, and as I come up to the corner looking out over the sea I can see Halifax it seems. At least my imagination does, and someday soon I will no doubt be seeing it. Halifax represents Canada to me and it is really all I hope for now—[that] is, to get back, back to Canada, to you, to the kiddies. As I comb my hair and see the white ones multiplying by the day, I wonder—the new wrinkles, the heavier beard, the harder look about my face—I wonder will they still love their daddy or will they be disappointed in him. Yes, no doubt I've changed an awful lot and I hope it meets with your approval.

Friday night I went to a dance with some of the boys as sort of a celebration. There was a very good orchestra. Some R.A.F. band. I had a few dances at the first, and then Hedley Munro, our orchestra leader, and I sat out the rest of the dance and listened to the music, which seemed to be more interesting than the women on the floor. You still come first darling in all respects. Do you know it will be fun getting acquainted again. Oh, I long for the thrill of you in my arms—I ache at times.

How are the kiddies? Giving you trouble are they? I don't know about Rollie, you say you couldn't get him into G-bourg. It does seem kind of bad to have to send him to a kindergarten. Yes, I should be home looking after those two little tykes and I hope it is soon.

Re that daughter of ours. Well now, oh, I guess we had, or I had, better wait and see. Financial problems may have something to do with that, but still a little girl would make our family complete, wouldn't she?

I love you darling,
Daddy

↝

*Letter from Dorothy Starbuck.*

Dale Hill,
Southfleet,
Gravesend
Nov. 12th, [1943]


Dear Hazel,

. . .


I had a letter from Clarence and he expects to get his Christmas
leave at the end of this month. So, we shall be seeing something of
him. As it is getting near Christmas, he is very homesick. Poor lads,
it must be heartbreaking to be so far away, especially [for] the married ones. We had a man just come back from the Middle East, they
live quite near us. There are two children, a boy 10 and a little girl 8.
The father has been away over 3 years and the little girl did not remember him and for a time resented him. It must be very puzzling
for a child's mind to have an almost unknown man turn up after
they have had their mother's whole attention. . . .

We have been having some air raids again lately. Nothing very serious, but enough to be trying. You just get nicely tucked into bed
when the siren goes, the guns start firing—they make a terrible noise.
I usually get up, because my mother being elderly, you cannot get
her up in a hurry if you had to. And I think she is better dressed as
the nights are getting cold. And you never know if, when the planes
get in the gunfire, they will let go their bombs to get away. We had
one on the outskirts of the village about 2 weeks ago, but no one was
even scratched, although lots of glass was blown out of windows.

Well dear, I will write again when I have seen Clarence. Thank you
again for your kindness.

Love,
Dorothy

Canadian Army England
November 13, 1943

Dear Mummy,

Received a parcel yesterday with peanut butter and bars, and, darling, how about sending a raft of razor blades in the next parcel? The blades we get here are not so hot.

I also received three nice letters from you and I hope your request from Ted Culliton comes to something. That would be swell. Is there any way I can help from this side? I can't for the life of me think of any feasible reason to ask for a transfer back to Canada. [Edward "Ted" Culliton, a Liberal, was the Member of the Saskatchewan Legislative Assembly for Gravelbourg from 1935–1944 and 1948–1951.]

. . .

We, that is, the brass band went on a tour playing for inspections and we played for five generals' inspections in twenty-four hours. We got back last night and I don't care for any more like it. And to boot I'm two days behind in my work, which means Saturday and Sunday are well taken care of. And we have to play for a dance tonight. By the way, thank you for that music. As it happens, I saw the show last Wednesday and wanted the piece, and [what a] coincidence, I get it in a parcel from Canada. Nice number, isn't it? I'm going out and see if I can't find an orchestration of it for the band.

. . .

Gosh Hazel, every time I think of the possibilities that might pop up re Culliton, I get all thrills. It seems to be too much to hope for. Oh darling, do you think it can be done?????

Well, the Sgt. just came in with an armful of work, so I'll say bye-bye.

All of my love darling,
Daddy

P.S. Thank Rollie for the nice letter. He is doing alright at school isn't he?

☙

Canadian Army England
December 1, 1943

Dear Mummy,

At long last here I am. Just got over a bout of the flu, spent six days
in bed. I am still all stuffed up with cold, but feeling fine.

Thanks for the swell parcel, everything was in perfect shape. And
thanks for the Xmas cards. Have you received the ones I have sent?

Oh yes, someone very nicely made off with my fountain pen last
Friday, so I'm back to the old style again, darned it all! But, I guess
there is no use crying over spilt milk. The only thing is they can't be
bought over here anymore so I guess I'll just have to struggle along.
If I ever get another pen and pencil I'll sure know what to do with
them.

Received your letter of the 21st of Nov. today, it sure was nice. I
don't quite understand this Culliton stunt—what and how??? Can't
help over here? I'm physically fit, no family troubles, just fed up,
and that isn't reasons enough to get me home. If Culliton does pull
enough strings to get me back, he has a lot more influence than I
ever gave him credit for. Oh, but I do hope he can make it.

So, Murray wants to know when Clarence is coming home. Tell him
if Clarence had any say about it he would have done so long ago.

Just a few more days and Xmas. I wonder if it will be as lonely as
the others. I was rather counting on being away on leave for Xmas,
but due to financial embarrassment I believe I'll have to stay in the
barracks area or forfeit my leave. It will no doubt be a poor way of
spending a leave. I expected to get a raise, but it doesn't seem to
come through. It would be nice to get two or three dollars a payday
more, but red tape and regulations sure slow things up.

You say you heard that Mickey was in Italy? You heard wrong, because I was speaking to him today.

. . .

So, you wonder if you could thrill me; now Hazel, just to think of you does a little something to me. So what you wouldn't do to me when you do get hold of me—gosh, I just don't know! It will be swell. Am I behaving? Yes—a plain and frank answer—because I happen to love you.

Daddy

p.s. Send more razor blades and hankies.

⁂

Canadian Army Overseas
December 23rd, 1943


Hello Mummy,

Received second Xmas parcel, everything was swell. And you still
keep repeating I don't write weeks on end. Haven't you got any of
my mail at all? There always is a possibility of some of it being lost,
but not all of it.

Playing for a dance tonight, a regimental dance, will tell you all
about it tomorrow. We will be leaving in a few minutes.

Received a parcel from the Women War Workers, and one from
Aunt Olive, one from Dodo, and one from Yvonne. So, I've plenty
for Xmas, which is going to be awful quiet as I've no place to go.
I'm getting terrible lonesome already. I'm still doing plenty of painting and orchestra playing; frankly, I'm kept darned busy. As for having evenings to myself, it seems to be a thing of the past—dances,
practices—no wonder I don't write so often. Time flies so fast and
the first thing I know a week has gone by and no letters written.
A promise: Hazel, it won't happen again. I know how much I look
forward to your letters; it hurts when none come. So, I'll be careful
to write often. "I love you."

Hedley Munro asked me to spend my next leave with him and his
folks, or rather relatives, in Motherwell, Scot[land], about thirty
miles from Glasgow, so I think I will go with him for a change.

It will soon be time to leave for the dance, so this won't be very long.

How are the kiddies? Should have some pictures of myself to send
home soon; I really enjoy the ones I have of you and the kiddies—
they are all thumb-marked from handling.

For some reason I keep humming "Yours" all the time tonight, and I feel quite lonely. So, at the dance tonight, "Yours" will be for you. It is getting quite old, but I still like it.

Bye-bye Mummy, the boys are gathering up the instruments.

All of my love,
Daddy

❧

Canadian Army England
December 28, 1943


Hello Mummy,

Rather slow getting around to write aren't I? And I owe you so
many letters too. So, the New Year being just about here and a
resolution: to write much oftener if it is at all possible.

Thanks for the lovely parcels and cards. I'm glad you received mine
on time. I'm sorry I didn't send a wire; when I went in to do so all
the cablegrams to Canada had been suspended.

Well, I had a swell Xmas dinner: turkey, goose, and pork. Well put
up too, but no cranberry sauce. Next Christmas Eve we will have
dinner together. That is a date, and darling, it will be the nicest
Xmas of my life. I'm sick and tired of it all, wondering what to do
with myself, etc. I didn't get my leave as I expected to, had to forfeit
it on account of I was broke or very near it. In this country, one
needs at least fifty dollars to have a decent leave, on less than that
you can't go anywhere or do anything as we are stationed in a city
and things are so darned expensive. For instance, that card I sent
you cost 6 shillings, about $1.30, so you can see what it is like.
And if we go to a show it is 75 cents, at least for a decent seat. And
seventy-five cents a week for laundry, and the odd meal out—my
goodness, what would it cost me if I was spending my money on
drink or something like it. Occasionally I have a pint of beer before
dinner, but never any more. I just don't care for the stuff over here.

Gee, it was a lonely Christmas. We went to a show in the afternoon
and at night we went to the canteen. The regiment gave everyone a
few pints of beer and we sang songs till about 10, and then I went
back to my room, empty and cold, so I stripped, jumped into the
tub and rolled in.

Now we are in the thick of the change of books (pay books), so I am real busy for the next few days. I'll write again on the second or third.

I hope you had a better Xmas than I did. Give the kiddies a big hug and a kiss for me.

All of my love,
Daddy

☙

# LETTERS 1944

Canadian Army England
January 2, 1944


Hello Darling,

Happy New Year, and I do hope to wish you the next one while you
are in my arms and I can look down into your eyes and say a happy,
happy New Year, Hazel.


. . .


I've got a leave coming up in a couple of weeks and it is the same
old story. I am broke, and don't think I will be able to scrounge
enough to take it. So, I am going to ask if you can spare some, say,
about twenty-five dollars. I hate to ask but I have no one to turn to
but you, and I have already forfeited one leave for the same reason.
I'd rather take it this time as one practically has to admit that this
next leave will no doubt be about our last in this country. I hate
to ask for any from home as you no doubt could put it to much
better use than I could—if you are short don't send any.

Received two of your airmail letters today and they sure were swell.
So, you are a little worried about Rollie's health. I suppose he is just
like I was as a kid, all legs and neck and sickly looking. But I got by
fairly well. After all these years and this Army life, I'm still A1 cate-
gory, so I guess we needn't worry about Rollie. He will be alright. I
suppose Murray is altogether a different type. He probably has a little of the Mitchell to counterbalance the Bourassa slimness I hope.
It would be too bad if I were to raise two long drinks of milk. . . .


. . .


Well, I had rather a quiet New Year's. Went out for dinner, or rather,
was invited out for dinner by an elderly Englishman and had a very
nice meal and a pleasant evening. New Years Eve, I was standing
outside the pay office and this old gent came up and asked me

point blank if I would care to have New Year's dinner with him and his wife. As their two boys were in Italy, and his wife thought that maybe some Canadian away from home isn't going out to dinner New Year's, [they] would like to have a couple in for dinner. He seemed very nice, and as I had no place to go I accepted and had a very nice time. And [I] have a standing invitation to go up to their home any evening I care to. I haven't done that yet but intend to tomorrow night if we aren't too far behind in our work.

Well, I'll say night-night. It is getting a little late and the fire is out. My fingers are getting stiff. Oh, if I could only pull a chair to the stove and rest my feet on the oven door with you at my side, I'd be the most satisfied man in the world.

All my love darling, and all the best in the New Year.

Love,
Daddy

ↄ

Canadian Army England
January 11, 1944

Hello Mummy,

Received the air letter you wrote on New Year's Day. And thanks
for the kiss, do you know you have nice lips—at least the imprint
is very inviting.

Young Huel from G-bourg is attached to our regiment for a few
months and he was in to see me and we had quite a few nice talks.
He hasn't much use for the Canadian wives. He says it is something
awful the way they carry on, and he feels bad for our boys over here
with wives in Canada. Being a lieutenant, he said that he got around
a lot and was certainly surprised at how weak the women were. A
few drinks, he said, and nothing mattered but the immediate; they
seem to forget all about their husbands. With all his slurs about
married women, it didn't phase me in the least, because I figure I
am one of the lucky ones. And the finish of your previous letter
makes me all the surer, when you said, "I've kept myself for you."
Thank you darling, and I can say the same even after these long
years. And I hope that the last year apart has just gone by.

I asked you for a little money in my last letter. I could still use it,
but as I said, if you need it, a leave is nothing, more or less. So, it is
up to you. By the way, if you send me any have it cabled over; otherwise, it will no doubt be too late.

So, you had a rather quiet New Year's. I'm glad you enjoyed the
New Year's dance. I didn't go anywhere, only to dinner at Bakers'
and haven't been back since.

. . .

How is your health darling? Are you feeling better again as you still
are working? How are the kiddies? Maybe I should answer Rollie's

letter—has he any trouble reading my letters? I can hardly imagine having a son old enough to read. So Murray sings does he? I'll be he is cute. Darned it all Mummy, I do want to get home so bad. Have you heard any more from Culliton?

. . .

Well bye-bye darling,
all of my love,
Clarence

෮

*Letter from Dorothy Starbuck.*

Dale Hill,
Southfleet,
Gravesend
Feb. 6th, [1944]


Dear Hazel,

Clarence has had his leave at last. If he had left it another fortnight
it would have been six months since we saw him. He looked much
better than when we saw him before. I think the spell in bed with
the flu did him good, and his nerves seemed steadier. Not that I saw
much of him, just at breakfast and supper. He was away with Percy
all day, because the very night he arrived our store in Gravesend had
all the upper part burnt and everything had to be got out. Clarence
helped get things straightened out.


. . .


It was not much fun for Clarence working nearly all his leave, but
he said he was glad to be able to help us and he seemed quite happy
over it. I expect he will write and tell you all about it.

I was only saying today how strange it is that Clarence has always
fitted in in our family. He has never bothered me. He just seems to
fit in, and my brother and I always refer to him as our lad.

I was telling him this week that I hope someday in the not-too-
distant future he will be able to bring you and the family to see us.
I think he would be quite happy over here if only you and the boys
were with him.

I was glad to hear from Clarence that you are all well. I think his
illness was partly caused by worrying about you and the kiddies.

We all hope that many of the boys will be able to join their families soon now. It does seem that this year may hold many unexpected things for us. May the Lord bless us all and bring us peace.

Love,
Dorothy

☙

Canadian Army Overseas
February 15, 1944


Hello Mummy,

Gosh, it has been a long time since I've wrote. I have just come
back off leave with Starbucks. Had a grand time, but quiet. I had
to borrow a few pounds and I hope that cheque you sent gets here
soon. I'm sorry I asked you for it now, but I can still use it.

As you will notice I have left the Pay Office [return address on letters has changed]. I'm "C" Company Orderly Room clerk now,
which is a much easier job and now I should have plenty of time to
write. I sure have been getting bounced around lately, and I'm sure
dissatisfied. My only desire is to get home. You ask about action.
Things are certainly pointing that way Hazel, and as for getting
home before this is all over [that] is more than I can expect, but
I expect that it will be this year.

We still have the orchestra and play for a few dances—a pastime. . . .

How are my little men doing? Rollie still doing all right at school
I hope? And no doubt Murray is getting to the age now where he
will take an awful lot of handling too.


. . .


. . . After this do, I'll get a job with someone else for the time
being and get on our feet and then strike out for ourselves. And
someday, hope to see your dreams of a nice home and security
realized. It would be nice wouldn't it? You and I and the kiddies.

I love you Mummy,
all of my love,
Clarence


ひ

Canadian Army Overseas
March 1st, 1944


Hello Darling,

And are you ever. Received this pen today, it is nice and writes well, and I'm hurrying to thank you for it. I have just opened the parcel and haven't read the clippings yet, and I also notice some of Rollie's and Murray's handiwork. How are they? Still giving you a lot of trouble?

You asked about a leave that I didn't spend at Starbucks'. I've spent my last four there, and the biggest portion of the 2 previous ones. So, I don't quite understand, unless you misunderstood Dorothy. They were expecting me long before (I didn't get my leave), so maybe that is the leave.

Well Hazel, you are rather peeved at me again because I don't write often enough. I'll admit I don't, and doing all this clerical work an awful lot of my spare time is taken up with different things. I have to type, etc. But maybe I shouldn't look for excuses—after all you are my wife and I love you. Don't let your imagination run away when at times I don't seem to write any too often.

General Montgomery inspected us yesterday and gave a nice talk and told us we would be on the second front, which is to be expected darling. But you needn't worry. It will not be another Dieppe and I'm in a much different job now than I was then.

Just had my old watch fixed after two years. It cost me £2, 10s ($11.00) to get it fixed. If I had of known that, I think it would still be in my kit bag. At any rate, I've a watch.


. . .

Well Hazel, we have been a long time apart, and with what I have learnt, and experiences of the past, make me more than sure that our married life when again reunited will be ideal. I'm certainly looking forwards to many a happy year with you and our family. And as you say, eventually, a nice home. That is one of my ambitions darling. Yes, security and comfort, a big order. Others have achieved it, so there is no reason why we can't.

I have put my name in for commission. I don't know how I will make out. I have to pass several boards and different exams. At one time it was quite easy to make it, but I was given to understand that it is much harder now as they are trying to make a better "standard of officer personnel." So here is hoping. At any rate it will be months yet before anything happens, and it is one way of getting home for awhile.

All of my love Mummy,
Daddy xxxxx

[p.s.] A hug and kiss for the boys.

ↅ

s. Sask. R.
c.a.(o.)
April 12, 1944


Hello Mummy,

Finally, here I am. We have been having quite a hectic time—
schemes, etc.


. . .


So, the kiddies want their daddy to come home. No more than he
wants to come home, I assure you. I hope your intuition is right
and I do get home this year; heaven knows this has been long
enough.

I'm sorry about not sending at telegram on your birthday. We were
on a scheme at the time, and I was so darned miserable, wet and
cold, that I couldn't think of anything but [to] feel sorry for myself.
Selfish maybe, but it sure wasn't fun.

By the way, all our mail is being censored, and knowing that makes
a letter rather hard to write.

Dorothy wrote me a letter telling me about your troubles back
home. And she mentioned that she gave you a little advice. I don't
know what it was—at any rate, she is a good head.

How are the kiddies anyway? Rollie still holding his own at school?
If I don't hurry home I won't be there for Murray's entrance to
school either. Wish Rollie a happy birthday for me. Give him a
hug and a handshake for me too. He must be past the kissing stage
now—more for black eyes and bloody noses now—8-years-old, no
wonder. I've got a few gray hairs, [and] it makes me realize that
time marches on and waits for no one.

Yes, Hazel, if we were only together away from all this hubbub—
quiet evenings at home, you and I and the kiddies.

Well bye-bye darling,
all of my love,
Daddy

P.S. Could do with the odd bit of eats. Parcels are still darned nice.
Love.

☙

s. Sask. R.
April 24, 1944


Hello Mummy,

I am the chap who you asked to write oftener, so here is the beginning of a few more letters.

Received the money quite awhile back and I wrote of it in different letters. Don't tell me that as few letters as I have written that some of them have been lost. No wonder you heard from me so seldom.

How are the kiddies? I was going through my snaps last night and my how the little fellows are changing. I won't know them at all. They really look like little men, especially Rollie. Is he still doing alright at school?

Have you heard from Dorothy Starbuck lately? She writes me a letter a week. They are nice people, it would be nice if you could meet them someday.

. . . Incidentally, I have bought a fifty-dollar bond in your name to be taken out of my pay, so much per month. It will be paid for in November, so you should be getting it about then. It is not much towards the nest egg, but will help and I can get along without it.

I have received all the parcels to date and cigs too. Thanks a million, and keep up the good work, they are always welcome.

Gosh, it has been a long time since I've seen you. We will have to get acquainted all over again won't we? But it will be fun.

What a miserable day. Windy and cold, but the scenery is grand again. The apple trees are in bloom, and flowers by the millions. Even with all the nice scenery, give me Canada any day—at least we know what to expect from the weather.

How is your Dad keeping? What does he say about the whole situation—you being alone, farming, and the future.

. . .

Well darling, I guess I'll call it a letter. I am in the best of health and always look forward to the day I get back to you and the boys.

All my love,
Clarence

☙

Pte. Bourassa C.O.
L12541
s. Sask. R.
May 3, 1944


Hello Mummy,

Received your letter of the 19 April last night and I will answer the same questions again. Re: the $25—received it ages ago. Thank you again. And also have received parcels. I don't quite understand this six weeks between my letters—some must be lost.

Thank you for the promised folder, and I assure you I shall acknowledge receipt as soon as I get it—not at Xmas as you say. I'll admit my letters are scarce enough, but surely not that bad, Hazel.

. . .

It would be nice to get home Hazel, nothing I would sooner do, but I'm afraid it is impossible, being in perfect health and family matters running smoothly (which is nice). As for the suggestions you made for causing reasons enough to get me home, I don't think much of them; they would rather upset the apple cart, wouldn't they?

I wrote Rollie a letter yesterday, and also one to you. So maybe if I keep up the good work, you won't mind.

Yes, I'll admit the time I am spending in the Army is going to make things hard to get back into the running after the war. I'll know practically nothing about merchandising or anything that pertains to it. It will be like starting all over again, getting up-to-date, etc., etc. I hate to think of it. But we can take it, can't we darling? As you say, nix on Lafleche unless it presents something really worthwhile (if that is possible). I wonder where we could get a little assistance to start up on our own. I wonder about Dad and his promises— there may be something there. I'm sure going to play it for all it is worth; I took an awful jolting on account of him once re the Fir Mountain store. That, I will bring up to him again, and how! As for McLaughlin's suggestion, I would like to talk to him about it. What do you think? I'm not worrying an awful lot about it anyway darling, because we will make out. And as you say, maybe I am learning a little more about life and it's "what one shouldn't do," etc.

Well darling, I'll say bye for now. Get well quick and take care of yourself. I'm fine, and don't worry.

All of my love,
Clarence

ↅ

Pte. Bourassa C.O.
L12541
s. Sask. R.
c.a.(o.)
May 5, 1944


Dear Mummy,

I wrote you an air mail letter yesterday, but it seemed so incomplete. So, I am writing again and I hope this doesn't take too long getting to you.

I'm fine and find time passing quite quickly—training, office work, and orchestra. I feel as if I will soon be home now; surely, this isn't going to last much longer.

I'll admit I haven't been writing an awful lot lately, but from now on I will. I miss your mail too darling, and I'm just getting my just desserts.

Yes, I will be home soon, I hope. Speaking naturally, in figures of months, but not too long now. And then we will have to start all over again. And my ambition is still the same—a store of our own. I feel certain that we would make a success of it no matter where it may be. Your experience and my little bit should make a fair team. Now where and how are we going to get the necessary funds? Where it comes from, I don't care, just as long as we can get started. I wish I was home now and working on it. I wonder if Dad will help? If he offers to, I am certainly going to take advantage of it. And maybe someone else might give me a break. At any rate, I'm not worrying, because without a doubt I'll get work when I get back but it won't something we can call our own. And the quicker we get it the better, because I'm not getting any younger and I'm spending the prime of my life in the Army. Have you any suggestions? What about this McLaughlin angle—do you think there is anything [in] it? What is or has happened to Ted Culliton's suggestions and vague promises?

Well, it is dinner time now darling so excuse me I'll continue this during the afternoon. I hope it's good, because I've an appetite like a horse lately.

Hello, here I am. The dinner was just an Army meal, enough and substantial, but that old good home flavor was conspicuous in its absence. It sure will be grand to see the last of an Army kitchen. One thing certain, when I get back on civvie street I won't be a picky eater—anything cooked at home will be a banquet. How is Lee doing with his noodles? Still putting on Sunday feeds? I often think of them and wouldn't mind a feed of it.

Looking forward to the odd parcel as a change in diet and mostly flavour.

. . .

Nice weather, long evenings, do make me awfully lonely for you and the kiddies.

All of my love and kisses,
Clarence

ROLLIE'S NOTE: *The following letter was received in Lafleche May 13, 1944, but the date Dad sent it is unknown.*

Pte. Bourassa C.O.
L12541
S. Sask. R.
C.A.(O.)


Hello Mummy,

Just a few lines. I've missed your letters lately, but I suppose everything is disrupted again for a few days.

Well Hazel, we are on field pay, and with the purchase of the bond I'm in a bad way. Could you wire me about $10.00? I need it. The fact is I owe nearly that much and there is a possibility of a short leave in the very near future. I hate to ask, but I need it, and as we are on field pay I can't draw what I have coming to me but will have the credit balance transferred to you to pay back the ten dollars.

I bought a fifty dollar bond and had it transferred to you. It will be paid in full in six months.

You should see the tan I have acquired the last few days. I look like an Indian, and I have my hair clipped very sort Army-style proper, and I'm in the pink of condition—a lot of sleep, enough to eat, and plenty of exercise.

I haven't seen any of the other boys for weeks. They never come around as they are in other companies and have acquired new friends in their respective companies, and we all get lazy. I spend most of my time with the Orchestra boys.

What is doing around the old hometown these days now that spring is here? Do you play tennis, golf, or anything like that? What do the kiddies do? Does Rollie still beat it off on his own or does he

stay pretty well to home? If he is anything like I was he sure won't
stay home, ask Mother.

. . .

Do you know that I often lie awake and worry about you darling?
Because no matter how sick you might be, you would not tell me.
Don't do that, I want to know.

All my love,
Daddy

P.S. Is the ten a deal? I'll return it in a few weeks.

ℰℐ

*Letter from Dorothy Starbuck.*

Dale Hill,
Southfleet,
Gravesend
June 9th, [1944]


Dear Hazel,

I received your letter dated May 6th this morning. As you know, the 2nd front has started and we have not heard from Clarence for nearly a month—then, the letter was censored. We haven't the faintest idea if he has gone over or not. I listen to the radio reports to see what regiments have gone, but so far have heard nothing. And as far as I can see we cannot hear for a time and must have patience. We have been expecting this for a long time. Every leave Clarence has had we expected it to be the last from this side, but when it actually came it was a shock and made you feel sick and sorry.

. . .

Don't worry if you don't get letters, I don't expect to. They have all been tied very tight. I see by the papers they have been kept in sealed camps and not allowed to come in contact with anyone outside. The secrecy probably saved many lives, so we must put up with it.

I will let you know when I hear any news, but I expect you will hear first.

Love,
Dorothy

⁊

Pte. Bourassa C.O.
L12541
s. Sask. R.
C.A (O.)
June 2[?], 1944


Hello Darling,

At last, here I am again. Received the money order a few days ago,
thanks a million. Also received the 300 cigs the other day just in
time, and I'm certainly looking forward to the others you say are
on the way.

. . . as my application is in for my commission, my officers suggested I acquire a little practical experience and it sure keeps me
plenty busy. At any rate, I feel a good deal better and in the pink.
As to how we'll make out when the final selection board meets and
I have my trials, is simply a question mark. But, I'm certainly
going to try now that I have put my foot into it.

Thanks for the snaps, they were grand. Would you send me
Camille's present address, I believe congratulations are in line.
Gosh, the kiddies have grown.

So, Camille married an Englishman and no doubt expects to live
in England. Well, poor girl, if I know Camille she is going to miss
good old Canada a lot more than she realizes now.

How are my two little men anyway? Received Rollie's letter and am
answering. Also enclosing a note for Murray as Rollie suggested in
his letter.

Received a parcel of eats from Mother yesterday. Can you imagine a
tin of sauerkraut and a tin of sausage—sure made a grand meal!

Just had my hair cut and as it fell into my lap I was astonished at the amount of white ones among it. My goodness Hazel, you will hardly recognize me when I get back.

I was speaking to Mickey last night and mentioned Kay in our conversation. I casually asked if he had heard from her, and he said that he hadn't received an answer to his last letter and was hurt as he still considers Kay his best friend and would certainly like to write her but wouldn't till she answered his letter.

Take care of yourself darling,
All my love,
Clarence

&

Pte. Bourassa C.O.
L12541
s. Sask. R.
C.A.(O.)
June 28, 1944


Hello Darling,

Received the 1000 cigs you and Mother sent. Thank you, smokes
are certainly welcome. Also received two letters or air letters.

You keep asking about Rollie, but I have answered that question at
least twice so some of my letters must be getting lost. So, I'll answer
it again. I don't like the idea any too well. This G-bourg business, it
didn't do me an awful lot of good. But if Rollie is too much to handle, send him there for a year, which wouldn't do him any harm. In
fact, it would do him a world of good, and as he is at the age where
he may go all wrong if not properly handled. Yes, I sure should be
home to look after our little men and give you a rest. Don't let it
get you down Hazel. This isn't going to last forever. Now that
things have started we should be home in a few months.

By the way, how are those little trees I planted a few years ago? Have
the boys pulled them up yet or are they still showing a few signs of life?

. . .

I've learned how to play cribbage and spend a lot of our spare minutes playing the game. It is a good pass time, and whenever we have
ten or fifteen minutes to ourselves out comes a cribbage board and
a deck of cards and away we go. It is a very interesting game.

So the CCF took it in Sask.? Must have been quite a time. I can
just imagine G-bourg election night. So Ted C[ulliton] lost out.
Who took his seat? Not something like Houze, I hope. Well, I
guess it was bound to happen some time or other.

So Dad gave you to think that maybe he would help a little after this is over. I hope so, but no strings before I accept a thing. I rather appreciate my independence, and I imagine [I] could do better if I didn't have someone else's opinion to contend with.

I'm [in] a rather awkward position here, writing on my knees. Oh, thank you for the leather folder, darned nice, and certainly handy.

Well, take care of yourself darling and don't work too hard. I'm in the best of health and hope this finds you the same darling.

Give the boys a big hug for me and say hello to Wilfrid for me. And also thank Ab Sewell for the smokes, I will be writing him.

All my love,
Clarence

༄

Pte. Bourassa C.O.
L12541
s. Sask. R.
C.A.(O.)
July 8, 1944


Hello Mummy,

Received your letter of the 25 June yesterday. It was swell letter
and thanks for the clippings.

We are now somewhere in France and having plenty to eat and
good food too. So, we are doing alright by ourselves.

So, the kiddies, or rather Rollie, has the measles. Did Murray get
them too? You do have your troubles! Well darling, this will soon be
over, so I should be home soon and take over some of your cares
and worries, if I don't add to them.

Gee, when you mention noodle feeds in your letters my mouth sure
waters. That is going to be part of our celebration when I get back. I
suppose that I will be so glad to get home that I won't be able to eat
for days. Pardon the odd blur, as there is a light shower coming up.

So Lafleche is getting too much rain. Do you know that is hard to
believe, all I can remember is the farmers praying for it.

. . .

Well darling, I guess I'll close for now. I'm OK and in good health.
Explain to everyone else that I won't be writing to very many of
them. It will take most of my spare time writing you, which is
going to be often.

Bye-bye, love and kisses,
all my love,
Daddy

[p.s.] Give the kiddies a big hug and a kiss for me.

Pte. Bourassa C.O.
L12541
s. Sask. R.
C.A.(O.)
July 11, 1944


Hello Darling,

Received two of your letters today, one of the 25 June and one on
the 3 July—thank you.

Oh yes, that question you insisted on. When you come to meet
me—this fall I hope—come alone, because I will be able to see the
kiddies later and it will be a rest for you as well as a second honeymoon. How does that sound? It sure suits me to a tee.


. . .


I'm fine and still looking forward to parcels and smokes; that is absolutely all we can depend on for a change in food and smokes.
They issue us six smokes or six cigs a day—not very many.

The Canadian Legion is putting on a show for us tonight, I am
hoping to go to it. "Orchestra Wives," they say it is good. Oh, yes,
music and the Army at present don't mix; all our instruments are
packed away. Do you ever see the Palmers? She told me she would
give me some addresses if we ever got into France. Well, here we
are and it would be nice to see someone with relatives back home.
That is, if we ever get time.

Well darling, I'll write again soon, so, so long for now. I'm fine and
pray God to keep me so.

A big hug and kisses for the boys,
all my love,
Daddy

*Clarence's last letter.*

Pte. Bourassa C.O.
L12541
s. Sask. R.
C.A.(O.)
July 16, 1944

Hello Darling,

I have been receiving your letters quite regularly and in very good time. Thank you.

Well, I'm in France, right in the thick of things one would say. And I'm fine, getting plenty to eat, and plenty of sleep—if the guns don't get too noisy.

Am I ever getting a fill of fresh fruit—cherries, red currants—ripe now, and ours for the picking as there is no one to gather them in and they are going to waste. So, I'm wasting as few as possible; in other words, I eat all I can of them.

We had the brass band instruments unpacked this morning and played for three different church parades. After about six weeks of a lay off I rather enjoyed playing.

So, the trees are still coming along fine, that is nice to hear. Well, if you don't know how to play cribbage, don't worry, I'll show you how; and anyway, we won't have time to bother with cribbage for quite awhile after I get back.

So, you are still worried about what I would do if I were to come back to Lafleche. If I would spend hours at Tuffy's or the poker joint, etc. Don't worry about that, I've rather lost that wanderlust. I like peace and quiet, and much more so since I've come to war-torn France.

Well, no more kids eh! Not even a daughter? We will have to talk that over when I get back.

Don't worry about saving too much—just don't go short in the meantime. Save what you can spare, and I am doing the same. I've bought a victory bond that you should be receiving about the first of November, as I am paying so much on it a month.

As for staying at Lafleche, I'm certainly not fussy. Any place will suit me fine. Yes, a few more weeks and nine years of married life will have gone by, and a rather messy nine years, thanks to me. I'll make that all up to you darling and I hope to spend the next fifty years' anniversaries with you.

Well, I guess I'll close as military security etc. makes these letters rather dry, doesn't it?
All of my love, and I do miss you darling more than you realize.
Bye-bye, love and kisses,
Clarence

P.S. I'm forgetting the kiddies. Hugs and kisses for them.

❧

ROLLIE'S NOTE: *It was July 29th, mid-afternoon. Mr. Spence, the Canadian Pacific telegraph operator and station agent in Lafleche, arrived at our door with the telegram below. I remember my mother running across the street to our neighbours to have someone look after Murray and me so she could go to my grandparents and others with the news. The most vivid image I have as an eight-year-old was waking up in the night, hearing my mother crying and calling out my dad's name. Why there was no other adult around to stay with us, I don't know.*

CANADIAN PACIFIC
TELEGRAPHS
*World Wide Communications*

W.D.NEIL, GENERAL MANAGER OF COMMUNICATIONS, MONTREAL.

CANADIAN PACIFIC COMMUNICATIONS

STANDARD TIME INDICATED

OK 45/42 blue GB 2 extra Rept dely

Ottawa, Ont. July 29/44.
122 PM

S MU 1442

Mrs. Hazel G. Bourassa,
Bafleche, Sask.

18058 Minister of National Defence regrets to
officially reported missing in action twentieth july 1944 stop
inform you that L12541 Private Clarence Ovilla Bourassa has been
when further information becomes available it will be forwarded
as soon as received .

Director of Records.

Dale Hill,
Southfleet,
Gravesend
Aug. 14th, [1944]


Dear Hazel,

It was a shock to get your airgraph, but it must have been a worse one for you as I suppose you did not know Clarence had gone to France. We had a letter from him dated July 4th, but he made no mention of going then. Almost at once, a letter came from the Canadian Legion saying they were sending on a kit bag belonging to him, so we guessed what was happening. I did intend to write to you but in both his letters Clarence said he was writing to you, but anyway you would not have received the news any quicker. Don't worry more than you can help. He may be a prisoner, or he may have been wounded and picked up by the French people. We have heard of a man my brother knows who came down in France from an airplane and arrived back 9 months after, and another who was 2 years getting back.

I know Clarence would hate being a prisoner, but it may save him from worse things.

I don't think Clarence was meant to die yet; I will tell you why. In the ordinary course of events he would have been on leave at the end of July and at the beginning of August, and that very week we had our house damaged. The back windows were blown out and in the room where Clarence would have been sleeping the whole of the ceiling came down. Huge pieces of heavy plaster fell on the pillows, and any- one sleeping there would have been badly hurt, if not killed. Several houses around were also damaged, but luckily no one was hurt.

I have washed and mended Clarence's clothes that needed it, and I shall keep them until the news is more definite, hoping that he will be able to collect them himself.

The war is moving so quickly now, let us hope it will soon be over.

Keep hoping and praying.

Love,
Dorothy

&

ROLLIE'S NOTE: *Eerily, an undated postcard from Dad arrived.*

*Postcard*

[no date]

A few yards down the road from Starbuck's.

I am having a swell time Hazel. I'm on leave—will be going back in a couple of days. I'm leaving all my extra clothes here this time, as instructed that we must get rid of it.

All my love,
Daddy

&

CD 1X

## CANADIAN PACIFIC TELEGRAPHS
### *World Wide Communications*

W.D.NEIL GENERAL MANAGER OF COMMUNICATIONS, MONTREAL

52-49 CB 2 Exa D.L.
    Roport DeLy.
        446 PM.
Mrs Hazel Grace Bourassa,
LaFleche,Sask.

11694 MINISTER OF NATIONAL DEFENCE DEEPLY REGRETS TO INFORM YOU THAT
L 12541 PRIVATE CLARENCE OVILLA BOURASSA PREVIOUSLY REPORTED MISSING IN ACTION
HAS NOW BEEN OFFICIALLY REPORTED KILLED IN ACTION TWENTIETH JULY 1944 STOP
IF ANY FURTHER INFORMATIONS BECOMES AVAILABLE IT WILL BE FORWARDED AS SOON
    AS RECEIVED.

        Director of Records.

    K/AU 1650.

ROLLIE'S NOTE: *After word was received that Dad was killed, my mother received many pieces of correspondence. Among letters from family and friends, were the following.*

South Sask. Regt.
Cdn. Army Overseas
10 Aug., 1944

RE L-12541, PTE. BOURASSA, C.O.

Dear Mrs. Bourassa,

You will no doubt have heard before this of the death of your husband, who was killed in action on 20 July 44. Please accept our sincerest sympathy in your bereavement.

Pte. Bourassa was well-liked by all who knew him in this Regiment, and he gave unstintingly of his talents, both musical and artistic, in addition to his duties as a solider.

Our prayer is that God may be your guide and comforter in this hour of sorrow.

Yours very sincerely,
John K. Kemp, Capt.
O.C. "C" Coy.

၄၅

Canadian Legion
War Services
Lafleche Branch No. 204
B.E.S.L. [British Empire Service League]
August 29th, 1944


Dear Mrs. Bourassa:

It is with deep regret that we learn that Clarence has been "Killed in Action" in the service of his country. At a time like this it is hard to put into words what one would like to express. Knowing that he died to uphold our way of life and for a just and righteous cause, the liberation of the oppressed has some consolation. If there is anything we can do to assist you or any advice you may require with regards to business matters do not hesitate to call on us, we are willing to help in any way we can.

"He shall not grow old as we that are left to grow old,
Age shall not weary him nor the years condemn,
At the going down of the sun and in the morning,
We will remember him."


Fraternally,
E.R. Ridgway,
Secretary.

❧

*Airgraph*

September 5th, 1944

Dear Hazel,

I received your airmail letter yesterday. I had heard the news indirectly from a girl who has a boyfriend in the same regiment, but as it was unofficial I hoped it was not true. I am glad Clarence did not suffer. I will write later in the week when I have sorted my thoughts out a bit.

Love,
Dorothy

❧

Dale Hill,
Southfleet,
Gravesend
Sept. 6th, [1944]


Dear Hazel,

I am going to try and answer your letter. We shall all miss Clarence, for although we knew that one day he would be returning home, there was always the hope that he would be coming to visit us. He did even speak of bringing you here and staying if he could get a job. In his last letter he said, God willing, he would spend another leave with us, but we must not blame God for man's devilry. But, I do think that Clarence always felt he would not come out of this. In fact, when he first came over he said so. But lately, after coming out of Dieppe, he did not say anything and talked a lot about going home and what he would give to be able to get home. And almost the last letter he wrote from this side he said he was getting lots of mail from home and was feeling content but longed for the war to end. I wonder what his real thoughts were. He had a wonderfully active mind, but found it difficult to express himself and consequently gave people a wrong impression. He was such a mixture of gaiety and sadness, child and man, that very few folks understood him.

Now Hazel, you have some very great decisions to make and if you ever care to come to this country we shall always welcome you and the boys. You will have to rebuild your life as we have got to rebuild our house. I think I told you we had two bombs drop within a few hundred yards of us in a fortnight, and we cannot use any of the top rooms. The first bomb blew the ceiling down in the room Clarence used to have; the second blew the window frames out and the fireplace to pieces and brought down all the upstairs ceilings and damaged some of the downstairs. So, we are living in 2 rooms and a bit, but hope to soon start on the repairs. If you could see Clarence's room now you would think something devilish had played havoc there.

Write to me sometimes and let me know how things go, will you? I will send Clarence's belongings off as soon as I can get them packed up and find out the best way to send them—my brother is going to make inquiries.

. . .

All my love,
Dorothy

౭౩

**BUCKINGHAM PALACE**

The Queen and I offer you our heartfelt sympathy in your great sorrow.

We pray that your country's gratitude for a life so nobly given in its service may bring you some measure of consolation.

*George R.I.*

27 Sept. 44

Dear Mrs. Bourassa,

It is with much regret and under sad circumstances that I write to you at this time to offer my sincere sympathy in the passing of your husband, Pte Bourassa C.O., who was killed on the 20th of July 44.

Pte Bourassa was an excellent soldier and was very well-liked by everyone in our Company. His bravery and willingness to do his part made him "one of the boys," which is the highest compliment that soldiers can pay to a comrade. We were in position near Ifs and your husband was killed by a sniper during the afternoon of the 20th.

I know that a letter of this nature is of little compensation to you, but as I thought very highly of Pte Bourassa I felt that I wanted to write to you personally to inform you that your husband was an asset to our Regiment, of which we are very proud, and also inform you that as a comrade his loss was deeply felt by all of us.

He is buried side-by-side with comrades who died for the same cause and we, who are still living, deeply feel that they have not died in vain. You will be notified as to the location of the cemetery where your husband lies at rest.

In closing, will you please accept once again my sincere sympathy in your sad bereavement.

Sincerely,
B.A. Beer, Capt.
"C" Coy.
S.S.R.

౿

Dale Hill,
Southfleet,
Gravesend
Oct 2nd, [1944]


Dear Hazel,

I expect you are wondering why you have not heard from me or
why Clarence's belongings have not turned up. Well, they have been
packed up for a month and I have been trying to find out the best
way to send them. The parcel is too big for the ordinary mail service.
Anyway, I have been advised to write to the War Office and I am
awaiting their reply. If that does not answer, I will let you know and
perhaps you can find out [on] your end the best way to go about it.

Well, dear, how are you feeling? I still find it very difficult to realize
that Clarence is not alive. I still keep feeling that he must turn up
again. I have not told my mother he was killed, she knew he was
missing and I have left it at that. She has had so many shocks lately
and is breaking up fast. She had a bad illness last winter and we did
not expect her to get over that, and Clarence was very sweet to her.
She thought a lot of him and has had his photograph copied in oil
colours. We have a camp of the Balloon Barrage men next door to
us and one of them paints in oils. He is very clever at copying photographs and it is really lifelike, so much that we are glad it has been
sent away to be framed—it seems to haunt you somehow.

Don't thank me for what I did for Clarence. I hoped it helped him
a bit—I think it did, and it helped me a lot. These young folks save
me from becoming a crabby old maid, and we have had enough of
them in our family. Two of Father's sisters, and three of Mother's,
did not marry and what a life they led . . . they were spoilt when
they were young, and because they cannot get everything their
own way (and who can these days), there is terrible trouble.

. . . but don't forget if ever you care to come this way, there will always be room for you and the boys—the more the merrier. We are not well-off, but things seem to manage to go round alright.

Love,
Dorothy

☙

Minister of Agriculture (Canada)
October 24th, 1944


Mrs. Hazel Grace Bourassa,
Lafleche, Sask.

Dear Mrs. Bourassa;

I regret to note your husband's name in the casualty list which
appeared in the press recently.

It is to be regretted that your husband in company with many others
should be called upon to make the supreme sacrifice. Mrs. Gardiner
joins me in extending deepest sympathy to you in your great loss.

When this cruel war is ended we shall long remember his personal
sacrifice that others may enjoy freedom.

Yours sincerely,
James G. Gardiner

~

*Airgraph*

October 24th, 1944,


Dear Hazel,

I got in touch with the Canadian Military H.Q. and they are sending Clarence's belongings to you—the parcel left us on Oct. 18th.



Love,
Dorothy

☙

Dale Hill,
Southfleet,
Gravesend
Nov. 20th, [1944]


Dear Hazel,

. . .

I can quite understand how you felt over the memorial service.
We had our Remembrance service on Nov. 5th, the Sunday before
Poppy Day . . . it was strange that it should fall on Clarence's birthday. I put a Remembrance cross on our War Memorial with his
name and rank on it.

. . .

As for the photograph, the lad who painted it has left here some
weeks ago. Goodness knows where he is now, overseas perhaps,
many of them are. But, if he should come this way again I will certainly ask him to make another copy. The one we have belongs to
my mother, but we will see how things are later on.

I expect by now you have my airgraph saying Clarence's belongings
have been sent off. There is also a parcel on the way. I hope the boys
will like the books; not knowing them, it is rather hard to choose,
and there is not much to choose from. Poor lads, how their daddy
did love them.

Well, I must close now and do some work. It is washing day, but it
is raining. We have had a lot of rain lately.

Love,
Dorothy

෬

ROLLIE'S NOTE: *The painting of my father's portrait remained with the Starbucks until 1958, when it was shipped to my grandparents in Lafleche. It now hangs in my residence in Regina.*

THE PAINTING OF CLARENCE, ARTIST UNKNOWN.

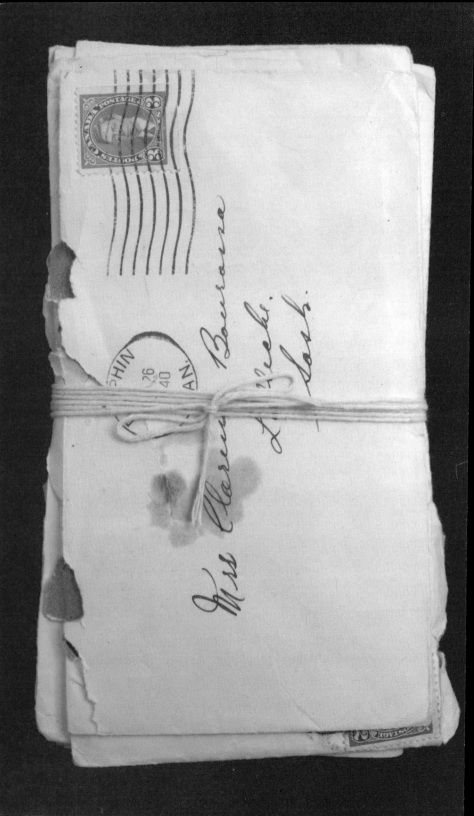

# AFTERMATH

*Letter from Dorothy Starbuck.*

Dale Hill,
Southfleet,
Gravesend
March 24th, [1945]


Dear Rollie,

I had a letter from your mother this morning and she tells me you are first in your class. I was a friend of your daddy's and I know how much he loved his sons. I am sure he knows all about your success and is feeling very proud of you, although he cannot write and tell you so or send you anything.

Your daddy was like Jesus—he gave his life for us, and now he has gone to live with God. But he knows what you are doing and loves you more than ever. Tell Mommy I will write to her soon and give her my love and a big kiss.

Auntie Dorothy

☙

*Letter from Dorothy Starbuck.*

Dale Hill,
Southfleet,
Gravesend
July 4th, [1945]


Dear Hazel,

Very pleased to get your letter—it was only about 8 days coming. Fancy Clarence's belongings taking all that time to come. I looked up the receipt I had for them and it was dated Oct. 19th, 1944. I expect lack of shipping space was the trouble. The hanky must be mine. I did have one like it, but I do lose them and never know where they go. To tell you the truth, I did the job in a hurry; that is what I do when I get a job I don't like. I make up my mind it has got to be done and make a dash at it.

Clarence may have got more of your snaps and had them in his pocket. The ones I sent he left with his civvie clothes in August 1943. He took out one of you and the two boys in a group and put it in his wallet, but he had the others all out and looked at them the last time he was here in January 1944.

I should not worry too much if the boys will not tell you the details of his death. I should think the tale that he died in action the most likely. I don't think the others want to talk about it and I doubt if they really know what did happen. If they were where we think they were, in the Falaise Gap, the fighting was so heavy they would be too dazed to know what happened.

We found that in this country during a bombing raid the people actually working on the job did not know what was going on around them. It was only the onlookers who knew, and there would not be many onlookers in a battlefield. . . .

I am glad you will soon be moving into your new home. It will give you fresh interest to get all your things arranged in it. We are still waiting for the men to come and repair ours, but now that some of the men are coming home there should be more labour. . . .

I think you will hear sometime where Clarence is buried; probably through the War Graves Commission. They took very good care of them after the last war. . . . I expect they will have to make out a complete list before any official notice is given.

. . .

I am thankful we know he did have a funeral. So many were just reported missing and that is the end. No one knows what did happen to them.

Must close now and go to bed.

Love,
Dorothy

❧

ROLLIE'S NOTE: *Over the next two years my mother received the following three letters regarding where Dad was buried.*

Department of
National Defence (Army)
Ottawa, Canada
17th July, 1945

Mrs. Hazel G. Bourassa,
Lafleche, Sask.

Dear Madam:

Information has now been received from the overseas military authorities that your husband, L12541 Private Clarence Ovilla Bourassa, was buried with religious rites in a temporary grave located at Ifs, approximately two and a half miles South of Caen, in the Department of Calvados (Normandy), France. Marked map is enclosed.

The grave will have been temporarily marked with a wooden cross for identification purposes and in due course the remains will be reverently exhumed and removed to a recognized military burial ground when the concentration of graves in the area takes place. On this being completed the new location will be advised to you, but for obvious reasons it will likely take approximately one year before this information is received.

Yours faithfully,

J.B. Rading [?]
for C.L. Laurin, Colonel,
Director of Records,
for Adjutant-General.

❧

Department of
National Defence (Army)
Ottawa, Canada
8th March, 1946

Mrs. Hazel G. Bourassa,
Lafleche, Saskatchewan

Dear Madam:

Information has just been received from overseas that the remains
of your husband, L12541 Private Clarence Ovilla Bourassa, have
been carefully exhumed from the original place of interment and
reverently reburied in grave 3, row E, plot 4, of Bretteville-Sur-Laize
Canadian Military Cemetery, Bretteville-Sur-Laize, France. Marked
map is enclosed. This is a recognized military burial ground and
will receive care and maintenance in perpetuity.

The grave will have been marked with a temporary cross which
will be replaced in due course by a permanent headstone suitably
inscribed. While it cannot now be stated when this work of permanent commemoration will begin, before any action is taken you
will be communicated with and an opportunity will be given you
to submit a short personal inscription of your own choice for
engraving on the headstone. Therefore, if you should change your
address would you be good enough to inform the undersigned.

Yours faithfully,

J.B. Rading [?]
for C.L. Laurin, Colonel,
Director of Records,
for Adjutant-General.

℘

Department of
National Defence (Army)
Ottawa, Canada
7th August, 1947


Mrs. Hazel G. Bourassa,
1045 Third Avenue North West,
Moose Jaw, Saskatchewan


Dear Mrs. Bourassa,

I am forwarding herewith a photograph of the grave and marker
over the burial place of your late husband, L12541 Private Clarence
Ovilla Bourassa, the location of which is grave 3, row E, plot 4,
Bretteville-Sur-Laize Canadian Military Cemetery, Bretteville-
Sur-Laize, France.

Any errors appearing in the inscription will be corrected when the
permanent headstone is placed.

Yours faithfully,

J.B. Rading [?]
for H.M. Jackson, Lt.-Col.,
Director of Records,
for Adjutant-General.

೧

THE PHOTOGRAPH OF CLARENCE'S
GRAVE AND TEMPORARY MARKER
THAT HAZEL RECEIVED WITH THE LAST LETTER (*left*), AND THE PERMANENT
MARKER LATER ERECTED (*right*). THE INSCRIPTION AT THE BOTTOM
ON THE LATTER READS: "AND I SHALL SEE HIM FACE TO FACE AND BE
WITH THOSE I LOVED ONCE MORE."

IN 2003, ALMOST 60 YEARS AFTER CLARENCE'S DEATH,
DALLYN JOHNSON, ROLLIE'S GRANDSON AND CLARENCE'S
GREAT-GRANDSON, VISITED THE GRAVE IN FRANCE.

ROLLIE'S NOTE: *It wasn't until the war was over and the Canadians
had returned home that we learned more about how Dad was killed.
Freddie James from Woodrow, Saskatchewan, was with Dad and the
S.S.R. They shared the same tent during that last campaign and Freddie knew Dad well. In a visit to Lafleche, Freddie met with my grandmother and he told her of the circumstance's of Dad's death. My
grandmother wrote down Freddie's account and gave it to my mother.*

*Freddie said that during the last days Dad looked old (about 40)
and his hair was very grey, almost white. It was raining, and they were
crawling through a muddy wheat field near Ifs, a small village a few
miles from Caen. A shell landed in the midst of the group, exploded,
and Dad and the officer beside him were killed instantly by shrapnel to
the back of the head. Freddie said, "they never knew what happened."
It was two weeks before the bodies were recovered for burial, and
Freddie said that the German's had stripped them of their watches
and rings—anything of value. There were no coffins, so the bodies were
wrapped in blankets and buried with Catholic rites in temporary graves.*

*Several years later, after Dad was laid to rest in his final burial place,
word was received that the Government of Saskatchewan was naming
locations in the province's north after native sons who lost their lives in
World War Two. My mother received the following letter.*

Regina, Sask.,
Sask. Resources Bldg.,
August 23, 1951

Mrs. H. G. Bourassa,
Lafleche, Sask.

Dear Mrs. Bourassa:

It may be recalled a recommendation was made some time ago on
behalf of the province that a Saskatchewan lake, island, bay or river
be named in honour and memory of your husband, Clarence Ovilla
Bourassa.

I am happy to advise that the Canadian Board on Geographical
Names officially approved the name on August 2nd, 1951. A map
is being forwarded under separate cover showing the location of
Bourassa Creek. As soon as revised maps of the area are published
a copy will be forwarded.

A report has been included in the official records of the province
and the Dominion Government associating for all time the sacrifice
of your husband with the feature named in his honour. It may be
of some comfort to us who are left that a part of the native province
will perpetuate for all time the name of one who gave all in defence
of the country in the last war.

Yours sincerely,
J.H. Brockelbank,
Minister of Natural Resources

ROLLIE'S NOTE: *Bourassa Creek, named after Dad, lies in northern
Saskatchewan near the Alberta border, approximately halfway between
the Clearwater River and Lake Athabasca.*

ℭ

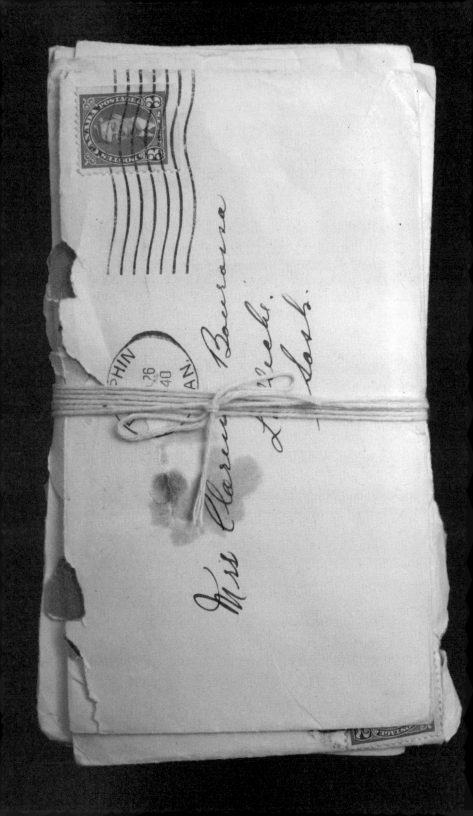

# EPILOGUE

# EPILOGUE

A memorial service for Dad was held at the Catholic church in Lafleche and a table draped with the Union Jack and Red Ensign flags represented a casket. A full high mass along with the Legion's military service seemed to go on forever. I remember the folks gathering around my mother, brother and me, saying things to me such as "it's so nice your mother has you to look after her," "you'll be such a comfort to her," and "you're the man of the house now." I don't believe much of this registered on an eight-year-old. Nothing had changed, it was still just the three of us in a little two-room house—the same as it had been the last four years.

Days, weeks and months went by until VE day. Then the war was over. The world, Canada, and every community large or small celebrated. In Lafleche, the festivities began with a victory parade down Main Street. Children of the men overseas were selected to represent different countries and their leaders, and I was chosen to be Charles de Gaulle of France. A red, white and blue sash was draped over my shoulder and pinned at my waist and I was given a card with one of de Gaulle's quotes regarding the Allies' victory written on it. I had to read this onstage. Being what seemed to be the centre of attention somewhat took away any immediate feeling of loss I had, and, then, a rare luxury, we went to a movie.

The film was "The Fighting Sullivans," the story of four brothers growing up during the Depression and all joining the Marines. Throughout the movie the youngest was always late or chasing after his brothers yelling, "wait for me." All four were killed when their ship was torpedoed, and the ending of the film showed the three oldest walking through the clouds to heaven, when you heard, "wait for me," and the youngest came running to catch up. All of a sudden the reality of losing my father hit hard. I started crying and saying I wanted my daddy. It was as if calling out, something or someone would bring him back. Returning home, we sat huddled on the couch, both Mom and me crying, and Murray joining in because we were.

I've been asked if I ever felt as if I had to grow up too quickly—having at a young age to "be the man of the house." Maybe, but I don't think I realized it at the time. But being "the man of the house" did mean there was wood to chop, sidewalks and the yard to keep clean, and I had to look after Murray when Mom went out. I've also been asked if I ever felt "cheated" because I didn't have a father, and if I sought out other male role models when I was growing up. I don't believe these things ever crossed my mind. Our home and family—my Mother, Murray and I—was what I grew up with and it seemed normal. And as for "role models," men were few and far between in Mom's life at that time. I do, however, remember one 'gentleman' in particular, saying as much as he liked her, but he wasn't ready or willing to take on the responsibility of two kids. And, at the time, that seemed okay with me—I didn't want the family we had to be changed in any way. Mom never remarried.

During the 1940s, "wartime houses" were being built across Canada and Mom applied for one in Moose Jaw. We soon were "city bound." Murray and I stayed at our neighbours in Lafleche while Mom moved what furniture we had to our new place. After things were settled in she met us at the railway station on a cold evening in November and we walked with what little luggage we had to our new home. I still remember the fascination of having running water.

Money, or more specifically the lack of it, became an everyday part of our lives. It was very seldom we bought bread. It seemed Mom was constantly rolling dough, and the house always smelled of fresh baking. Occasionally, Mom would send me with a note to the butcher or baker with a handful of coins, and the butcher would check Mom's list and find out how much money I had, and I always seemed to have the right amount. Mom had an obsession, as did many who lived through the Depression and Dirty Thirties—to save every cent possible and spend only out of necessity. To this day, every expense, bill, or purchase is recorded to the penny whenever she shops. But Mom never implied or gave us the feeling that we were "poor." We always had enough to eat; however, it was quite obvious we were living day to day. I remember taking a note and my sleigh to the local coal company and having a burlap bag filled with coal.

My world was Mom, Murray and me. There was always just the three of us, even at Christmas. The Legion, though, did hold a Christmas party for the "war kids," and gave us Japanese oranges and bags of candy. An allowance was unheard of; in fact, I don't think it was even a word then. But, Saturdays were special. Murray and I were given 15 cents each to go to the afternoon movie matinee. Mom wanted everything for her boys. When the Moose Jaw junior band was formed, Mom was one of the first parents to register her boys.

At age 10, I got my first paper route and had 40 customers. The paper cost 25 cents a week and you had to collect from everyone. After collecting from the subscribers the money would be spread out on the kitchen table and my take-home pay usually averaged $2.40 a week. Mom had opened a bank account for both Murray and me, and the money was deposited in the account with a small amount reserved for "spending money."

Summer saw Murray and I back in Lafleche on my grandparents' farm and staying with folks in town. On the farm I worked dawn to dusk doing everything from cleaning the barn to milking, from picking stone to stooking sheaves. At the end of the summer my grandfather would hand me an envelope to take home—my wages!

Back in Moose Jaw, I had school, my paper route, band, and now our neighbour, a manager at Eaton's, had me working Saturdays, unloading trucks and stacking shelves. At age 14 my maternal grandfather moved to Manitoba where he had purchased land just north of Camp Shilo, where 10 years earlier my father began his military career. For two months, six days a week, we cleared bush, broke land, and fenced his property. At age 15, I became a telegraph messenger during the summer months. At this time, Mom began work at the Armed Forces Base in Moose Jaw, and, suddenly, we could afford things. The coal bin disappeared, and an oil tank was installed with a new space heater and an electric stove.

In high school, I occupied my time playing football, basketball and hockey, and singing in the choir and in a quartet at various functions, getting out of classes to sing at funerals at the church a block away. I also played clarinet and saxophone in a dance band. A love of music, it seems, was something I inherited from my father.

From being a telegraph messenger to holding various other positions with the railroad, I found myself working full-time through grades 11 and 12 (midnight to 8 a.m.). Halfway through grade 12 sports were out of the picture, I started missing band practices, and my grades were slipping. The day of my high school graduation, my world took a big turn.

I'd had no time for girlfriends, but all the other guys had dates for the grad. I asked the girl next door if she would be my date and she accepted. There we were, rented tux, corsage, and enjoying the ceremonies and banquet until the post-grad party. Then the bottles appeared and I experienced my first encounter with alcohol. I became very drunk and very sick, and my friends drove me home, set me on the front step, rang the doorbell and took off. I found out later that my date phoned her father to take her home. Mom was not pleased, to say the least.

By the time school was over a friction had built up between Mom and I that eventually reached a point where by mutual consent I packed my belongings and moved into the YMCA. All of a sudden all I had was my job on the railroad. I had no school and all the "freedom" in the world. Life was a blur for almost 2 years—parties, girls, eating in restaurants, and no one telling me what to do—but thanks to the work ethic instilled in me at an early age, I never missed a day from work.

Eventually, the novelty of this lifestyle began to wear off. My friends were in university, were finding jobs and careers, and were leaving. And although I did have a steady girlfriend, and her parents had accepted me into their home, there was a void. I eventually phoned my mother. But there was still a tension, and Murray finished grade 10 and moved to Alberta to work for our uncle.

On February 5th, 1956, my life turned around. The prettiest girl in the world, one with bright, blue-green eyes and an infectious smile, walked into my world. Her name—Bernice (Bea) Darlene Knox. She was from Limerick, Saskatchewan, just 12 miles from Lafleche. We were married on August 25th that year, six months from the time we met, and almost to the year, on August 8th, 1957, our daughter arrived. It wasn't until then that the tension between my mother and me started to ease.

We were in our early twenties, with a family of three, a boy and two girls, and I found myself working shift work and trying to make ends meet. I was doing odd jobs for people, including working in a sign shop, and I had the realization that this was not the life I wanted. With what money we could spare I signed up for a correspondence course in commercial art and sho-card lettering (just what my father had dreamt of), and all of a sudden life returned to "normal." I was going to school, working full-time on the railroad, part-time in the sign shop, and trying to look after a home and family. If it wasn't for Bea and her encouragement and continual drive I don't know if I'd have continued at that pace, but upon completion of the art course I promptly applied at another school to take illustration and design.

And then my break. The local television station's graphic artist was going on holidays and they needed someone to fill in for a couple of weeks. The next thing I knew, I was at the drawing board at the TV station each day until 4:00 p.m., then heading to my job on the railway. Then the TV station manager called me in to see if I would consider working full-time. Bea and I talked it over. There would be a substantial drop in pay at the beginning, but TV was in its infancy with a future. No more shift work and a chance to have a normal family life. We had purchased a "revenue home" with a basement suite, and as we were a block away from a technical school, Bea took in boarders. For two years she cooked and kept house not only for our family but for four students attending school. We slowly got ahead and built our lives.

It has now been close to 66 years since my father's death, and once again I reflect upon a question I've been asked—did I ever feel cheated because I didn't have a dad while growing up. I would have to say no. There certainly were times during my late teens when his presence surely would have been valuable, but I do believe that his guiding hand was there, that somehow he exerted an influence. I also believe that his gift for music and his artistic ability was passed on to me, and for that I am thankful. Also, my mother's strength, developed through all the hardships she had to endure, has resonated in both her sons. She showed them that hard work and perseverance could be rewarding, and I believe we've inherited a legacy to be proud of.

*Rollie Bourassa*
*February 11, 2010*

၎

HAZEL worked at the Canadian Forces Base in Moose Jaw until her retirement in 1979. She recently celebrated her 96th birthday and continues to live in Moose Jaw.

MURRAY, married with 3 children and 9 grandchildren, lives in Salmon Arm, B.C., where he retired after a lifetime in the automotive industry, working from the ground floor up to owning dealerships in Dawson Creek and Salmon Arm.

ROLLIE, married with 3 children and 9 grandchildren, carried on his father's skills in the field of the arts, receiving certificates and diplomas in art, illustration and design. He worked for many years in radio, television, and public relations, and he has been the recipient of numerous awards (local, provincial, and national). His art can be found in galleries, offices, and homes around the world. He and his wife Bea reside in Regina, where Rollie continues to be active in the arts and the community.

CLARENCE'S FAMILY CELEBRATING HIS PARENTS 60TH WEDDING AN-
NIVERSARY IN 1971. LEFT TO RIGHT: FRANCOIS (BROTHER), DELORES
(SISTER), T.H. (FATHER), CLARA (MOTHER), CAMILLE (SISTER), YVONNE
(SISTER), ELNORA (SISTER) AND BOB (BROTHER).

ROLLIE (LEFT), HAZEL AND MURRAY ON HAZEL'S 90TH BIRTHDAY.

This book is set in *Adobe Garamond Pro*, an Adobe Originals design, and Adobe's first historical revival. It is a digital interpretation of the roman types of Claude Garamond and the italic types of Robert Granjon. Type designer Robert Slimbach has captured the beauty and balance of the original Garamond typefaces while creating a typeface family that offers all the advantages of a contemporary digital type family.

Claude Garamond (ca. 1480-1561) cut types for the Parisian scholar-printer Robert Estienne in the first part of the sixteenth century, basing his romans on the types cut by Francesco Griffo for Venetian printer Aldus Manutius in 1495. After his death in 1561, the Garamond punches made their way to the printing office of Christoph Plantin in Antwerp, where they were used by Plantin for many decades, and still exist in the Plantin-Moretus museum. In 1621, sixty years after Garamond's death, the French printer Jean Jannon (1580–1635) issued a specimen of typefaces that had some characteristics similar to the Garamond designs, though his letters were more asymmetrical and irregular in slope and axis. Jannon's types disappeared from use for about two hundred years, but were rediscovered in the French national printing office in 1825, when they were wrongly attributed to Claude Garamond. Their true origin was not to be revealed until the 1927 research of Beatrice Warde. In the early 1900s, Jannon's types were used to print a history of printing in France, which brought new attention to French typography and the "Garamond" types. This sparked the beginning of modern revivals; some based on the mistaken model from Jannon's types, and others on the original Garamond types. Garamond is considered to be distinctive representations of French Renaissance style; easily recognizable by their elegance and readability.